A Handbook of the Scottish Gaelic World

A Handbook of the Scottish Gaelic World

Michael Newton

FOUR COURTS PRESS

Set in 11 on 14 point AGaramond for
FOUR COURTS PRESS LTD
Fumbally Lane, Dublin 8, Ireland
e-mail: info@four-courts-press.ie
and in North America
FOUR COURTS PRESS
c/o ISBS, 5804 N.E. Hassalo Street, Portland, OR 97213.

A catalogue record for this title
is available from the British Library.

ISBN 1–85182–540–1 hbk
ISBN 1–85182–541–x pbk

Fhuair sinn taic bho Urras Brosnachaidh na Gàidhlig
agus Comunn Gàidhlig Inbhir Nis son an leabhair seo fhoillseachadh.

The assistance of the Gaelic Language Promotion Trust
and the Gaelic Society of Inverness is gratefully acknowledged.

Printed in Great Britain
by MPG Books, Bodmin, Cornwall

Roimh-Ràdh

Tha cothlamadh san fhacal 'Gàidhealtachd'. Chaidh a ràdh turas gum b'e Gàidhealtachd a bha ann an Alba gu léir aig aon am; agus is fìor sin anns an t-seagh gu robh buaidh aig a' Ghàidhlig, a bheag no a mhór, air a h-uile cearna de Alba, uair no uaireigin. Tha ainmeannan àiteachan a' sealltainn gu robh sin mar sin, go ruige crìoch Shasainn. Agus mhair Gàidhealtachd ann an iardheas Alba, an Siorrachd Àir agus an Gallaibh mu Dheas, go deireadh an t-seachdamh ceud deug co-dhiubh. Ach se an dùthaich ris an can sinne, o chionn àireamh mhath bhliadhnaichean, a' Ghàidhealtachd: Alba tuath air Cluaidh, monadh Shruighleidh, móran de Shiorrachd Pheairt, Braighe Aonghais, agus taobh an iar Siorrachd Obar Dheathain.

Se 'Gàidhealtachd' eile a tha ann an dùthchas nan Gàidheal, is i a' toirt leatha eachdraidh, mac-meanmhain; sgeul is ursgeul; ceòl is òrain; litreachas tro na linntean, go ruige ar latha-ne fhìn; rosg is bardachd is dràma; agus a h-uile gnè ealain a tha ann. Boinidh sin fhathast ann an iomadh dòigh do Alba air fad.

Chuige seo cha do rinneadh oirdhirp mhór air cunntas cruinn a thoirt air na cuspairean sin comhla. Ach a nise tha an leabhar nodha seo againn: dùthaich agus dùthchas nan Gàidheal gan cumail ann am beachd ar sùil. Tha an obair air a stéidheachadh air rannsachadh dìcheallach agus air fios-rachadh a chaidh a tharraing á iomadach tobar eòlais. Agus, os cionn gach nì, tha a' Ghàidhlig aig an ughdar: dh'ionnsaich e an cànan. Leughaidh agus sgrìobhaidh e a' Ghàidhlig is nì e comhradh innte gun strì. Tha a shealladh fhéin aige air gach cùis a bhoineas dha ùidh; is tha e a' cur sin an céill gun fhathamas do dhuine seach a chéile. Dùisgidh an leabhar seo, tha mi a' smaoineachadh, iomadh cat grìosaich; is bu mhath nan doireadh an dùs-gadh ceum air thoiseach sin 'na ar cuid sgoilearachd. Chan iarrte gum biodh a h-uile duine riamh uile gu léir air an aon ramh ann an rannsachadh sam bith.

Tha roinnean am measg nan sgoilearan mar thà. Air aon rud, bu mhath le cuid dhinn an fhìor Ghàidhealtachd a lorg ann an seann seòl beatha nan Gàidheal. Ann am beachd dhaoine eile, se na thathar a sgrìobhadh an diugh an rud as prionnsabalaiche – na tha a' mìneachadh is a' cur an céill ar suidheachadh is sinn fo bhuaidh is fo bhinn cumhachd an t-saoghail mhóir. Their cuid againn nach eil sna seann sgeulachdan, na seann òrthaichean beannachaidh is cronachaidh (tarraingeach is mar a dh'fhaodas iad a bhith) is anns gach cleachdadh aosda a tha nise air a dhol á fasan ach nithean a dh'fheumadh cnàmh ann an cùrsa nàdair co-dhiubh. Canar nach eil na Gàidheil diofraichte o shluagh sam bith eile: gu bheil e an dàn a h-uile nàisean atharrachadh a réir gluasad na h-eachdraidh; is nach robh agus nach eile na Gàidheil ag iarraidh fuireach air cùil-fraoin tìm càil nas mutha na tha daoine eile. Bha sgeulachdan, romansaichean, òrthaichean is a leithid rim faotainn air feadh sluagh an domhain. Bha geasalachd is saobh chreideamh a cheart cho cumanta. Dh'atharraich iad, chaidh iad á sealladh, chaidh iad á bith. Ach masa h-eadh, cha do chuir sin gun do chnàmh an darna cuid aigne no cainnt.

Tha buidhnean eile ann a rithist a bhios a' tagairt gura h-e creideamh a mhill a' Ghàidhlig: gura h-e gu h-àraid an t-Athleasachadh a rinn am fàsachadh. Tha an fheadhainn a tha de caochladh beachd a' cur na ceist: masa h-e, cionnas nach robh a' bhuaidh sin aig a' chreideamh ann an dùthchannan eile; rud nach robh. Se a tha ann, their iad, ach gun do ghabh ministearan Gàidhealach na h-Eaglais Stéite an t-àite is an inbhe a bha aig na baird fhoghlamaichte o shean. Agus se sgoiltean na h-eaglais (gu sonraichte ann an aidmheilean soisgealach) a bha a' teagasg leughadh is sgrìobhadh sa Ghàidhlig.

Tha fios aig na h-uile gura h-e Crùn agus Pàrlamaid Alba a rinn léirsgrios air Rìoghachd Innse Gall agus Arra Gàidheal tacan math man dàinig iomairt an Athleasaiche. Uime sin, theirear, is cinnteach nach fhaod a bhith nach eil adhbhar nas doimhne na iomlaid creideimh ri lorg ann am beatha nan Gàidheal ann an Alba.

Tha an rannsachadh a rinn an Dr Mìcheal Newton riatanach, ionmholta, luachmhor. Chan e a mhàin gu bheil an leabhar a' deanamh farpas ann an tomhas air gach puing dhar n-eachdraidh: tha e cuideachd a' fàgail rèidhleach gu leòr aig a' ghinealach a tha ri tighinn am beachdan fhéin a chur an céill. Agus tha e rèidh, soilleir, furasta a leughadh. Tha mo bheannachd-sa aig an obair. Guma soirbh leis an leabhar is guma fada a bhios e an clò.

IAIN MAC AONGHAIS

Contents

Acknowledgments

This book is the result of many conversations, discussions, debates and inquiries with friends and adversaries too numerous to mention or remember. My work will no doubt bear the mark of my training with William Gillies, Ronald Black, and Dr Roibeard Ó Maolalaigh of the Celtic Department of the University of Edinburgh.

I am also particularly indebted to esteemed friends and colleagues Dr Margaret Bennett, Jonathon Dembling, Robert Dunbar, Kristen Fikkan, Alasdair MacCaluim, Allan MacDonald (of Glenuig), Dr Alastair McIntosh, Dr John MacInnes, Wilson McLeod, Thomas William Moore, Sharon Paice-MacLeod, James MacDonald Reid, Dr Dòmhnall Uilleam Stiùbhart, Seumas Watson and Frances MacEachen (Cape Breton), and Dr Alex Woolf. Wilson McLeod and Dr Dòmhnall Uilleam Stiùbhart were kind enough to provide detailed comments on drafts of the book.

I would like to thank Wayne Holder, John and Amanda Graham, and Kristen Fikkan for loaning me computer equipment to write this book at its various stages of development. I also give my thanks to the staff of Edinburgh University Library, Edinburgh Central Library, the National Library of Scotland, the School of Scottish Studies, and the Celtic Department of the University of Edinburgh for their help in accessing textual materials.

Finally, this book would not have been possible without the encouragement and support of my parents, and the inspiration and guidance of Dr John MacInnes.

List of Illustrations

(Illustrations appear between pages 160 and 161.)

ILLUSTRATION CREDITS

4: Edmund Burt, 1754, *Letters from a Gentleman in the North of Scotland to his friend in London*, London. 5, 6, 7, 8: Thomas Pennant, 1774, *A Tour in Scotland and Voyage to the Hebrides in* 1772, London. 9, 10, 11: James Drummond, 1881, *Archaeologia Scotica: Sculptured Monuments in Iona & the West Highlands*, Edinburgh: Fellows of the Society of Antiquities of Scotland. 12, 13, 14: Joseph Anderson, 1881, *Scotland in Early Christian Times*, Edinburgh. 15: H.D. Graham, 1850, *Antiquities of Iona.* 1, 2, 3: Matthew Stout.

Introduction

The term Dark Ages was originally coined to describe the conditions of much of Europe in the wake of the Roman Empire, yet the term is inappropriate to describe Gaelic society in Scotland and Ireland in this period. As Germanic raiders wreaked havoc on the former territories of the Roman world, Gaeldom enjoyed a Golden Age, as native intellectual institutions were invigorated by the additional input of Latin learning. It was these Gaelic-speaking leaders who gave their name to Scotland and who made it one of the first nations of Europe.

Scotland's true Dark Ages came after the Gaelic-speaking kings were Anglicized and the last Gaelic province, the Lordship of the Isles, was dissolved. Later governments treated the Celtic Fringes as zones which needed to be subdued lest rebellion and anarchy spring from them.

Fortunately, many of the artefacts of the Gaelic Heroic Age, especially poetry, survive and tell us a great deal about the people and events which helped to shape the history of Scotland. Songs of praise to warriors of the seventeenth and eighteenth centuries continue to be sung to this day and still serve to inspire musicians and poets. Yet we need to consider the cultural context in which these works were created to fully appreciate them.

This book focuses on Gaelic clan society in the classical period, between the twelfth and seventeenth centuries. Gaelic society proved itself to be adaptable as it underwent a number of transformations in social, economic, and political structures through the ages. Despite these changes, the ethos of clan society continued to reappear and reassert itself even while the institutions of which it was a part were in the process of disintegrating.[1]

While on-going, innovative analysis of economic data and historical events is important in giving us a complete picture of Gaelic society, it does not necessarily provide an insight about the inner life and perspectives of the human community. There is a huge corpus of literature of many sorts to inform us of this side of their being, a literature which self-consciously looks back to the ancient past and takes pride in its pedigree and continuity.

Gaelic communities are heirs to a tradition which historically covered a much wider geographical spread and included a more distinctive range of expressions than remains today. More than two and a half centuries of hostile, alien institutions, established after native Gaelic institutions were destroyed, have restricted the breadth of a self-determining Gaelic culture. Unless sensitive and thoughtful planning is taken into consideration in the present Gaelic renaissance, there are already indications that Gaeldom might atrophy into a cipher for Anglo-American global culture.

Contemporary Scottish culture presents a bewildering mix of apparently contrary images and has been characterized as having a discordant, dysfunctional nature. As has been explored in Irish Studies, we must ask: is this neurosis inherent in Scottish culture itself, or is it a result of divisive historical circumstances?[2]

The tendency of recent years has been to speak of Scotland as the Mongrel Nation, as though Scotland was a disparate collection of languages and cultures to be accounted for by a multiplicity of racial origins. While there is diversity in any nation, culture or community, the Mongrel Nation myth is an artefact of modern times and an expression of Scotland's current identity crisis. It is possible to see the conscious recognition in earlier times of the features of a common Scottish tradition springing from Gaelic, and wider Celtic, roots.

This book attempts to provide a holistic understanding of the elements of Gaelic culture, especially as articulated by the Gaelic record itself, from its own point of view. The dynamics of cultural imperialism, assimilation and appropriation to which the Highlands have been subjected is symbolic of the history of Scotland as a whole, and an understanding of those processes is key to the de-colonization and re-integration of the Scottish as well as the Gaelic psyche.

Many indigenous cultures which have sustained oppression from modernist societies have responded in recent years by asserting the merits of their own value and belief systems. This is not merely a romantic appeal to primitivism but a serious discussion about cultural paradigms. It is a fact that Scotland, like other industrialized societies, was once very different and we need to understand and assess this historical reality and its cultural consequences to evaluate the costs of the transition. A more complete and balanced understanding of the past should empower us to plan the direction we are headed in the present.

In order to understand and appreciate other cultures on their own terms, we need to be able to liberate ourselves from the biases of our cultural background. Learning about another culture is a process of self-revelation, of exposing what ideologies underlie our own worldview, as one cannot articulate a critique of ones own place unless one can also stand in a radically different place.[3]

Scotland is beginning an exciting period of change and of redefinition. The nation as a whole has the chance to appreciate the significance of Gaelic culture in its own formation, to explore its potential and to use these resources as a platform to build on towards the future. Scotland is not the only beneficiary of an informed discussion about its indigenous culture; descendents of the Gaelic Diaspora around the world have begun to explore their ancestral heritage. We can learn much about Scotland by comparing its history to the experiences of similarly marginalized cultures, and in turn Scotland can make a contribution to the revitalization of other peoples who value their heritage and the wondrous diversity of humankind.

CHAPTER I

Thinking about culture

Culture – the matrix of life

It is a basic assumption of the social sciences that a human being is a social animal. We are all born into a family, come to interact with a community and think of ourselves as being members of some nation or ethnic people. We learn what it means to be a member of our society, what our identity is and how we relate to others around us. Culture is, in part, the commonly accepted values, customs, beliefs and practices which allow the individual to interact meaningfully with his community.

> We must needs live in and with the help of *some* culture … No social gathering, no meal, no establishment or perpetuation of a human relationship, is conceivable without some idiom to set the scene, limit expectations, and establish rights and duties.[1]

Culture optimally allows both the community and individual to develop and flourish. 'A man who experiences the benefit of community life is a more complete individual.'[2] Individuals inherit the knowledge, practices, customs and beliefs developed and transmitted by their communities, and in turn are able to contribute to that body of tradition.

This does not mean that people are necessarily consciously aware of the constituent elements and values in their culture, however. These are usually as transparent to the mind of the individual as water is to a fish. 'Men and societies frequently treat the institutions and assumptions by which they live as absolute, self-evident, and given …'[3]

The exact definition and boundaries of a culture are not rigid and may be quite difficult to quantify with any precision. We might think, then, of cultures as being like families, with particular traits and characteristics in common with others when there are common ancestors or mutual influence. The closer two families are related and the closer their spheres of interaction, the more they are likely to have in common.

Scale is also an important factor. A man from York might think of himself as belonging to that distinct community while in Yorkshire, but when he goes to Essex, he might be conveniently labeled a Yorkshire man. When he goes to Scotland, he is simply an Englishman. When he goes to Japan, he could be identified as an Englishman or perhaps as just a European. 'We need to see ethnicity as not just at the level of small bands or groups, but as a multiple, concentric and (sometimes) overlapping phenomenon.'[4]

Although, as a development of Greek thought, modernist culture loves to specialize knowledge and to departmentalize life, real human culture actually does not fragment according to compartments and categories, such as religion, science, economics, politics, and so on. Instead, the whole matrix of life is interwoven in a complex, multi-layered web, held together by the unifying force of *myth*.

> One cannot reduce any culture to its explicit functions – political, economic and legal, etc. No culture is wholly transparent in this way. There is invariably a hidden nucleus which determines and rules the distribution of these transparent functions and institutions ... It is only if we try to grasp this kernel that we may discover the foundational mytho-poetic nucleus of a society.[5]

The modernist usage of the term 'myth' equates it with 'lies' and untruths, obscuring its significance and historical function in society. It is commonly heard in phrases such as, 'Oh, that's just a myth!', meaning that there is no truth in it. The origins of the dismissal of the power of myth in society is apparent in the writings of Herodotus and Plato, who, in the development of rational thought, tried to distinguish *mûthos*, 'fictive narrative', 'legend' from *lógos*, 'word' or 'true story'.[6] In other words, they believed that with logic they would surpass irrational primitivism. As modernist society is based upon the foundations of Platonic thought, it is no surprise that we too give little conscious esteem to the role of myth.

As more recent scholarship has analyzed the components and operation of culture, the role and importance of myth has become clearer. Myth is not exclusive to the ignorant or superstitious, but an inescapable fact of human consciousness: no language or culture can exist without a mythic core. Modernist culture also has its own mythology.[7] 'In myth are expressed the thought patterns by which a group formulates self-cognition and self-realization, attains self-knowledge and self-confidence, explains its own source and being and that of its surroundings, and sometimes tries to chart its destinies.'[8]

We might define *ideology* as a more formally articulated form of myth. It usually has a political function in society, expressing a particular interpretation of phenomena or events to propagate a particular point of view. History itself is never free of myth and ideology, since without some frame of reference or filter through which to sift out and interpret events, it would merely be a chaotic mass of actions without meaning.[9] In this sense, all history is propaganda in that it propagates a particular point of view. The questions we should pose to any particular reading of history are, whose mythology is it, whose cause does it advance, and why has it been chosen?

Myth not only influences our perceptions of the past, and thus helps us to explain the present, but it also guides us in our decision-making and helps determine our future. Myth also has a central role in the continual reformation and molding of society. Culture is not static but dynamically evolving according to its perceptions of itself, its needs, its resources, and its goals.

Cultural theorists point out that culture is never completely homogeneous, that it has variations over geographical space, between class distinctions, between genders, between age groups, and so on. It is certainly true that one can see variations, according to social and historical circumstances, in culture across these different variables. Different ideologies may compete simultaneously among the members of a society, people adopting that which justifies their own position and ambition.

It would be naive to deny, however, that there are not emergent patterns in terms of values, beliefs, aesthetics, cultural icons, and behavior which characterize societies and unite them across differences.

In order to talk meaningfully about culture, we need to define our terms carefully. Characterizing cultures and bestowing names is always a difficult act, fraught with complexities. Names are important references, however inadequate they may be when scrutinized closely.

The term 'Western culture' is a misnomer because not all peoples in the west of Europe were involved in equal degrees in creating it, and it is now a culture which, through the channels of industrialization, capitalism and mass media, has taken hold in all corners of the globe. Two other terms will be used in this book. The first is *modernism* and *modernist culture.* These refer to ideologies which emerged in Western Europe by the time of the Renaissance, developed in the alchemy of Christianity from the raw ingredients of Greek philosophy and the Judeo-Christian tradition.[10]

> Modernism is a complicated concatenation of ideological presuppositions, including ideas that progress is inevitable, that the power of science and technology is unlimited, that humankind represents the apex of creation, and that the natural and cultural worlds can be understood on the basis of a machine metaphor.[11]

The term modernist is misleading if one thinks of it as only referring to a time period, the modern age, as we could speak of any culture that survives into the present day as being modern. It rather refers to specific cultural myths, ways of life, and organizing principles, and the social relations and means of production later engendered by these paradigm shifts.

The current phase of modernist civilization could be called *techno-consumer culture*, as technology and consumerism are the two primary *cultural foci* of the modernist world at present. Economic forces primarily work through and are justified by consumerism and its attendant institutions, and these in turn feed into the development of further technology. Technology provides the means of production and distribution which make consumerism possible on the scale on which it currently exists, and the myths which envelope technology pervade our lives and even our thoughts and language.

The term 'traditional society' is not a very precise one, for tradition and myth is universal in all human cultures. When people use the term 'traditional society', they are usually referring to small-scale non-urban societies, organized on a kinship paradigm, reliant on oral, rather than written, modes of communication and discourse, without what we would consider complex technology. The term *primal culture* will be used when referring to a society with the above characteristics. *Modernist* and *primal* are useful reference points to extremes of cultural organizational styles, though in reality few societies lay at either extreme but are somewhere on the continuum between them.

A dynamic, organic entity

While individuals have an influence over the development and 'movement' of their cultures, a culture is larger than any one individual and has much more weight resisting change than any one individual can assert. Culture is more than just the unordered whims of individuals, for human personality itself is shaped by the community which outlasts the life span and influence of its members.

Without a coherent set of values and beliefs, the community would die and have to be reborn with every individual. It would not be able to provide a sense of rootedness, stability, purpose and moral standards in times of crisis and uncertainty, transmitted from one generation to the next without conscious effort.[12] One of the most important channels for the encapsulation and dissemination of culture is language.

> Language is the great container of culture. Because of the stability of every language, each generation has been able to carry over and pass on a significant portion of previous history, even when it has not been otherwise recorded. And no matter how much the outer scene changes, through language man retains an inner scene where he is at home with his own mind, among his own kind.[13]

We are molded by culture and are given definition within its conceptual space. Some of us might react to it, fight against it, criticize it, break its laws and strive to change its values, but we are nonetheless framed by its parameters.

None of this is to claim that culture never changes. Cultures, especially those in contact and competition with other cultures, are subject to change. But we don't need to assume, as modernist culture does, that change is 'inevitable'. This is, in fact, one of the myths of modernist culture.[14] A critical line of inquiry is: Who is effecting the change? Who stands to benefit and who to lose? What are the costs and what will the effects be on other aspects of the culture?

Changes in any one part of culture's intricate web of inter-linked threads will have a significant impact on all other parts, although they may be hard to predict or even to notice immediately. It is apparent in hindsight how, for example, changes in religion can cause changes in politics, a shift in perspective about science can affect the arts, and so on. None of the repercussions of change can be constrained within any one sphere of activity or thought.

This issue of the side effects of change might be illustrated by an example. There is a common myth in modernist culture that technology is inherently 'neutral', that it contains no particular values or attitudes within itself, and that it is merely the way in which technology is applied which determines what effect it has.[15] The values inherent in any particular technology become more obvious when it is introduced into a society which did not produce it, which does not have pre-existing values and categories that are compatible with it. The introduction of European farming technology to Cherokee society had far-reaching implications:

> It involved overturning many of the values and practices of Cherokee life and replacing them with others that seemed immoral, sacrilegious, and repugnant ... Farming itself was not an issue: the Cherokee had farmed for thousands of years. But this new kind of farming involved deep changes in the relationships between the sexes and with the land ...[16]

Technology does not develop in all cultures from a mere struggle to maximize gains and minimize effort, as modernist thought believes. It occurs within culturally-specific parameters, which 'can rarely be isolated from religious, social, cultural or ecological considerations'.[17] Every technological item is a culturally specific artefact. The desire to innovate, which in modernist society has surpassed our needs and transcended any sense of morality, in other societies 'remained within the limits of existing social and cultural traditions'.[18]

Change is never total: cultures carry a great deal forward with them from the past. In his study of the development of modernism, Lewis Mumford explains how, in every new phase or stage of civilization, the elements of the previous age are not entirely discarded, but become a new layer in the foundation of the new age.

> For culture is a compost in which many traits temporarily disappear or become unidentifiable, but few are ever completely lost ... The [dominant traits] are what give each historic phase its style and color: but without the substratum of active persistents, and without the vast underlayer of remnants, whose existence remains as unnoticed as the foundation of a house until it sags or crumbles, no fresh invention in culture could achieve dominance. If one bears this in mind, it is legitimate to characterize a cultural phase by its largest visible new feature: but in the total body of a culture the persistents and the remnants, however hidden, necessarily occupy a far larger area and play a more essential part.[19]

Discussion about cultural change will focus around the difference between *internal innovation* and *external acculturation*.[20] When a culture develops something according to its own internal principles and resources, on its own accord, we can say that it has produced an internal innovation. When it has displaced an old form in preference for a new form taken from an external source despite a clash of internal values or principles, we can say that this is a sign of external acculturation. The difference between these processes can only be determined on a case-by-case basis, and we must ask what values and beliefs characterize the change, who is affecting the change, and why it is taking place.

The introduction of new farming technology into traditional Cherokee life, quoted above, caused a conflict of principles and was clearly an external acculturation. It was an introduction into Cherokee society that was alien to it, incompatible with its internal cultural matrix and was unlikely to have been a development within the natural course of Cherokee life.

Although gambling has been practiced in Native American culture for thousands of years – it seems to be a nearly universal feature of human societies – it is a mistake to think that today's gambling casinos on Native American reservations, and all the social ills that accompany them, are a natural development of traditional culture that would have occurred without the influence of an external, cash-based culture. This is, instead, an example of external acculturation, despite the fact that such money-making ventures can be initiated by Native Americans themselves, who have few other options in the world in which they live.

When two different cultures come into contact with each other, the reactions of the members of the native culture can be typically divided into three camps: the *traditionalists*, the *syncretists* and the *assimilationists*. Which of these reactions prevails will depend on the relative health and self-confidence of the two cultures and on the particular circumstances. While the traditionalists would argue for maintaining (or restoring) their culture uninfluenced by outside ideas, the syncretists try to adapt and accommodate various aspects of the new order into their culture, while the assimilationists prefer to leave their inherited culture behind and adopt the new one wholesale.

The assimilationist ideal can seldom be achieved quickly or completely, for the patterns of the original culture usually influence the ways in which the new culture is adapted. Likewise, the traditionalist ideal can seldom be achieved because contact with the external culture often influences perceptions about culture and cultural change, and traditionalist movements have frequently introduced great innovation.[21]

Whether we look at Native American society, Gaelic society or any other society which stands at the cross-roads of tradition and Modernism, there is debate, sometimes even violent conflict, about which path to follow. The differing responses and lack of agreement can lead to factional in-fighting which only strengthens the position of the newcomer and creates a stereotype of the native as innately prone to division.

Culture, race, and individuals

Race is a concept that people in the modernist world take for granted. It seems obvious to us that a fundamental way of identifying people is by their racial origins. The whole idea of race and racialism is, however, a cultural construct – that is to say, it is a category invented in modernist culture that does not exist in every culture, and was even thought of differently in the recent past.

The ideology of racialism – of dividing people into races – was developed by empires which sought to control the people whose lands they invaded and to justify their conquests. But the ideology of race was highly flexible and changed to suit the needs of the ruling elite.[22] In other words, the concept of race is inextricably part of the political agenda that created it.

In reality, race and culture are totally independent dimensions to a human being's identity. A person can be of 'pure' African stock and yet be American by his culture, or of Scottish ethnic origin and yet be thoroughly English culturally. Being a Scot or a Gael is a cultural identity, the result of socialization, not a racial trait, just as is being English, American or French. Having the surname MacDonald only suggests that one has a Gaelic ancestor – it does not mean that a person with that name is a Gael or a Scot.

While skin colour or facial features may suggest a particular racial background, ethnic groups have continually moved around, inter-bred, evolved new features and lost old ones. There is no such thing as a 'pure-bred' race and there is no one-to-one correspondence between race and geographical location. It is not race which determines our values, our traditions, our festivals, our worldview and our mother tongue, but culture. Thinking along racialist lines is the relic of an oversimplified Imperialist ideology which does not stand to scrutiny.

We can differentiate between at least three factors. We can identify a broad racial origin for people, we can identify what culture they were raised in, and we can determine what their *allegiances* are. Although the first two factors are essentially beyond a person's control, a critically-minded person should be able to choose to give his or her allegiance according to what is just – if a sense of justice is not over-ridden by self-interests.

There are a number of examples of this, especially where peoples from very different origins have come together. In Peru, for example, 'Racial allegiance is defined by where a person is from, what he wears, how he sees himself, and most of all by what language he speaks.'[23]

Native Americans assimilated Europeans into their tribes. Such was the effect of 'going native' that Benjamin Franklin noted, 'When white persons of either sex have been taken prisoners young by the Indians, in a short time they become disgusted with our manner of life, and ... there is no reclaiming them.'[24] Likewise, many of the descendants of English colonists sent to conquer Ireland were Gaelicized in language and culture, much to the dismay of English officials who accused them of becoming 'more Irish than the Irish themselves'.

The ideology of racialism has had a very political role. Although the same ethnic origins characterize the people of both Britain and Ireland (albeit in slightly different ratios) – Celts, Anglo-Saxons, Vikings and Normans – the ideology of England gives a glorious Teutonic/Gothic lineage to its people, disregarding other peoples. The ideology of Ireland is that of a Gaelic people, opposed to the waves of invaders. Both of these ideologies hide a more complex truth, but play important roles in providing a unifying myth for society.

With the strong conviction transmitted by culture through the process of socialization and its constant reinforcement, stepping outside its bounds, criticizing it and rejecting its values is in reality a very difficult proposition. It is, however, possible and because it is possible massive shifts in the cultural matrix do happen.

It is important that we disentangle people's origins from their role in the cultural dynamic in which they are involved. People may be involved in cultural processes, consciously or unconsciously, which may be completely at odds with their own ethnic origin.

The European conquest of America would have impossible, particularly in the first phases, without exploiting the pre-existing rivalries between Native American tribes. Cortés, the first conquistador of Mexico, recognized that the best way of augmenting his vastly outnumbered army in order to subdue the Aztecs was to employ their traditional enemies, the Tlaxcalans.[25] Interpreting the battle between the Aztecs and the Tlaxcalans as a civil war, however, would be ignoring the larger scale dynamics of the conflict and, more importantly, the final result in cultural terms: Europeanization.

Native Americans, as individuals or groups, were to feature as important players in the conquest of America into the 'Indian Wars' of the late 1800s. Whether due to blinding loyalties, antagonisms, desire for personal gain, or a lack of other options, it seems ironic to us in hindsight that Native Americans were active participants in the downfall of their cultures. Other apparent contradictions of an opposite nature also exist, such as John Ross, known to his people as Kooweskoowee, a man more Scottish than Cherokee by ancestry, yet completely committed to the Cherokee nation in his role as Chief in a time of extreme crisis.[26]

The cultural processes in which people are involved in go far beyond their ethnic origins and often beyond immediate comprehension. We can form a more meaningful analysis of an event or process of events not by focusing on the origins of the people involved but on the values inherent in the ideology which directs those events, on the centre of control of the process, and on the cultural outcome of those events.

Imperialism and cultural myth-making

Science and technology were catalysts in the formation of modernist culture. 'By the eighteenth century ... Mechanical progress and human progress came to be regarded as one ...'[27] The more technically advanced a culture (or race, according to the thinking of the times) was, the more 'progressed' they were as human beings. There was an assumption, which still lingers in popular modernist thought, that a sort of evolution has brought Western society from the darkness of primitivism into the light of the modernist age:

> The traditional model of social evolution is usually taken to be a straightforward pattern of linear development ... Social development was seen as the natural progression through a number of states, from nomadism and primitive communism through feudalism to industrial capitalism.[28]

This was in reality little more than an ethnocentric narcissism which, like racialism, convinced early modern Western society that it was the pinnacle of human achievement and was therefore justified in taking over the other peoples of the world and bringing them into line with themselves.

This naive ideology is no longer accepted by scholars, for anthropologists in particular have confirmed that all human societies are highly sophisticated 'organisms', despite differences in social organization and technology. It is now acknowledged that societies cannot be placed in a linear sequence from 'early' to 'advanced', or from 'unworthy of existing' (or 'needs developing') to 'progressed'. The more balanced approach

> recognizes each culture as unique and valuable in its own right ... From this perspective the basic cultural forms, from hunting-gathering to advanced industrial societies, form no linear sequence of evolution but rather are mosaics built over time and place by countless generations ...[29]

The ideology of cultural evolution – usually expressed in racialist terms – was, however, a common rationale for taking control of the land, resources and social institutions of other peoples and 'modernizing' them. It was a way in which dominant powers could convince themselves and others that they weren't really committing a violent act of cultural genocide – which they were – but rather a humane act of human progress.[30]

By the end of the sixteenth century the English imagined themselves as taking over the role of the Romans in spreading a sophisticated Empire to the uncivilized peoples of the world.[31] The queen of England recommended that the earl of Essex come to Ulster in 1574 as she believed he could 'bring in that rude and barbarous nation to civility ...'[32] Barnaby Rich argued in 1578 against the criticisms that the English were too severe in Ireland because, he declared, the Irish preferred to 'live like beasts, voide of lawe and all good order', and that they were 'more uncivill, more uncleanly, more barbarous and more brutish in their customs and demeanures, than in any other part of the world that is known.'[33]

In the 'wilderness of America', in particular, the Englishman equated the wild Indian with the wild Irish, and the ideology and stereotypes developed in the subjugation of Ireland continued to inform the 'Anglo-Saxon' conquest of America well into the twentieth century. Theodore Roosevelt stated just this, justifying the dismantling of Native American culture, shortly before becoming President of the United States in 1901:

> It is our duty toward people living in barbarism to see that they are freed from their chains and we can free them only by destroying barbarism itself ... Exactly as it is the duty of a civilized power scrupulously to respect the rights of weaker civilized powers ... so it is its duty to put down savagery and barbarism.[34]

The Gaels of Scotland experienced a similar cultural attack. Rooting out the language and culture of the Highlanders and replacing it with English became a religious calling to many reformers, who made claims such as: 'Our poor people are from their Cradles train'd up in Barbarity and Ignorance. Their very Language is an everlasting Bar against all Instruction ...'[35]

When Highland society collapsed in the mid-nineteenth century and was on the verge of starvation, rather than owning up to the intentional sabotage to and neglect of the Highlands done by the government, the Highlanders themselves were blamed.

> It is the fact that morally and intellectually [the Highlanders] are an inferior race to the Lowland Saxon ... and that before they can in a civilised age be put in a condition to provide for themselves on the charity of the hard-working Lowlander, the race must be improved by a Lowland intermixture; their habits, which did well enough in a former stage of society, must be broken up by the force of Lowland example.[36]

It has been demonstrated, moreover, that the myth of progress in Scotland, especially during the Scottish Enlightenment, became equated with Anglicization. This caused the Gaelic peoples to be denigrated as a 'failed civilization', and inhibited esteem for the distinctively Celtic cultures that created Scotland's past. The Scottish psyche was thus divided and lost the ability to synthesize a unifying ideology of nationhood, critical to the formation of nation-states in the eighteenth and nineteenth centuries.

> The Scots [of the Union] also held a very different view of the civilizing process from other nations. They became committed to theories of progress which induced considerable scepticism about the value of so-called high civilisations of the pre-modern world. As a result, Scots lost the potential for historical creativity and nationalist myth-making allowed by alternative theories of civilization ...[37]

This myth persists in Scottish perceptions of the past and present to this day. We must ask what the social and cultural consequences of the suppression of a Gaelic identity, and the promotion of an Anglo-Teutonic myth, have brought to Scotland and who stands to gain from them.

The myth of cultural 'natural selection' still lingers in the minds of people. Rather than acknowledging the role that Euro-Americans had in destroying Native American societies and the natural resources upon which they depended, many people will still say that they were 'doomed to die anyway', as though some Darwinistic process would have weeded them out of existence had Europeans never come.

Likewise, many people still state that the Scottish clan system was 'becoming obsolete' anyway, failing to recognize the fact that Gaelic society was a highly sophisticated one, dynamic and capable of adaptation. The old Gaelic order did not simply die: it was deliberately strangulated. Believing that it was doomed for failure gives people an excuse to blame its demise on 'natural, uncontrollable forces' rather than on deliberate political and military actions against it.

Cultural dynamics and control

Modernism accepts change as inevitable, as a worthy goal in and of itself. 'Change itself became, in this complex of ideas, not merely a fact of nature – as it is – but an urgent human value; and to resist change or retard it in any way was to "go against nature".'[38] This developed out of the idea of history as a linear sequence, whose ultimate goal was the Christian paradise and, under the influence of individualism, human 'betterment'.

Although some kind of change does occur in all cultures, the myth of progress is alien to primal cultures. Such societies are by nature conservative, in the strict sense of the word that they prefer to maintain the established order transmitted to them by tradition. 'For the archaic mind humankind has no task higher than to live in an eternal mythical present, maintaining through ritual the sacrality and timeless harmonies of natural existence.'[39] Were society to step out of line with the precedents set down in mythic time, social collapse and universal chaos would ensue.

> The whole weight of culture, down to modern times, has centred on its ties with the past, so that even fresh departures would be disguised as a replenishing of old sources. With good reason, archaic societies distrusted innovators and inventors as heartily as Phillip II of Spain, who classed them, not without reason, as heretics.[40]

The modernist will no doubt answer that blind allegiance to tradition is what keeps people from 'advancing'. But the myth that advancement in science and technology has direct benefit to humankind and the planet as a whole is betrayed by the fact that modern technology has unleashed forces of oppression, exploitation and ecological disaster unparalleled in human history. People in many parts of the world have come to realize that the modernist myths of progress and development are nothing more to them and their societies than

> a euphemism for exploitation, a new colonialism. The forces of development and modernization have pulled most people away from a sure subsistence and got them to chase after an illusion, only to fall flat on their faces, materially impoverished and psychologically disoriented.[41]

The theories of *cultural invasion* and *cultural conquest*, particularly based on colonial experiences in the Third World, provide models for understanding how a culture can be colonized, both physically and mentally, by an invader. After the invading group establishes a physical presence, they disrupt the social order of the colonized, impose their own worldview, and assert that this is to be the natural order of things.

> In order for cultural invasion to succeed, it is essential that those invaded become convinced of their intrinsic inferiority. Since everything has its opposite, if those who are invaded consider themselves inferior, they must recognize the superiority of the invaders ... The more invasion is accentuated and those invaded are alienated from the spirit of their own culture and from themselves, the more the latter want to be like the invaders: to walk like them, dress like them, talk like them.[42]

Cultural conquest is a set of stages of alienation from the 'old native' identity – 'impoverished, backward, inferior, primitive'[43] and finally unreal and illegitimate – to identification with and slavish imitation of the 'new ascendancy' identity. The invaded group loses its ability to think and act independently, as it assumes it is innately inferior, and it becomes dependent upon the invaders. 'The effect consciously sought by colonialism was to drive into the natives' heads that if the settlers were to leave, they would at once fall back into barbarism, degradation and bestiality.'[44]

The distinction between race and culture is important in this analysis, because the conqueror and the conquered can be racially indistinguishable, and conquest and control happen through a manipulation of culture. A member of the conquered can assume the role of the suppresser, regardless of his origins, by changing his cultural allegiance and assuming the role of the master in this game of domination.

Culture largely defines the way we think about ourselves. We automatically develop at a very early age the sense of belonging to some social group. If the dominant voices in society convey the impression that our social group is capable of success, then we too come to believe that we are personally capable of great achievement. If the dominant voices in society convey the impression that our social group is inferior and doomed to failure, then we too are likely to internalize this doom into our own psyches and to lack self-confidence in ourselves.

The conquered may eventually attempt to re-assert themselves in some way, but if they have lost their own worldview, their own distinctive set of values and cultural norms, they may only look for *external validation* through the paternal approval of the culture of their conquerors. A culture surely has been conquered when it is incapable of expressing its own self-worth except according to the standards of its conquerors. The constant need to look outside the bounds of Scotland to find examples of success and the lack of internal role models is one of the symptoms of the inferiority complex of modern Scotland.

It may be very difficult indeed for the oppressed to resist employing the same labels and categories made by their invaders, especially if the stereotypes created of them are supposed to have 'redeeming features'. These supposed virtues may be exaggerated beyond their previously balanced functionality to try to meet the expectations of the outside world. The desire of Anglo-American culture to find a peaceful, ecologically-friendly society projects an alien agenda upon Native America's warrior society and obscures its complex relationship with the environment. Some Native Americans were not slow to sell an image which met the expectations of an audience hungry for these stereotypes. Such are the paradoxes of marginalized cultures.

It is important to realize the difference between the model of cultural invasion and the classic Marxist model of class oppression. What we are dealing with in the English-Scottish, English-Irish and English-Native American contexts is not a class struggle but a cultural struggle. Although it is commonly the case that control and suppression is accomplished by assimilating ruling castes, cultural invasion must necessarily happen first, as a preliminary step, before class division can be used as a tool in cultural conquest.

Almost all societies group themselves in hierarchies. This does not mean that there exists a cultural conflict within them, however. Clear evidence for cultural, and not class, conflict was even given by Marx himself, who sought to eliminate cultural divisions in order to unite people according to class for revolution: 'The ordinary English worker hates the Irish worker ... [and] in relation to the Irish worker he feels himself a member of the ruling nation ... His attitude is much the same as that of the "poor whites" to the "niggers" ...'[45]

Likewise the Cherokee leader John Ridge complained in 1823 of similar attitudes of Anglo-Americans towards Native Americans, who are 'frowned upon by the meanest peasant ... the most stupid and illiterate white man will disdain and triumph over this worthy individual.'[46] Even modern political intellectuals are eager to sacrifice Native American identity to the cult of the Marxist class struggle: 'Vargas Llosa proposes finishing off the Indian in the name of social Darwinist capitalism, Martínez Peláez in the name of Marx. Neither will allow Amerindian culture even the right to exist ... The heroic task of socialism is "deindigenization".'[47]

Some Gaelic leaders were being criticized by their dependents in the late seventeenth century not for being of a different class, but for abandoning their allegiances to their culture and being assimilated into Anglo-British society. Once they adopted non-Gaelic identities and allegiances, they could use their privileged position within Highland society against it.

It has even been said that what happened to the Gaels was not too different from what happened to 'working class people' all around the world. This attitude betrays a fundamental naiveté about class and culture. Economic and social conditions forced people from other parts of Europe to emigrate to America and other colonial destinations, but myths of racial inferiority were used to justify the eviction of Gaels from their homes.

There are numerous examples of peoples in Europe who have been 'modernized' without having been told that they had to abandon their language and culture to do so. Icelandic society was very similar, even into the twentieth century, to Gaeldom, yet today they are a proud, independent, industrialized nation, still speaking the Scandinavian language that their ancestors did a thousand years ago. They take special care to resurrect old words and coin new Icelandic ones when new concepts enter Icelandic life. They take a keen interest in their old sagas. Their entry into the 'modernist age' did not require them to despise the culture of their ancestors.

Cultural invasion and conquest, in short, are tools to establish the dominance of one culture at the expense of the self-esteem and independence of another culture. When the colonizer successfully violates the other's norms and institutions, and declares its culture invalid, the colonized culture becomes convinced that it is inferior to the dominant culture and atrophies into a subordinate, subservient, impoverished 'lower-class'.

It is a legacy of this cultural colonialism that many Gaels internalized a sense of inferiority and lost the conviction to carry their language and culture forward to a new generation. The effects of accepting a subordinate, inferior status can be seen in the entire nation. Scottish teenagers are, according to a 1997 World Health Organization survey, the least self-confident and most prone to depression in Western Europe.[48] Without self-esteem, a society cannot make sacrifices and toil together, recover from crises and imagine a better future for itself and work towards it.

Celtic, Gaelic and Scottish

The marketing of the name 'Celtic' has brought great profits to people selling Celtic art, Celtic music, Celtic spirituality and Celtic clothing and has caused great confusion to those whose only experience of Celtic culture are these commodities. Does Celtic mean anything other than a 'feel-good factor', an exotic window dressing for selling products?

The term *Celtic* refers to a cultural family, identified by language, within the larger Indo-European family. A simplified explanation of the development of the branches of the Indo-European language family can be displayed via the family tree (the item on the left in Figure 1.1). This shows how changes in the sounds, words and grammar of the languages lead to the formation of new branches. It is difficult, however, on such a diagram to illustrate inter-relationships between languages, as language development is not just a matter of linear evolution and differentiation but also a process of overlaying earlier substrata and interacting with neighbouring languages with whom there is no 'vertical' connection. The item on the right in Figure 1.1 gives a slightly different interpretation of the relationship between the Indo-European languages.

In theory, all of the Indo-European languages and cultures derive from a common ancestor from which they evolved thousands of years ago. There are many words in the different languages, called *cognates*, whose common ancestry attests to the kinship of the different Indo-European languages. The word 'mother' is, for example, *màthair* in Gaelic, *mater* in Latin, *mat'* in Russian and *matar-* in Sanskrit, testifying to the fact that this was a word inherited from the older common language which underwent systematic changes. As the different peoples went different directions, acclimatized to different environments, developed and borrowed new ideas and encountered new people, so did their languages change.

The Celts were one of the groups to emerge from this general Indo-European stock. 'The Celts were distinguished in various ways, by social organization, religion, dress, methods of warfare, for these were matters of which the early historians took account; but the main distinction then, as now, will have been that of language.'[49]

Despite the lingering reverberations of racial ideology, we should not think of the Celts as a race, but as a culture identifiable by language. The peoples of Europe cannot be distinguished from each other by race but by their languages and by the cultures that are coupled with these languages. We should be wary about projecting modernist beliefs about race into primal societies and pre-modern Europe, as other notions of identity were predominant.

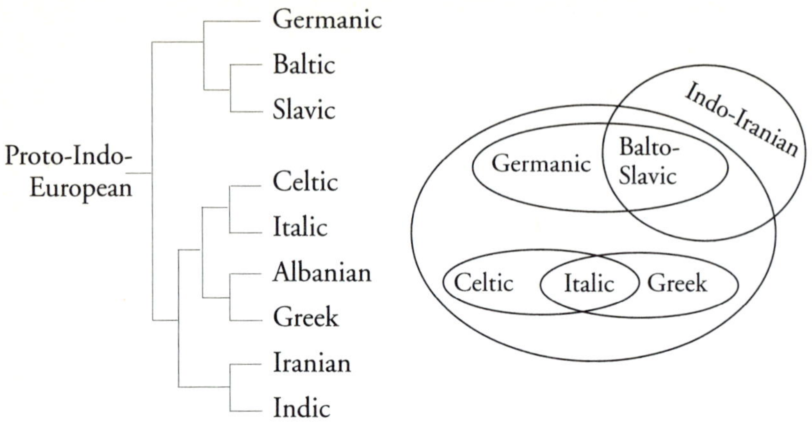

Figure 1.1 – Two models of Indo-European language relationships

A variety of physical features are described in the accounts of the Greeks and Romans. The Celtic warrior of Gaul was, according to the ideal recorded by Classical historians, fair skinned, blonde and blue-eyed, but we can see many other physical descriptions in early sources. In his *Agricola*, for example, Tacitus tells us that the people of Britain are not all of one stock, but resemble various neighbours across from them on the Continent of Europe. While his descriptions are useful, we should beware of his inferences regarding origins, as we know that these peoples were all culturally Celtic:

> The physique of the people presents many varieties, whence inferences are drawn: the red hair and the large limbs of the inhabitants of Caledonia proclaim their German origin; the swarthy faces of the Silures, the curly quality, in general, of their hair, and the position of Spain opposite their shores … those peoples, again, [in Britain] who adjoin Gaul are also like Gauls …[50]

Although the hero-warrior of Gaelic tradition is most often characterized like that of the fair Gaulish warrior caste – 'Good figure, chalk-white teeth, blue eyes, golden hair are the stock conventions'[51] – there is considerable variation in the way that physical characteristics are praised in Gaelic poetry and folktales. In love songs, hair colour can as easily be *bàn* (fair) as *donn* (brown), *dubh* (black), or *ruadh* (red). Colours have special associations in Gaelic tradition[52] and colours in Gaelic names refer specifically to hair colour. The variety of hair and skin colours in Ireland were explained in Gaelic accounts according to the legendary pre-historic peoples of the insular Celtic world, the Fir Bolg, Tuatha De Dannan and the Milesians.

The Celtic peoples have always been interacting and inter-mixing with other peoples. There has been interaction with the Germanic and Nordic worlds, with the peoples of the trans-polar Arctic North and those of the Mediterranean. Sea travel was extensive and common in pre-historic times and Britain and Ireland were within access of many early peoples.

We don't really know what the term 'Celtic' originally meant, where it came from, if the Celts really called themselves this or if it was a label given to them by others. The ethnonym *Keltoi* first appears in Greek sources by the end of the sixth century BC, where they are said to dwell in Gaul (roughly corresponding to modern day France) and in south-western Spain.[53]

By the middle of the first millennium BC, we have evidence of Celtic languages being spoken in a wide continuous arc from Ireland across to Italy.[54] There is also evidence of Celtic place-names in Austria, Bohemia, southern and western Germany, France, Britain and Ireland with many common elements.[55]

The later Celts are usually separated into a P-Celtic/Q-Celtic linguistic divide, on account of one group (Gaul and Britain) which started pronouncing their *qu* sounds as *p*, as opposed to a more conservative group (in Iberia, Scotland and Ireland) which retained the original *qu* sound. This P-Q division is really a 'short-hand' for a number of related sound changes, but we shouldn't think that this was any sort of significant division between peoples, especially between early Ireland and Scotland: 'around the first century BC the resemblance between Goidelic and Brittonic was extremely close and [any differences were] insufficient to hinder mutual understanding ...'[56]

The oldest recorded name for Britain is *Albion*, written down *c.*500 BC.[57] It is a Celtic name meaning 'the habitable surface of the world',[58] and is the name still used by Gaelic speakers for Scotland: *Alba* (locative) *Albainn*. The fact that this name was established by this early date for the whole island suggests that the Celts had been established there for a good while. Later, a new group of Celts who called themselves *Britonnes* arrived and gave their name to the island (although Gaelic preserves the earlier pre-Brittonic name *Alba*).[59] The early form of P-Celtic in Britain is hence called *Brittonic*.

Brittonic developed into different dialects amongst the different peoples in Britain. One of these dialects is Welsh, the living language of Wales, and Breton, the living language of Brittany. Other forms have not survived.

Cumbric is the name given to the dialect that was once spoken in the areas which are now the south of Scotland and the north of England.[60]

It is important to get a sense of the Celtic foundations of Scotland to understand the continuing influence of those persistents in Scottish life. All of Scotland was once Celtic, Brittonic south of the Clyde-Forth line, and Pictish and Gaelic north of it. The Picts, until recently, were treated as a people shrouded in mystery, and much wishful thinking driven by anti-Celtic prejudice attempted to give the Picts a non-Celtic identity. Research on their place-names, personal names, artefacts and practices, however, show them to be Celtic.[61]

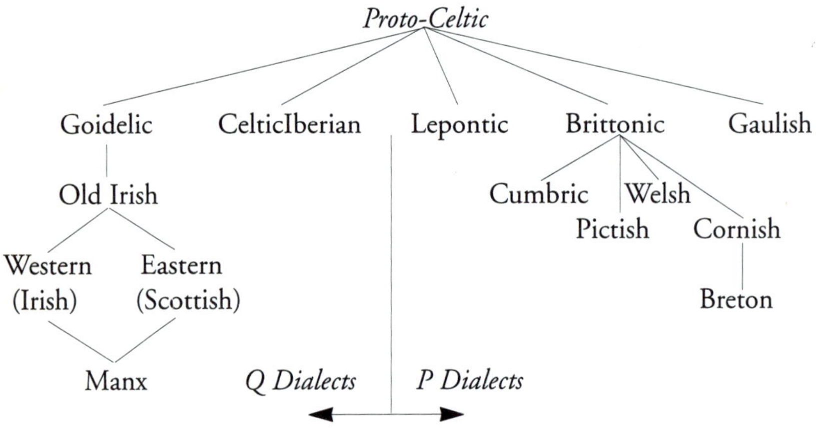

Figure 1.2 – Languages within the Celtic family

The Celts are a family of related cultures. A person cannot simply be a Celt, he must also be something more specific – Welsh, an Irish or Scottish Gael, a Breton – if he is really Celtic, just as a Native American must be something more specific – a Cherokee, a Navajo, a Sioux, and so on. Celtic is an abstract term for a family of identities which have similar characteristics but are not identical to each other.

Despite the fact that the Celts had no centralized political structures and were frequently at war with each other, the term 'Celtic' is not just the 'Other', referring to a diverse assortment of European barbarians. Dr Proinsias Mac Cana has pointed out that the Irish were able to maintain their independent diversity exactly because they had a common culture: 'each individual kingdom was small enough not to require such structures, while in the country as a whole cultural-religious homogeneity was such that centralized government was unnecessary.'[62] The ethos of the warrior-centred Heroic Age could only be maintained by keeping the 'tribal' units small enough. 'The underlying principle was one of co-ordination rather than consolidation.'[63]

A skeptic might equally discount the notion of '*Greeks* as the name for the ancient populations of the modern nation-state of Greece because such names describe groups whose languages were far from identical, and who were also Athenians, Spartans, Euboeans, Phocaeans or even Macedonians'.[64] Did their lack of political unity and constant in-fighting discount the usefulness of the concept of Greekness?

One must also keep in mind that many features once common throughout pre-industrial Europe survived longest in the 'Celtic Fringe' and are now mistakenly thought of as being specifically 'Celtic', such as bagpipes, step-dancing, fiddle music, keening, wakes, pre-Christian nature celebrations, and so on. We must be careful to use the term Celtic in ways which are accurate and meaningful.

Although there have been upheavals and cultural shifts in Scotland, particularly associated with the loss of Gaelic and the subsequent overlay of a Germanic language and culture (Lallans 'Scots'), it is important to recognize the many persistents and continuities in the matrix of Scottish culture. 'In Scotland, although we must bear in mind the existence of two strong deeply-rooted cultures, seasonal customs and beliefs in both culture areas show an essential kinship. The differences seem to be in expression and temperamental reaction.'[65]

A study of the customs of birth, marriage and death throughout Scotland comes to a similar conclusion:

> No sooner have we concluded that Scotland is a small nation of many regional variations than we are faced with a rather paradoxical concept: the universality of customs throughout the nation. The reader will recognize many aspects of tradition which are replicated from one area to another, sometimes with slight variations, and at other times virtually identical to a custom already encountered in an entirely different region.[66]

So too can we see similarity in the customs of the seasonal festivals across Scotland, patterns which can be explained in terms of Celtic origins.

Folktales and songs in Lowland culture have motifs in them which betray Celtic origins. Historians too point out that the discontinuities in Scottish culture have been vastly exaggerated, particularly due to the myth that Progress in Scotland was due to the sudden arrival of the Anglo-Saxon race and culture. 'Less important than the arbitrary dating of a watershed in Scotland's history is the realisation that in every century in Scottish history until the nineteenth, the forces of continuity outweighed those of change.'[67]

The culture of the Highlands in particular displays a 'considerable degree of homogeneity'.[68] This pattern of local variation of a common culture is matched by a common language with regional dialects: 'Scottish Gaelic is remarkably uniform ... [The] differences in Gaelic are all differences of *cainnt* "speech" as opposed to *càna(i)n* "language" ...'[69]

J.G. Campbell wrote in his compilation of folklore in the Highlands and Islands, 'The beliefs of one district do not differ essentially from those of another.'[70] In her study of the material culture of Highland folklife, I.F. Grant observes:

> Although there were sometimes local differences in customs, the shape of implements, pronunciation and vocabulary and in songs and traditional stories yet, by and large, there was a predominantly Gaelic culture and similarity in methods of agriculture and social organization and new developments were widely diffused.[71]

It is indeed remarkable, in studying Gaelic oral tradition, how songs or tales specific to one clan, person or place could be found throughout the Gaelic-speaking region. Tales about events and people in the Hebrides, for example, were recorded in nineteenth-century Eastern Perthshire. Songs by mainland bards, such as Iain Lom, could be heard everywhere from Lewis to Argyll. The Gaelic oral tradition was not merely one of regions or localities within the Highlands, but 'the art of a nation'.[72]

The legends of the Fianna – the Gaelic equivalent of Arthur and the knights of the Round Table – were exemplary myths localized by the Gaels wherever they travelled. Fenian lays and tales have been recorded everywhere from Kintyre to Lewis to Dunkeld to Loch Lomond, and the names of the Fianna feature in place-names in Scotland as far south as Gowmacmorran in Lanarkshire.[73] The characters of the Fianna were even known amongst the Lowlanders of Medieval Scotland, appearing in such works as Barbour's *The Bruce* and Sir David Lindsay's *Ane Satyre of the Thrie Estaits*.[74] Hector Boece says in his sixteenth-century work *The History and Chronicles of Scotland* that tales about Fionn mac Cumhaill ('Fingal') were in common circulation and similar to those of King Arthur.

The word for a Gael in Gaelic is *Gàidheal* (plural *Gàidheil*). The early peoples of Britain had an intuitive understanding of a close link between language and nationality. The Welsh word *iaith*, for example, means both language and nation.[75] When Bede, in the eighth century, enumerates the peoples in Britain – Britons, Picts, Gaels and Anglo-Saxons – he equates their language and ethnic identity.

As the common Gaelic name for Ireland is *Éire*, an Irishman is called an *Èireannach* in Gaelic and a Scotsman (regardless of his speech) is called an *Albannach* (plural *Albannaich*).[76] The old ethnic term relating to the Celts of Britain was applied in Welsh specifically to non-Romanized Pictland, *Prydein*, and this term appears in Gaelic (shifting the 'P' to a 'C') as *Cruithin*.[77] The Picts in Gaelic are called *Cruithnich* (plural). The other P-Celtic peoples, who occupied Strathclyde and all of Britain south of the Firth-Clyde line, are called *Breatannaich* (plural) in Gaelic and Britons in English. This is the origin of the name Dumbarton, 'the fort of the Britons', which is called *Dùn Breatann* in Gaelic.

Regardless of the fact that, in early times, more specific 'tribal' designations were used to refer to other Celts, and there was no generic ethnonym meaning 'Celts', the Celts knew who they were not. The term *Gall* (plural *Goill*) was initially used to denote a person from Gaul – someone from outwith the insular Celtic context – but upon the arrival of Germanic invaders, it was subsequently applied to Vikings, Anglo-Normans and English. It is never used in reference to other insular Celts.

Gall eventually came to mean, in Scotland, the more specific 'Other' who was always present: the Lowlander. This is in distinction, however, to the *Sasannach* 'Englishman'. This terminology indicates a Gaelic perception that the Germanic peoples who became 'naturalized' in Scotland were different from those who lived south of the Scottish border. 'All we can say from the evidence of Gaelic tradition is that the integrity of Alba, Scotland, is never in question. The inhabitants of the Lowlands are unquestionably *Albannaich*. But within that framework, there are more detailed perceptions.'[78]

Despite mutual interchange between *Gàidheil* and *Goill*, there has been an on-going tension between the two. There is a common reaction amongst Lowlanders today who seem threatened by a growing interest in Gaelic that the Gaels are 'no more Scottish' than they are. This is not the Gaelic point of view, however. In Gaelic tradition, the Lowlanders are interlopers who have ousted the Gaels from their rightful place in Scotland, both in terms of status and territory. Edmund Burt, an English officer stationed in the Highlands in the 1720s, observed:

> They have an *adherence one to another, as Highlanders*, in opposition to the people of the Low-Country, whom they despise as inferior to them in Courage, and believe they have a right to plunder them whenever it is in their Power. This last arises from a Tradition, that the Lowlands, in old Times were the possessions of their Ancestors.[79]

We must take care, however, how we interpret the idea of 'plunder' and cattle-raiding within the context of Gaelic society. The Gaelic economy from earliest times was based on the mobile 'cattle' unit[80] and the reiving of cattle between tribes was designed to 'assert status or claim redress for real or assumed breaches of established relations … As in India the new elected monarch had to carry out a successful cattle-raid as an integral part of the protracted ceremonial of royal inauguration …'[81]

Thus cattle-raiding was not thought of as theft in a modern sense, but an accepted form of inter-clan aggression, although it caused Gaels to be stereotyped as 'lawless' in Lowland tradition. The Highlands were, and continue to be, an extremely law-abiding society. The conflict was in the two different traditions of what law was understood to be.

It is interesting, despite this apparent dichotomy, that according to Gaelic tradition, it is the Lowlander Thomas the Rhymer who figures as a Messiah role for the Gaels.[82] In a similar role to that of Arthur and Merlin in Welsh tradition, and Fionn mac Cumhaill in other Gaelic traditions, Thomas is sometimes described as the prophet who has foreseen the rightful return of the dispossessed Gaels to their proper place in Scotland, and sometimes as the Sleeping Warrior who will himself be the leader of that revolution.[83]

CHAPTER 2

A Gaelic history of Scotland

The Celtic peoples of early Scotland were gradually subsumed into a Gaelic identity which was itself altered by their influence. They were beleaguered in the south by Germanic invaders and in the north and west by Viking raiders a short while later. It was soon apparent that, while these people would not necessarily be sent packing home, that they might be useful allies and, with time, be integrated into the Scottish nation. We need not assume that this was seen to put the integrity of the nation into jeopardy: it was the Norse and Anglo-Saxon areas which were the remote peripheries of the time, while the large interior of the nation remained Celtic and maintained links with the centres of learning and culture in Ireland.

Even by the time of the Anglo-Norman settlements in the 12th century, Norsemen (apart from those in the Northern Isles) were well on the way to being re-Gaelicized, and many of the descendents of the Anglo-Normans soon went native. The question of how and why an alternative Anglo-Teutonic identity came to dominate Scotland and overshadow its original Gaelic identity is complex, but neither economic determinism or cultural Darwinism can explain how Gaelic has dwindled in significance in Scottish history and the popular imagination. What is important to understand is the process by which the institutions created by Scotland's Gaelic kings came to be dominated by an Anglo-centric ideology increasingly hostile toward and dismissive of its Gaelic origins.

The result of generations of Scots going through schools which not only ignore Scotland's Celtic past but are dismissive of the idea that the Celts, and particularly the Gaels, had anything worthy of calling a civilization has cultivated a widespread prejudice. The hostility to Gaelic that surfaces when it is in the public spotlight is the worst, most paranoid, symptom of the 'Scottish cringe' which may be remedied by education and a broader view of Scotland's history.

A single chapter can only provide the emergent patterns and broad brush strokes of history, with a hint of some of the counter-currents. A number of issues raised in this summary will be explored in greater detail in further chapters.

Celts, Romans and Christians

Archaeology reveals that there has been a special connection between Scotland and Ireland since very early times. From Neolithic stone tools and building designs to metalworking, there are close affinities between the material cultures of ancient Scotland and Ireland.

Dwelling and defensive sites in Scotland are developments of wider Celtic styles, but are particularly close to Irish construction styles. The *crannog*, an artificial island built a short distance from the shore of a loch, was resorted to in times of danger and easily defended from attackers. These structures date from as long ago as 700 BC and some crannogs in the Scottish Highlands continued to be occupied into the eighteenth century. The crannog is specific to Ireland and Scotland and the similarities and great antiquity of these sites has caused debate about their origins, but the latest hypothesis is that they were 'invented' in Scotland and brought somewhat later to Ireland.[1]

Recent research on the construction styles of ancient dwellings has shown that a distinctive style of home, in which a living hall with a central hearth and an adjoining circular chamber, can be found in Ireland, the Hebrides and Orkney, suggesting a shared tradition of construction.[2]

The *broch* is a strikingly distinctive-looking defensive tower, unique to Scotland, which appears by *c.*100 BC. Almost 500 brochs, from as far north as Shetland to at least as far south as Stirlingshire have been recognized.[3] These Pictish brochs are a development within the wider Celtic tradition of defensive fortifications.[4]

None of these archaeological artefacts, of course, tell us anything about the languages that the people spoke or what they considered their identity to be, and they very seldom offer more than a tantalizing hint at their ways of life and systems of belief. The continuity of the styles of buildings, the uninterrupted occupation of particular sites and the continued reverence of sacred sites, however, attest to a remarkable degree of cultural stability from early in the first millennium BC well into the historical Celtic period. 'Archaeology demonstrates that basic material culture, the everyday domestic equipment and fashions in buildings, was common to the Picts, Britons and Scots, who built the same kinds of houses and forts and used the same kinds of tools and weapons.'[5]

The reality of a Celtic culture in the middle of the first millennium BC over a wide swathe of Europe has already been mentioned in the first chapter. The gradual development and distribution of Celtic speech and culture over a large area by continual social interaction has been called the model of *cumulative Celticity*, attempting to account for the Celtic peoples not in terms of invasions and mass migrations but in terms of cultural exchange.[6]

The term *Pict* first appears in a Roman source in AD 297, already associating them with the Gaels.[7] We don't know if the tribes of northern Scotland called themselves 'Picts' or if this was a name given by the Romans to them.[8] Although this ethnonym eventually referred to the northern tribes of Scotland as a whole, our earliest information describes more specific groupings of peoples.

The three main tribes, the Decantae, Smertae and Lugi, assigned to the area where the distinctive Pictish symbol stones are believed to have originated, around the Moray firth, all have names which are paralleled in other parts of Celtic Britain, Gaul, or Ireland.[9] Names of rivers and lochs are usually the oldest names in any country, surviving changes of language and population shift,[10] and many river and loch names in the ancient Pictish 'heartland', such as the Tay, the Dee, and the Lossie, are definitely Celtic.[11]

The Pictish element *aber-* means a 'confluence of water, a river mouth', and occurs in place names, such as Aberdeen, all over Pictland south of the Moray firth in neat correspondence with the Pictish element *pit–*. *Aber–* is clearly Celtic, as it also occurs in Wales and is based on the same root *beir* as the Gaelic *inbhear* (Englished as Inver). An examination of the second element in *aber* place name compounds reveals Celtic roots with close correspondences in Gaelic: Aberbervie ('the boiling water', Gaelic *berb*), Aberbothrie ('the deaf (silent) one', Gaelic *bodhar*), and so on.[12]

The personal names of Picts which appear in Roman and early Christian sources are clearly Celtic: Agricola mentions Calgacus (the Swordsman), Dio Cassius mentions Argentocoxos (Silver Leg), and Adomnán gives us names like Mailchon (hound-servant).[13]

While our information is brief and fragmentary, there is no suggestion that the Picts were fundamentally any different from their southern Celtic neighbours, a fact that a propagandist like Tacitus would not have missed.[14] Many who have tried to give the Picts a non-Celtic identity have grasped at the claim of their use of matriliny, but even this has been shown by recent scholarship to be no different in practice from that of their neighbours.[15]

The Picts began unifying themselves, even by the Roman period, into two main groupings divided north and south by the natural geographical boundary of the Mounth[16] (a Pictish name equivalent to the Welsh *mynydd*, absorbed into Scottish Gaelic as *monadh*).[17] King Bridei mac Bile, when he defeated invaders from Northumbria at Dunnichen Moss could already claim high-kingship for all Picts by 685.[18] This very rapid centralization brought the centre of Pictish power to the southern kingdom of Fortriu, where it would form very strong links with the Gaelic kingdom of Dál Riada.

History and tradition records a great deal of exchange and inter-migration between Pictland and Ireland. The Cruithin, long established in Ireland, were P-Celts in origin and there are Irish tales and historical records of Pictish nobles taking exile in Ireland.[19] The presence of P-Celtic war bands in northern Ireland in later seventh and early eighth centuries has been connected with the political upheaval following Germanic invasions in the south of Scotland.[20] Tacitus tells us of an Irish prince exiled in Britain and this has been connected with the Irish tale of Tuathal Techtmar.[21] Thus, even from a very early stage, the Celtic peoples of southern Scotland and northern Ireland are closely intertwined. This link lingered on, for Cormac's Glossary of the tenth century 'betrays considerable knowledge of Welsh'.[22] A great many early Irish tales describe nobles sent to Scotland in exile, which would not have happened if Scotland was an alien, hostile territory where communication was impossible.

The Celtic dialects of Ireland and Scotland of this period, while they may have had points of difference, were in the main very close. That mutual comprehension happened is illustrated, among other things, by place-names and personal names. Many Pictish names were given Gaelic forms when recorded by Gaels, demonstrating that they understood their meanings.[23] Many of these names were common to P- and Q-Celts and were very similar to each other.

We must be careful not to project modern geographical and political boundaries where they did not exist in the past. The Gaels were adept at sea-travel and, has been discussed above, had been traversing the narrow stretch of sea between Ireland and Scotland for centuries. Current scholarship is demonstrating that Gaelic settlement in coastal areas of Scotland across from Ireland is much older than previously believed. The most important political connection between Irish and Scottish Gaels in the early Christian era was that of the kingdom of Dál Riada, which later tradition claimed to have been established in Scotland by the royal house of Fergus mac Eirc around the year 500. This family ruled a Gaelic population which was divided into three tribal-territories, the Cenél nOengusa in Islay, the Cenél nGabráin in

Kintyre, Gigha, Jura, Arran, and Cowal, and the Cenél Loairn in Lorne, Mull, Tiree, Coll and Ardnamurchan.

During the centuries of Gaelic-Pictish interaction, 'bilingualism' of the two dialects must have been the norm, with a gradual shift from a Pictish to Gaelic form of language. Place-names provide the best evidence for this linguistic transition. The Pictish element *aber-* was translated to Gaelic *inbhear-* in a number of place-names[24] and many place names in Scotland which were coined by Picts were translated (or transliterated) into Gaelic.[25] Some Pictish terms borrowed into Gaelic demonstrate that distinctive administrative concepts from Pictish culture survived the linguistic shift.[26]

This evidence shows that there was no wholesale slaughter of Picts or massive invasion of Gaels, but a long process of cultural assimilation, in which the two people came together as a Gaelic kingdom built upon a wider Celtic foundation. The cultures and histories of the Celts of Ireland and Britain, especially in areas of close geographical proximity, were interdependent and cannot be neatly separated from each other.

There was probably no more influential player in the process of nation-building, and nothing more indicative of the Gaelic hand in that process, than the church. The Christian church came in the wake of the Roman Empire and carried with it the status and learning of the Classical world. As the church, lead by Gaelic-educated church leaders, spread across Pictland, so did the status and influence of Gaelic culture propagate through these institutions. Iona, the hub of the Gaelic church, was placed strategically to access Gaelic, Pictish, and Brittonic kingdoms.

There was no separation between church and state. Men like Columba took prominent roles in the church exactly because they were members of ruling dynasties, and the leaders of the church took an active role in the matters of state. An angel spoke to Aedán mac Gabráin, promising that he and his descendants would rule Dál Riata successfully if they obeyed Columba's wishes.[27] The church, in turn, needed the patronage of kings to survive and flourish. 'The literate clergy were a mandarin class which forged a role for itself as the advocates and interpreters of high kingship.'[28] The figure of Columba continued to play a role in the inauguration of Scottish kings until the thirteenth century.[29]

At the level of the common folk, the saints were a vital link between the old faith and the new. The oldest folklore in Gaelic oral tradition concerns the activities of the saints, and written saints' lives contain ample evidence of the affirmation of the power of Christianity by recourse to native Celtic beliefs and values. The cults of saints took over the sanctity and traditions of pre-Christian sites all around Scotland.

Europe's first international human rights treaty, *Cáin Adamnáin*, 'The Law of Innocents', was penned by Adomnán, an abbot of Iona and a nobleman of the Cenél Conaill dynasty. This law, which protected women, children and clergy from the ravages of warfare, was ratified in 697 by the kings of the Picts, of the Dál Riatic Scots, of the Strathclyde Britons, and of many Irish kingdoms, and the law took effect in both Scotland and Ireland. 'It is singular testimony to the widespread common Celtic (and now Christianized) culture extending from Ireland across Dalriada and Pictland to Lindisfarne ...'[30]

Although the Roman Empire made very little impact on Scotland[31] and had minimal direct contact with Ireland, the Classical learning of the Roman world did come to Gaeldom through the medium of the church. There is evidence of a great deal of syncretism as Christian theology and Classical learning were harmonized with self-confident and sophisticated native Gaelic institutions. This allowed the Christian worldview to be accepted into a pre-existing mytho-historical framework without denying the validity and importance of Gaelic tradition.

There is little doubt that the absolute integrity of native pre-Christian tradition was compromised in this process, but the synthesis of these two traditions produced a highly successful union. While the Germanic hordes spread chaos around the remnants of the Roman Empire, Gaeldom 'in the Dark Ages became the chief custodians of the classical learning that had passed to Europe from Greece and Rome'.[32] Gaelic literature is the earliest written vernacular literature in Western Europe, with works such as *Amrae Cholaim Chille* being written in the sixth century. The sophisticated, syncretic Gaelic law system was written down as early as the seventh century.

With the sophistication of these ecclesiastical-based centres of learning, it is little wonder that the burgeoning Gaelic church was to have a lasting impact on the culture and political structures in Scotland: 'the Gaelic language has deeper roots in Scottish soil than any other institution except Christianity'.[33]

Forging the nation

The creation of the kingdom of Scotland would not have been possible without the ideology of kingship and the development of hierarchical relationships between leaders of particular regions and the centralized monarchy. Just as the *rí túaithe* (tribal king) in Ireland could be subject to a *ruirí* (over-king) who in turn might have a dependent relationship with a *rí ruireach* (king of over-kings), so too the Pictish kings of Scotland seem to have shared this common Celtic hierarchical principle of kingship.[34]

The dynasties of Brittonic Strathclyde, Pictland, and Gaelic Dál Riata had been interacting and intermarrying for some time, and hence a noble of a particular origin sometimes became the king of another people. Bridei son of Bili, a Strathclyde Briton, was the king of Pictish Fortriu for a time and by the eighth-century Pictish kings had Gaelic names and held Pictish and Dál Riatic kingships at the same time.[35] This points to early attempts to consolidate Pictish and Gaelic kingdoms well before the arrival of Cináed mac Alpín (Kenneth mac Alpine), a Gael who took the kingship of Picts in 842.

Although Kenneth mac Alpine justified his suitability for kingship by claiming descent from Áed Find, king of Dál Riata, his ancestry is still uncertain. Whatever his origins, he could not have held any kingship or achieved military victories unless he was of some royal lineage and enjoyed the support of clients who were willing to join his war band.[36]

The disruption of Viking raids and settlement in the west turned the Gaelic focus eastwards into Pictland. The greater centralization of the kingdom and concentration of power in the hands of Gaelic kings no doubt sped the process of Gaelicization among the Celtic peoples now subsumed under their control. Sites which had been important Pictish centres of power were now employed as the seats of Gaelic institutions: new laws were proclaimed at Forteviot in Fortriu, *Dùn Chailleann* (Dunkeld, 'the fort of the Caledonians') became a leading church centre, and the new Gaelic dynasty established itself at the old Pictish seat of Scone.[37]

The more the Picts were Gaelicized and receded from historical memory, the more that folkloric elements made up for the lack of recorded details. The tale that Kenneth mac Alpine slaughtered the Pictish nobility treacherously during a banquet is an ancient folklore motif found far and wide around the world.[38]

Kenneth was, despite his Gaelic origin, considered a king of Pictland and it is not until 900 that terminology changed to reflect a Gaelic identity for the new kingdom as a whole when Donald II was styled *Rí Alban*. The Gaelic identity of the kings and institutions brought the name Scot and Scotia, first coined by the Romans to describe the Irish, to the country we still call Scotland. 'Alba was inescapably part of the Gaelic world: the same language, 'high culture' and major saints' cults were shared from Munster to Moray.'[39]

During the time that these consolidations were taking place in the inside of Scotland, however, Angles and Vikings were invading the peripheral areas of the kingdom. When the Anglian kingdom of Bernicia tried to push northwards, they were met by an alliance led by Áedán mac Gabráin, king of Dál Riada, at the battle of Degsastan in 603. The temporary success of the Germanic peoples introduced what was to later become the English language into the lowlands of southern Scotland. Decisive victories by the Picts in 685 and 756 prevented the Angles from moving further north into Pictland.

The invasions of Norse raiders in the late eighth century and their establishment of kingdoms of their own soon thereafter was to complicate matters for both Celtic and Germanic peoples alike. There is evidence for the settlement of Norsemen in the Northern and Western Isles from about the middle of the ninth century onwards, but more significant politically were rival Norse kingdoms based at Dublin and York. While the loss of the far north and west to Norse settlers may have been a territorial setback, the Danish conquest of the expansionist Anglian kingdoms in Northumbrian gave the Scots kings the chance to consolidate the core of the kingdom. They also soon learned how to exploit the rivalry between Danish York and Norwegian Dublin to their own advantage.[40]

While Norse settlement was heavy enough in the Northern Isles to replace the Celtic elements, there is sufficient evidence that re-Gaelicization was not slow in coming to the Western Isles and west of Scotland. By the middle of the ninth century, a hybrid Gaelic-Norse people called the *Gall-Ghaedhil* emerged and the Gaelic language was re-established by the eleventh century.[41]

By the tenth century, the Scottish kings were reasserting their power southwards, particularly as the kingdom of York was being taken over by Wessex. The king of Wessex acknowledged Scotland's possession of Lothian in 973 and Malcolm II's victory in 1018 secured southern territory as far as the Tweed. Strategic marriage and politicking in the north defused Norse threats until the Treaty of Perth acknowledged Scottish control of the Hebrides in 1266.

The Western Norse not only enthusiastically adopted a Gaelic identity for themselves, they began restoring the Gaelic cultural centres which their forebears had brought to ruin. Somerled, a *Gall-Ghaedheal* with a Norse name, renovated Iona and attempted to restore its Irish links in 1164. He and his dynasty emphasized their Dál Riada ancestry in their conscious construction of a Gaelic principality which was to be the primary patron of traditional learning and culture for generations to come. Other than in the Northern Isles and the tip of Caithness, the Norse were absorbed into Gaelic society and are remembered in Gaelic tradition as the archetypal enemy.

The securing of the borders of Scotland by Gaelic-speaking kings helped to secure the expansion of Gaelic culture into the corners of the kingdom. A new layer of Gaelic settlement is visible in place-names of the south-west from the ninth century onwards, while a Gaelic aristocracy and their Gaelic-speaking followers were established in the south-east by the opening of the twelfth century.[42] Gaelic place-names in the Lothians such as Gilmerton and Gilchriston are testimonies to the Gaelic magnates who brought their Gaelic-speaking retinues to secure and consolidate the contested frontier of the Scottish kingdom. 'From Cape Wrath to the Clyde-Forth line ... was a land whose inhabitants, the Scots, were overwhelmingly Celtic, speaking almost universally the 'Scottish', that is, the Gaelic, language, and observing social and religious customs that must be explained largely in Celtic terms.'[43] The battle-cry of Scottish soldiers in 903, 918 and 1138 was said to be '*Albanaigh, Albanaigh!*' (Gaelic for 'Scotsmen, Scotsmen!'). 'The new feudalism of the twelfth century came into contact not with a receding Celtic culture but with a still-expanding one.'[44]

Feudalization and clanship

At the same time that the Scottish kingdom was being unified and stabilized under its Gaelic kings, economic-political reformers of a new order were taking Europe by storm. Feudalism turned kingship from rule by royal authority over noble subjects into a stricter hierarchy of a regal landlord who granted land to vassals belonging to the crown in exchange for loyalty and military duty.[45]

Many English nobles refused to submit to William the Conqueror after his 1066 conquest of England and some sought refuge in the Scottish court. Among them were heirs to the old Wessex throne. King of Scots Malcolm III married the young English princess Margaret, whose preference for English ways was impressed upon her sons. 'The way was opened for continental and English influences of every kind to pour into Scotland, most conspicuously in the life of the church but by no means confined to religious faith or ecclesiastical organization.'[46]

When Malcolm III died in 1093, the choice of the kingdom's magnates was his brother Dòmhnall Bàn who immediately 'drove out all the English who were with King Malcolm before'. Political struggles immediately ensued, with the sons of Malcolm seeking Anglo-Norman military backing to regain the throne and willing to submit to the English king to get it. When Edgar was made king of Scotland in 1097, he acknowledged his fealty to the English King William, and when his brother Alexander I succeeded him in 1107, he too seems to have paid homage to the English King Henry I, whose illegitimate daughter he married.

Just as significant as the makeup of the ruler was the makeup of the church, which was the primary institution of learning and cultural prestige in medieval Europe. Margaret set a number of church reforms into motion, including bringing monks from Canterbury to Dunfermline. King Edgar granted Durham monks a priory at Coldingham and King Alexander brought canons from Yorkshire to a priory he founded in the heart of the kingdom at Scone, marking the beginning of 'a planned colonization of the religious orders of western Christendom in Scotland'.[47] The replacement of learned Gaelic churchmen by Anglo-Normans at important national centres went a long way towards de-rooting the Gaelic-specific foundations of these institutions which were dependent upon noble patrons.[48]

The feudal movement in Scotland was accelerated by King David, who had spent his adolescence at the English court and was described as being the paragon of Norman knighthood. When David assumed the Scottish throne in 1124, he ushered in further church reform, feudal land grants and the establishment of royal burghs. The new parish system was often closely related to feudal land grants, making it function as part of the policy of royal control and consolidation.[49]

David granted the first feudal settlers estates in the south of Scotland, as when Robert de Brus was granted lands in Annandale and the Steward was granted lands in Renfrewshire. Such feudal nobles brought with them Anglo-Norman and Flemish clients and a contingent of retainers from their English estates. A second phase of more intense feudal colonization including a higher proportion of Flemish settlers was begun in the north, attempting to secure areas such as Moray, which had revolted against David in 1130. Feudalization was no doubt considered a development necessary to unite the kingdom and strengthen its defenses against threats from powerful enemies already equipped with this form of social and military organization.

Although human settlement must have already been widespread on the landscape, David's establishment of burghs introduced towns and commerce previously unknown to Scotland. A burgh was a legal entity recognized by the king which privileged a community of burgesses with the right to trade and gave them exemption from toll charges throughout the kingdom. About fifteen burghs appear to have been founded during David's reign, largely populated by Flemish immigrants experienced in commerce. Scottish burghs were usually placed in the fertile coastlines of the Lowlands, where they could exploit natural resources and have access to the sea routes where they could trade in the burgeoning European markets.

As towns were 'dangerous places, prone to warfare, disease and fire ... their populations needed regular human replacement, which could come only from the countryside.'[50] The industry of the burghs required low-cost manual labour available in the outside community. It was from the feudal and burgh settlers that the Lowland dialect of English developed ('Lallans'). The constant interaction between burgh and countryside, and the growing economic force of the burghs, had the effect over time of changing the language and culture of the originally Gaelic-speaking communities that were situated around them.

It would be wrong to see all native Celts as entirely passive or overlooked by the processes of feudalism, however. A number of rivals contested David for the throne, a common event under the Celtic system of tanistry. King Lulach's grandson Angus died in 1130 in an attempt to oust David. Angus had been allied to Malcolm mac Aedh, whose father may have been deprived of the earldom of Ross. Malcolm allied himself with Somerled of Argyll and fomented rebellion until he was finally captured and imprisoned in 1134. Somerled himself claimed royal descent and was killed in 1164 while leading an invasion through the Firth of Clyde.

Another contender known as Donald Macwilliam threatened the throne from his power base in Moray from the 1160s to 1187. It is likely due to this source of unrest that two fortresses were built in the Moray area in 1179.[51] It was by the prowess of Roland of Galloway, itself recently pacified from rebellion, that Donald was defeated. Further generations of Macwilliams continued to threaten the established kings until 1230, although by 1214 Moray was being secured by the settlement of loyal feudal subjects.

There is, on the other hand, evidence that a number of native Gaelic families entered into the new feudal order and were important 'in promoting acceptance of the new ideas that flowed from Norman England ...'[52] The best examples are the MacDuff earls of Fife, who appear to have been the premier family among the native nobility. Not only do the MacDuffs act as chief witnesses on royal charters (an innovation of the feudal age), but they were the first native family on record to be given a feudal land grant. Others, such as the earls of Lennox and Strathearn, followed.

> On the eve of the first War of Independence (*c.*1290), seven (eight if Dunbar be included) of the thirteen earldoms of Scotland were still in the hands of old native families, and of the five held by 'outsiders' four ... had been acquired by marriage with an heiress of the original family.[53]

Incoming families, where circumstances were conducive, were assimilated into Gaelic society, such as the Grants, the Menzies, the Chisholms, the Murrays, the Frasers, and the Stewarts.

> The families of the territorial lords who held the countries of Atholl, Badenoch, Mar, Argyle, Ross, Sutherland, &c. Notwithstanding their being mostly of Low-country extraction, yet in process of time they adapted the language and manners of their Highland vassals, in whom their strength consisted.[54]

Regardless of the elevated position of social leaders in the Highlands, they had a close and interdependent relationship with their followers, who, being largely Gaelic in culture, were able to quickly absorb such people into a Gaelic ethos.

Unlike England, Ireland or Wales, the feudal settlement happened not by conquest but by royal decree as a deliberate organizational policy, although it often needed a certain degree of force to be executed. This provided a mechanism whereby, in the socio-economic spheres of influence of the burghs, Gaelic society had a slow but steady transformation into an Anglo-Norman-Flemish culture over a number of centuries, without the residual legacy of a foreign occupation.[55]

Despite the ongoing process of Anglicization among the nobles and around the burghs, it is significant that Alexander III was made king in 1249 in Scone by Gaelic officials, as the Chronicle of Melrose says, 'in the ancestral manner'. This suggests that the people of Scotland would not have considered him a proper king without the Gaelic ritual of kingship: the blessing of the clergy, the recitation of his pedigree by a Gaelic poet, the transmission of the rod of kingship, and so on.[56]

When the line of Gaelic kings came to an end, with the death of Margaret the Maid of Norway, the sole surviving descendant of Alexander, in 1290, the vulnerability of succession by primogeniture was all too apparent. Scotland was, in the interim period, ruled by elected 'Guardians', who asked King Edward I of England for advice in choosing between a number of competitors. Edward came to a meeting on the Scottish border with an army of troops from his vast dominions demanding to be acknowledged as overlord of Scotland. The majority of the competitors were willing to submit to Edward's demands, being Anglo-Norman feudal lairds with lands and interests in England as well as Scotland.

John Balliol, lord of Galloway, was chosen for the throne, and although he swore fealty to Edward as his superior, his actions as king demonstrated more of a loyalty to Scottish interests than Edward could bear. When the nobles of Scotland petitioned the Pope to free Scotland from the submissions made to Edward in 1291 and 1292, and encouraged Balliol to ally the kingdom with France, Edward felt it necessary to mete out punishment.

When the English defeated the Scottish defense, John was stripped of kingship and all the regalia that symbolized Scotland's identity as a nation, including the Stone of Destiny – items which originated in the nation's Gaelic past – were taken to England. Scotland became an impotent colony. Within a year, however, the flames of defiance were fanned in the Gaelic north into a popular rising aimed at restoring the kingdom. Wallace and Murray were the rising's acknowledged leaders, though it is significant that the MacDuffs, Scotland's premier native nobility, joined the cause, along with Robert the Bruce.[57]

Although the Bruces were a feudal Anglo-Norman family, the young Robert's mother was of the native Gaelic nobility of Carrick. He was fostered in boyhood with a prominent Irish nobleman. His commitment to the Gaelic identity of the Scottish kingdom was manifest in his ability to exploit the people and landscape of Gaelic Scotland as well as in his choice of the Gaelic symbols of nationhood. Scotland's most famous political manifesto, the Declaration of Arbroath, comes from his reign and begins by recounting the nation's Gaelic origin legend. Bruce was installed as king of Scots in 1306 at the traditional site of Scone but soon was forced into exile in the Gaelic west.

His decisive victory at Bannockburn, to which he brought both St Andrew's cross and Columba's *Brecbennach*, was greatly supported via Ireland and the

Gaelic west.[58] Bruce cut the Gordian knot of mixed feudal loyalties by demanding that Scottish lords give up any lands they held in England. Bruce also forfeited lands from those who had not been loyal to his cause and reapportioned them to those who had fought for him. Among those who benefited from their support for Bruce were the Stewarts, the Campbells, the MacDonalds, and the MacRuairis. So important was the Gaelic West in these struggles that John Major wrote in his 1521 *History* 'That great-souled Robert Bruce in his last testament gave this counsel to those who should come after him, that the kings of Scots should never part themselves with these [Hebridean] islands ...'[59]

Angus Òg of Islay's lands in Kintyre were exchanged with vast lands among the southern Hebrides. Further acquisitions by Angus Òg and his son John through marriage, inheritance and crown charter created an extensive sea-board territory whose rulers, the Clan Donald, deserved the self-assumed title *Rígh Innse Gall* (king of the Hebrides) (commonly called in English 'the lord of the Isles'). Not only did this sub-kingdom extend, in its prime, to nearly the entire west coast of Scotland and into the north of Ireland, but the number of fighting men could rival that commanded by the crown itself.[60] The importance of the lordship in Gaelic terms is, however, not its size or military force, but its role in maintaining a stable and peaceful political order under which traditional culture could flourish. The realm of the lordship of the Isles created a Gaelic Scotland in miniature when the process of Anglicization was well underway in the rest of the kingdom.

The choice of Iona by the lordship and Columba as patron saint are examples of the pan-Gaelic ethos it re-established as the conscious heir of the territory of Dál Riada. The *aos dána*, professional hereditary classes of literary men, lawmen, musicians, artisans and medics, were supported by the lordship.

The area of the lordship was the largest and most powerful province in Scotland in the fifteenth century, enough so to sometimes challenge the authority of the crown itself. In terms of the old Gaelic laws of succession, Donald lord of the Isles was legitimately qualified to be king of Scots and attempted, in the battle of Harlaw (1411), to fasten his hold on the earldom of Ross and press toward even bigger claims.

That the lords of the Isles could act against the interests of the Scottish monarch, especially when he was weak, was demonstrated in 1462, when they and the Douglases plotted to divide Scotland between them as subjects of Edward IV of England. The lordship itself did not, however, claim to be or attempt to create a separatist state. Despite the rivalries and conflicts with individual monarchs, the lordship maintained a commitment to their identity as Scots and a loyalty to the old line of Gaelic kings descended from Malcolm III.[61]

Besides vassal clans throughout the Isles and western seaboard, the lordship formed alliances and contracts in the Highlands, such as with Clan Chattan and Fraser of Lovat.[62] It was the rivalries between internal factions of the Clan Donald, and raids made by Alasdair of Lochalsh to assert his supremacy, that provoked King James IV to declare the lordship forfeit in 1493. Six major risings in the Isles attempted to restore the lordship until the death of Domhnall Dubh in 1545. The stable order that the Clan Donald dynasty had held became all too apparent when anarchy and strife erupted in the sudden power vacuum. The various branches of the Clan Donald divided into independent clans and former vassal clans vied and feuded with each other for territory and power.

The most successful and aggressively expansionist of the emergent clans was the Clan Campbell, whose poets asserted its claim for assuming *Ceannas nan Gàidheal* (the leadership of the Gaels). The Campbells straddled both Highland and feudal-Lowland culture, exploiting whatever devices suited them. They usually acted as the agent of the Scottish crown in the Highlands, as opposed to the more traditionalist stance of the Clan Donald, and the contest between these two forces, 'a dialectical opposition of resistance to and collaboration with the central authorities',[63] is a recurring theme of Gaelic tradition.

Anglicization and polarization

The first evidence of the awareness of a difference between Lowland and Highland cultures is the famous comment by John of Fordun in the 1380s:

> The manners and customs of the Scots vary with the diversity of their speech ... The people of the coast are of domestic and civilised habits, trusty, patient, and urbane, decent in their attire, affable and peaceful, devout in Divine worship ... The Highlanders and people of the Islands, on the other hand, are a savage and untamed nation, rude and independent, given to rapine, ease-loving, of a docile and warm disposition, comely in person, but unsightly in dress, hostile to the English people and language, and owing to diversity of speech, even to their own nation, and exceedingly cruel.

This character-sketch of the 'aboriginal' framed in terms of the conflict between savage and civilized is familiar in colonial contexts to the present-day. Still, Fordun allows that the Gaels – whom he calls 'Scots', to distinguish them from the people speaking English – were intelligent and loyal subjects if they were ruled properly. Fordun must be exaggerating the extent of English-speaking territory, for Gaelic still covered many Lowland areas and had only recently receded in others.[64]

While there is an implication that the Gaels were cruel and warlike, and certainly later propaganda was to capitalize on this claim, should we assume that Gaelic regions were particularly so in this era? The destructive raids of the Wolf of Badenoch in the late fourteenth-century Highlands characterized the lawlessness of the times, but the perpetrator of these deeds was a member of the royal house of Stewart, not a native Highland chief. As the concept of kinship was still widespread throughout Scotland, blood-feuds could be found in both Highlands and Lowlands. It is hard to discern a great difference between Highland and Lowland society in these terms in the fifteenth and sixteenth centuries.[65]

Up until this era, the Gaels were important in the identity of the kingdom of Scotland since they represented the origins of the nation. As long as the ideology of royal kingship was dominant, the king needed a noble lineage which reached back into the mists of time, a lineage which was known to be Gaelic. Scottish society at all levels was keen to claim some contact with royal lineage. The Gaelic foundation legend of the nation still held ground in popular imagination in the sixteenth century, for John Major (1521) tells us, 'from whomsoever the Irish traced their descent, from the same source come the Scots though at one remove'.

Into the sixteenth century, Lowland writers were willing to admit to the primacy of Gaels and Gaelic speech in Scotland, although they had different explanations as to the decline of the language. John Major tells us that 'at the present day almost half of Scotland speaks the Irish tongue, and not so long ago it was spoken by the majority of us.' Boece states that the Lowlanders learned English through frequent commerce and on account of attrition through warfare. The Highlanders, however, 'hes baith the writingis and langage as thay [the ancient Scots] had afore, mair ingenius than ony othir pepill.' Bishop John Leslie (1578) is even more adamant that the Highlanders preserved the identity of the ancient Scots: 'not onlie mair than 2 thowsand yeirs they haue keipet the toung hail vncorrupte; bot lykewyse the maner of cleithing and leiuing.'[66] George Buchanan likewise calls the

Gaels the ancient Scots and refers to the Gaelic terminology differentiating *Gàidheal* from *Gall*:

> A great part of [Galloway] still uses its ancient language. These three nations [Wales, Cornwall, Scotland], which posses, the whole coast of Britain that looks toward Ireland, preserve the indelible marks of Gallic speech and affinity. But it is worthy of particular notice, that the ancient Scots divided all the nations who inhabited Britain, into two classes, the one they called Gael, the other [*Gall*].[67]

Gaelic terminology and cultural concepts were also absorbed to some degree into Lowland speech and culture in this period, although some of these items only enjoyed a short life span before they were squeezed out by English. One of the few areas to be researched thus far, Scots Law, reveals significant borrowing. This again suggests that the nature of feudalism in Scotland allowed for a great syncretism, and hence greater continuity, than it did in the other Celtic lands.[68]

Nonetheless, the power and prestige of a nation is with its nobility, and Scottish nobles had by now long used English as the language of the court and administration. Language seldom fails to carry cultural and symbolic significance. Even the Lowland Scots of the burghs thought of themselves as English (and their language 'Inglis').[69] Despite their linguistic and cultural identity as Anglo-Saxons, Lowlanders did not think of themselves as English in a national sense. In the sixteenth century they appropriated the term 'Scot', which had previously referred to the Gaels, for themselves and applied the term 'Erse' to the Highlanders on account of their similarity to their Irish relations.[70] The Gaels, in turn, had little affection for the Lowlanders, the *Goill*, who they 'hate, on account of their differing speech, as much as they do the English'.[71]

That the ascendancy of an Anglo-Norman identity had an effect even in the Highlands is evidenced by the re-writing of the traditions of 'progressive clans' of certain Celtic origin. The Campbells added a 'p' to their name in the 1470s and claimed an origin with the family of Beauchamp, deriving their name from De Campo Bello (although the Campbells kept their Britonnic and Gaelic connections as well). The account of MacKenzie origins was reworked to claim the Anglo-Norman noble Colin Fitzgerald as founder.[72]

In the ensuing clash of cultures, the Lowlands, the seat of wealth and power, saw the Highlands as a 'problem', and indeed it is common until the present day to hear of the 'Highland problem'. Perhaps the best example of the conflict of these two cultures is found in the poem *The Flyting of Dunbar and Kennedy*, a poetic dueling match *c.*1500 between William Dunbar from Lothian and Walter Kennedy from Ayrshire. Kennedy staunchly defends Gaelic from Dunbar's attack, accusing his ancestors of treason and upholding Gaelic as Scotland's true language, a fact which Dunbar never refutes:

> Thow lufis nane Irische, elf, I understand
> Bot it suld be all trew Scottis mennis lede;
> It was the gud language of this land
> And Scota it causit to multiply and sprede
> Quill Corspatrik, that we of tresoun rede
> Thy forefader, maid Irisch and Irisch men thin
> Throu his tresoun broght Inglise rumplis in …

Prejudice inherited from Biblical and Classical cultures that the North was a primitive and ungodly place made it necessary for Lowland Scottish intellectuals formulating a new national history to defend its civilization against charges of barbarity. European colonization of the Americas stimulated new debates about civilization and the role of state and Empire. The European Renaissance created a model of civility and civilization based on the Classical world.[73]

John Mair justified imperialism by stating that barbarians were already slave-like by nature, leaving little doubt that his comments applied to the 'Wild Scots' as well as newly discovered peoples. Only the Lowlanders were governed by reason and capable of civility, he asserted, traits they had in common with the English. King James VI and I wrote similarly that the Native Americans, like Highlanders, Borderers and Islesmen, were beastly and slavish, unlike those who had, in the fashion of the Romans, transcended the bonds of the kin-group to become citizens of an ordered civil society.[74] Such ideology, expressed and adopted by the king himself, was used to rationalize the attempt to destroy native Gaelic institutions.

Although there is evidence that some of the Highland clergy were exposed to the religious disputes that triggered the Reformation,[75] Protestantism was by and large a phenomenon of urban society and confined to a few Lowland areas until a very late stage. The movement in the Lowlands was galvanized by the persecution of heretics and by xenophobia against the French influence of Mary Queen of Scots. Two Reformation settlements, in 1560 and

1564, were recognized by the Scottish Parliament.[76] The Reformation in Lowland society caused a profound re-orientation away from the traditional ties with Catholic countries such as France and Ireland and towards England.

The Reformation in England was fueled by the messianic conceit that England was an 'elect nation' destined to lead the world's struggle against the Antichrists in Rome and the Turkish Empire. Reformers in Scotland encouraged the idea, articulated a number of times particularly after the disaster of Flodden, that the new religious settlement extend itself to a new entity, the entire island of Britain. This proposal drew on the mythic significance of Britain of the Roman Age, claiming that both peoples were ethnically of the same stock, and were not foreign to one another but nearer to any other nations in 'maner, form, language and all condicions'.[77] To the men who devised these plans of union and invented the idea of 'Great Britain', the Scotland that mattered was Lowland. The Reformation formed part of the ideology to create a homogenous English society in Britain and Ireland and marks a renewed attack on the Celtic languages and cultures.[78]

It is ironic, then, that the Reformation could only make any initial progress in the Highlands by adapting to the patterns of Gaelic society. There was no bourgeoisie from which to recruit ministers, but rather learned and tacksmen classes.[79] The first book to be published in any of the Celtic languages was a Classical Gaelic translation of the Book of Common Order (1567), accomplished under the patronage of the earl of Argyll, one of the first converts to the new religion.

Unions and conquests

When James VI of Scotland became James I of England in 1603, he fueled the craze for prophecies and apocalyptic writings which would demonstrate that his reign had divine approval and was destined to establish a new World Order. While the invention of the British idea by Lowland Scots gave them access to a much more powerful entity, it soon became clear that the smaller and weaker member would have to conform to the larger and richer member.[80]

James VI had already begun the attempt to tighten control and 'civilize' the Highlands in 1587, making clan chiefs responsible for the actions of reivers and brigands, requiring proof of charters for lease of Crown lands, raising rents, and re-negotiating feu-duties. This was to initiate the cultural reorientation of chieftains from warlords in a kin-based society to landlords and merchants, replacing oral agreements, local consumption, and customary dues with written records, a cash economy, and 'normalized' economic transactions.[81]

As burghs had created Lowland civility, and trade and commerce was believed to engender civilization, the planting of burghs filled with loyal Protestant subjects was planned, and in a few cases carried out, in the Highlands. Others advised more aggressive colonization and military occupation. Not only did attempts between 1598 and 1609 by the 'Fife Adventurers' to colonize the Isle of Lewis fail, but the attempt to replace Gaels by Lowlanders in Kintyre resulted in many of the Lowlanders going native.[82]

On the whole, however, the plantations were effective. It became clear that Ireland and Scotland were part of the same 'problem' that thwarted conquest. Gaelic chieftains in Ireland were dependent upon professional mercenaries from Gaelic Scotland. Ulster was the area least dominated by English forces and the place from which Gaelic risings were most likely to emerge. Not only did one branch of the Clan Donald control the Scottish coastline across from Ulster, another branch was highly successful in expanding their lands in northern Ireland itself. Rivalries between Ulster chieftains split loyalties and manpower in the Gaelic rising. Campbell of Argyll quickly wrested Kintyre and Jura away from the Clan Donald.[83] Ulster, the crucial link between Irish and Scottish Gaeldom, was broken and planted with loyal subjects of the Crown beginning in 1609.

The most notorious of clan persecutions of this era was against the Clan Gregor. The MacGregors had been harried by the expansionist Campbells since 1570, but a battle close to the Lowlands provided a rationale for them to be evicted and their name outlawed. The seventh earl of Argyll was given the responsibility in 1611 'to lay mercie asyed, and by justice and the sword ruit oute and extirpat all of that race'.[84] These series of events were well known throughout the Gàidhealtachd in song and story and must have betokened worsening conditions to all that heard them.

In 1609 nine Gaelic chieftains were abducted and forced to sign the Statutes of Iona, which were designed specifically to Anglicize leaders and institutions of Gaelic society in order to bring them under control of central government. Among the items listed in this agreement was the 'planting of the gospell among these rude, barbarous, and uncivill people' by Protestant churches; the outlawing of bards who were traditionally on circuit between the houses of noblemen; the requirement that all men of wealth send their heirs to be educated in Lowland schools where they would be taught to 'speik, reid, and wryte Inglische'.[85]

This was followed by an Act in 1616 which sought to establish schools in every parish in the Highlands so that 'the youth be exercised and trayned up in civilitie, godlines, knawledge, and learning, that the vulgar Inglische toung be universallie plantit, and the Irische language, whilk is one of the chief and principall causes of the continewance of barbaritie and incivilitie amongis the inhabitantis of the Ilis and Heylandis, may be abolisheit and removeit ...' Up to this time Classical Gaelic and Latin were the languages of status and learning in the Gaelic world.[86] An explicit ideology of civilizing the Gaels by exterminating their language and replacing it with English through school education was easier to pass in law than it was to execute, but it reflects a mounting official strategy.[87]

The effects of the Statutes, however, in requiring heirs to be educated in English in Lowland schools and in requiring chieftains to spend more time on official business in the Lowlands became almost immediately apparent. There are complaints in Gaelic sources from 1626 onwards that at least some clan chiefs were spending too much time away from home, neglecting their proper traditional duties, spending excessive amounts of precious clan money and becoming strangers to their people.[88]

The Statutes of Iona redoubled the efforts to make chieftains culturally and economically 'normalized' with the rest of Scotland. A greater degree of dependence upon cash and emphasis on rents played easily into the hands of the Campbells, who were adept at giving financial loans to land holders secured against their estates. Not only could they exploit the ill circumstances of their debtors, the Campbell house of Argyll had the judicial privileges to manipulate legal technicalities to their advantage.[89]

Although James VI had been subtly promoting the Episcopalian religion of the English church through his new united kingdom, his son and successor Charles I was far more aggressive. In 1638, the National Covenant was signed by leaders agreeing to defend the king himself but to oppose his Episcopalian policies. A Covenanting army marched into England and forced the king to accept the Scottish Parliament's abolition of Episcopalianism and the right of the Parliament to challenge the king's authority. In this flux of authority, the Gaels of Ulster attacked the planters in 1641, aiming to regain control of Ulster and the English colony of Dublin and build a 'Catholic Confederacy' which could demand religious rights. Alasdair mac Colla Chiotaich, whose father had struggled against Campbell expansion, joined the rising as a promising young military leader. Alasdair is the last great pan-Gaelic warrior hero, celebrated in larger than life dimensions in story and song.

The Scottish Covenanters entered into a Solemn League and Covenant with the English republicans in 1643. The rising in Ulster joined the King's Royalists when Alasdair mac Colla lead an army from Ireland to Scotland. Under the leadership of Alasdair mac Colla and James Graham, marquis of Montrose, the Royalists won battles and terrorized Campbell lands for over a year.

When this army was finally defeated, the king gave himself up to the mercy of the Scottish Covenanting army in England. They handed him over to the English parliament when he rejected their demand to make Presbyterianism the religion of England. Gaels were shocked by the betrayal and execution of Charles in 1649. As the reign of Cromwell began military garrisons at Fort William and Inverness were built.

The sustained conflict between Covenanters and Royalists escalated the intensity and scale of warfare in Gaeldom. It sowed bitter division between clans as they were inexorably drawn into British politics and forced to choose sides. The news of these violent battles reinforced the stereotype of Highlanders as rebellious, bloodthirsty savages.[90]

The eighth marquis of Argyll, who was an ardent Covenanter against Charles I, was beheaded for treason when Charles II was restored to the monarchy in 1660. It came, then, as a bitter disappointment to the majority of Highland clans, who had been loyal to the king, that the restored regime showed them no gratitude but instead gave its support again to the house of Argyll, who continued a ruthless strategy of territorial expansion. Not only did the earl of Argyll press debtors into liquidation, turning them into landless, 'broken men' who increased the lawlessness of the Highlands, but he had the legal status to protect his underhanded subterfuges.

When Charles II died in 1685, his Roman Catholic brother James VII succeeded him. James was forced to flee to France due to growing hostility to Catholicism and his son-in-law Prince William of Orange seized the throne. The 'Jacobite cause' was born among the followers of James, and the high level of support among Highland clans caused William concern. One of the first actions of William was to force Highland tenants to pay unpaid rents for the 'erecting of English schools for rooting out the Irish language, and other pious uses'.[91]

Scottish Jacobites were defeated by William in 1689, who required thereafter that all Highland chieftains take personal oaths of loyalty. Despite the lack of real threat to the throne, the delinquency of the chieftain of the MacDonalds of Glencoe provided Highland-loathing Dalrymple with the opportunity to demonstrate the uncompromising severity of central government. Although Campbell of Breadalbane – under threat of being labeled a traitor 'not true to King nor Government' – oversaw the orders, the slaughter of thirty-eight MacDonalds was not a clan feud but an official government act following King William's sanction to 'extirpate Highland rebels'.

As part of the 1690 revolution settlement, the Presbyterian Church was established as the national Church of Scotland, albeit in a form which kept it tied to the political interests of the London government.[92] Where conversion in Gaelic areas occurred, it was largely due to the personal choice of clan chiefs. A few of them, like Campbell of Argyll, were early converts who lent the crucial support to make the operation of Protestantism in the Highlands possible.[93] Lachlan MacLean of Duart was converted when he was fostered in the earl of Argyll's household.

Because of its lack of widespread acceptance amongst Gaels,[94] the Established Church made renewed efforts to win the Highlands for Presbyterianism, the Williamite reign and the English language. The Assembly's Act of 1699 *Anent Planting of the Highlands* attempted to focus efforts on supplying all of the Highland parishes with Gaelic-speaking ministers, who were in very short supply. Although Gaelic was recognized as the necessary medium for missionary activity – and the fear of the Counter-Reformation played no small part in making Protestantism make such concessions – it was clearly the long-term goal to supplant it with English.[95]

In 1709 the Society in Scotland for Propagating Christian Knowledge (SSPCK) was established in order to expedite the 1696 Act by providing further funding sources. All manner of incentives and punishments were used to stop children from speaking Gaelic.[96] After a number of years of unsuccessful attempts at English-only teaching methods, it was realized that literacy in Gaelic was a much more effective means of teaching and a bridge towards fluency in English.

The Act of Union amalgamated the English and Scottish parliaments in 1707. In a sense, this was the logical extension of processes of convergence which had been ongoing since at least 1560. Whatever threats, bribes and incentives worked for the decision-makers seemed to matter little to most Scots, who were outraged and ashamed by the take-over. Iain Lom lists a number of guilty greedy nobles who are to be punished according to their crime:

Nam faighinn mo raghainn
Is dearbh gu leaghainn an t-òr dhuit
A-staigh air faochaig do chlaiginn
Gus an cas e do bhòtainn.[97]

But if I were to have my wish
I would certainly melt down gold for you –
Pouring it down in the shell of your skull
Until it fills up your boots.

Final conflict

Disaffection for the policies of the throne and the London government came to a head on the death of Queen Anne in 1714 and the arrival of the Hanoverian King George I to take her place. Shouts of 'God save the King' by burgh officials in Inverness were overpowered by the popular response 'God damn them and their King'.[98] In this state of unrest and dissatisfaction, the Jacobites seized the opportunity for a rising, one which many thought would succeed. The earl of Mar gathered twenty-six clan chiefs to Braemar under the pretense of a deer hunt in 1715 and raised the banner for exiled James. The poetess Sìleas na Ceapaich sang in her song of incitement:

Ach Alba éiribh còmhla
Mun geàrr Sasunnaich ur sgòrnan
Nuair thug iad air son òir uaibh
Ur creideas is ur stòras
'S nach eil 'n diugh 'nur pòca.[99]

But arise as one, oh Scotland,
Before the English cut your throats
Since they deceived you with gold and took
Your credit and your possessions
Which is no longer in your pockets.

The response was, however, mixed. Few of the western clans were involved and splits within clans were detrimental. Even the Clan Campbell was divided between sides. The end came quickly as a stalemate on Sheriffmuir two months later. The Jacobites who participated in the rising had their estates forfeited to the York Buildings Company and some of them fled into exile for safety. General Wade was appointed commander in Scotland in 1725, building military garrisons and roads in order to hold law and order for the Hanoverian regime.[100]

No other event in Scottish history has inspired such heated debate as the Jacobite rising of 1745. It has been analyzed as an inter-dynastic struggle, as an international power play, as an internal Civil War and as a desperate move by a selfish and ambitious young man. Historians will argue about the complexities of the rising from all these perspectives with a wide variety of evidence, but the perceptions of contemporary Gaels is expressed in a large corpus of song and story.

The poetry of this period, whether by poets in traditional loyalist clans or in 'progressive' Protestant territories like Argyll and Sutherland, is overwhelmingly Jacobite. This is a reflection of the values deep within the matrix of Gaelic society and the conventions of bardic tradition that necessarily accorded with the ideals of Jacobitism: loyalty to the rightful ruler, the signs that presaged a Gaelic resurgence, the right to reject tyranny and the yearning for religious tolerance. The breadth of evidence and its longevity in oral tradition, argue for the operation of Jacobite literature throughout Gaelic society.[101] Gaelic songs of the '45 display none of the false sentimentality, romanticism or defeatism common in the English-language productions of later days. In the pre-Culloden phase, although there is the occasional sense of anxiety and recklessness, the overall mood is one of jubilant expectation.

Whether or not the Jacobite sympathy expressed in such verse was transformed into action is another question. The losses for many in the 1715 rising were very real, and a number of clan chiefs had by now become entrepreneurs in the Empire with too much at stake to risk another forfeiture.[102] While the loyalties of many clan chiefs may have been pulled into the orbit of English society, many of their followers retained their sense of loyalty to Gaelic ideals. Some companies of soldiers were taken out under the false impression that they were fighting for the prince, rather than against him, and some defected to the prince's side when they learned of the deception.

The conflict was not a rebellion of Catholics against Protestants, as Episcopalians vastly outnumbered Catholics and numerous Presbyterians fought as Jacobites as well. If the rising succeeded, said the propagandists, the church and state would finally be at peace with one another. The Hanoverian side, however, was less compromising. Cumberland destroyed every Episcopal church he could in the Highlands. Presbyterian ministers in the Highlands in general not only served as spies for the Hanoverians but attempted to discourage their congregations from committing revolutionary acts.[103]

The Gaels who fought with the Jacobites did so not only in the hopes of restoring the proper king to the throne, but in hopes of restoring Scotland's independence. This aspiration was stated in a declaration read at Glenfinnan at the outset of the campaign:

> Having always borne the most constant affection to our ancient kingdom of Scotland, from whence we derive our royal origin ... we cannot but behold with the deepest concern the miseries they suffer under a foreign usurpation ... We further declare that we will with all convenient speed call a free parliament ... so the nation may be restored to that honour, liberty, and independence, which it formerly enjoyed ...

It is not surprising in this light that the Jacobite army was less than enthusiastic about moving the campaign from Scotland to England.[104]

There are many references in Gaelic verse that the rising was a conflict between the forces of Gaeldom and the forces of England, regardless of who was employed on either side. The long-standing Messianic prophecy in Gaelic tradition that the wheel of fortune would turn again in the favor of the Gaels, who would be returned to their proper place in the kingdom of Scotland, was exploited in Jacobite propaganda.[105]

While in hindsight the rising may seem foolhardy, the promises and expectations of further military and economic backing made it seem more reasonable at the time. Although decisive victories were easily won early in the campaign, the Hanoverian regime prepared to make a serious confrontation. At Culloden in 1746, an ill-prepared Jacobite army was crushed. Alasdair mac Mhaighstir Alasdair lamented the loss of the battle, but did not yet expect that the war was over:

Nach nàir dhuit féin mar thachair dhuit
O Albainn bhochd tha truagh
Gann làn an dùirn de Ghàidhealaibh
Fhàgail ri h-uchd buailt'?
Nach smuain thu do chruadal mór
Shliochd Scòta sin nan lann?
Us diùbhlamaid air muinntir Dheòrs'
Fuil phrionnsail mhór nan Clann.[106]

Are you not ashamed of what has befallen you
O poor Scotland
With hardly a handful of Gaels
Left in the fore of battle?
Will you not remember your vast hardiness
O war-like sons of Scotia
And let us avenge on George's men
The great royal blood of the clans.

Many held out the hope that the Jacobite forces would rejoin and that the Hanoverian atrocities had readied the Gaels to join unanimously against the merciless regime.[107] Although the Gaels were divided in the rising, punishment inflicted in the form of slaughter, rape, pillaging and vandalism was carried out through the Highlands. While anecdotal evidence suggests that some Gaels in the Hanoverian forces did what they could to soften the violence,[108] every area in the Highlands has its catalogue of brutalities.

The Hanoverians responded with severity by dismantling Gaelic society and passing measures to break its pride. Jacobite leaders either fled into exile or were punished or executed by the government, their estates being forfeited and run by newly installed managers who would force socio-economic change into place. The Gaels would themselves pay for their own undoing.

> The rents and profits [from the Annexed Estates after 1752] were to be used 'for the Purposes of civilising the Inhabitants upon the said Estates, and other Parts of the Highlands and Islands of Scotland, and promoting amongst them the Protestant religion, good Government, Industry and Manufactures, and the Principles of Duty and Loyalty to his Majesty, his Heirs and Successors, and to no other Purpose whatsoever'.[109]

The system of land-holding was reorganized to undermine the previous traditional rights of chieftains and tacksmen. A more personal insult, however, was the 1746 Disarming Act which forbade Highland civilians from bearing arms or wearing the symbol of the warrior-Gael, the plaid. It was soon noted, 'The barbarous policy of Edward the First did not more effectively destroy the spirit of the indignant Welsh by the murder of their bards than the prohibition of the ancient garb that of the poor Highlanders'.[110]

The defeat at Culloden has been invoked continuously in Gaelic poetry ever since as a symbol of the oppression and injustice that Gaels have endured from the English-speaking world.[111] While the English and Lowland mind, gazing back over the course of centuries, could only see the inevitable collapse of an inferior culture, the Gaelic mind perceived a causal link between the Anglicization of the Scottish nobility and the triumph of an oppressive anti-Gaelic regime. In the year 1800, the Gaelic tradition bearer Uisdean Mac Dhòmhnaill made the statement:

> *...is e buille as truime fhuair a' chànail-sa riamh gun deachaidh an teaghlach rìoghail do Shaghsan agus gu robh mór uaislean na Gàidhealtachd 'gan leantainn; bha iad sin aig tabhairt cleachdaidh agus cànail Shaghsan air an ais. Bha barrachd coimeasgadh bho'n aimsir sin eadar Gàidheil agus Gaill agus bha riaghladh na Rìoghachd uile ag oid-hirpeachadh gus a' chànail 'chur as ...*[112]

> ...the worst blow that our language ever received was the removal of the Royal Family to England, and the attendance of our men of rank and influence at Court; who were carrying back to their country the manners and language of England. There was more intercourse from that time on between the Gaels and the non-Gaels and the entire weight of the government was trying to kill the language off ...

Clearance, exile, and inferiority

The prophecy of deliverance from their enemies by the long-awaited Messiah figure turned into a bitter illusion, especially after Charles Edward Stewart died heirless in Rome in 1788. Although social leaders and institutions had been increasingly diverging from traditional Gaelic norms since the seventeenth century, the post-Culloden period marks a watershed in the history of the Gàidhealtachd because of the finality of control which the new instruments of Anglicization had achieved.

John Ramsay of Ochtertyre observed the results of these deliberate policies first-hand and wrote:

> The whole weight of the Government, for a number of years, was employed to dissolve every tie between the chief and the clan, and to abolish all distinctions between the Highland and Lowland Scots. Even the gentry who had not been engaged in the rebellion found it expedi-

ent to drop some of their national customs ... their successors have no longer the same attachment either to their people or to ancient modes of life. They affect the manners of the Lowland gentry ...[113]

The tenantry could now be removed at will by the landlords, who soon realized that people could not produce the profits that the new economic system required. Although increasingly difficult conditions had compelled some people to emigrate, the first large-scale clearances, where people were forcibly evicted from their homes, happened in Glengarry in 1785. This removal of Gaeldom's proudest warriors sent a shock throughout the Gàidhealtachd: 'The collapse of the Glengarry house was throughout all the Highlands felt to be a whole race calamity ... That disappearance was like the fall of a fixed star from the Celtic firmament.'[114]

Although Dr Samuel Johnson, the famous English scholar who toured the Highlands in 1773, was not always able to see across the cultural and linguistic divide that separated him from the Gaels, one of his more insightful remarks confirms that post-Culloden Gaeldom was oppressed in a number of ways by all of the institutions that existed around it.

> There was perhaps never any change of national manners so quick, so great, and so general, as that which has operated in the Highlands, by the last conquest, and the subsequent laws ... Of what they had before the late conquest of their country, there remains only their language and their poverty. Their language is attacked on every side. Schools are erected, in which English only is taught ...

While Johnson displays a great deal of sympathy for the suffering of the people, he reveals elsewhere his belief that Scotland must inevitably be civilized by England for its own good, invoking the darling of modern Imperialists, Rome.

> Yet what the Romans did to other nations, was in a great degree done by Cromwell to the Scots; he civilized them by conquest, and introduced by *useful violence* the arts of peace ... Till the Union made them acquainted with English manners, the culture of their lands was unskilful, and their domestick life uninformed ...

The severity of the treatment of Gaels had to find some cultural and political rationale, and the idea that the Celts were inferior was already well established in the Anglo-British tradition. Johnson's use of terms such as 'savage' and 'barbaric' a number of times in his short travelogue when discussing Gaels and their ways of life reflects attitudes of his cultural superiority. His Lowland companion, James Boswell, gives us an even more explicit parallel when he remarks on Johnson's servant, 'I observed how curious it was to see an African in the north of Scotland, with little or no difference of manners from those of the natives.'

The rending of the fibre of Gaelic life made cultural conquest possible: 'When a people are taught to despise the modes of thinking, customs and prejudices of their ancestors, and to consider as barbarism and vulgarity all that in their childhood they were accustomed to regard as excellent and elegant – the whole web of thought and feeling is unravelled, and cannot be readily or easily made up in a new form.'[115]

It is into this social chaos, and into the distraught and anxious minds of an oppressed people, that religion created an alternative form of leadership and a 'cosmological revolution in Gaelic society'. Lacking the native institutions and secular social leaders that had previously acted in the interests of Gaelic society, the church filled the power vacuum with little opposition.[116]

The clergy of the Established Church were largely educated men from the upper classes of Gaelic society, an 'aristocracy of learning'. The eighteenth-century rescue operation for Gaelic oral tradition, particularly motivated by the 'Ossianic controversy', was undertaken by such ministers. For as long as native Gaels who were loyal to their culture and balanced in their approach to secular and sacred were the dominant religious leaders, the secular arts retained some degree of esteem and status in Gaelic society.[117]

Still, the Established Church was, after all, the establishment: it was an arm of an institution based in the Lowlands whose interests were bound to the landlords, factors and the better-off single tenants. As ministers were dependent upon the landlords for their stipends, few ministers were willing to publicly question authority.

The church had a mission to 'civilize' the Highlands according to the norms of English-speaking society. The cultural loyalty of the ministers to the State can also be seen in their use of the pulpit to promote the ideology of Britishness. Sermons contained news of British imperial victories and even used such events as central themes. Anglo-British culture infiltrated church thinking widely, making the Highlands as much a heathen mission field as the lands of the Native Americans, which the SSPCK also attempted to evangelize. The Gaels, according to theory, had a place within the British Empire as loyal soldiers who would make it possible to bring civilization to the world.[118]

The expanding territories of the Empire created a channel into which to move the troublesome population and avoid settling more difficult issues at home. Alasdair Campbell deplored the deportation of Gaels from the Highlands into the far-reaches of the world when so much of Scotland lay empty, observing that 'Any one the least conversant in ancient and modern history is fully aware that the predominant passions of adventurers are, inordinate ambition and an ungovernable degree of avarice.'[119] For the apologists of the Empire, it was 'a bread and butter question. If you want to avoid civil war, you must become imperialists'.[120]

In a narrow economic sense, the Empire provided labour for a dispossessed population. In a broad cultural sense, it succeeded in draining Gaelic Scotland of much of her two most important assets, her human population and self-confidence.

The government had guaranteed that Highlanders were politically impotent and economically vulnerable. Highland landlords had greater powers over their tenants than any in contemporary Europe. A number of factors combined, particularly with the Potato Famine of 1846-7, to make Clearance a recurring catastrophe of the nineteenth century and one which still scars the Highland landscape and psyche.[121]

The poets of the Clearances generally strove to defend the traditional ideals of the Gaelic community against what was seen as destructive outside forces.[122] This was particularly embodied in the form of the landlord, or the Lowland shepherd and his flocks of sheep which displaced the native peoples for the sake of the landlord's profit: 'Since the introduction of sheep into the Highlands, and before rapacious Lowland sheep farmers, the people disappeared as surely as the Red Indians from the advance of the Whites'.[123] The poetry of the nineteenth century, wrote W.J. Watson, was the 'wail of a dejected and harassed people'.[124]

Just as the idea of 'Great Britain' had been invented by ambitious Lowland Scots to justify the merger of Scotland and England on the grounds that they were of the same ethnic stock, so too could they justify their participation in the Empire with the ideology that Lowland Scotland was from the same Anglo-Teutonic stock as England, untainted by Celtic blood. 'Lowland Scots were reassured that as Teutons they were not mere helots of an English Empire, nor a subject colonial people, but a branch of the dominant race which rightly belonged at the imperial high table.'[125] This ideology depicted the Germanic peoples, whether called Anglo-Saxons, Goths, Norse or Teutons, as destined to rule over inferior subject people.[126] Although the supreme sense of superiority, particularly in conquest of enemies, had been a part of English nationalism for a long time,[127] theories about race gave a pseudo-scientific rationale to this conviction.

The creation of the idea of 'Celtic peoples', the 'Other', by British intellectuals was an integral aspect of defining who the 'Anglo-Teutonic peoples' were. While the Celts were lazy, retrogressive, effeminate and emotional, the Teutons were hard-working, progressive, masculine and rational, and hence inherently superior at running an Empire.

After the 'rebels' had been crushed at Culloden, the Highlanders no longer posed a threat to the Anglo-British State. Especially after the popularity of MacPherson's Ossian in the 1760s, the Highlander came to be identified as a 'noble savage'. While the new fashion for pseudo-Celtic literature created a new market for those who were willing to write on 'Celtic' themes according to the tastes and expectations of the English audience of the times, it did not allow real Celts to express their own worldview or values. The popular portrayal of the 'lost world' of the Celts 'reinforced its disconnection from the reality of industrialization and empire'.[128] The 'Celtic revival' was so uninformed about authentic Celtic culture that it produced an utterly alien art form that the rest of the world still believes is Celtic.

> The special brand of romanticism attributed to the Gael and his poetry is a romanticism of the escapist, otherworldly type, a cloudy mysticism, the type suggested by the famous phrase, 'Celtic Twilight'. This Celtic Twilight never bore any earthly relation to anything in Gaelic life or literature. It was merely one of the latest births of the English literary bourgeoisie, and its births are to Gaelic eyes exceedingly strange ...[129]

The ever-deepening social and cultural crisis in the Highlands, and the lack of faith in ministers who were in the pockets of landlords, culminated in the Disruption of 1843 when a number of ministers and their congregations separated from the Church of Scotland and formed the Free Church of Scotland. At their best, the unfettered positions of these ministers allowed them to speak against the moneyed interests which conflicted with the interests of the Gaels. Such ministers 'developed an early form of liberation theology in the fight for social justice',[130] inspiring people to act against injustice by drawing upon the language and examples of the Bible.[131] It has also been noted that Gaelic was the language of the Free Church in many places after the Established Church had abandoned it.

At its worst, however, the Free Church could be a 'recluse religion', turning its back on the evils and injustices of the world by establishing an alternative internal community. It was the excesses of this form of the Evangelical Movement which rejected the world and all that was worldly, including Gaelic secular culture, especially music, song and dance.[132] The view that the world was a vale of tears, full of suffering and unfairness, that justice was for God and that man should resolve his own inner battle, could lead to political indifference and inaction.

On the other hand, literacy in Gaelic had been gaining ground in the mid-nineteenth century largely due to church-based education[133] and, despite Clearance and emigration, there were still native Gaelic speakers in most districts throughout the Highlands as defined in the Middle Ages. The government, however, not only lacked the sympathy to support Gaelic education, but 'were unable to visualise any solution for Highland and Hebridean poverty except emigration, and their method of encouraging the people to emigrate was to educate *all* of them as potential emigrants'.[134] The Scottish Education Act of 1872, which made nationally organized, de-Gaelicized, education mandatory, destroyed the progress which had been made in Gaelic education during the 1800s.

Young men in the Gàidhealtachd preferred to suffer the consequences of war than to stay at home and suffer the shame of cowardice. Gaelic regiments suffered tremendous losses in the First World War and many areas were almost completely emptied of their young men. While many people gave themselves loyally and willingly to the causes of two World Wars, the irony of Gaeldom's sacrifice of itself was not lost on all:

Hitler gheall e Lebensraum
Dha shluagh ma gheibh e bhuaidh;
Cha b' ionnan sin 's na Hitleran
A bhris spiorad mo shluaigh;
Na Hitleran breun Breatannach
A mhurt mo thìr mu thuath
Gu Lebensraum do chaoraich
Is na daoine sgiùrs' thar chuan.[135]

Hitler promised Lebensraum
To his people in victory
He is different from those Hitlers
Who broke the spirit of my people
Those stinking British Hitlers
Who murdered my northern land
To make living-space for sheep,
Who scourged the people across the ocean.

Conclusions

The lack of racial differences allowed cultural change to move in all directions between Celtic, Nordic and Germanic peoples. Different circumstances in different areas at different times produced alliances across 'racial boundaries' which had the effect of changing cultural make-up over time: Picts became culturally Gaelic under the national institutions of Scotland; the Western Norse became culturally Gaelic as they gave their allegiance to Gaeldom and assimilated their families and institutions into Gaelic ones; the Gaels of the Lowlands became culturally Anglo-Norman as they were absorbed into feudal institutions; and so on. Over time cultural assimilation wiped away racial origins and new myths of identity and race emerged.

So long as Gaelic society remained intact, cultural changes in Gaelic areas tended to occur through the medium of the kin-group. The allegiance and policies of the chieftain were implicitly adopted by his followers. Thus, as has been demonstrated all around the world,[136] assimilation of society *en masse* to new values and modes of living is most effectively accomplished by assimilating the elite first and the prestige and leadership such people have will eventually 'trickle down'.

Once the bonds of kinship were loosened, however, other institutions, particularly the church and school, came to have a bigger impact on Gaelic society. Without any higher native institution to keep such powers in check, education and the church, when directed and informed from outside Gaelic society, could have a profoundly detrimental impact on it.

Internal innovation tended to transform society from within when culture was self-confident. External acculturation was easier for outside forces to accomplish when self-confidence was weak and the results of assimilation only reinforced these weaknesses.

In Ireland, cultural innovation was developed particularly under the aegis of the church. Because there was no centralized political structure which an incoming invader could conquer and exploit to affect cultural change, Irish society was able to absorb newcomers and reassert itself until its native leaders were driven into exile in the seventeenth century.

In Scotland, however, the nation was developed as a centralized infrastructure and hierarchy at a very early stage. Feudalism was implemented through this internal infrastructure although the results, culturally speaking, depended on the particular power and economic structures of each area. In most Highland areas, newcomers were vastly outnumbered by and dependent upon the native stock, who could thus absorb them in time. The result was syncretic, more Gaelic than Anglo-Norman.

The Lowland burghs, and large foreign populations that established them, overpowered and assimilated those Gaelic areas around them, creating a language and culture which, while it bore the marks of native Gaeldom, was gravitationally held within the orbit of Anglo-Norman culture and continually reshaped by it.

It is clear from many examples throughout this history that people experienced and perceived historical events according to what they understood their identity to be. The Norse invasions were not simply seen as a series of isolated raids on various tribal groupings, but a threat to Gaelic civilization in general. The loss of the Glengarry MacDonells was not simply the departure of the people of one 'culture region' who had been former rivals and enemies, but the sign that Gaeldom as a whole was suffering.

The Lowlands too clearly perceived history through the lens of their identity. Once their connections with Gaeldom became more and more distant, the language and culture they shared with England made cultural and political union with England possible and, to some, desirable. This perception of a common Germanic-ness was in contrast to the alienness of the Celts, who were seen to be obstacles to Progress. The intensity of the attack on Gaelic culture was directly proportional to the degree to which Lowland society was culturally and politically wedded to England, at least in part because of its own insecurity as a disparaged periphery of the Anglo-British world.[137]

Some Scottish kings expressed hostility towards Gaeldom, but policies became notably more aggressive upon the Union of Crowns. Although numerous attempts were made within Scotland to 'control' the Highlands, it was only after the Union of Parliaments that the military finally destroyed and replaced the native institutions of Gaelic society.

Despite this, it must be remembered that there have been Gaelic-speakers in Scotland from before the arrival of the Romans to the present day. The English language (in its various dialects) has only become universal in Scotland since the Second World War, and it has not yet displaced Gaelic.

CHAPTER 3

Gaelic oral tradition

Songs, poems, legends, and other oral narratives are a primary resource for understanding Gaelic culture, providing an inside perspective into Gaelic society. They give us the names of people involved in important events, illustrate customs and values, and give voice to the thoughts and feelings of ordinary men and women over many generations.

Furthermore, the worldview of Gaelic society is embodied in this remarkable oral literature. There is a consistent and pervasive style and set of conventions in these texts which characterizes the mind-set of Gaelic society and is a mirror to it. The images, conventions, and rhetorical structure of Gaelic literature may seem quite alien to us today, and hence the poetry, for example, often seems disjointed and full of clichés. Once the elements of Gaelic literary style are studied in their proper cultural context, however, they provide a unique window into the Gaelic world.

> The Gaelic sense of identity is conditioned and sometimes actually shaped by information that emanates from these historical legends as well as from other, less formally organised categories of tradition. Poetry and legend combine in tradition to create a native view of history.[1]

The primal context

Perhaps the best introduction to the discussion of poetry and oral tradition is to reconstruct the social context of primal societies, and to focus on the role of poetry and poets in such societies.[2]

The word is believed in primal societies to have great power, to be a magical force in itself. Such primal beliefs are apparent in the Bible passage, 'In the beginning was the Word, and the Word was with God, and the Word was

God … All things were made by him.' Language and words, for primal societies, are truly magical elements, conjuring up tribal history, expressing one's inner thoughts to the outside world, evoking beauty, fear, love, hate, and the much of the range of human emotion and knowledge. Until the development of modern linguistics, the origin and development of language was an unfathomable mystery.

Primal societies believe in the existence of an Otherworld of powerful beings, usually ancestors, who have influence over the mortal world, and song and poetry are almost invariably the means of communication with this Otherworld. One owes one's personal and cultural existence to one's ancestors, from whom wisdom and the precedents of life come. 'Wisdom is the universal virtue of early societies. It provides a guide for everyday living and allows every person to make some kind of sense out of the world.'[3] Those who guard the tribal wisdom and communicate with the Otherworld have a very elevated office in primal societies.

Names are always serious preoccupations in primal societies, for names are thought to reveal the character of the thing that they name, and knowing the name of something can give you power over it. People may have different names in different contexts, be awarded with a new name as part of a rite of passage or upon some achievement, or be praised or shamed with a nickname that encodes some prior event. 'The notion of magic rests on the idea of a rational universe in which words and language play a very important part.'[4]

The magic of words and language does not work, however, unless the words are true. The praise of an ally will be hollow and limp if the poet makes false claims, and the undeserved shaming of innocent man will turn a satire back on the poet. Primal societies are concerned that truth be constantly maintained, and that the recounting of the past and tribal wisdom be authenticated from trustworthy sources. Thus we read the advice in the Old Irish tract for princes, *Audacht Morainn*, written *c.*700

> … Let him preserve justice, it will preserve him … let him not exalt any judge unless he knows the true legal precedents … The true ruler, in the first place, is moved towards every good thing, he smiles on the truth when he hears it, he exalts it when he sees it.[5]

The *ríg* (ruler) was the sacred representative and ruler of his tribe in early Gaeldom and he was expected to maintain *fír flaithemon* (ruler's truth) on behalf of his people and territory. The *ríg* who succumbed to falsehood lost his honour-price, caused his tribe and territory damage, and was removed from office.[6]

Poets are usually the people who preside over the use of words, names, wisdom, and verbal lore in primal societies. Poets have a profoundly social function in transmitting the tribal wisdom, seeking to maintain truth, and acting as an intermediary between this world – and its human representatives – and the Otherworld.

The role of people in primal societies is tightly bound by what is inherited by an individual – gender, family profession, caste, etc. – and their standing is dependent upon honour. In small-scale societies, people are aware of the actions and attitudes of others around them, and are inter-dependent upon them for survival. People have clearly defined roles and expectations, and breaking these norms could mean death for the individual or even the whole tribe.

> The dynamics of traditional societies are based upon status and role. Public aspect is important; and the emotions of honor and shame are the important social forces … One has a strong sense of one's honor and what one can do and what is due to one.[7]

A person who lost his honour – who betrayed his social role, who reneged on his obligations, who told lies – lost his standing within the tribe. To be ostracized from the tribe was tantamount to a death sentence, as it was the only institution that provided support and protection. Survival outside of it was usually impossible.

To maintain one's honour was thus paramount. Everything was done by contract in early Gaelic society, and the measure of a man was the number of clients he could attach to himself. A man with a good reputation could attract many clients, thus raising his honour-price (*enech*) and allowing him to have more power and influence. One often had to assert one's status and defend one's reputation, and this was a common source of conflict: ' "Face" as a motive and occasion of political, including military, action cannot be underestimated in this period.'[8]

The poets of primal society remind people of their roles, informing them with the tribal wisdom, voicing their honour when they fulfill their obligations, and shaming them when they violate the sacred codes. 'The poets are the creators of public opinion and public judgment and hence are of great social value.'[9] The Gaelic word *cliù*, corresponding to 'reputation' in English, has as its root 'what is heard'.

Poets thus play a central role in the smooth operation of society. Unlike the role which they have been relegated in modernist society – that of the wild-eyed loner creating works of art expressing individualistic visions – the poet in primal societies has a highly practical and functional role, maintaining the social order, expressing the feelings and concerns of his tribe, and celebrating the many events of its life-cycle.

People's roles in primal society might be divided into an idealized schemata of four classes: kings, priests, warriors, and commoners (even though real societies are often more complex, and roles often overlapping). Each of these four classes has a different kind of participation in oral tradition, and a different relationship with the poet.

The poet's role in counseling the king, in celebrating his successes and exposing his failures, has already been noted. The king may commission the poet to create songs of praise to spread his fame, and to record the regal lineage from which he descends, and thus prove his worthiness of the sacred office. The poet may compose a special ode and perform some special ritual when the king is inaugurated in order to connect him with the powers of the Otherworld and the gods of the territory.

The poet can inform the priest, and these two roles are combined in many societies. Communication with the Otherworld, and the magical rites necessary to enable such communication, is invariably in song, poetry or some elaborate or arcane speech, and the knowledge coming from such sources – such as prophecy – is often in the form of poetry.

The warrior is protected by the spells of the poet, is incited into battle when the poet recounts the great deeds of his ancestors, is taunted by the insults of his enemy's poet, and is celebrated – either in victory or in death – by the eulogy of the poet.

Poetry may bless the labour of society in the form of charms, and the motion and energy of labour is often accompanied by song to keep it synchronized and to keep the labourers entertained. Labourers may be lulled into a soothing trance by songs, or they may challenge and tease each other with impromptu verses. Mundane knowledge about practical tasks may be encoded in poetry and proverbial lore. Mothers sing their infants to sleep, men woo their sweethearts with love songs, and so on.

The tribe as a whole will have a body of myth and legend which records its ancestors, its origins, its identity and future, the precedents and 'culture heroes' which explain its operation, and significant events in historical or sacred time. Such material will often be narrated at tribal gatherings, such as inaugurations and seasonal festivals. The tribe may have a body of myths which is recounted to individuals at their rites of passage in order to explain their new roles and responsibilities.

While many examples of poetry which fit this primal context survive from Irish sources,[10] very little early material survives from Scotland. Regardless, the poetic expressions of the Scottish Medieval period, in both learned Classical tradition and vernacular folk tradition, show many of the same concerns and characteristics.

The classical Gaelic order

Sometime around the twelfth century, for reasons not yet completely understood, the poetic order of Gaeldom transformed itself both in terms of the poetry it produced and in terms of its operation in society. Once the old order of monasteries in Ireland, which had provided a stable base for previous generations of Irish poets, began to decline, a new settlement with the secular world for patronage and support was established. Powerful Gaelic lords became the patrons of trained poets, who became the professional intelligentsia of the new Gaelic order.[11]

The language, metres and conventions of poetry became technically defined and regulated to a remarkable degree during this period. Lexical and grammatical treatises dictated the use of language to poets in training, resulting in 'a mediaeval exercise in language planning'.[12] Scores of different metres were delineated according to the basic building blocks of poetry: alliteration, syllable count, rhyme, and so on. Trained poets throughout Gaeldom were so good at creating compositions within these restrictions that a poem written in Ireland in 1250 does not deviate in language or style from one written in Scotland in the late seventeenth century.

Although the term 'bard' was borrowed into English from a Celtic source, one must be careful about using this word in a Gaelic context. Like the rest of society, the poetic order was hierarchical, with the *file* in the upper ranks and the *bard* in the lower ranks. Poets were among a number of highly skilled, hereditary, and aristocratic professionals, such as artisans, clergy, law-men, and physicians, whose education was maintained by the patronage of the Gaelic nobles, who in turn expected the services of these professionals.

A *file* who was qualified to be taken in the service of a Gaelic lord as his official poet had the title of *ollamh*. He was given land on the lord's estate, was given special gifts and privileges, and was exempt from the customary dues of the lord's dependents. In turn, he was expected to compose poetry for significant events, such as births, marriages, deaths, and warfare, and to uphold the good reputation of the lord. He was given a *duais* (fee) for poems commissioned by the lord. He was a counsellor to the lord, and might be expected to deal with legal matters – writing documents and witnessing charters – and to act as an ambassador or diplomat on behalf of the lord. He frequently also maintained a *duanaire* (poem-book), a collection of official poetry concerning the dynasty.[13]

He was also expected to train the next generation of poets, and sometimes was asked by the chieftain or other gentry to be the tutor of their children. A student – only the sons of poets who were literate and had a good memory were accepted – spent about seven years studying linguistic and metrical tracts, including numerous exemplars from these style-books, as well as the mythological, historical, genealogical, and literary tradition which he was heir to. The poetry schools ran from *Samhainn* (the beginning of November) to 25 March.[14]

Students were given tests in composition by the *ollamh*, who assigned them a topic and a metre in which the poem was to be written. They were to compose the verses during the next day, keeping themselves in the dark and having no recourse to writing but using only their memory. The *ollamh* entered their rooms the next evening, lit the room, and allowed them to commit the poem to writing. They then dressed themselves, entered the common room, and performed their pieces for their instructors, who judged them.[15]

Gaelic poets have a long tradition of composition in the dark, and the continuity of this practice is indicative of their deliberate maintenance and cultivation of the mystique of the poet and poetry. It is also suggestive of the role of the poet as the seer, and the phrase *Chì Mi* (I can see) opens many Scottish Gaelic poems to the present day.[16] The Gaelic poet knew that he inherited the powers of the ancient pre-Christian druids, and he did his best to maintain a sense of awe in his abilities and, thereby, his position of privilege in society.

An ode written by a *file* was not performed by him, however, but by the bard in his company. The ode

> was perform'd with a great deal of Ceremony in a Consort of Vocal and Instrumental Musick. The Poet himself said nothing, but directed and took care that everybody else did his Part right. The Bards having

> first had the Composition from him, got it well by Heart, and now pronounc'd it orderly, keeping even Pace with a Harp, touch'd upon that Occasion; no other musical Instrument being allowed for the said Purpose than this alone, as being Masculin, much sweeter and fuller than any other.[17]

It should be noted that there is little distinction in Gaelic between a song and a poem: traditional poetry was meant to be recited to music, though these odes may seem more like chanting than singing to the modern ear. Most of the terms associated with the performing of a song in vernacular Gaelic – *gabh*, *can*, *labhair*, *abair* – are equally valid for prose, song, and poetry.[18]

The *bard* is the lower rank of poet, who often took the role of *reacaire* (from a Latin word which appears in English as 'reciter'), performing the poetry of the *file*. He was thus familiar with the language, metres, conventions, and style of *filidheacht*, though he could not compose verse with the same technical demands. There is a class of less demanding metres recognized as properly belonging to the *bard*, and these came to prominence in Scotland in the seventeenth century.[19]

Women seem to have been excluded from the ranks of the *file*. There are only a handful of Classical Gaelic poems written by women which have survived, and they were composed by noblewomen who were given the educational opportunities afforded to people of their rank.

The *file* was proud of his exalted station, and was quick to remind the *bard* of the latter's inferior station in the poetic order. This is particularly clear when the system of patronage of the native learned order was being extinguished in the seventeenth century, and *filidh* (plural) suddenly found themselves competing with the inferior vernacular poets. An excellent practitioner of *filidheacht*, Cathal Mac Mhuirich, satirizes a vernacular bard, while at the same time he sees the declining fortune of Gaeldom:

As sona trá tarla dhuit
gan amus d' fhoghlaim ordhuirc
bheith fa lán modha go mear
le dán dona gan déanamh ...

Leanmhuin ghlún nginealach cáigh
fios a n-einigh 's a n-iomráidh,
dob fhearr dhúinn dul red tréidibh
's cúl do chur rér gcéidchéimibh ...[20]

You have blessed by fortune,
Without bothering with education,
To be held in such regard
For a poor, unpolished poem …

(I have been) following everyone's genealogy,
Recording their honour and repute –
Better that I should follow your own trade,
And abandon the path of my youth …

Because poets were held in such high esteem, their praise desired and their satire feared, they could also take advantage of their rank and be a burden on those who they encountered. Thus there is, from the earliest records, a distrust and fear of the poets and their unchecked powers.[21] A band of poets called the *Cliar Sheanchain* imposed themselves on people's hospitality and are the subject of anecdotes which describe how they were defeated in poetic combat.[22] There are other anecdotes about beggar-poets who attempted to abuse the privileges of the official poet, such as when one encounters an amateur poet named David:

Ciod a chuireadh bàrd, bleadaire na bonnaich,
Gun bhalg-min air a dhronnaig?

(Bleadaire)
Sìol is fodar do m' each!
Biadh is deoch air a' bhòrd!
On tha mi fo chlèith a' bhàird
Gabhaidh mi tàmh mar mo chòir!

(David)
'S filidh mise 's cha bhàrd
On is e as àirde cliù;
Chan ionnan is thusa, 'bhiast:
Tathann do bhiadh mar an cù![23]

What would cause a poet, a bannock-begger,
To go without carrying a bag of meal?

(Beggar)
Grain and fodder for my horse!
Food and drink on the table!

Since I am of the order of bards,
I will take my proper leisure!

(David)
I am a file, and no bard,
Which is a higher rank;
You, beast, are no match,
Barking like a dog for your food!

The official poet in action

It was expensive to maintain poetic schools and the Gaelic professional classes, and so their fate was tied to that of the Gaelic nobility themselves. For as long as Gaelic society continued in its traditional character, in which pedigree and honour were paramount, the poets were a necessary element in the social machinery. 'Highland families required a special sort of validation for the aristocratic system to work',[24] and the authorization to rule was the domain of the *file* in the ideology of Gaelic society.

One of the few glimpses we have of the king's poet in the royal Scottish court is a poem commonly called the *Duan Albanach*, which appears to be an ode delivered to King Malcolm III (d. 1093). The poem is an enumeration of the rulers of Scotland, rejoicing in the supremacy of the Gaels and in the lineage of Malcolm:

A éolcha Alban uile,	O you learned company of Alba,
A shluagh féuta foltbhuidhe,	O you noble golden-haired company,
Cía céudghabháil, an éol duibh,	Do you know what the first conquest was
ro ghabasdair Albanbruigh?[25]	Which won the land of Alba?

This poet is thus at the focus of the learned men of the nation's royal court, revealing his knowledge of the past and conferring his blessing upon the king. A fragment from an inaugural ode to the Scottish king may have survived in a section of a poem commonly known in English as *The Prophecy of Berchán*:

Go mes for cráobhaibh caola
Go cuirm go ceol go caomhna
Go n-ith go mbliocht go mbúar mbras
Co n-úaill co n-ádh co n-erbhas.[26]

May there be fruits on slender branches
Ale-feasts, with music and merriment
May there be corn, milk, hardy cattle,
Pride, success, honour.

These images remind us of the contract between the king and his kingdom, that the land and people will prosper so long as the king fulfills the duties of his office truthfully.

The Anglicization of the successors of Malcolm III undermined the Gaelic culture of the court, however, and the last recorded appearance by a royal court poet was in the inaugural ceremony of Alexander III in 1249.[27] Despite this decline in the royal court, the professional poets continued to operate in other parts of the nation where Gaelic culture continued to flourish.

A number of other poems exist which evoke the royal ancestors of rulers as a way of bolstering their claims for supremacy. While the poets of the Clan Donald continually recall legendary figures such as Conn Ceudchathach and Colla Uais, the poets of the Campbell of Argyll attempted to diversify their royal lineage by adding descent from King Arthur!

Cathal Mac Mhuirich states how the leaders of society would lose their status without the claims of legitimacy provided by the poets:

Gan neach re cuimhne a gcéimenn
do ríomh chreach no caithrémenn
gan snas ar fíorbhun a bhfis
glas ar an gníomhrudh d' aithris.

Beid a maithe fa mhéala
do dhíoth lochta a leisgéala
's a n-uaisle budh dheacht fa bhroid ...

With no one to recall their deeds,
To enumerate forays or exploits,
No elaboration of the authenticated facts:
This will hinder their deeds being told.

Their gentry will be at a loss
From the lack of advocates,
And their nobility will surely be regretful ...[28]

The poet composed battle incitements for warriors and armies, although these may have been in vernacular Gaelic rather than in high-register literary Gaelic.[29] One of these is commonly called the *Harlaw Brosnachadh*, as it appears to have been composed to incite the Clan Donald at the outset of the battle of Harlaw in 1411. The seventeenth-century antiquarian Martin Martin, although he erroneously calls the poet a 'druid', nonetheless gives us a vivid description.

> Before they engag'd the Enemy in Battle, the Chief Druid harangu'd the Army to excite their Courage. He was plac'd on an Eminence, from whence he address'd himself to all of them standing about him, putting them in mind of what great things were perform'd by the Valour of their Ancestors, rais'd their Hopes with the noble Rewards of their Honour and Victory, and dispell'd their Fears by all the Topicks that natural Courage could suggest.[30]

The poet also acted as an ambassador, taking the pleas of his patron to the court of another chieftain, such as when the *ollamh* of An Calbhach Ó Domhnaill of Ulster was sent in 1555 to seek the support of Campbell of Argyll. Poets did not simply agitate for war, however, they also sued for peace and sought to prevent unwise bloodshed. When Colla Ciotach's sons were captured and held hostage in the Lowlands, Cathal Mac Mhuirich urged him in verse to stem his anger and prevent the escalation of warfare.[31]

The poet frequently indulged in what may seem to be hyperbole when addressing his subject: Campbell of Argyll was likened to the god Lugh to inspire him when going to Flodden; the Clan Donald were claimed to be the best race in the world; the generosity of Torquil MacLeod of Lewis was compared to the famous legendary figure Guaire; and so on. We need not think of these 'idealized chiefly portraits' as idle flattery, however: the poet could withhold, or understate, his praise if it was not merited. The poet was meant to prescribe the ideals which the chieftain was meant to aim to achieve.[32]

So long as his position in society was secure, the poet did not have to compromise the truth of his words for fear of the consequences. A poet could even cause death to the subject of his satire. A poet who made unjust satires, however, had to compensate his victim according to his honour price and the poison could backfire on him.[33] One *file* warns John Stewart of Rannoch of the sting of satire:

Nárab tusa thollas oram:	Let it not be you who angers me:
nimh na n-aoir ní an cogadh soirbh;	The sting of satire is no easy fight;
's fearr dhuit gach radháil ón teine	You would be better off scorched by fire
ná a gabháil mar eire oirbh.	Than to take this burden on yourself.[34]

As the native intelligentsia, the *filidh* were instrumental in maintaining the conceptual identity and unity of Gaeldom and Gaelic culture. The Gaelic poets in both Ireland and Scotland were seen by English authorities as architects of Gaelic resistance; the Cromwellian campaigns of 1649-52 in Ireland purposefully destroyed the poet schools; the Statutes of Iona, and legislation before and after it, sought to undermine the support for and authority of the poets. Gaelic literature implicitly, and sometimes explicitly, expresses a conceptual cultural solidarity.[35]

The Scottish Gaelic vernacular tradition

The boundaries between *file* and *bard* were already blurring in the seventeenth century. When acting as *reacaire*, bards became familiar with the style and substance of the high-register *filidheacht* and translated it into a vernacular register, accessible to all and not just the formally educated. The bards had adapted the *file*'s syllabic metre in vernacular poetry by the sixteenth century. The 'strophic' metres particular to the *bard* were themselves hardy survivors of an ancient style of praise poetry which had only been temporarily eclipsed by the prestige of the *file*.[36] This loosening of restrictions also allowed female bards to rise to prominence and indeed many of the best poets of this era are women.

In reality, only a handful of chieftains – especially Campbells, MacDonalds, MacLeods, and MacLeans – were likely to have had the resources to employ the expensive *file*, while other chieftains would have settled for the less costly class of *bard*. While particular bards probably had preferred verse styles and may have differed in the functions they served their chieftains, the prominent theme in their poetry is that of clan affairs. The bardic ('strophic') metres were thought to be inappropriate for religious and romantic subjects.[37]

The Scottish bards of the seventeenth century can be seen as taking on the mantle of the *file*. Praise of chief and clan, the satire of enemies, incitement to war, and political commentary and persuasion are all represented in their output.

Although the discussion of the oral tradition has thus far focused on its aristocratic origins and context, it is vital to realize that this was the crucible which created the worldview of Gaelic society.

> Gaelic panegyric is not merely the celebration of great men in life and death, although it is of course that. It is also a system which reflects the entire Gaelic experience in Scotland and the siege mentality which that experience created as the Gaelic nation strove to maintain an identity. The historical realities of this precarious situation ensured that an artist was honoured in proportion as he celebrated those qualities and those values that were necessary for the survival of the nation. That is the reason why the warrior's role is the apex of the panegyric code. We can see how the system works with centripetal compulsion, ever bringing us back to this central symbol: the warrior who is protector and rewarder.[38]

This panegyric code operates throughout society to such a degree that the rank of neither the poet or the subject of the poem can be easily discerned in most Gaelic poetry.[39] The vernacular songs sung in the court of the chieftain were popular amongst his humblest retainers.[40] A striking example of this is the testimony of Duncan Campbell, who describes the topics of discourse amongst the natives of Glen Lyon when Queen Victoria was crowned in 1838.

> [My grandmother] and others of her generation enjoyed the liberty this occasion gave them for going … to the history of Scottish kings as far as Kenneth Macalpin, which had come down by oral tradition. Long afterwards when I read the *Duan Albanach* I was much surprised to discover that the substance of it was retained to a remarkable extent in the oral and local traditions which our aged people recalled and told …[41]

Likewise, James Logan tells us that the people were keen to learn the clan sagas and legends which circulated amongst the learned orders.

> The delight which the Gael had in the recitation of their traditional history was extreme. The duty of preserving and relating their legends was properly the province of the bards, who were supported for the purpose, but the whole population were accustomed to acquire the *sgeulachds*, or historical narrations …[42]

The poet of traditional Gaelic society, of whatever rank or origin, considered himself or herself the spokesperson of the community, voicing its concerns and convictions.

> Gaelic traditional poetry was in the main one of celebration and participation. The poet produced an artefact which enabled his audience to participate in their culture; to act out culturally reinforcing roles. The poetry was largely oral-based; much of it was meant to be sung. In such circumstances innovation was not at a very high premium. The verse had to make an immediate impact, and skill in versification and verbal wit culminating in the well-wrought memorable phrase was therefore the basic requirement.[43]

Community poets continued to compose songs of praise which buttressed the traditional values of the community by praise and dispraise, blessing and curse. A late poem for a clan chief evokes the ancient theme of immortality through poetry transmitted from generation to generation:

Fad 's a shiubhlas a' ghrian,
Dol gu deiseal nan nial gu h-àrd
Gus an leagh le teas dian
Na beanntainnean sìos gu làr
Cluinnear iomradh do ghnìomh.[44]

For as long as the sun travels,
Going clockwise around the skies above,
Until intense heat will melt
The mountains down to the ground,
The report of your deeds will be heard.

Satire was also invoked to protect the community from attacks from the outside, such as the response of this poet to the 1872 Act of Education which forced Gaelic out of the curriculum:

Dùisgibh, bhàrdaibh, le'r teangannaibh
Is thoiribh sgiùrsadh smearail dhoibh;
Is sìnibh orr' le sgeigearachd
A ghreadas gus a bheò iad.

Na caomhnadh sibhs' an aiteam ud
Mas deas no tuath is dachaidh dhaibh;
Fàgaibh truagh nan craicionn iad
Gam maslachadh nur n-òran.[45]

Awaken, o poets, with your tongues
Give those folk a good thrashing;
Pour derision over them
Which will blight them as long as they live.

Do not spare any of that crowd
Whether the north or south is home to them;
Leave their bodies wretched,
Shaming them in your song.

Satire was one of the responses of the Gaelic community to the Clearances, and it is said that some tenants were threatened with eviction because their songs were politically subversive.[46]

Song was an omnipresent feature of life in Gaelic society, accompanying every task, synchronizing group efforts, uplifting the spirits of the solitary and keeping the minds of all engaged and active.

> Song was an integral part of a whole culture which embraced the life of the community in all its facets … there was scarcely a form of human activity, literally from the cradle to the grave, into which song did not enter …[47]

Songs were a natural way to pass the time while working in a world in which tasks were performed by humans, rather than by machines. Singing was something that everyone was expected to be able to do, and the widespread ability to compose verse spontaneously was noted by many writers, such as when Martin Martin says that the people have 'a quick vein of poesy'. Such improvisational skills were particularly exercised during 'flytings', versified contests between two rivals sometimes representing their clans or homelands. Such emulations could be very provocative indeed, although improvisational verse of a less aggressive nature, such as teasing maidens about suitors, was also common.[48]

The vitality of song within Gaelic culture promoted its recognition as a badge of cultural identity.[49] Songs from the era of the Clearances commonly complain that the noise of the Lowland shepherd and his flock have replaced the Gaelic songs. The twentieth-century Lewis poet Murchadh Mac Phàrlain remarked on the continued survival of the Gaels with the statement 'Yet still we sing!'

Despite the social imperative of the Gaelic oral tradition, song was also a vehicle for personal emotional expression and release. There is not so much a sharp divide but a continuum between speech and song in Gaelic, and heightened emotion can be 'spoken' in many of the same ways as song in terms of melodic phrases, musical cadences, and poetic eloquence. Such practices in Gaelic society allowed people to communicate their innermost feelings and to assuage them in that process.[50]

The Gaelic panegyric code

Both Classical and vernacular poets used many of the same techniques and motifs in their poetry. Poets were familiar with, and had memorized, hundreds of poems which provided models and exemplars which their audience would also be familiar with. A poet would very frequently choose a familiar poem which expressed an idea or theme similar to the one that he had in mind, and rework it to be his own composition. There are many Classical poems with similar opening statements or sentiments, and many vernacular songs which borrow well-kent choruses.

The opening line often stated the aim or theme in Classical verse but it did not typically proceed with a linear storyline, such as is common in the classic Ballad. The story and characters in the poem were often assumed knowledge, and such information would be related outside the song itself. The poem was more typically a 'kaleidoscope of poetic images', one phrase suggesting an image which the next phrase might expand upon, a collage of variations ever returning to the central theme of the poem.[51]

As panegyric was the strongest ingredient in the making of the poetic tradition, many of the techniques of Gaelic poetics revolve around describing and praising the background of the subject, naming his ancestors, his homeland, the setting in which he lives, and his deeds and that of his people. Thus does Iain Lom delimit his subject Sir Donald MacDonald of Sleat:

Mhic Shir Seumas nam bratach	O son of James of the banners
O bhun Slèite nam bradan …	From Sleat of the salmon …
Do theaghlach Rìgh Fionnghall	You are of the stock of the king of the Isles
Oighre dligheach Dhùn Tuilm thu …	The rightful heir of Duntulm …

As seen in the above example, personal and place names are often conferred titles and epithets that evoke cultural and historical resonances for those familiar with the implications of these terms. The salmon is a noble animal in Gaelic cosmology, and thus ennobles the place associated with it, and so on.[52]

There is also a common convention of naming other clans and districts as the allies of the subject. Place names and clan names not only enhance the standing of the subject by claiming the allegiance of other political units, but they place the person in a cultural network which reinforces the sense of solidarity, a unified Gaelic nation of people and place, even if the conceits are more ideal than real.[53] Thus does Alasdair mac Mhaighstir Alasdair include the Campbells in his roll call of the clans to support the Prince in the Rising of 1745:

Gun neartaich iad do chàmpa	They will strengthen your camp
Na Caimbeulaich gu dearbh,	Indeed, the Campbells,
'N Diùc Earragh'alach mar cheann orr'	The duke of Argyll as their leader
Gu mòralach mear prionnsail …	Majestic, gleeful, princely …

A poet praising Campbell of Argyll begins his list of allies with the MacDonalds:

Cóir ar tús ag cur san chaithréim
Clann Domhnuill chuige ón tír thuaith;
na fearchoin as dána an doghruinn …[54]

It is proper to place first in the battle-roll
Clan Donald of the north;
The boldest man-hounds in the strife …

The poet enumerates the attributes and qualities of the subject, or at least those which the subject is prescribed to attain. These include generosity (especially to poets), bravery in war, intelligence, learning, devotion to God, ferocity in battle, faithfulness to truth and justice, and others.

The subject may also be cast in a number of social roles and functions: he is a hunter of deer (a good hunter was also a good warrior); he is a leader of men; he is the protector of his people; he is a warrior commanding a ship; he provides for the poor; and so on.

The comely physical features of the subject are described in detail: he or she has soft, white skin and long, curly, fair hair; he is tall, and has a commanding stature; he has beguiling blue eyes; she has lips that taste of honey and full, rounded breasts underneath her blouse; he wears a handsome plaid and carries intimidating weapons; and so on.

The social leader also had to maintain a household arrayed in the traditional style: many guests would frequent his house, play board games, music, and dancing; he generously dispenses food and wine; he is a patron of the arts and the poets; and so on.

The Classical poets were especially versed in traditional lore, being able to recount the myths, legends, and collective literature of the past and to employ them to good use in their poetry. Allusions might be made in order to make a comparison with a legendary figure, to highlight precedents which should be followed in the present, to recommend a course of action based on a well-known mytho-historical anecdote, or simply to draw upon a rich store of literary resources. The poet *Fionnlagh an Bard Ruadh* who tries to regain the favour of the MacGregor chief reminds him that Conall Clogach reconciled himself with chief Conchobhar, and that Conall's plight was 'well-nigh a type of mine'.[55] The poet Iain Dubh mac Iain exclaims at the beginning of his incitement to the rising of 1715 'This is the time when the prophecy will be proved to us!'

Poetry calls upon a symbolic vocabulary of metaphor and kenning. Just as the rhetorics of Gaelic tradition are aligned along the poles of praise and dispraise, so too are there representatives of each of the classes of nature which imply praise and dispraise. That is to say, the poetic tradition has split the birds, fish, animals, trees, and other natural categories into noble and ignoble members, according to various criteria, and these members are used to imply praise and dispraise in poetry. Some examples are:

	Praise	*Dispraise*
Birds	Eagle	Buzzard
Fish	Salmon	Eel
Animals	Deer	Frog
Trees	Oak	Alder

The use of these symbols allows the listener to form a striking, concrete visualization of the message of the poetry. Note that it is metaphor, and not simile, which the poet employs, and these can be extended with many details: 'You are the holly tree which is always green, and which no snow can wither.' The tree is an especially common symbol, which has many features analogous to humans and human society: the tree is tall, withstands the elements, has a sturdy base, is fertile and full of fruit, provides shelter, and so on.

Gaelic poetry commonly indulges in understatement and double negatives. 'You were not miserly' implies that the subject was very generous. A string of negatives builds up to a superlative: 'You were no sapling, no withered branch, no gnarled, defective twig, but a full-grown, sturdy oak.'

These techniques are commonly stated in the negative in order to break expectations and express grief and lament. 'The hall which you frequented is now silent and empty' expresses the loss of the patron who maintained the goodly household. 'The land is barren and sullen since your death' is an echo of the ancient belief in the marriage between ruler and territory, and all of the tribe and nature are represented as mourning the death. 'We are like a flock without a shepherd' or 'we are like chicks without a nest' emphasizes the role of the subject as a social leader and protector.

The following are excerpts from an example of the bardic metre and theme, though it was composed in 1880 for an ordinary citizen of southern Perthshire:

Mar chraoibh tha mi gun rùsg	I am like a tree without bark
No mar loingeas gun stiùir	Like a ship without a rudder
On latha chàirich iad thu	Since the day they put you inside
's na dèilean.	the coffin planks.
'S i do chomhairle ghlic	It is your words of wisdom
Nì mi ionndruinn a-nis;	That I miss now;
Bha i luachmhor dhomh,	They were valuable to me,
tric is feumail.	frequent and useful.
Tha Baile Chalasraide 'n tràth-'s	The town of Callander is presently
Dubhach tùirseach mu d' bhàs	Grieved and afflicted by your death
'S beag an t-ioghnadh dhaibh bhith	It is no surprise for them to be
cràiteach deurach.	Pained and in tears.
'S iad chaill an ceann riaghailte	They have lost a lawful leader
'S am fear iùil bu mhaith ciall	And a sensible guide
An sàr-cheann-uidhe bha riamh	One who was sought out who was ever
mar stèidh dhaibh.	Like a solid base for them.
Do na bochdan 'nan airce	To the poor in their affliction
Bu tu 'n dìon 's an cùl-taice	You were their shelter and their support
Bheireadh biadh dhaibh	Who would give them food
is pailteas eudaich.	And ample clothing.

Bha buadhan 'inntinn toirt barr
Ann am breithneachadh àrd
Cosnadh cliù dhà is gràdh
nan ceudan.

Regarding important matters,
His mental faculties were superior
Earning him reputation and the love
Of hundreds of people.

Bu neo-lochdach a ghluasad
Stòlda faichilleach stuama:
Bha mòr-mheas aig an t-sluagh
gu lèir ort.

His carriage was flawless,
Composed, watchful, modest:
There was no one who did not have
The greatest esteem for you.

Ged chuir iad thu 'n tràth-'s
Chladh na leacainn fuidh 'n làr
Chaoidh cha dealaich mo ghràdh
's mo spèis riut.

Although they have now sent you
To the graveyard, under the soil,
My love and affection for you will
Stay with me forever.

All of these techniques can be reversed in order to dispraise or satirize a subject. 'You are the twisted alder whose wood is useless' would be taken as a great insult, as it names an ignoble tree, a negative attribute (twisted rather than straight), and the implication that the person is without purpose in society.

Satire, or at least poetic reproach, was also used for political persuasion and social control within the community. The following is part of a poem written by a priest in Strathglass in the early eighteenth century who attempted to shame Lord Lovat into releasing an imprisoned fellow priest. He does so by stressing his improper actions, his ensuing lack of allies, his lack of loyalty to the truth and to earthly and heavenly kings, by evoking negative imagery, and by naming a prophecy which depicts his family as failing and weak:

Mhic Shimidh, mosgail a d' shuain
Èirich suas is cuimhnich d' olc:
Rinn thu do-bheairt nas leòr,
Tha deireadh do sgeòil a' teannadh ort!

'S misd' thu MacCailean a bhith uat
'S misd' thu an taobh tuath gun bhith leat
'S misd' thu gun mheall thu 'n dà Rìgh
Seal mun chuimhnich thu do lease.

Tha nathraichean-neimhe 's an fhraoch
Nach cuir thu le draoidheachd gu tosd;

Tha tuirc-neimhe ri do thaobh
Feitheamh ri gaoith 'fhaotainn ort.

Tha fàisneachd a' tighinn gu teachd
Gun dèanar ort creach gun tòir,
Gum faicear do cholluinn gun cheann,
'S gum bi do chlann mhaoth gun treòir.

Simon of Lovat, awake from your slumber!
Arise and realize your misdeed:
You have done enough mischief
The end of your days is coming to you!

You are the worse without Campbell of Argyll,
The worse of lacking the North as an ally;
The worse of deceiving both Kings
Shortly before you remembered your lease.

There are poisonous serpents in the heather
That you cannot silence with wizardry;
There are venomous boars next to you
Waiting to pick up your scent in the wind.

The prophecy is coming pass
That you will be brought to ruin without force
That your body will be seen headless
That your effeminate children will be weaklings.[56]

This poem reminds us of the close relationship between the secular poet and the priest in Gaelic culture. Both of them tapped Otherworld power with their mastery of the sacred word, both could ex-communicate members of their society, both were held in awe and reverence, both were drawn from the same 'aristocracy of learning'.[57]

The power of satire extended even beyond human subjects. The belief in the ability to drive away rats via satire is evidenced in Old Irish texts, and many such satires survive in Gaelic tradition. One poet even wrote satires to the braxy, hoping to scare off the disease.[58]

Curses and imprecations form another branch of this kind of verse, but while a great many curses were flung spontaneously at enemies, only a few of these have been recorded and survived. One of these concerns a fourteenth-century power struggle between a Campbell noblewoman and her son, who tried to keep her imprisoned. When he hit her with an arrow as she was making her escape into a boat, she made the curse:

Fhir ud thall a' bhogha bhàin	Yonder man with the white bow
air an tràigh air ùtraich	Cavorting on the shore
Dhia! Gun cluinninn gàire nan eun	God! May I hear the noise of fowl
air do bheul a' bìdearsaich!	Feeding on your face!

The young man did die in this manner, according to the tale.[59] Blessings, charms, and invocations of a more beneficent nature survive in much greater numbers, many of them appearing in the collection made by Alexander Carmichael known as the *Carmina Gadelica*.

The panegyric code is not confined to human subjects alone. The popular song which praises the mountain *Beinn Dobhrain* has been shown to follow these same conventions, the mountain taking the place of the chieftain who keeps a generous hall for his guests (the deer), maintains the proper relationship between members of the tribe (hunters and animals), and so on.[60] A twentieth-century poet from Cape Breton even praised the newly installed radio-antennae in his community by extending the well-developed tree imagery of Gaelic panegyric.

Wider oral tradition in society

Almost every activity was accompanied by song. The use of songs during communal labour is described in many early accounts.

> These songs greatly animate every person present, and therefore, when labourers appear to flag, a *luinneag* is commonly called for, which makes them for a while forget their toil and work with redoubled ardour. In travelling through the Highlands in harvest, the sound of these little bands on every side … has a most pleasing effect on the mind of a stranger.[61]

A number of these *òrain bhuain* (reaping songs) survive. One of these is a flyting song in which the reapers divided themselves into two bands, representing the MacDonald and MacLeod factions which appear in the song. 'While working with all their might to be first at the other end of the field which they were reaping, [they] sang this song with so much fervor that they unconsciously cut themselves with their sickles.'[62]

The term *iorram* seems to have originally referred to a particular kind of poetic metre which was used in clan panegyric.[63] By the seventeenth century onwards, it has been restricted in usage to refer to rowing songs, which was the main function of group work songs amongst the men of the islands and western seaboard.

> They are sung on board of ships and buirlings by the sailors, when they row or work, to deceive the time. The subject is generally the life and actions of some chief or relation. The language is such, as to express the sentiments and actions described; the music, expression, and strokes of the oars, coinciding in such exact time, both the sailor and passenger forget their hardships and fatigue, even in the most inclement seasons.[64]

There seem to have been different song styles which were chosen from according to the speed and rhythm of the rowing.[65] The rowers sang the chorus of the song, while the verses were sung by a soloist an the helm of the boat, who announced his intentions by shouting, '*Suidheam air stiùir is èigheam creagag!* (I shall sit at the helm and I'll call out the rowing!).'[66]

Women sang *òrain bhleoghainn* (milking songs) to the cattle, which soothed them and made them give more milk. Mothers and nurses sang children to sleep with *tàlaidhean* (lullabies (literally 'enticements')), many of which are tragic and sorrowful in nature, suggesting that they were just as important as a catharsis for the mother as they were as sedatives for the baby.

The largest genre of female choral work songs was that sung while fulling tweed, called by the later period *òrain luaidh* and in English 'waulking songs'. Males were excluded from this process, and many subjects were discussed in this exclusively female process that would not have been voiced in mixed company. The *òran luaidh* tradition drew to it a number of songs from other traditions, such as rowing songs, clan panegyrics, and Fenian ballads, that would have otherwise been lost.[67]

Dancing is performed to *puirt-a-beul*, literally 'tunes from mouth', and there is a very large repertoire of these in Gaelic to the present day. Most are humorous, some are absurd, and a few are bawdy, but all are rhythmically interesting and highly danceable. Observers in the nineteenth century wrote about the penchant for dancing.

> The cultivation and practice of poetry and music are chief amusements of the Gael, and connected with both is dancing. If the Scots excel in the former, they certainly of all nations are pre-eminent in partiality to the latter. Their passion for this pleasing and healthy exercise is indeed so strong, that it seems part of their nature.[68]

There were a number of direct connections between song and dance.

> Most of the Highland Reels and Strathspeys were wedded to verse. It might be some incident of love or war that was sung, and this gave special interest and charm to the song. Often also, there was a correspondence or likeness of sound and movement between the words and the music which added to the effect.[69]

Duain na Fèinne (Fenian poetry (also called Ossianic lays)) were the songs of highest prestige in Gaelic tradition. Most appear to have been originally composed in the syllabic verse of the *file* between the twelfth and fifteenth century, which helps to account for their high prestige. By the time they were recorded from oral sources they had been adapted to vernacular forms. Veneration for them was such that they may have been used to work magic.[70]

One of the most important concerns of primal societies is that the dead are laid to rest properly. The church has always disapproved of the ancient practice of keening the dead (*tuireadh* or *caoidh*), but only finally extinguished it in the nineteenth century. The keen was partly choral and partly solo, largely improvisational, and drew upon the motifs of panegyric poetry already discussed.

A number of other genres of the oral tradition can only be mentioned in passing, including *pìobaireachd* songs, psalm-singing, devotional songs, humorous anecdotes, prophecy, and so on. There is a great breadth of diversity in Gaelic song tradition from the perspective of the insider, and the remarkable tradition-bearer Nan MacKinnon vaunted confidently, 'If all the music of the world was cut off, the music of the Western Isles would serve the whole world'.[71]

The cèilidh house

The typical context for the exchanging of songs, poems, tales, legends, anecdotes, dances, and news of all sorts was the *cèilidh* (house-visit). This institution was crucial in disseminating the lore and values of society from the oldest generations to the younger ones of both genders. It demanded active minds, excellent memories, faithfulness to the original version of the 'text', respect for the elder tradition-bearers and the honoured guest of the house, and participation by all.

Every community had at least one *cèilidh* house which was frequented nightly during the winter months when nights were long and there was not much work to do out of doors. Many of the adults would simultaneously be weaving ropes, mending clothes, or doing other simple tasks as they listened. One of the classic descriptions of the *cèilidh* house in the early part of the nineteenth century was given by Hector Urquhart.

> In my native place, Pool-Ewe, Ross-shire, when I was a boy, it was the custom for the young to assemble together on the long winter nights to hear the old people recite the tales, or *sgeulachd*, which they had learned from their fathers before them. In these days tailors and shoemakers went from house to house, making our clothes and shoes. When one of them came to the village we were greatly delighted, whilst getting new kilts at the same time. I knew an old tailor who used to tell a new tale every night during his stay … It was also the custom when an *aoigh*, or stranger, celebrated for his store of tales, came on a visit to the village, for us, young and old, to make a rush to the house where he passed the night, and choose our seats, some on beds, some on forms, and others on three-legged stools, etc., and listen in silence to new tales …[72]

There were other occasions for exchanging this information, however, and it is clear that the social interaction therein could serve a number of different purposes.

> It was usual for the young women of a *baile*, or hamlet, which consisted of from four to twenty families, to carry their work to the houses of each other's parents alternately. In these societies oral learning was attained without interrupting industry, and the pleasure of instructing and receiving knowledge was mutual. The matron, visited on one

> evening, perhaps excelled in genealogy; while another was well versed in general history; one may have been adept at poetry, and another an able critic; &c. The Highlander, after his daily occupations, hastened to join the society of the young women, where he met his beloved, or had the pleasure, in her absence, of repeating the last sonnet he had composed in her praise, for which he either received applause or encountered disapprobation.[73]

The young men and women might flirt via the messages in the songs they sang.[74] People challenged each other with riddles, attempting to earn the title *Ridire nan Ceist* (king of Riddles) for the evening. The information discussed was not mere entertainment or escapism, however: there was much lore with great practical value, and people were expected to put the wisdom they absorbed to practical use:

> Before the year 1800 there was many a one of the Highlanders who could tell the names of his ancestors for many generations back. Also, although they could neither read nor write, they took note of the time, and he who did not always learn the day of the month and the age [that is, phase] of the moon, was considered a man void of intelligence. The people who were of old would tell when the new moon would come, when it would be full or in the quarter, as well as though they had an almanac. They trusted much to their memory and when anything remarkable happened, they had a proverb to illustrate it.[75]

Gaelic proverbs number in the thousands, commonly entered speech, songs, poetry, and tales, contain practical knowledge (information about weather, the seasons, use of resources), moral advice (how to raise children, how to behave), and encapsulate wit and humour.

There are also hints that people were aware of the function of these social occasions in maintaining the cultural heritage of their ancestors and consciously cultivated that link with the past. The singing of Ossianic ballads was considered the recollection of past deeds done by ancestors, which singer and audience were expected to hold in the highest regard: the man who sang *Bàs Dhiarmaid* (The Death of Diarmad) to the Revd Alexander Pope refused to do so with his cap on.[76] Elsewhere it is stated:

> The favourite songs of the bards are said to have been those celebrating the renown of their ancestors. The praises of great men were

> accompanied with a sort of religious feeling. It was not only useful to the living to extol the virtues of former heroes as an excitement to their imitation, but was reckoned extremely pleasing to the deceased – it was indeed thought the means of assisting the spirit to a state of happiness, and became consequently a religious duty.[77]

The *cèilidh* house was also a lively venue for the discussion and debate of important social and political issues in the life of the community. Debates were sometimes exchanged in verse between two people advocating the two sides of an argument, with the audience either immediately signaling their approval or disapproval, or else implicitly supporting one side by keeping the song active in the local repertoire.[78]

There are a large number of songs from the eighteenth and nineteenth centuries debating the virtues and vices of items newly come into the Gàidhealtachd from the Lowlands, such as tea. Drunkenness must have been a hot topic of debate, especially during the era of the Evangelical Revival, for there are many songs taking sides about whiskey and other forms of alcohol. Bards were involved in the controversy over the whether or not pubs were to be allowed to operate in a particular neighborhood in the 1960s, and villagers

> looked to their local bards for perspectives on an issue and for articulation of their own feelings. The local song-maker retained this crucial role in Gaelic society as both a medium of and a catalyst for public debate until very recently. He serves as a record of opinion, like the bards of classical Gaelic society, and also expresses his own biases in song. His opinions are often given more credence than those of a 'normal' (i.e., non-song-making) citizen, as he had a reputation for thought, cleverness, and eloquence.[79]

A significant feature of oral tradition is the manner in which all of these elements – proverbs, songs, tales, riddles – intermingle with each other: proverbs are often explained by tales, or refer to characters and situations in them; songs employ proverbs to make pithy remarks; songs are dependent upon tales to explain the characters and situations in them; and so on. This is mirrored by the fact that the best tradition-bearers are typically generalists, commanding a large number of items from all of the genres of oral tradition. 'But though each prefers his own subject, the best Highland story-tellers know specimens of all kinds. Start them, and it seems as they would never stop.'[80]

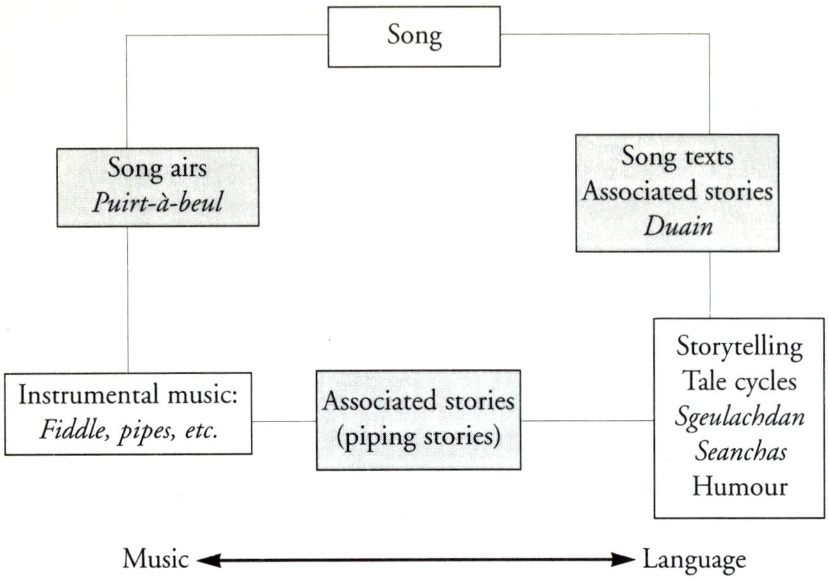

Figure 3.1 – The continuum of Gaelic oral tradition
(after John Shaw 1992-3)

Gaelic music cannot be perceived from an inside perspective as simply 'folk music' because so much of it originates in the Classical tradition of the native aristocracy. Although many of the songs do bear the hallmarks of folk song, clumping all of Gaelic song together under this label would ignore important internal distinctions.

Modernist society distinguishes between passive consumers and virtuoso performers. Music and song in the Gaelic world are functional and not merely aesthetic, and one of these functions is the maintenance of community. Tradition-bearers did not consider themselves to be celebrities but rather links in a chain of transmission from the past to the future.

> It came as a surprise to me that a person of Joe Neil's gifts of memory and narration would have so little to say concerning his own life … Joe Neil views his own personal story as relatively insignificant next to the tradition of which he is an active part. Many of the finer exponents among the older people in Cape Breton (– singers, bards, reciters, fiddlers, pipers and step-dancers – are inclined to regard per-

> forming gifts as a part of the shared cultural store, rather than the exclusive property of gifted individuals.[81]

As the *cèilidh* was a local institution, based in a community, run by and for the members of that community, it was automatically tailored to the needs, concerns, and environment of that community. People told stories regarding their ancestors, sang songs about events significant in their own communities, created proverbial lore relevant to their own flora, fauna, and sense of place, and engendered an ethos of self-reliance.

Decline of the oral tradition

The decline of the Gaelic oral tradition cannot be separated from the assault on the Gaelic language and culture as a whole. The recurring complaint of scholars sent by John Francis Campbell in 1860 to collect folklore was that the local ministers had ridiculed and silenced the old people for their tales, and the school-master continued this policy of denigration with the young.

The reality of the oppression of Gaelic society must have also caused many to lose esteem for the grandiose songs of old and all that went with them. John Ramsay of Ochtertyre notes at the end of the eighteenth century that, 'The Highland muses are said to have dropped their wings more since the last rebellion than at any preceding period.'[82] Duncan Campbell notes that the forced removal of the fighting men of Glengarry, the subject of so many panegyrics, to Canada 'turned war-songs and proud *pìobaireachd* into hollow mockeries or pathetic laments, took the pith out of the oral traditions.'[83]

The incorporation of the Gàidhealtachd into the twentieth-century Anglo-American world of mass-media has accelerated the demise by projecting images of wealth and glamour which undermine a sense of self-confidence and discourage people from sustaining their own traditions. Local heroes and family ancestors are upstaged by stars from Hollywood and London, time-honoured traditions are displaced by the latest fads, local singers cannot compete with technologically-enhanced voices from the stereo, and so on. This is, of course, a universal phenomenon since the advent of radio and television. It has been observed as a break in the line of transmission in Cape Breton, where 'The youth were quick to adopt radio, and the net effect was that the control of culture was removed from the community.'[84]

Despite the forces against Gaelic and its oral tradition, tradition-bearers have survived to the end of the twentieth century, passing onto us a rich treasure from the generations before them. Most of them have a great affection for, and dedication to, this heritage, consciously sustaining what they have inherited. The death of these traditions has been witnessed by those to whom they signify the end of community and the end of life itself:

> I am reminded, finally, of an old man in Barra who, in 1970, tired of returning home to an empty house as television took over from the *cèilidh*, one night painted THE END in large white letters on the end of his thatched cottage. It remains an appropriate symbol for the passing of one tradition and the arrival of the brave new world …[85]

John Lorne Campbell, the scholar most active in recording and promoting Gaelic oral tradition in the twentieth century, argues that Gaelic songs are not just literary compositions of great beauty but also cultural resources of significant consequence.[86]

Many modern writers comment that Gaels, and other non-industrialized peoples, enjoyed telling stories and singing songs simply because they had no other entertainment. This is to overestimate the superiority of global, electronic mass media and to underestimate the satisfaction that people find in participating in their own local forms of expression. The comments of one nineteenth-century Highlander are typical:

> *Lasaidh mo chridhe fhathast le sòlas nuair a chuimhnicheas mi air cleachdaidhean agus gnàths nam beann. Cò neach a thogadh anns a' Ghàidhealtachd nach d' fhiosraich an tùs òige, an deòthas inntinn leis an èisdeadh sgeòil na Féinne. Cha dì-chuimhnich mi ri m' bheò an toil-inntinn leis an èistinn ri seanchas nan aosda nuair a labhradh iad mu euchd nan laoch bho'n tàinig iad. 'S cinnteach mi gun do chuidich seo ri clann nan Gàidheal a thogail suas ann am barrachd buaidh os cionn gach sluaigh anns an domhan – mar a bha am beachd air àrdachadh le bhith cluinntinn cliù agus treuntas an sinnsear a ghnàth 'ga luaidh … Iadsan a dh'fhiosraich an rùn cridhe leis an èist an Gàidheal ri seanchas mu chinneadh, chan ioghnadh leò mar a chumadh air chuimhne iad …*[87]

> My heart still burns with delight when I remember the traditions and customs of the Highlands. What person, who was raised in a Gaelic community, did not experience in their early youth the mental excite-

ment that comes when the tales of the Fianna are heard. I will never forget for as long as I live the enjoyment with which I listened to the lore of the old people when they would speak about the exploits of the warriors from whom they were descended. I'm sure that this enabled the Gaels to be endowed as they grew up with qualities superior to other people of the world – since their ideas were elevated by constantly hearing references to the fame and excellence of their ancestors ... Those who know the love with which the Gaels listen to the lore of their ancestors will not be surprised that they are remembered ...

CHAPTER 4

The organization of society

The primacy of the individual is the great axiomatic principle of modernist life and the structure and assumptions about society as we now know it follow from this idea. Large-scale, anonymous government institutions provide us the services – education, health, transport, defense, and so on – that our immediate community, most of them relations, would have rendered in kind to us in the past.

The immediate benefits of this system are that it frees the individual to pursue his or her own personal agenda, to create a life and career unbounded by conventions of the community, and to engage in the specialization of knowledge and work. The immediate problems with this system are that it forces us to disengage from our community, to invent a new identity which would have been largely inherited in the past, and to lose the breadth of experience and tradition that is central to the human experience.

People are becoming increasingly isolated, further removed from each other and the rhythms of nature which give them life and meaning. Religious cults and rampant consumerism prey upon the hunger of the soul which this anomie and unrootedness cause. Many people today long for the sense of belonging and purpose taken for granted in primal societies. The narrow confines of life in techno-consumer society – the unnaturally accelerated pace, the commodification of every aspect of living, the sacrifice of all for greater productivity and quantities of production – make a mockery of the idea of 'freedom'. The only freedoms allowed are those dictated by capitalist enterprise, which often uses the word 'freedom' as a euphemism for 'freedom to exploit'.

The development of individualism has a long history but was part of the ideology of progress in Western Europe. The idea was well established by the eighteenth century that the final 'polished' stage of cultural development – the commercial stage – was characterized by class differentiation and personal possession of property.[1]

It has already been shown in Chapters One and Two that as early as the sixteenth century the Lowlanders characterized the Highlanders as living in a primitive stage of society where kin-based allegiances surpassed the civil duties of citizens in nation-states. The elimination of kin-community was a target of the political and social reforms of King James VI.[2] The supposed slavish nature of Highlanders to their 'tyrannical' chiefs was a common condemnation into the mid-eighteenth century. 'The Highlanders have been oppressed and inslav'd by their Chiefs, yet oppress'd and inslav'd after Such a Manner, that they have joyfully submitted to their tyrants, and glory'd, nay triumphed in their base and ignominious Servitude.'[3]

In other words, the Highlanders were pictured as an uncivilized people who the English-speaking world was eager to reform or replace. The Highlanders themselves, however, had a very different notion of the ideal society, the nature of inter-personal relationships, and virtuous conduct.

Clans and kinship

Highland society, on the one hand, was never a totally closed system, impervious to influence or change. Feudalism, in particular, had an impact on land-holding and political institutions: 'Highland society was based on kinship modified by feudalism, Lowland society on feudalism tempered by kinship.'[4] On the other hand, many of the most important features of Highland society were forged in ancient Gaelic times and can be studied in early Irish textual sources. The lack of complete contemporary documentation of Highland institutions can often be remedied by reference to early Irish texts.[5]

Kinship was the organizing principle of Highland clans, although in reality not everyone in the same clan was related. This is a virtually universal phenomenon.

> All of the Traditional societies with which I am intimately familiar, and I suspect all the indigenous Traditional societies of the world, are founded on institutions which are defined by kinship. This does not necessarily mean blood kinship ... The clan is a political institution which claims an ideology of kinship but which is also based on a historical reality.[6]

The people who operated as members of a clan all accepted the authority of a common leader, as Duncan Forbes of Culloden noted.

> A Highland clan is a set of people all bearing the same surname and believing themselves to be related to one another and to be descended from a common stock. In each clan there are several subordinate tribes who own their dependence on their own immediate chief, but all agree in owning allegiance to the supreme chief of the clan or kindred and look on it as their duty to support him in all his adventures ...

Despite the ideology of kinship, people who were of different origins could find themselves dependent upon a particular chieftain, living upon his estate, and effectively becoming members of his clan. They often took his surname as their own.[7] The world of a Highlander was largely determined by the highly local parameters of his clan and chieftain.

> The Highlanders are divided into tribes and clans under chiefs and chieftains and each clan is divided into branches ... who have chieftains over them ... Next to the love of the chief is that of the particular branch from which they sprang, and in a third degree they love the whole clan and name, whom they will assist, right or wrong, against those of any other tribe with whom they are at variance.[8]

There are a number of terms in Gaelic for referring to lineages and kin. The term *clann* itself appears in family names by *c.*1100 in Scotland (in the Book of Deer), but most of the known clans are named after founding ancestors who can be dated to the era 1150 to 1350. The MacDougalls, called *Clann Dùghaill* in Gaelic, are named after a *Dùghall* who lived in the later twelfth century.[9] The term *cinneadh* was replacing *clann* in the Gaelic of both Scotland and Ireland in the sixteenth century, although this process did not affect any kin-group names.[10] The term *fine* refers most specifically to the ruling family of a particular clan, although it could be extended to imply the clan as a whole.

Over time, the children of a ruler would in turn reproduce and their children would be the progenitors of new *sliochdan* (lineages). If they needed to assert their own individual identity as a separate branch from the main root of the clan, they might coin a title based on the founder of their branch: Clan Ranald is a branch of the Clan Donald descended from *Raghnall*, the second surviving son of the first lord of the Isles. The two main branches of the MacLeods are called *Sìol Tormoid* and *Sìol Torcail* after the two sons of Leòd, the progenitor of the clan.

People were not merely individuals, but part of a network of kin with whom they shared responsibilities and rewards. '*Cha duine, duine 'na aonar* (A person by himself is not a person).' There are many Gaelic proverbs which relate the binding force of kinship, such as '*Cha nigh na tha de uisge anns a' mhuir ar càirdeas* (All of the water in the ocean could not wash away our kinship)'.

It was not that people were forced by necessity to be amongst their kin, whom they would otherwise prefer to leave: they wanted to be amongst their own relations. '*Is miann le triubhas a bhith a-measg aodaich, ach is miann leam fhèin a bhith a-measg mo dhaoine* (Trousers like to be amongst clothes, but it is my wish to be amongst my people).' Life was more fulfilling and richer for sharing it: '*Is sona gach cuid an comaidh; is mairg a chromadh 'na aonar* (Everything shared brings happiness; pity he who would stoop by himself).' The recent loosening of these ties has been distressing: 'In these modern times I often hear the horrid and unnatural assertion that it is disagreeable having one's relatives all round one. So much for the culture of the twentieth century!'[11]

Children were expected to respect their elders, who passed on the culture and wisdom of the ancestors and who were worthy of their respect. 'Young people are bred, not only with a profound reverence for their parents, but with a kind of implicit confidence in the elders of their tribe.'[12] One of the most insulting accusations was the charge that a person showed disrespect for his parents.

Parents were responsible for the proper raising of their children. '*An leanabh a dh'fhàgar dha fhèin, cuiridh e a mhàthair gu nàire* (The child who is left to himself will bring shame to his mother)'. Parents would be dependent upon their children in their old age. '*Is mairg aig am bi comhaltas gann agus clann gun rath* (Pity those without foster-siblings and whose children have no success)'.

Because the actions of an individual had a large impact on the rest of the kin-group, they had to consult them before making important decisions. The classic example of such a decision is marriage, as such a union is not merely between two individuals, but between two kin-groups, and involves a potential exchange of wealth and territory. There are a number of tales and anecdotes about the affront given by those who marry without the approval of their families. Hugh MacDonald of Sleat, brother to the lord of the Isles, was advised against marrying a second time in 1469 without first consulting the Council of the Isles.[13] A woman pleads in one song:

Ach mas fear thu a tha air mo thì-sa
Ruig an tìr an còir dhomh 'bhith
Faigh toil m' athar is mo mhàthar
Cead mo chàirdean 's còrdaidh sinn ...[14]

But if you are a man truly in pursuit of me
Go to the land I ought to be in
Appeal to my father and my mother
Get my kin's permission and we'll make ready ...

Ancestry is a prevailing concern of primal societies, for the characteristics of ancestors are thought to be passed on to their descendants. One would be concerned to know of the traits of a particular family before choosing to marry someone with whom one would have children, for they could inherit qualities from both sides. These inherited qualities were thought to be overriding factors in life. '*Is buaine dùthchas na oilean* (Inheritance is more lasting than what is learnt).'

Ancestry was the deed of title for one's station in life and one's endowments. People were eager to make connections with ancestors who embodied particular qualities, sometimes with more creativity than genealogical authenticity. The kings of Scotland, and many of the other leading noble families, were careful to emphasize their descent from the early kings of Dál Riada, who they saw as their cultural predecessors and the key to their political power.[15]

A person saw it as his duty to respect and follow his ancestry. '*Cuimhnich air na daoine bhon tànaig thu* (Remember the people from who you descend); *Lean gu dlùth ri cliù do shinnsre* (Follow closely to the reputation of your ancestors).' Unlike the modern notions of Scotland as a 'mongrel nation', Highlanders boasted of their pure Gaelic ancestry. 'The Highlanders are exceedingly proud to be thought an unmixed People, and are apt to upbraid the English with being a Composition of all Nations.'[16]

Kings and chieftains

In early Gaelic society, the *ríg* (king) of a *tuath* (a local tribal grouping) was surrounded by an aura of sacredness. His reign was punctuated by ritual activity and constrained by *geasa* (taboo). The king was to be a flawless paragon who was married to the goddess of the territory, and he was to exercise his duties faithfully in order to secure the needs of his people. A king was thought to have failed in these obligations if he was satirized, maimed, or defeated in battle, or if famine or pestilence came to his land.[17]

The king had officers to assist him, most importantly the master-poet who had inherited his office from the druid. Many of the institutions surrounding kingship reveal its sacred nature, and this is particularly apparent in the role of the *file/ollamh*, who was 'the mediator and the manipulator of the supernatural powers which affected the king and through him his kingdom.'[18] According to the early Irish laws, for example, 'It is the poet's duty to be with the king at *Samhainn* and to protect him from enchantment.'

The chieftain of Highland society inherited many of these characteristics. The belief that the chieftain had a special relationship with the territory can be seen particularly in laments in which nature mourns the death of the king or chieftain. When Prince Charles Edward Stewart was born in 1720, his anticipated return to Scotland was pictured as restoring the bounty of the land.

> *Bidh gach tulach 'na iomairibh réidh*
> *'S fàsaidh cruithneachd air aodainn shliabh …*
> *Cuiridh coille trom-bhlàth os ar cionn*
> *Cuiridh 'n talamh gun airceas de bharr*
> *Tacar mara cur làin 's gach lìon …*[19]

> Every hillock will become smooth fields
> And wheat will grow on hillsides …
> The forest will produce fruit over us
> The land will yield harvest without restraint
> The provision of the sea filling every net …

When he died in 1788, William Ross sang:

Tha gach beinn, gach cnoc 's gach sliabh	Every mountain, hill and moor-side
Air am faca sinn thu 'triall	On which we saw you travelling
Nis air chall an dreach 's am fiabh	Has now lost its comeliness
O nach tig thu 'chaoidh nan cian	Since you will never ever return

The king was important ideologically as the focus and embodiment of the ideals and identity of his people. This is particularly true in the formation of Scotland, which united a number of different ethnic elements. The Scottish dynasty was the stable bedrock upon which the kingdom was built. Authors in the Middle Ages, and even into the seventeenth century, were aware of its origins in Dál Riada:

> We do not pretend to be amongst the great and rich kingdoms of the earth; yet we know not who can claim preference in antiquity and integrity, being of one blood and lineage, without mixture of any other people, and have so continued above two thousand years; during which, no foreign power was ever able to settle the dominion of a strange Lord over us, or to make us forsake our allegiance to your Majesty's royal ancestors, our native and kindly kings; whereas most of the other kingdoms are compounds of diverse nations, and have been subjugated to princes of which did design universality, are all broken in pieces ...[20]

The *ceann-cinnidh* (chief) of Highland society provided a similar focus, and Anglo-British commentators made him out to be a tyrant and a threat to the central government. 'The ordinary Highlanders esteem it the most sublime degree of virtue to love their chief and to pay him a blind obedience although in opposition to the Government, the laws of the country and even the laws of God ... He is their idol, and they profess to know no king but him ...'[21]

While feudalism brought with it the practice of primogeniture, which dictated a strict father-to-son succession, the older Gaelic practice of tanistry allowed any male whose great-grandfather had been leader to succeed him. The male chosen during the life-time of the current leader to replace him was called the *tánaise* (borrowed into Lallans as *tanist*). While the last echoes of tanistry in the succession of the kings of Scotland seem to fade away in the thirteenth century, it may have been practiced by at least some clans into the seventeenth century.[22]

Each system of succession had its advantages and disadvantages. At its worst, tanistry could bring periods of strife as possible candidates fought each other, and even murdered each other, to eliminate competition. Primogeniture tended to preclude such debates and struggles with its simplicity. Heirs could be, however, flawed mentally or physically, and tanistry did not saddle people with inadequate leaders. Even under tanistry, however, successors tended to be the sons or close relative of the previous ruler, as one needed to be close to the centres of power to draw upon the necessary wealth, military backing, and expertise to succeed.[23]

The king (or chief) was chosen by a body of men representing the interests of the kin-group. 'They reckon their chief, whom they choose for their patron: tho he be not of their name.'[24] The lord of the Isles appears to have been chosen by the Council of the Isles, and some, at least, of the clans appear to have chosen their chiefs in some sort of election, 'and having elected them associate them with a council of elders'.[25]

A nobleman who had a large following of dependents could make a better case, with or without show of force, than one without such support: 'the claimant who had the strongest party in the clan, especially if sanction'd by the will of the deceas'd, was generally acknowledged as heir.'[26]

While the office of the king (or chief) was sacred, the man who performed this role was not: he was subject to rules and regulations. He was dependent upon his followers for his own power, and therefore was no stronger than the will of his people to follow him and no more wealthy than his people made him. There are many Gaelic proverbs to this effect. '*Is treasa tuatha na tighearna* (The common people are stronger than a lord); *Is àirde tuathanach air a chasan na duine-uasal air a ghlùinean* (A commoner standing on his feet is taller than a nobleman on his knees); *Far nach bi nì, caillidh an rìgh a chòir* (A king will lose his rights where there is no wealth).'

> Nothing can be more erroneous than the prevalent idea, that a highland chief was an ignorant and unprincipled tyrant, who rewarded the abject submission of his followers with relentless cruelty and vigorous oppression. He was, on the contrary, the father of his people: gracious, condescending, and beloved, far from being ruled by arbitrary caprice. He was taught from the cradle to consider the meanest individual of his clan, as his kinsman and his friend, whom he was born to protect, and bound to regard. He was taught too, to venerate old age, to respect genius, and to place an almost implicit dependence on the counsels of the elders of his clan.[27]

A chief was 'not allow'd to part with territory (even) for the preservation of his life … the habit of making all private considerations subservient to the good of the community'.[28] John Major stated likewise in the early sixteenth century that the Scottish king 'holds his right as king of a free people, nor can he grant the right to anyone against the will of that people'.[29]

There are a number of examples of chiefs and chieftains who were deposed and replaced. After some ten years as chief of the Mackintoshes,

Farquhar's 'friends of the name of Clanchattan were altogether dissatisfied with his way of managing affairs. Therefore he willingly renounced his inheritance and birthright in favour of his uncle ...'[30]

As in many other warrior-societies, the chieftain-to-be had to prove himself to be a capable leader in battle. It has been shown that in traditional Gaelic warfare, 'It was above all the leaders, and not the rank and file, who were expected to man the gap of danger and sacrifice their lives in defense of their followers.'[31]

> Every Heir, or young Chieftain of a Tribe, was oblig'd in Honour to give a publick Specimen of his Valour, before he was declar'd Governor and Leader of his People, who obey'd and follow'd him upon all Occasions.
>
> This Chieftain was usually attended by a Retinue of young Men of Quality, who had not beforehand given any Proof of their Valour, and were ambitious of such an Opportunity to signalize themselves.
>
> It was usual for the Captain to lead them, to make a desperate Incursion upon some Neighbour or other that they were in Feud with; and they were oblig'd to bring by open force the Cattel they found in the Lands they attack'd, or to die in the Attempt.
>
> After the Performance of this Atchievement, the young Chieftain was ever after reputed valiant and worthy of Government, and such as were of his Retinue acquir'd the like Reputation ...
>
> A Heap of Stones was erected in form of a Pyramid, on the top of which the young Chieftain was plac'd, his Friends and Followers standing in a Circle round about him, his Elevation signifying his Authority over them, and their standing below their Subjection to him. One of his principal Friends deliver'd into his Hands the Sword wore by his Father, and there was a white Rod deliver'd to him likewise at the same time.
>
> Immediately after the Chief Druid (or Orator) stood close to the Pyramid, and pronounc'd a Rhetorical Panegyrick, setting forth the antient Pedegree, Valour, and Liberality of the Family, as Incentives to the young Chieftain, and fit for his imitation.[32]

This description of an inauguration mirrors the description of the ancient Gaelic rite performed for the king of Scotland described in the previous chapter. The inauguration of the lords of the Isles was likewise consummated by the bestowing of a white rod of lordship (*slat tighearnais*).

The loyalty of the people to their proven leader was apparent in their daily lives:

> The Islanders have a great respect for their Chiefs and Heads of Tribes, and they conclude Grace after every Meal, with a Petition to God for their Welfare and Prosperity. Neither will they, as far as in them lies, suffer them to sink under any Misfortune; but in case of a Decay of Estate, make a voluntary Contribution on their behalf, as a common Duty, to support the Credit of their Families.[33]

For a while after the dissolution of the clan-system after the defeat of the Jacobites in 1746, many clansmen continued to give money toward the upkeep of their chieftain, although he was often in exile, and they were already burdened by taxes levied by the government.[34]

The chieftain was responsible for the welfare of his own people. As a chieftain's strength was in the men who were in his command, it was in his interest to look after them. He would postpone or even cancel rent in times of scarcity[35] and attend to the needs of the poor: 'Gentlemen are very charitable to their poor: some will have 20 or more every meal in the house.'[36]

The role of the chieftain in feeding the hungry and supporting the needy is frequently met in Gaelic poetry.

Ga mhèid 's gun cost thu 'chìsean ris
Chan fhaic thu dìth air tuathanach;
Do bhantraichean 's do dhìlleachdain
On 's e do nì-se 'dh'fhuasglas orr';
Dèanamaid ùrnaigh dhìcheallach
Gun cùm an Rìgh a-suas duinn thu ...[37]

With all of the income that you spend
You will see that no tenant goes without;
(The plight of) widows and orphans
Is relieved by your wealth;
Let us make an earnest prayer that God
Will keep you in good health you for us ...

The breadth of his responsibilities for the upkeep of his people is suggested by the following passage:

> When a Tenant's Wife in this or the adjacent Islands dies, he then addresses himself to Mackneil of Barray, representing his Loss, and at the same time desires that he would be pleas'd to recommend a Wife to him, without which he cannot manage his Affairs, nor beget Followers to Mackneil, which would prove a publick Loss to him. Upon this Representation, Mackneil finds out a sutable Match for him; and the Woman's Name being told him, immediately he goes to her, carrying with him a Bottle of strong Waters for their Entertainment at Marriage, which is then consummated.
>
> When a Tenant dies, the Widow addresseth herself to Mackneil in the same manner, who likewise provides her with a Husband, and they are marry'd without any further Courtship …
>
> If a Tenant chance to lose his Milk-Cows by the Severity of the Season, or any other Misfortune; in this Case Mackneil of Barray supplies him with the like Number that he lost.[38]

Similarly, when a number of the followers of Colin Campbell of Glenorchy in 1570 were raided, he promised that they would be recompensed and protected from his own savings: 'Spare neither my gear nor your own, for God leaving us our healths we will get gear enough.'[39]

The dependence of people upon their chieftain, and their desire for a strong one, is reflected in such proverbs as '*Is mairg aig am bi an tighearna fann* … (Pity he whose lord is weak); *Cò ris a thèid mi gam ghearan is gun Mhac Mhic Ailein am Mùideart?* (Who can I go to to make my complaint if the chief of Clan Ranald is not in Moidart?)'.

Nobility and hierarchy

Everything in Gaeldom was arranged and performed according to social rank. This is exemplified by the care taken in arranging the seating of guests at dinner carefully according to their station.

> Every family had commonly two Stewarts, which in their Language were call'd [*Màrsal Taighe*]: the first of these serv'd always at home, and was oblig'd to be well vers'd in the Pedegree of all the Tribes in the Isles, and in the Highlands of Scotland; for it was his Province to assign every Man at Table his Seat according to his Quality … and this was necessary to prevent Disorder and Contention …[40]

That a nobleman could be violently outraged when his rank was dishonoured is illustrated by an incident which is said to have occurred when the lord of the Isles was hosting a dinner at his castle in Mull in the fifteenth century. John MacDonald assumed the office of *Màrsal Taighe* for the evening, and took advantage of this by seating others in less favorable positions than his own. He proceeded to address them in the most insulting way possible:

> 'Now', saith he, 'I am the oldest and best of your surnames here present, and will sit down; as for these fellows who have raised their heads of late, and are upstarts, whose pedigree we know not, nor even they themselves, let them sit as they please'. MacLean, MacLeod of Harris, and MacNeill of Barra went out in a rage, and ... determined, as soon as an opportunity offered, to be fully revenged of John MacDonald for the affront, as they thought, he had given.[41]

The respect offered to nobility is shown metaphorically in a proverb employing tree imagery: '*Bidh an t-ubhal as fhearr air a' mheangan as àirde* (The best apple will be on the highest branch).' The Revd Norman MacLeod found it necessary to scold the upper ranks of Gaeldom who had become estranged from their humbler relations by the mid-nineteenth century: '*Ged a b' ubhlan iad air a' ghèig a b' àirde, bu mheanglain sinn uile de'n aon chraoibh* (Although they were the apples on the highest branch, we were all shoots from the same tree)'.

Amongst the specialized, high-ranking professions in Gaelic society was that of the warrior. 'They were well train'd in managing the Sword and Target, in Wrestling, Swimming, Jumping, Dancing, Shooting with Bows and Arrows, and were stout Seamen.'[42] The chieftain kept ranks of fighting men called *buannachan*[43] and a bodyguard of chosen warriors called *Lèine-chneas* (or *Lèine-chnios*). New recruits from the *tuath* (common-folk) were sometimes taken into this privileged profession on account of their renowned strength or prowess. By about 1600 the formal social barriers to the *tuath* entering into warfare had disappeared on account of the increasing need for fighting men in the face of escalating warfare, even though the former associations between social divisions were not altogether forgotten.[44]

Despite the strict assignment of rank, and operation according to rank, people were not segregated from each other because of being inferior in status. Rather, everyone celebrated their ties of kinship and inter-dependence with the noble leaders of society, and these ties engendered a sense of innate self-esteem amongst the Highland people as a whole. There was constant intercourse between ranks, and it has been noted that tanistry created a society which had a remarkably high percentage of nobles in comparison with most of the rest of Europe.[45]

There is ample anecdotal evidence to illustrate the fluid dialogue between all members of Highland society. When describing how everyone, including the chief, danced together at the harvest feast, Miss Grant of Rothiemurchus observed that 'a vein of good breeding ran through all ranks, influencing their manners and rendering the intercourse of all most agreeable'. Duncan Campbell of Glenorchy, who died in 1631, is pictured amongst his dependents in his elegy.

Dob iomdha um nóin a mbrugh Bhealaigh
Brughaidh, biatach, barún ríogh
Ag feitheamh ar fheidhm Thriath Tatha …[46]

In the hall of Bealach at noon there were many
Yeomen, hospitallers, and barons
Waiting on the charge of the lord of the Tay …

Medieval scholars appear to have remarked at the pride of nobility amongst all Scots, for John Major wrote in 1521 about this at length:

> Most writers note yet another fault in the Scots … I am not able to acquit the Scots of this fault, for both at home and abroad they take inordinate pleasure in noble birth, and (though of ignoble origin themselves) delight in hearing themselves spoken of as come of noble blood … Poor noblemen marry into mean but wealthy families. In this way some of the Scots ennoble their whole country.[47]

Visitors from other nations often remarked at the self-regard of common Highlanders, in contrast to the cringing peasants of their own societies. 'The poorest and most despicable Creature of the name of MacDonald looks upon himself as a Gentleman of far Superior Quality than a man of England of £1,000 a year.'[48]

Gaelic society is often characterized by the English-speaking world as being a uniformly poor, 'peasant' society. Gaels, however, saw themselves as a sophisticated and hierarchical, yet inter-dependent, society. The poet Iain Crichton Smith contrasted the community on Lewis where he grew up in the early twentieth century with Anglo-British society:

> In a society which is still concerned with class to a great extent, it is important to say that the community in which I grew up was a classless one. It is possible that, seen from the outside, the islanders might be characterised as belonging to a peasant society. Seen from the inside, however, the islander does not think of himself as a peasant nor does he consider himself as being set in a particular social scale. Indeed, questions of that nature have never really troubled him ... The criterion in such a society always was, not what class does such or such a man belong to, but can he do the things that are necessary?[49]

That association with native nobility propped up the pride and self-confidence of Gaelic culture is apparent in the dissolution of Gaelic society, when chieftains became alienated from their people, who could no longer find role-models and paragons of native culture:

> The altered relations of the peasantry to their superiors involved deep-reaching consequences. Gradually the lairds and chief withdrew from familiar intercourse with the people, and the gentry of middle rank – the tacksmen and *duine-uasals* of the clan – in course of time disappeared. It was the presence of this upper class that gave to Highland society its peculiar character. The common man was strictly dependent on the lairds and tacksmen for his little holding, but at the same time they owed their power and military importance to his goodwill and readiness in their service. Thus, the obligation being reciprocal, the dignity of the lower orders was preserved.[50]

Ties that bind

Fosterage is one of the ancient Celtic customs which endured in Gaelic Scotland into at least the seventeenth century amongst the nobility, and even longer amongst the lower ranks of society.[51] It cultivated inter-dependence between families within clans, and furthered links between clans. A *dalta* (fosterling) was to be taught a number of skills, according to rank and gender. A boy was returned to his parents at seventeen, and a girl at fourteen, although they maintained close bonds of affections with their *comhdhaltan* (fostered-siblings) and foster-parents (*muime* (foster-mother) and *oide* (foster-father)), whom they were obliged to help support in their old age.[52]

> As a rule one of the chief's sons was handed over as an infant, practically, to one of the tacksmen or other members of the clan, and there he remained, as one of that family, during the years of his pupilarity. The lower classes usually considered this trust a very great honour, and by no means a service for which any direct reward was to be given or expected. So much was the condescension thought of that when a son was born to a chief it was not uncommon to find a contention arising among members of the clan as to who was to be favoured with the fostering of the boy-child. The one who succeeded sometimes had to face a considerable measure of jealousy, and even ill-will, from others less fortunate; and time after time feeling ran so high against him as to cause a feud … Against this, however, were to be placed the advantages of a direct family connection with the chief, and the gain therefrom of a higher standing and a more influential position for the lucky one among his fellow clansmen.[53]

There are a number of proverbs which relate to the intense bonding between fosterling and foster-family. '*Is caomh le fear a charaid, ach is e smior a chridhe a chomhdhalta* (A man's relation is beloved to him, but his foster-sibling is as the pith of his heart); *An uair a theid a' ghrian fodha, teichidh m' fhaileas, ach grian ann no as cha teich mo chomhdhalta* (My shadow will flee when the sun sets, but my foster-sibling will not flee whether or not the sun is there)'. It is significant that the Gaelic terms for foster-parents are cognates with the English terms of affection 'mummy' and 'daddy'.

> The lower order of people value themselves much on their connections with the rich. Connections often arise from the time that a mother, wife, or sister, gave suck to [that is, nursed] the gentleman's child; whence they call them *comhdhaltas*, co-fostered, or fosterlings. This appellation is used by all the family, as well as by the child whose mother's milk suckled the great man's child. The familiar epithet is no less useful to the rich than to the poor man; because, if the rich man countenances the poor, the last, in return, will think himself interested in protecting the flocks, and other effects of the rich; so that this tie of friendship being reciprocally useful, is continued for generations.[54]

These arrangements were formal contractual agreements, of which some documents have survived to attest to the practice. The natural parents generally paid a fosterage fee in cattle to pay for the service and to guarantee that their children were maintained according to their rank. This fee would be reclaimed by the parents if any problem arose, or else:

> When the child returned to the parents it was usually accompanied by all the cows given by both the father and the fosterer, with half of the increase by propagation. Those beasts were considered as a portion, and called *Crodh Mhic a Làimh*, of which the father had the produce, but was supposed not to have full property in, but to owe the same number to the child, as a portion to the daughter, or as a stock for the son.[55]

That fosterage could change the fortunes of a clan is claimed by a history of the Campbells, which records how they assisted the MacEacherns: 'The MacEachairns … haveing their force augmented by this new relationship of [*co-dhalt*]-ship, with the Knights of Lochows Family, a relationship be the by, more binding in these countries, even in my own time, than that of blood.'[56]

The bond of 'manrent' allowed the kinship network to be extended by adding new dependents to the chieftain's domain. Men entering into this agreement offered their personal services, and that of their clan if they were a chieftain, to a more powerful lord in exchange for the latter's protection and leadership.[57]

These bonds could have implications for the whole clan. Campbell of Argyll offered to transfer his bond of manrent of the entire MacLaren clan to Campbell of Glenorchy in 1559, if they themselves chose to have him as their chief and protector. Cameron of Lochiel placed himself in the service of the earl of Huntly in 1547 'by the advice of his kinsmen and friends and clan', and Huntly in return paid him a fee and officially acquitted the Camerons of past crimes.[58]

The bond of friendship, while it is not defined anywhere as to how it differed from manrent, appears to have been more of an alliance of equals, rather than a vassal-lord relationship.[59] Such an alliance appears in stories such as that of the renowned hero Conall Gulban:

> The king of Ireland went back and he married the king of the Iubhar's sister; and the king of the Iubhar and the king of Ireland made *comh-cheangal* 'a league' together: if straits, or hardships, or extremity, or anything counter should come upon either, the other was to go to his aid.[60]

That this kind of bond was engaged in is confirmed by Martin Martin:

> Their antient Leagues of Friendship were ratify'd by drinking a Drop of each other's Blood, which was commonly drawn out of the little Finger. This was religiously observ'd as a sacred Bond; and if any Person after such an Alliance happen'd to violate the same, he was from that time reputed unworthy of all honest Mens Conversation.[61]

The practice of cementing alliances with blood is referred to in the proverb '*Is milis fuil nàmhaid, ach is milse fuil caraid* (The blood of an enemy is sweet, but a friend's blood is sweeter)'. This is explained 'It was once the custom to taste a friend's blood to indicate undying affection and fidelity'.[62]

While it has been shown that the chieftain was expected to be concerned with the welfare of his clan, individuals could rely upon the support of the entire community, who felt it their responsibility to share their meager wealth with those in need. Seeking aid from neighbors was known in Gaelic as *faoighe*: 'It entailed no stigma upon the craver, and was by no means confined to the lower classes of society. On the other hand, refusal of the thing craved is represented as extremely dishonouring to the person refusing.'[63]

Although the Scottish Parliament passed an act against 'thiggers and sorners' (people asking for neighborly aid and free lodging) in 1414, and the even more comprehensive Statutes of Iona of 1609 attempted to eliminate such customs,[64] vestiges of the practice of *faoighe* persisted into the twentieth century. The practice, known in Lallans as 'thigging', was summarized in the late seventeenth century:

> To *thig* is to beg assistance of Friends, which is very ordinary among persons of every Quality. Men thig Horses and corn; women thig cows, sheep and goats. When a person of Quality thigs he is attended with a great many servants, whereof one is the Spokesman and intimates to the Master of the House the end of their coming. By this means they get a great deal of one kind and other.[65]

The practice is further explained in the context of a Perthshire glen in the nineteenth century:

> While kinship near or far made it the duty of the comfortably-off to help those that were badly-off, usually through no fault of their own,

> it likewise filled the strugglers with such pride of independence that, however hardly tried, none of them took [to] the road as beggars going with meal-pokes from door to door. What a lonely woman did was, at clipping time, to go around the fanks *air faoigh ollamh*, in other words, to ask for puckles of wool, which she took home and spun and so turned into money. Men who drifted into helplessness often quartered themselves for the end of their days on well-to-do relations who did not grudge them their keep.[66]

Faoighe was also commonly resorted to when a newly married couple was attempting to gather a stock of cattle and the necessary equipment to support themselves.[67] Like any social custom that relies upon honesty and integrity, however, it could be abused by those ready to take advantage of Highland generosity.

Women

Most of the discussion thus far has revolved around the men of the ruling elite. The emphasis upon the warrior-hero is illustrated by the Gaelic panegyric code, reflecting the fact that 'even more so than in Ireland, the culture of the early modern Scottish Gàidhealtachd was imbued with a strong patriarchal ideology … From a perspective within the boundaries of the culture itself, it seemed natural, axiomatic and incontrovertible.'[68] Behind this general description of gender, however, are a number of exceptions and complexities.

As in other non-industrial societies, women's primary function was in producing descendants for her husband and clan. We need not believe, however, that her role as wife and mother made her a mere reproduction machine:

> She borrowed a kind of sacredness from the tie which united her to her husband … independent of mental charms or personal attractions, was endeared to the husband by this tacit homage, and by a tie, more prevalent by far here, than in polished societies. She was the mother of his children; to her he was indebted for the link that connected him with the future descendants of his almost idolized ancestors.[69]

At an economic level, people were maintained by their parents in their youth and by their offspring in their old age. A good wife not only maintained domestic affairs properly, but raised children who would be to the profit of the entire family in coming years. Quite a number of proverbs relate to the importance of a wife in a successful household. '*Is e fortan no mì-fhortan fir bean* (A man's wife is either his fortune or his misfortune); *Is fhearr bean ghlic na crann is fearann* (A wise wife is better than a plough and land)'.

A man and his wife were a working unit which ideally should work in unison for the same purpose. '*Am fear a labhras olc mu 'mhnaoi, tha e a' cur mì-chliù air fhèin* (The man who speaks ill of his wife ruins his own reputation)'.

A woman moved into the home of her husband and as an 'outsider' who had a powerful role in the family, she could be at the centre of tension and conflict (especially if the husband's extended family was also in the home).[70] Women were liable to be excessively haughty with their female peers about their households and this rivalry was seen as a destabilizing force in society: '*Cha tèid àrdan nam ban fon ùir* (The pride of women will never be buried)'.[71]

A bride's family contributed a *tochradh* (dowry) (a word borrowed into Lallans as 'tocher') when she married. A woman was entitled to recover the wealth she contributed to the marriage in the case of divorce.[72] A woman belonging to the upper ranks of society generally came with a *tochradh* of forty to sixty cattle, although some of them were also accompanied by retainers, including fighting men.[73] Marriage was one of the ways in which clans sought to gain wealth and territory, and such wealth could be lost when a daughter left her kin-group:

> The habit of giving cows as a *tocher* to the daughters of the house [noblewomen] made them in the olden time very anxious that they would marry among their own kinsmen, or at least in their own clans, as it would be an enriching of the enemy to give their cows to them, and hence the frequency of elopements in those days. A young man sorely exercised about which was the better thing for him to marry, an old woman who had a tocher, or a young one who had none, went to his father and spoke thus –

Comhairle iarram oirbh, an ceò	I would ask you for advice, unknowing myself,
Cò i feòil is fhearr, a dhuine,	Sir, which flesh is preferable,
Seann bhò 's i làn saill,	An old cow, laden with lard,
No atharl' òg am feòil thana?	Or a young one whose flesh is thin?

And the reply was a sensible one:

Cha chuir seann bhò laogh mu chrò	An old cow will not add calves to the fold:
'S i 'n atharl' òg feòil is fhearr ...[74]	The young cow is the better flesh ...

Women, likewise, could find themselves in unsatisfactory marriages with older men on account of their wealth and no small number of songs complaining of this predicament exist.

Mur biodh crodh, cha ghabhainn thu,
Mur biodh crodh, cha b' fhiù thu,
Mur biodh crodh 's na laoigh 'nan cois
Cha laighinn air do chùlaibh.

Bheirinn comhairle chèillidh ort
Nan èisteadh tu gu ciùin rium
Nan sguireadh tu de d' bheumannan
Bho'n 's tu mo chèile-pùsta.

'San oidhche 'chaidh mo phòsadh leat
Bu deònach air a' chùis mi;
Mus tàinig ceann na madainne
Gum bu mhath leam anns an ùir thu ...[75]

If not for the cattle, I wouldn't have taken you,
You wouldn't be worthy, if not for the cattle,
If it weren't for the cattle with their calves,
I wouldn't lie down next to you.

I would give you sensible advice –
If only you would listen quietly to me,
If only you would hold your blows –
As you are my partner in marriage.

The night that I was married to you,
I was willing in the arrangement;
But before the next morning was over
I wished you were under the ground ...

Giving birth to a man's children forged a strong link to him. This, combined with the leniency about marriage and legitimacy of children born out of wedlock in Gaeldom,[76] gave many low-born women an incentive to become the mistresses of noblemen, or at least fantasize about the prospects. 'The desire to bear illegitimate children to some handsome aristocrat, or envy of women raped by a handsome aristocrat, is fairly common'[77] as a motif in women's songs. 'I would bear you five, or six, or seven sons' can be found in many women's songs, but the following example is remarkably frank in its eroticism:

Nam bu toigh leat siod, 'fhir bhàin,
Bhiodh falt mo chinn 'gad chumail blàth;
Gum biodh mo chìochan a' cumail dìon ort
Ged rachadh mo riasladh 's mo chur gu bàs.

Shaoilinn fèin nach bu pheacadh trom
Ged shiùbhlainn fraoch leat is talamh lom
Gach nì fos n-ìosal a bhiodh tu 'g iarraidh
Bu leat do mhiann dheth 's chan iarrainn bonn.[78]

If it be your pleasure, fair-haired man,
My hair could keep you warm;
My breasts could give you shelter,
Though I be harmed and put to death.

I wouldn't think it any serious sin,
If I was to travel heather and bare land with you;
I would do secretly everything you want,
Have your desire, and I ask no payment.

The nurse of a child also formed a very close bond with it and it was believed that certain traits could be transmitted through breast milk. A number of Jacobite Highlanders were taken prisoner after their defeat at Culloden, and, according to tradition, General John Campbell, having heard Cumberland insult the ability of the Highland soldiers, bet than one of the prisoners could defeat the best swordsman from the English Hanoverian ranks. If the Highlander were to win, all of the prisoners under Campbell's charge were to be freed; otherwise, they would all be killed. The Highlander who accepted the challenge was missing a hand from the battle and sorely wounded, but was able to beat the larger and healthier Englishman. Campbell congratulated him with the words (in translation), 'Go home now and thank your mother, because she gave you such good milk.'[79] Similarly, a poet says of the lord of Coll:

B' i do mhuime bhean chìche	It was your wet-nurse
Rinn do chuislean lìonadh ...[80]	Who pumped up your veins ...

Women were prominent at the far ends of life as *mnathan-glùine* (midwives) and *mnathan-tuiream*[81] (keening women). These women were important enough to have had their livelihoods secured by their communities.

> *Bha bean-ghlùin agus bean-tuiream anns a chuile baile am Barraidh. Agus bha e mar fhiachaibh air muinntir a chuile baile fiar samhraidh agus fodar geamhraidh fhaicinn aig gach tè dha'n t-seòrsa gu àilgheas a' mhaoir air faobhar a' chlaidhe. Agus chan fhaodadh na daoine dìth no deireas 'fhaicinn air tè seach tè dhiubh seo, los gum bitheadh gach tè dhiubh murrach air a dleasdanas a dhèanadh dar a thigeadh e m'a coinneamh ...*[82]
>
> Every village in Barra had a mid-wife and a keening-woman. And everyone in every village was obligated to supply each woman of this sort with summer grazing and winter fodder, to the satisfaction of the bailiff (promising on) the sword's edge. And the people would see to it that neither of these women would suffer want nor loss any more than her peers, so that each of them could carry out her responsibility when the time would come ...

Whether the result was victory or defeat, women had an important role in the aftermath of war. In the case of defeat, women had to search amongst the corpses to find their kin and lament the dead in song. Keening gave women in an otherwise male-dominated society a chance to voice their anger, criticisms, and complaints publicly with relative impunity.[83] The later prohibition of women from accompanying the corpse to the graveyard, which exists to the present day in Protestant communities, was a step taken in extinguishing this practice with its overtly pagan associations.[84]

It appears that women celebrated the return of their men in victory with choral praise. An account of the journey of Edward I of England in the Highlands in 1296 mentions that the women of Strathearn 'came out to meet the king ... and sang before him, as they used to do ...'[85]

Although they mourned their relations killed in combat, it does not appear that women questioned or rejected the warrior ethos of their society. They only wished that their male progeny and relations fight, and die, honourably. The prayer of a mother whose son is going to war illustrates this:

Tha iùbhrach 's a' chuan, a ghràidh,
Tha an tràigh làn de m' dheòir;
Tha cnoc na faire 'na ghual, a ghràidh,
Tha farum nan ràmh 's an òb:
Am fear nach till, a ghràidh,
Cha bheò, cha bheò!

Tha sàir 'nan siubhal, a ghràidh,
Mar ghàirich nan tonn;
Is balbh an tuiream, a ghràidh,
Is àrd am fonn:
'S mur till thu tuilleadh, a ghràidh,
Is geal bàs nan sonn.

Cha bhi màthair mo mhic 's an streup
Ach bidh Màthair Mhic Dhè 's an streup;
O a Mhàthair nan gràs,
Fhuair do Mhac-sa tàir agus teum:
Na leig air macan mo ghràidh
Lapan am blàr nam beum …

Dh'fhalbh thu, a mhacain mo ghràidh,
Tha do dhàn an sgàil an sgleò;
Tha reul na h-oidhche fo smàl, a ghràidh,
Tha Caoineag nan càrn fo bhròn;
Mas bàs duit, a leanaibh mo ghràidh,
Biodh do chadal air làimh na h-Òigh.[86]

The galley is in the sea, my beloved,
My tears fill the shore;
The beacon-hill is ablaze, my beloved,
The inlet is full of the sound of oars;
He who will not return, my beloved,
Will not be alive!

The heroes are under way, my beloved,
Like the roaring of the waves;
The do not grieve, my beloved,
Their strain of song is loud;
And if you do not return, my beloved,
The death of heroes is resplendent.

The mother of my son will not be in the strife,
But the Mother of the Son of God will be;
O Mother of grace,
Your own son was mocked and spited;
Do not let my beloved son
Be a weakling in the fierce battle …

You have departed, my beloved son,
Your destiny is unknown;
The night-star is gloomy,
And the keening-woman of the cairns is sad;
If you die, my beloved child,
May your sleep be in the palm of the Virgin.

Formal education was limited to the clan elite, and this sometimes included females as well as males. Chief of the MacDonalds of Sleat Domhnall Gorm Òg had his two daughters tutored by the *ollamh* Cathal Mac Mhuirich, probably in order to avoid their being educated in the Lowlands by the Protestant establishment.[87] Poems in the Classical style attributed to three women have survived, one the widow of Clan Nèill of Gigha, another may be a daughter of Campbell of Argyll, and the third of the house of Stewart.[88] Composing Classical poetry, as these women did, required significant education.

The working of cloth was a specifically-feminine activity, and the environment in which this was done may have been one of several which was exclusive of males from very early times.[89] Songs sung by women in this setting, and composed by them for these occasions, allow us to see Gaelic society from their own perspective.[90]

While most of the *òrain-luaidh* (waulking songs) composed by women deal with their relationships with their families and with romantic interests, some of them also reveal political concerns. Examples can be cited which argue for backing one side of a dispute against another (especially against the interference of the central government). These 'demonstrate that some women, at that particular time and in these particular areas, were involved at least to some extent in public debates and in shaping political opinions among their people.'[91] Although the Jacobite waulking songs dealing with the '45 Rising were composed by Alasdair mac Mhaighstir Alasdair, he must have thought this female-medium of communication one which would have an influence on men of standing via the women who transmitted his highly politicized songs.

Women rarely took part in warfare directly but they frequently shamed men into action. When Charles Stewart of Ardsheil showed reluctance to lead his clan for the Prince in the '45 Rising, his wife rebuked him sharply. 'If you, Charles, are not willing to become Commander of the men of Appin, stay at home and take care of the house, and I will go myself and become their Commander.'[92] She is, in other words, implying that he is more suited to women's work than she is. Upon hearing her taunt he agreed to lead them.

Women played no small part in the religious conflicts of the sixteenth and seventeenth centuries. Some noblewomen were responsible for maintaining Catholicism in their clan territories, despite the Protestant regimes of their chieftain-husbands. Women of all ranks were the primary support of the poorly financed Counter-Reformation of the seventeenth century, which fought a 'guerrilla war' against the officially-sponsored Protestant movement. On the other hand, Protestant women could be just as pivotal in Catholic areas, as can be seen in the history of the church in MacKay territory.[93]

Women of the upper ranks of society could also be at the centre of the political events of their day, as is well exemplified by Lady Agnes Campbell and her daughter Fionuala MacDonald. 'The control these women could exert over their military dowries, together with their superior standard of education, allowed them to play a crucial rôle as brokers in Ulster politics during the late sixteenth century'.[94] Some women used their positions of influence and power to further the interests of their husbands or families. Seònaid Mackenzie advanced the ambitions of the Mackenzies, was involved in the commercialization of the MacDonald of Sleat estates (which she married into), and organized clan defenses against possible Campbell attack during her husband's absence.[95]

Women were especially responsible for the domestic affairs in the old Gàidhealtachd: cooking, cloth production, maintenance of clothing, rearing children, and so on. Some menial tasks were classed unworthy of men, such as dealing with goats, sheep, poultry, and cattle. Although women carried more than their fair share of the labour and toil of Gaeldom, their fortunes declined in the aftermath of Culloden. As men were drawn away from home fighting in foreign wars in the British army, women had to pick up the heavier labour previously done by men. Involvement in industries such as herring-fishing and Lowland harvesting pulled many women away from their families when they were needed and disrupted the familiar patterns of life.[96]

Territory, ownership and power

Power in traditional Gaelic society came from the bottom up: a leader needed followers, who needed land and resources. This structure is described in the Old Irish adage: '*Glenad cách a choimdid/ comad cách a chrích/ barr cáich a choimdiu/ bun cáich a chrích* (Let each man cleave to his lord; let each man protect his territory. The top of each man is his lord; the root of each man is his territory).'[97] This same basic pattern determined power and wealth in the Highlands:

> The glory of the chief was the glory of all his kindred and name: and the numbers and fidelity of his vassals and tenants, again, were what constituted the power and consequence of the chief. The produce of land, corn, cattle, fish, and game, were spent on the estate, but chiefly at the mansion-houses of the great, in generous hospitality. And in those time, the Highlanders were better fed, and, in general, finer men than they are at present. For now the cattle, the salmon, and the very game, are either carried or driven out of the country: nor has the faint dawn of commerce been yet able to supply that abundance which preceded it ... When the great landholders lived among the husbandmen, who were for the most part allied to them by blood, or at least the sameness of name, the people loved their chiefs: and each laird and lord was accounted rich or poor according to the numbers of tenants that possessed their lands.[98]

A clan's wealth ultimately depended upon the amount of productive territory under their control. Land was necessary for growing crops and grazing livestock, which in turn fed the men who defended these lands and sought to expand their holdings. People could occupy new lands peaceably by marriage, or forcibly by conquest. 'Indeed, politics, economy, marriage, kinship, possession of land and of property, were all woven together into an inextricable web in Highland society, to produce a culture which was both dynamic and self-perpetuating.'[99]

The right to land won by conquest occurs in all warrior-societies and is usually called *còir claidheimh* (sword-right) in Gaelic. It is acknowledged in the early Irish law tracts as a legitimate means of acquiring land[100] and such on-going antagonism was part of the normal dynamics of heroic societies. A poem celebrating the feats of Alasdair mac Colla boasts:

dúthchas do shíol Airt an fhoghuil
cairt an chloidhimh.

Cairt an cloidhimh dhóibh as dúthchas
do droing dhána;
minic chuirid síos gan séla
cíos is cána.[101]

raiding is the birth-right of Art's progeny,
the right of the sword.

The right of the sword is the heritage
Of that bold people;
Frequently do they impose, without official sanction,
tax and tribute.

A powerful chieftain created a network of kinsmen and allies to hold down his territory, so that the social structure of a clan became superimposed upon the landscape. Privileged members of the clan tended to be given the role of *fear-baile*, a 'tacksman', who was an administrator of one or more townships given such duties as collecting rents, organizing military operations, and other social functions.[102]

When a chieftain quickly extended his power into new territory, he needed ways of extending the social structure to fill this space, and bonds of friendship and manrent could be employed in this manner. Thus, the territory of a clan was not composed exclusively of members of one kin-group.

Figure 4.1 provides a hypothetical example of a clan's placement within its territory (the area within the oval). All members of this particular clan are darkened. The clan chief forms a bond of manrent with a nobleman who becomes a new tacksman in the chief's new territory. He brings in two other

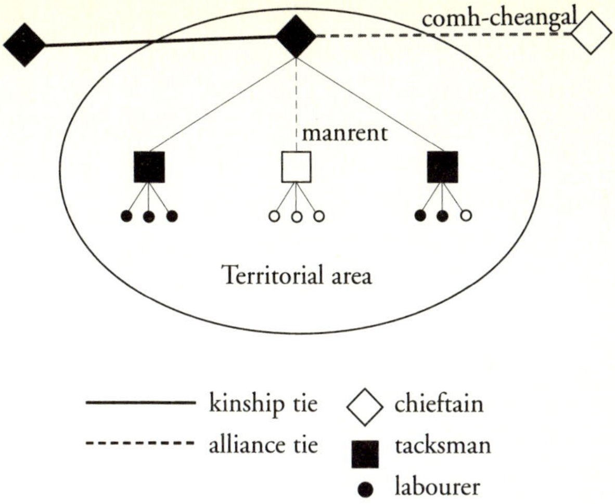

Figure 4.1 – Social structure and territorial arrangements
(solid elements indicate blood-relations)

tacksmen-kinsmen (black squares), who bring their dependents with them to work the land. Another of the chief's family (black diamond), however, stays outside of the clan territory, and may become a tacksman for another chieftain. Finally, the safety of the clan may depend upon an alliance of friendship with a neighbouring clan (white diamond).

Although sword-right encouraged conflict between clans, life within any particular community was peaceful and secure: 'a predatory expedition was the general declaration of enmity [by clearing] the pastures of the enemy … [but] in the interior of their own society, all property was safe'.[103]

Once people had occupied a particular territory for three generations, they had, by the conventions of Gaelic society, a right to continue holding that land. This right is one of the meanings of the Gaelic word *dùthchas*: '…the Notion they entertain, [is] that they have a kind of hereditary Right to their Farms; and that none of them are to be dispossessed, unless for some great Transgression against their Chief, in which Case every Individual would consent to their Expulsion.'[104] This practice was widespread throughout Scotland and associated with the words 'kindly' and 'kindness' in Lallans, affirming a common association with the kin-group.[105]

The officials writing the report of the Napier Commission in 1884, investigating the land-rights of Highlanders, noted that traditional Gaelic practices did not accord with written law.

> The opinion was often expressed before us that the small tenantry of the Highlands have an inherited inalienable title to security of tenure in their possessions while rent and service are duly rendered – an impression indigenous to the country though it has never been sanctioned by legal recognition, and has long been repudiated by the action of the proprietors.

An integrated sense of self

An individual in Gaelic society was nestled within a much larger context. 'In primitive cultures, before individuated minds and individual identities had been achieved, it was the persona of the tribe that necessarily established and maintained the identity of its members.'[106] Likewise,

> No highlander ever once thought of himself as an individual. Amongst these people, even the meanest mind was in a manner enlarged by association, by anticipation, and by retrospect. In the most minute, as well as most serious concerns, he felt himself one of the many connected together by ties of the most lasting and endearing. He considered himself merely with reference to those who had gone before, and those who were to come after him; to these immortals who lived in deathless song and heroic narrative; and to these distinguished beings who were to be born heirs of their fame, and to whom their honours, and, perhaps, their virtues, were to be transmitted. This might be supposed to cherish pride; but, besides this, it had a high moral tendency.[107]

There are at least three different naming schemes for naming an individual in Gaelic society, operating in different contexts.[108] One is the *sloinneadh*, an enumeration of (normally male) ancestors. A woman might be called, '*Màiri nighean Iain 'ic Dhomhnaill 'ic Iain* … (Mary daughter of Iain son of Donald son of Iain …)'. A *sloinneadh* consists of at least seven generations, and often many more. The primacy of this naming scheme again emphasizes the definition of an individual in terms of his ancestors. A *sloinneadh* is, however, most useful if one knows the individuals named in the context of the community.

The use of surnames inherited from one's clan became common at some point in the Highlands, although it is not yet clear how widespread this practice was at various times and places.[109] It does appear to have been more common on legal documents written by government officials than in actual Highland communities, although it has certainly become commonplace in modern times and is useful for reference by those from outside a community.

Finally, people are frequently given nicknames in their youth which stick to them throughout their lives. Such names might refer to an embarrassing anecdote, a distinguishing characteristic, or a memorable event. A nickname (*frith-ainm*, *far-ainm*) is most functional within a community, but sometimes travels with the individual.

Modernist culture can be characterized as continually segregating life into specialized and mutually exclusive categories: work vs. leisure; at home vs. on-holiday; secular vs. sacred; young vs. aged; sedentary work vs. vigorous exercise; and so on. This is not only part of our scientific heritage of reductionism, but is an inevitable result of the large-scale mechanisms that allow modern techno-consumer society to operate.

Traditional Gaelic society, on the other hand, can be described generally as integrated and fluid in its structure and operation. Although people had bursts of intense work, such as at harvest time, they had ample opportunity for leisure and numerous outlets for their creative energies. Their work was intermingled not only with song and music of their own making, but with the recognition of the ever-present sacred around them.

Not only did all of the ranks of society interact with each other, but people of all ages interacted with each other. As homesteads and villages consisted of all of the generations of families, the youngest generations were in constant contact with the oldest. The youngest were able to learn from them and to revere them for their wisdom, and to be constantly reminded of the realities of the cycles of life.

People knew not just a specialized trade, but had the skills necessary to build and repair their homes, to make and mend their clothing, to produce their own food, to read the weather conditions, and so on. Besides these merely functional skills, they were also well versed in the story and song of their ancestors, and frequently played at least one musical instrument.[110]

The structure dismantled

While the organization of Gaelic society might be seen by people from another culture as being chaotic, lawless, or anarchic, it projected a sense of order and stability for those inside of it. In the prophecies of most cultures about the end of the world, it is not just the physical universe which is destroyed, but the moral and social order which is indivisible from it. One of the eschatological tracts in early Irish tradition foresees that the apocalypse will come at a time 'without law, without precedent, without composition derived from truth of nature or of scripture or of precedent, for these rules were established from the beginning of the world to the end, against mutual dispute.'[111]

A cash economy breaks down the mutual inter-dependencies of kin-groups and makes the individual the primary unit of social organization.[112] This process began in the sixteenth century when central government attempted to make chieftains carefully accountable for clan land holdings, rents, and 'criminal' behavior. As clan elite were assimilated into the English-speaking world, they had a new need to generate income. The export of cattle southwards, particularly by the tacksmen, was the primary means of earning this income and the introduction of new wealth had an inevitable transforming impact upon the social structure.[113]

The unraveling of this social organization has worked its way to the heart of the Gaelic community in the latter half of the twentieth century. The cultural gap between generations is such that older Gaels can be heard to say that 'People no longer know who they are.'

While clan associations continue to operate for those long separated from their paternal leaders, it is ironic that many of those clan chiefs who still own lands in the Highlands tend to work against the interests of those few real communities which yet struggle to survive on former clan lands. The Lewis poet Iain Crichton Smith reflects on the losses borne by the Gaels of the islands in the wake of the decay of their communities:

> It is not right that a whole culture should have been treated in this way, that like the Red Indians and the Aborigines so many of our people should have had to leave their homes to inherit the worst aspects of a so-called superior civilisation … It is against such a failure that one can set the idea of community, the idea of a culture, and who would care to say that the islanders have turned their backs on a world that is viable and worth preserving?[114]

CHAPTER 5

The operation of society

Honour and warfare

Undoubtedly one of the most important cultural foci of Gaeldom was warfare. This is a genuine inheritance of the warrior-ethos of the ancient Celtic society which appears in early Irish and Welsh literature. The emphasis of warfare in earlier times was not to create larger political units, such as in the building of modern empires, but to assert status and win honour.[1] There was nothing to be gained by battling with an enemy of low status, or by conquering all of one's enemies, who are the means of maintaining one's fame. 'According to the heroic ideal, personal encounter, in which strength and skill counted, is the centre-piece of battle.'[2]

The destabilization of the Gaelic world in the wake of the break-up of the lordship of the Isles brought about a period known as *Linn nan Creach* (the Era of Plunder). This powerful Gaelic regime, which for a time was able to hold latent rivalries in check, gave way to a number of smaller, mutually antagonistic chiefdoms, each warring with each other for territory and resources. A chieftain needed to lead his clan to increase their wealth and prestige, and to decrease that of their enemies.

The emphasis in the heroic ideal is upon personal prowess, so not every method of warfare was equally laudable. Domhnall Cam mac Dhùghaill, a warrior of the MacAulays of Lewis, remarked about the year 1600 when heard about the invention of gunpowder, '*Tha latha a' ghaisgich seachad: tha an duine lag a-nis cho math ris an duine làidir* (The warrior's day is over: the weak man is now as good as the strong man)'.[3]

Although the Gaels did of necessity adopt firearms,[4] one can find a disdain for such non-heroic weapons into the eighteenth century, especially employed by the Lowlanders and English:[5]

'S iomadh laoch bu gharg an carraid
Nach iarradh gunna:
Lann chlaiseach dhubhghorm 'ga tarruing,
Toirt buaidh urram.[6]

There is many a warrior, fierce in conflict,
Who would not want a gun:
A shiny, grooved blade being drawn
Achieving victory.

The destiny for the accomplished warrior was everlasting fame in song and story. 'Heroic death with memorable words is the ideal.'[7] '*Is buaine bladh na saoghal* (Fame is more lasting than life).' His worst fear was to be the subject of shame or ridicule. '*Is beò duine an dèidh a shàrachaidh, ach cha bheò e an dèidh a nàrachaidh* (A person may live after his harassment, but he will not survive his disgrace).'

John of Fordun wrote in the fourteenth century, 'The Scots are a light-minded nation, fierce in spirit, savage towards their foes, who would almost as soon die as be enslaved, and account it sloth to die in bed, deeming it glorious and manly to slay, or be slain by, the foe in the field.' John Leslie, a one-time bishop of Ross, wrote in 1578 that the most noble warrior in the battle-company led a charge and those in his command sought to emulate his example and to defend him from harm.

When not engaged in warfare, the warrior loved to roam the hills and glens pursuing wildlife. A legendary king of Scotland, Dornadilla, was said to have kept himself suitably active:

> He spent a great part of his time in hunting, for he considered that exercise suitable to a time of peace, as healthful, and calculated to strengthen the body for military exercises, besides rendering the mind capable of enjoying the purest pleasures, and protecting it against the pernicious vices, which are produced by indolence.[8]

Every male, then, aspired not to be the stooping farmer, but the erect and mobile warrior.

> Their popular poetry was surely well suited to a country where little more than threescore years ago every person wished to be thought a soldier – husbandry, and even pasturage, being followed no further

> than necessity required. And till very lately, sheep and goats were regarded as the property of wives, being beneath the attention of their husbands; and the lowest follower would have thought himself dishonoured by entering a byre or assisting at a sheep-shearing.[9]

The mother of Iain Ruadh Mac Dhùghaill of Lewis praised him:

Cas a shiubhal nam fuar-bheann
Ghabh thu roghainn bha uasal:
'S tu gun treabhadh no buailtean air dòigh.[10]

A foot for travelling the cold mountains
Your chosen path was noble:
Never did you plough or tend cattle.

The most common form of aggression was *togail creiche* (raiding), usually for cattle. This has already been shown to be an integral part of the inauguration of new chieftains, as a demonstration of his ability to lead war-bands. 'This Custom being reciprocally us'd among them, was not reputed Robbery; for the Damage which one Tribe sustain'd by this Essay of the Chieftain of another, was repair'd when their Chieftain came in his turn to make his Specimen.'[11]

It is important to note that such heroic activities were a natural part of the social order of Gaeldom, and did not figure in Gaelic consciousness as 'lawlessness'. The Clan Donald is praised by a Classical poet as:

Clann gan uabhar gan éagcáir	A people without arrogance or injustice,
Nár ghabh acht éadail chogaidh[12]	Who seized only the spoils of war

Neighbouring Lowlanders, seen as usurpers of the rights of Gaels upon the Scottish soil, were thought of as legitimate targets for raiding:

Cuime am biomaid gun eudail	Why should we be without cattle
Agus sprèidh aig na Gallaibh?	When the Lowlanders have them?
Gheibh sinn crodh as a' Mhaorainn	We'll take cattle from the Mearns
Agus caoirich a Gallaibh.[13]	And sheep from Lowlanders.

The Lowlanders saw such activities as evidence of the lack of law and civility in the Highlands. A Gael was not to fight without aim or provoke senseless violence, however. '*Na sir is na seachain an cath* (Do not seek out or avoid warfare)'. A proverbial sword inscription read '*Na tarraing mi gun adhbhar, is na pill mi gun chliù* (Do not draw me without a reason, and do not return me without honour).'

The king (or chieftain) is in fact represented as peace-maker as well as war-leader. In a poem advocating the leadership of Campbell of Argyll over all of the Gaels, his rule is said to unite the clans and bring an end to warfare:

Ar ngabhâil ceannais gach cinnidh
Ceangluidh síothchain 'na síth bhuain;
Congbhuidh ó shin reacht is riaghuil,
Do bhir ceart gan iarraidh uaidh.

Ceangluidh sé gan cheilg da chéile
Curadh-uaisle Innsi Gall[14]

Since taking the leadership of all the clans
He forges a lasting peace;
Since then he keeps law and order
He maintains justice without being asked.

He will bind together, without guile,
The noble warriors of the Hebrides

One poet asked God to intervene in the troubled political affairs which led to the battle of Killiecrankie of 1689, remarking that kings should maintain peace and not provoke conflict:

Dhè 'dh'òrdaich na rìghrean	O God, who commanded the kings
'Chumail sìth ris gach duine:	To keep peace between people:
Bho is Tu-san as brìoghmhoir'	Since you are the most wondrous
Na gach tì dhiubh siud uile	Of all of those beings,
Casg fèin le d' mhìorbhail	With your wonders, put a lasting end
An t-srìth-s' gu h-ullamh;	To this strife;
Ceartaich robairean Sheumais	Correct James' plunderers
Bàth reubaltan Uilleim[15]	And the foolishness of William's rebels

It may seem paradoxical that another cultural focus of Gaeldom was law, for a formally and extensively trained body of lawyers began writing it down in the seventh century. This law-system, often referred to in English as 'brehon law' (derived from the early Gaelic word for 'judge' *brithem*), was in practice to some extent in Scotland and was partially absorbed into Scots law.[16]

Men given the office of judge helped to maintain the peace of the lordship of the Isles and to administer justice. 'There was a judge in every Isle for the discussion of all controversies who had lands from MacDonald for their trouble, and likewise the eleventh part of every action decided.'[17] Cathal Mac Mhuirich compared Iain Mòr Mac Leòid to the legendary early Irish king Cormac mac Airt, saying:

Ní bhíodh cúis 'na cúis fhrithir	No cause for anxiety arose
Ná diongnadh í d'fhóirithin	But he could address it,
Le breith gceirt sheinrechta a shen	By just pronouncement of ancestral law
Do sheirc eighrechta d' innremh.	From love of guiding his heritage.
Fá flaith derbhtha an dlighidh ríogh	He was a prince who demonstrated royal
Fá breithemh mhúchaidh míghníomh;	justice, a judge who arrest misdeeds;
Fer tighe do bhí ag Banbha	Master of Ireland's house,
Rí agus file foghlamtha.[18]	A king and a learned poet.

Cooperation and obligation

The highest moral imperative in Gaelic society was hospitality to all. This virtue was practiced despite inter-clan hostilities – '*Bheirinn cuid-oidhche dha ged a bhiodh ceann fir fo 'achlais* (I would give him food and lodging for the night even if he had a man's head under his arm)' – and often to the detriment of the hosts themselves. It is this 'sacred obligation' which has instilled the sense of generosity in the Gaelic peoples to this day. The Revd Donald MacQueen contributed the following notes to Thomas Pennant's 1772 book about his Highland journey:

> Of all virtues their hospitality was the most extensive; every door and every heart was open to the stranger and to the fugitive; to these they were particularly humane and generous, vied with one another who would use them best, and looked on the person who sought their protection as a sacred depositum, which on no consideration they were to give up … Hospitality was founded on immemorial custom, before the thoughts of men were contracted by weights and measures, and

> reckoned so far a sacred obligation as to think themselves bound to entertain the man …

It was expected that one's costs would eventually be recovered since generosity was reciprocal. '*Gus an tràighear a' mhuir le cliabh, cha bhi fear fial falamh* (Until the ocean is emptied with a basket, the generous man will never be empty-handed).'

All affairs in early Gaelic society were bound by contracts between parties drawn up by lawyers. Similarly, though not so formally, a Gaelic proverb states, '*Gach cùis gu cùmhnant* (Let every business be done by agreement).'[19] Such agreements were usually verbal, but this made them no less binding in force:

> The provisions upon both sides were easily remembered, and, in case of any dispute, could be adjusted by the witnesses that had been present. Nor did this often happen. A people who transact their business verbally are commonly more tenacious of their word than those among whom writ or oath is requisite. In such a case breach of promise would subject the party that failed to infamy and shame.[20]

People relied upon each other to an enormous extent, for there were tasks which required the co-operation and co-ordination of everyone in the community. Anne Grant of Laggan remarked of life in the late eighteenth-century Highlands:

> All of the intercourse of life was carried on by a kind of tacit agreement and interchange of good offices that would appear extravagant anywhere else. Yet here were so necessary that it was almost considered a crime to withhold them.

Three men were required to operate the old Highland plough, where the soil permitted such a luxury (the primitive spades the *cas-chrom* and the *cas-dhìreach* were used on more difficult soil but covered far less territory).[21] Reaping was done in large groups with song to keep sickles synchronized.

> The actual cultivation of the land was done by groups, either of joint tenants holding directly of the chief or of sub-tenants holding of his tacksmen. The custom of joint cultivation, of course, is not a pecu-

liarly Gaelic feature and was common to most northern countries, but the system fitted in well with the social organization of the clan.[22]

Dependents of a chieftain were obliged to pay to him rent and to render services to him. These customs can be seen in early Gaelic law and the grounds for them in traditional cosmology recall the sacred attributes of the king and his link with the goddess of the land:

> The ideological basis of the levying of tribute in the form of livestock and agricultural produce, therefore, appears to have been that kings ensured – indeed gifted – fertility, and the ruled were merely returning the products of that fertility, as food-rent, winter hospitality, and other services, to their rightful owners.[23]

Documents composed under Scottish feudalism reflect the older substratum of Celtic law in their references to 'cain and conveth, *fecht* and *slùagad*'.[24] The earliest surviving use of these terms in a Scottish context refers to the Convention of Druim Cett in 575, which met to resolve conflicts of interest between the Irish and Scottish branches of the Dál Riada.[25]

The Gaelic term *càin* (borrowed into Lallans variously as 'cain', 'cane', or 'kain') refers to the tribute given to an overlord, usually paid in food such as butter or poultry.[26] The term *coinnmed* referred to the obligation to provide the lord's military retinue with a night's food and lodging once a year, or to render to him the equivalent value.

That these Gaelic legal practices once ran throughout the Scottish realm is verified by the payments demanded by the bishops of St Andrews as far south as the Tweed.[27] The term *cuid-oidhche* ('a night's due', written in various forms such as 'Cuddiche') may have been a development of the practice of *coinnmed*, and Sleat is described in the sixteenth century as paying tribute in this manner. 'It pays the old duties – that is, of victual butter, cheese, wine, ale, and aquavitæ [whiskey], as much as their master may be able to spend any night on each merkland, although he had a company of 600 men.'[28] Lords might also require their dependents to contribute to the labour on their estates.

Men were required to join the military hosts of their lords when called upon. This service, called *slógad* or *slúagad* in early forms of Gaelic, can be found in many Latin documents from the twelfth century onwards and was easily incorporated into the feudal order. King Alexander II declared an ordinance in 1220 imposing heavy penalties upon those who disregarded this service, and further Acts in 1318, 1456, and 1481 sought to secure 'fencible men' for the Defense of the Realm.[29] Hosts continued to be raised at a moment's notice in the Highlands by passing around the *crann-tàra* (gathering-beam). It was said to have traversed Breadalbane, a distance of some 30 miles, in three hours when raising men for the 1745 Rising.

These goods and services are commonly referred to in the general sense as *cìsean* (taxes or tribute), and the people subservient to an overlord (via a number of social mechanisms) were said to be '*fo chìsean aige* (in tribute to him)'.

During the heady victories of Alasdair mac Colla, a Clan Donald poet encourages the clan to reclaim its former glory:

Cíos is cána ar úrleith Alban	Tribute and taxes over the greater part of
aimsir oile	Scotland once again,
Biaidh sin ag an droing mur dhlighe	Those people shall have as their right,
nó an roinn roimhe.[30]	Or else the portion they had before.

The just paying of tribute to an acknowledged overlord is contrasted in the nineteenth century with the unjust levying of taxes by a Campbell landlord, who was said by the poet to have usurped the previous, rightful rulers of Tiree:

Ged tha an t-eilean cliùiteach seo	Although this famous island
Do'n Diùc 'toirt chìsean,	Pays taxes to the Duke,
Cha b' ann le ceart no cruaidh lannan	It was not with justice, or by hard blades,
A fhuaireadh e le shinnsre.[31]	That his ancestors acquired it.

In times of peace, communities came together to enjoy each other's company.

> It was a custom at one time among the Highlanders to meet by arrangement on the first Monday of each quarter of the year – *a' cheud Di-Luan de'n ràithe* – to accept of hospitality and wish each other health and happiness during that coming period of time ...[32]

Such occasions would have also facilitated barter and trade, and the search for potential marriage partners. There seems to have been more conscious attempts to cultivate clan unity and the sense of a common purpose and identity, however, as well as to settle the business of the people. The gnomic text attributed to the early Irish king Cormac mac Airt begins a list of things which benefit a kin-group with 'meeting of nobles, frequent assemblies'.[33]

> But fond as the Highlanders were of the chase, and useful as it was to their subsistence, they did not pursue it to the neglect of more important avocations. 'Though hunting', says their proverb, 'be a good help, yet the chase is but a poor livelihood.' The great hunting matches were the means of preserving a social intercourse between tribes who lived far distant from each other. It was a means also of bringing the chiefs and principal men of the country together, and enabled them to adjust differences, settle future proceedings, &c.[34]

The Gaelic element *comhdhail*, which appears in Lowland place-names in such forms as 'cuthill', indicates places where assemblies met, particularly for legal and political purposes.[35] Particularly jovial and high-spirited were the celebrations of war-victories and hunting parties.

> Among the Scots Highlanders, the chief gave a great entertainment after any successful expedition, to which all the country round was invited. On an occasion like this, the whole deer and beeves were roasted, and laid on boards or hurdles of rods placed on the rough trunks of trees, so arranged as to form an extended table, and the *uisge-beatha* went round in plenteous libations. This was called the *slige-creachain*, from being drunk out of a shell. The pipers played during the feast, after which the women danced, and, when they retired, the harpers were introduced.[36]

Other large-scale celebrations were held at seasonal festivals. The festival of *Samhainn*, corresponding to the modern Halloween, marked the end of the old year and was the time when accounts were settled between partners in contracts. The winter tribute due to lords was expected at this time, and much of it was consumed in large feasts which helped to display and assert the social rank of all involved.[37]

Figure 5.1 is a model for the economic operation of a clan. Within the clan itself, the *ceann-cinnidh* (chieftain) distributes food from his stores to the various members of the clan according to their status and needs, bestows gifts and rewards upon particular individuals, and provides a sense of pride and esteem to the clan as whole through his benevolence and ritual displays.

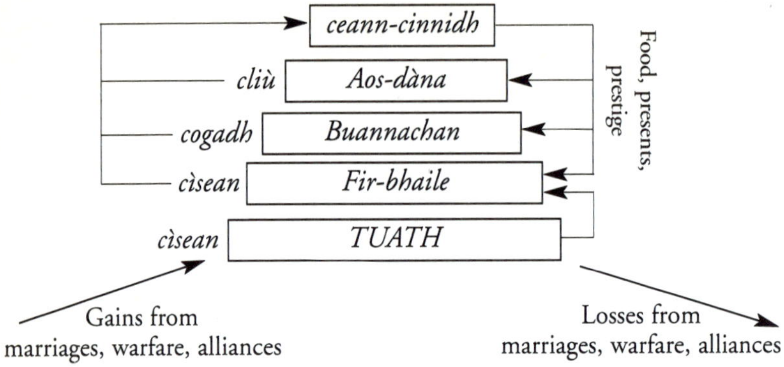

Figure 5.1: Theoretical model of clan operation

The *aos-dàna* (artisans in general, but particularly poets) created items (such as praise poems) which enhance the prestige and reputation of the *ceann-cinnidh* in particular and the clan as a whole. The *buannachan* (fighting-men) engaged in *cogadh* (warfare) in order to defend the clan against losses and to win spoils of war for the clan. The *fir-bhaile* (tacksmen), as local administrators, gathered the *cìsean* (rents and taxes) from the *tuath* (common folk and labourers), took a portion of that and passed the rest on to the *ceann-cinnidh.*

The clan as a whole obtained wealth and territory externally because of marriages into the clan, gains from warfare, and tributes from alliances with other clan groups. It was possible, however, for the clan to suffer losses from the same processes.

Values and morality

The Gaelic communities were rural and small in scale by modern standards, and highly familiar in character. 'Every man's personal character was known, and a brave, a sagacious, and a faithful commoner was sure of the esteem and confidence of his superiors.'[38]

Lying, stealing, murder, and other criminal behaviour within the clan would lead to swift punishment or banishment, and it was believed that the perpetrator of ill deeds would soon be found out. '*Cha bhi suaimhneas aig eucoir no seasamh aig droch-bheairt* (Wrong will not rest, nor will ill-deed stand); *Cha mhair a' bhreug ach seal* (A lie will not last for long).' It was expected that life within one's kin-group was safe, and that one's neighbours were trustworthy. Door-locks were considered a sign of evil-times: '*Cho mosach ris na glasan* (As contemptible as door-locks)'.

The Gaelic word *nàire* is usually translated into English as 'shame' or 'modesty', although it has a wider semantic range than this in Gaelic, referring to the sense of what is right, proper and honourable. It is a central concept in the operation of Gaelic society. '*Am fear a chaill a nàire is a mhodh, chaill e na bh' aige* (The person who lost his propriety and his manners lost all he had).'[39]

Status and honour are separate 'dimensions' in the assessment of a person's character in Gaelic society: different ranks had different codes of conduct, and a person could not elevate his rank by honour alone. Honour and shame could have a direct effect on a person's status, however, in that shaming someone, especially publicly, could deflate their standing.[40]

It was thus necessary to continually defend one's honour against insult and attack, and to constantly affirm one's status by public ritual of many sorts. In early Gaelic law, if a satire was made against a king, he was obliged to have the satire publicly revoked, or else he forfeited his honour-price.[41]

The care taken to seat people at feasts according to their rank was discussed in the previous chapter, and such occasions could lead to outbursts of aggression in the assertion of status and honour. The mere holding of such a public event – if it were lavish enough – was a statement in favour of the honour and status of the host, demonstrating that he was effective in defending his people's wealth, winning new wealth, and distributing it to his people.

The role of the poet in this scheme of things, then, should be clear. A poet can advance the honour of his patron like a modern public relations agent, reassuring the audience that the nobleman is fulfilling his responsibilities according to the prevailing social norms. The act of reciting a poem is a public display of status and honour.[42]

Poets constantly emphasize the generosity of their patrons. A chieftain who hoarded the wealth of his people would be reproached as being greedy and selfish. Often is a ruler praised with lines such as '*làmh a liubhairt an airgid 's an òir* (a hand for bestowing silver and gold).'[43]

D' ionnmhas nacha n-iarran féin	He seeks from wealth only
acht díon uaisle ar oilbhéim	To protect nobility from disgrace:
beg maoineadh a taisgidh táir	It is no gain for shameful hoarding
d' fhaicsin aoidheadh gan édáil.[44]	To see guests who lack treasure.

It is in this context that we can better understand the role of alcohol in Gaelic society as a symbol of the generosity of chieftains to their dependents. The distribution of wealth and alcohol in the royal hall often occur together in poetry:

Bhiodh do ghillean mu seach	Your servants, in turn,
A' lìonadh dibhe b' fhearr blas:	Would be pouring the best tasting liquor:
Fìon Spàinteach dearg aca 's beòir.	They had red Spanish wine, and beer.
Uisge-beatha nam pìos,	Whiskey in silver cups,
Rachadh an t-airgead 'ga dhìol	Paid for with silver,
Gheibhte 'n glain' e mar ghrìogan òir.[45]	In the glass they glistened like golden beads.

Drink was also a public display demonstrating the generosity of a patron to his subjects, the communion of the warrior society. As in many other nations, alcohol was drunk as a toast to others, living and dead, and the word uttered at such occasions is *slàinte* (health). Terms like *misgear* (drunkard) and *misgeach* (drunken), on the other hand, often imply dispraise in Gaelic poetry.[46] Although the widow of William Chisholm praises him for his ability to outdrink his peers, buying all of the rounds, she qualifies this by adding, '*bhith air mhisg cha b'e b' fhiù leat* (you did not esteem drunkenness)'.[47]

> Drink was tolerated, as increasing strength of mind, eloquence and gaiety; and its excesses were tolerated, in consideration of those happy results: but if a man drank till he became feeble and stupid, he was considered as exposing the weakness of his mind and body. A man was proud of drinking a great deal, without stuttering or sickening; but beyond that point all was contempt and disgrace.[48]

Drink was also a part of rituals. The ale of sovereignty in the inaugural ritual of kings and chieftains celebrated his marriage to the land goddess. The chief of the MacLeods drank a full bull's horn of wine as part of his ceremony of investiture.[49] The consumption of alcohol appears to have a connection with the commemoration of ancestors in some poetry. In any case, drink, though not excessive drink, was seen as a natural part of the celebration of life.

'N àm bhith triall gu d' fhàrdaich	When going to your residence
Gum b' e d' àbhaist mar bu dual	It was the custom that you inherited

Bhith tarrainn ort am bràithreachas	To be drawing together in brotherhood
Cur slàintichean mun cuairt	Passing around the toasts
Searragan is tunnachan	Flasks and casks
Gun chunnart air an luach	Their costs were of no concern
Sìor-òl nan corn sinnsearach	Constant drinking from ancestral horns
A dhìobhradh iad gu suain.[50]	That they would abandon for slumber.

It was vital to instill this honour code in children while they were young so that they would not bring shame upon themselves and their kin. '*B' fhearr a bhith gun bhreith na bhith gun teagasg* (It would be better to have never been born than to be untaught).' Another proverb, '*Ciall bà buachaille* (The sense of a cow is (determined by) the herdsman)', was said of children who behaved poorly because of inadequate supervision.[51]

It was expected that children needed to be disciplined. A song to Martainn a' Bhealaich by his wife advises him how to choose a nurse for their son:

Thoir dhachaidh leat tè shocair chiùin	Bring home a mild and gentle woman
A dh'ionnsaicheas mo mhac-sa dhuit.	Who will instruct my son for you.
Is ma bhuaileas i le gràdh e	And if she strikes him with love
Cuir gu blàth fo d' achlais i.	Put her warmly under your arm.
Ach ma bhuaileas i le fuath e	But if she strikes him with anger
Cuir gu luath dha'n chlachan i.	Send her quickly away to the village.

Such discipline not only led to mastery of one's self, but success in life: '*Am fear a thug buaidh air fhèin, thug e buaidh air nàmhaid* (The man who has conquered himself has conquered his enemy).'

Values and proper conduct were also constantly reinforced by the constant repetition of traditional songs and tales. The Fianna, in particular, were the celebrities and role models of Gaeldom. Many proverbs exist in Gaelic which explicitly list virtues as exemplified by the Fianna. '*Bha dorus Fhinn do'n ànrach fial* (Fionn's door was always generous to the traveler); *Cha do thrèig Fionn riamh caraid a làimhe deise* (Fionn never abandoned his right-hand friend); *Cothrom na Fèinne* (The chance of the Fianna (an expression meaning 'fair play))', and so on.

Affection and sexuality

Highlanders are described in early traveller's accounts as being both courteous and affectionate to one another:

> In defiance of the hardships these oppressed people suffer, they retain part of their former state and dignity, at their meetings and partings. They address one another by the title of gentleman or lady (*duine-uaisle* or *bean-uaisle*) and embrace one another most cordially, with bonnets off. And they are never known to enter a door without blessing the house and people so loud as to be heard, and embracing every man and woman belonging to the family.[52]

The lord of Coll is pictured as greeting the chieftain of the MacLeans in a most cordial manner:

> *Dh'fholbh thu 'nan coinneamh 's 'nan còmhdhail*
> *Le pòig is le fàilte*[53]
>
> You went over to meet them
> With a kiss and a welcome

The Gaelic word for 'kiss', *pòg*, is after all derived from the Latin phrase signifying 'a token of peace' and is part of Gaeldom's pan-European inheritance. Even so, other Europeans made note of the liberties which Scottish, and especially Highland, women enjoyed.

Æneas Silvius Piccolomini, who later became Pope Pius II, wrote after his visit to King James I that Scottish women were 'fair in complexion, comely and pleasing, but not distinguished for their chastity, giving their kisses more readily than Italian women their hands.' English officer Edmund Burt was surprised at the complimentary kisses given to him by married women, who, as he notes, 'had no further design in it', and Boswell recorded how Dr Samuel Johnson challenged one pretty young maid to see which of them would first tire of kissing. In his journals from the beginning of the nineteenth century, William MacGillivray gives us a glimpse of the affection of people of Harris:

> In taking my leave I took advantage of the custom prevalent in the isles, of kissing … After dinner, the ladies and I took a walk to South town, not as people walk in towns but after our own warm Highland

> manner – with my left hand upon Mary's right shoulder, and my right arm about Marion's waist.[54]

The unabashed public display of affection does not translate into loose sexual standards, however. A society with such an obsession about ancestry and lineage would not easily allow itself to degenerate into a mass of offspring with indeterminate parentage. All societies have ways of channeling and grounding sexual energy which could otherwise lead to waste and chaos. While Gaels may have appeared to others to have been less modest or demure than some of their neighbours, they did have their own refined sense of decency and virtue.

> How natural it must have been for a casual observer to suppose, from seeing men and women reposing in the same place, that the marriage rites were not in force. To judge of the ancient inhabitants by the rudest of the present Highlanders and Irish, who often sleep in the same apartment, and are sometimes exposed to each other in a state of semi-nudity, we should not come to a conclusion unfavourable to their morality … It may here be stated that the Gael have no word to express cuckold, and that prostitutes were, by Scots law, like that of the ancient Germans, thrown into deep wells; and a woman was not permitted to complain of an assault if she allowed more than one night to elapse before the accusation.[55]

The coldness of Highland nights was at least partially remedied by people sleeping together in the same bed: '*Is fuar leabaidh gun choimhleapach* (A bed is cold without a sleeping companion)'.

Pre-marital sexual relations, especially with noble men, were not particularly a matter for concern, although there were high standards for behaviour after marriage.

> [King] George IV was not personally liked by his Highland people. They had heard stories about his bad conduct to his wife, and of his relations with other women, including, what they could not forgive, other men's wives. They could be and were far more tolerant than the ministers and kirk-sessions about sexual immorality between unmarried sprigs of the upper classes and peasant girls, but they ground their teeth against adultery.[56]

A great deal of courtship happened during the summer at the sheilings, when the women would be tending and milking the cattle in the mountains. This pastoral practice is the subject of nostalgia in many Gaelic songs, and the setting of many romances.

During the winter courtship was commonly done by a custom known as *caithris na h-oidhche*, sometimes known in English as 'bundling', into the twentieth century. As the family would have known when their daughter had taken the fancy of some hopeful young man, they were better to be involved in the process than to try to subvert the inevitable passions of youth. The young woman would have her legs inserted into a large stocking and securely tied together. Once this precaution was in place, she was allowed to have her sweetheart come to spend the night with her.[57]

> The common, as well as the better sort of people, court sweet-hearts at nights, over all this country. The unlocked doors yield those lovers but too easy access to their favourites. The natural consequences of their rencounters often occasion squabbles in kirk courts, in which minister and elders take cognizance of the fornication committed in the parish …
>
> The woman, if she is pregnant by a gentleman, is by no means looked down upon, but is provided in a husband with greater eclat than without forming such a connection. Instead of being despised, numberless instances can be produced, where pregnant women have been disputed for, and even fought for, by the different suitors.[58]

There was no great stigma in Gaelic society about children born out of wedlock, although they seldom inherited the full status and wealth conferred upon children born in marriage.[59] Such children did sometimes, however, become minor gentry and found new septs.

Some of the sources reveal a stark frankness and humorous boldness about sexual matters. One proverb states, '*Is iomadh rud a nì dithis dheònach* (Two consenting persons can do many things)' and another, which was supposed to be the advice of a girl to her inexperienced lover, was, '*Is math do bheadradh, ach cùm air* (Your caressing is good, but keep going).'[60]

A traditional tale of the chieftain of Morar begins when he was out in the hills with his men and he saw a young woman following her cattle, lifting her petticoats up from the dew as she went. He said aloud 'That would be a handsome young woman if her two legs were not so slender,' to which she replied '*Is minig a bha ùth mhòr aig bò chaol-chasach* [A slender legged cow often has a large udder]'.[61]

Some songs, by definition performed for others to hear, delineate the physique of lovers:

Bu tu 'm fear mòr bu mhath chumadh,
o d' mhullach gu d' bhrògan …
Bu tu 'm fear slinneanach leathainn,
bu chaoile meadhan 's bu dealbhaich'
Cha bu tàillear gun eòlas 'dhèanadh còta
Math gearra dhut,
No dhèanadh dhut triubhais
Gun bhith cumhang no gann dhut –
Mar ghealbhradan do chasan
le d' ghearr-òsan mu d' chalpa.[62]

You were the tall man, most excellently
shaped, from your head to your shoes …
You were broad-shouldered, with a slim
waist, well-formed,
A tailor without skill could not make you
a doublet,
Or make trousers for you without making
them too tight or deficient –
Your legs like bright salmon,
with the hose around your calf.

The stages of life

Life is a constant process of growth, revelation, and entry into new stages of maturation. Every culture recognizes different phases of life and has ways of celebrating the maturation of the individual from one stage into the next, often by 'rite of passage' ceremonies.

The transition from one stage, or area, into the next is often considered dangerous, as one must pass through a 'liminal state' which is neither the one state or the next. Many cultures display an interest in liminality because of its paradoxical nature, and make it the subject of puzzles and riddles.[63] Rites of passage often reflect the vulnerability of being in this liminal state and the uncertainty of what lies ahead in the next stage of life.

The first rites of passage occurred at birth. The process of giving birth was dangerous for obvious medical reasons: childbirth was a common cause of death of women in non-industrial societies. The *bean-ghlùine* (mid-wife), who presided over the process, was well versed in these matters and was usually a mother herself.

The immediate physical danger of childbirth was paralleled by anxieties about the spiritual well-being of the mother and child. Women in childbed and newly born infants were believed to be particularly susceptible to Otherworld beings, who might steal away the mother or child and replace them with 'changelings'. They were thus under constant supervision and were administered special rites and charms for their protection by the mid-wife.[64]

The advantage of this anxiety and supervision is that any medical complications that a woman or infant might have would be quickly noticed and attended to. The child was finally considered safe from Otherworld harm after he had been baptized and christened.

A newly born child was welcomed into the world by being plunged into cold water, the shock of which started them breathing.[65] There are records of other rituals for infant and mother. Fire was carried sun-wise around them as further protection from malicious beings.[66] The first food given to an infant in some areas was the sap from a stick of ash,[67] a custom reminiscent of many around the world in which a newborn is given a token of the Tree of Life.

A person who survived the illnesses of childhood was unlikely to die of natural causes before reaching an advanced age – the health and longevity of the people of the Highlands and Islands was renowned. While many of the noble children would have been sent into fosterage for careful and studious training, the non-noble children would have enjoyed a more carefree pastoral life.

> The boys learned how to make and repair the milking and dairy utensils, to tend the flocks, shear [sic] the sheep, make and mend their own shoes; and to thatch, and make the heather and hair ropes so largely used by them; and perhaps the most desired part of their education was the shooting of a blackcock, the stalking of a deer, and the spearing of a salmon.

> The girls learned to emulate their mothers in skill of the dairy work, as well as in spinning wool for future webs on the distaff, and knitting stockings and hose of brilliant hues and rare patterns. They learned to know the herbs that were medicinal for man and beast, and the different plants used in dyeing the colours of their tartans. They learned to become useful wives, following in the footsteps of their mothers, as helpmates in the struggle for existence, neither fearing the snows and storms of winter, nor ashamed of the tawning of the summer sun.[68]

Folklorists have observed that heroic tales often elucidate implicitly the processes of social maturation. The tales of the Fianna derive at least part of their popularity because of their exploration of male development from youth to adulthood and of the alternating poles of existence between life in the 'wild' and life in domesticated society.[69] The older term for the Fianna is *fian*, derived from the same Indo-European root which produces Latin *venari* (to hunt) and English 'win'. 'In many cultures, hunting and warring in the wilderness constitute the designated vocation of the young male on the verge of manhood.'[70]

Although the Fianna were charged with the duty of protecting Scotland and Ireland from invasion, this exclusively-male band spent most of their time hunting and training in the warrior arts. According to one Scottish poem, they were to be given free lodging during the winter and were outdoors during the 'bright half' of the year.

Ó Shamhain go Bealltaine	From Halloween to May Day
Buannacht gach tighe d' fhianaibh;	Every house offered the Fianna lodging;
An t-sealg, fa sógh-seabhcaidhe,	The falcons were of good cheer
Aca i n-ionam an fhiadhaigh.[71]	Outdoors during the hunting season.

There are references to games of the Fianna which appear to be aggressive competitions between young men and the very initiation into the Fianna required passing strenuous tests.[72] There are hints that the initiation of a young male warrior required that he stalk and kill a boar at *Samhainn*.[73]

Gaelic law recognized a number of different sorts of marital unions, dependent in part upon the relative status of each partner and the degree of exclusiveness of their union.[74] The heroic ethos of warriorship carried over into the some of these marriage customs.

> A Scottish bride was expected to show a reluctance, and require a certain degree of violence, which was neither thought unbecoming in the man, nor a hardship to the woman; many instances being found of happy unions, accompanied with apparent force and cruelty.[75]

The 'winning' of a wife in such circumstances was similar to the winning of other spoils of war and displayed the ability of a man to advance his interests. Although this practice did lend itself to abuse, we need not assume that women were always unwilling abductees. There are anecdotes which suggest that they were co-conspirators in this demonstration of their future husband's heroic prowess and there was an entire literary genre called *aithed* about elopements, many of them instigated by women.[76] When the legendary hero Conall Gulban asked why the king's daughter was crying as he was carrying her away, she answered '*Mo thoirt air falbh bharr baile mòr m' athar fhìn gun aon deur fala a dhòrtadh air mo shon* (Because I am being taken away from my own father's holdings without a single drop of blood being shed on my account).'[77]

Marriage was not such a martial affair in most cases, however. Especially when families were not concerned about the political and economic consequences of marriage, people seem to have had a great deal of freedom in selecting partners.

> But there is hardly any country where parental authority is more passive than there. People marry very early, and without much regard to circumstances and hence their union is generally the effect of mutual liking ... Nor have parents the same reasons for crossing their children's affections as in countries where there is a greater inequality of circumstances ... It is, however, reckoned dutiful to consult them before entering into that state, because they may thereby expect their blessing, and a share of the little they have.[78]

There are numerous proverbs giving advice to young men and women about how to select a partner, such as '*Tagh do bhean mar as math leat do chlann* (Choose your wife according to how you would like your children to be)'. Once a bachelor had set his sights on a particular woman, he would normally go to her father's house in order to arrange the match. It was not himself, however, but his 'best-man' who did the bargaining in this betrothal ceremony, called a *rèiteach*. This session of negotiation was something of a verbal game of skill in which the best-man used metaphors based on the father's profession to try to 'procure' some item representing the daughter. The father, meanwhile, thwarted the aims of the best-man as long as he could, offering him each of the other women in the room. This exchange was witty and humorous, though often to the expense of everyone but the intended bride. In the end, however, the negotiations would be celebrated in grand style.[79]

The wedding was the scene of mirth and revelry which could last for several days. It may seem strange to us today, but the celebration of marriage was such a community affair that the whole party even participated in the bedding of the new couple.

> Wishing, if possible, to elude the public gaze, she attempts to steal away privately, when, observed by some vigilant eye, her departure is announced, and all push to the bridal chamber, The door is instantly forced open, and the devoted bride, divested of all her braws, and stripped nearly to the state of nature, is placed in bed in presence of the whole company. Her left stocking is then flung, and falls upon some individual, whose turn to the hymeneal altar will be the next. The bridegroom, next led in, is as rapidly demolished, and cosily stowed alongside of his darling. A bottle and glass being then handed to the bridegroom, he rewards the friendliness of those who come forward to offer their congratulations, with a flowing bumper. When the numerous levee have severally paid their court, they retire, and leave the young couple to repose.[80]

Nuair bha gach nì ullamh,	When everything was ready,
Do'n leabaidh chaidh an cupall,	The couple went to bed,
Is chruinnich a' chuideachd	And all of that company
Ud uile le chèile;	Gathered together;
Le aighear, le furan,	With joy, with hospitality,
Le botal, le cupan,	With a bottle, with a cup,
Tost leapaich gun tug iad,	They gave a bedding-toast
'S gun cuir mi e 'n cèill:	Which I will repeat for you:
'Gun gluais sibh 's an fhìrinn	'May you travel in the truth
An ceumannan dìreach	On the straight path;
Bithibh stuaimeil is sìobhailt	Be moderate and civil

'S na dìobairibh cèill;	And never abandon reason;
Ur sliochd-sa biodh lìonmhor	May your progeny be numerous
Feadh ghlacan na tìre	Throughout the land,
'S ur n-iar-oghachan chì sibh	And you will see your great-grandchildren
A' dìreadh ur ceum.'[81]	Following in your footsteps.

The mother of the bride greeted her the next morning and arranged her hair in the *brèid beannach* (pointed coif), indicating her status as a married woman. The first man who encountered her after this ritual of marital status had the honour of conferring a blessing upon her in verse, praising her beauty in the new headdress and giving her advice about marriage.[82] Honeymoons did not exist, for there was no concept of a need to escape from living in one's village amongst one's kin. 'Now we hear of the honeymoon trip from the Highland hamlet. Verily! things have changed.'[83]

Rather than fearing death and avoiding contact with it, people accepted it as an inevitable stage of the progression of life. '*Feumaidh an talamh a chuid fhèin* (The earth (that is, the grave) will get its share); *Am fear a gheibh gach latha bàs, 's e as fhearr a bhitheas beò* (The man who finds death each day is the man who lives best).'[84] Death in modernist society is the concern of specialized businesses, and it is not too much to suggest that the inability of people to complete their grieving for a loved one is not unrelated to their removal from the process of death and burial.

These matters were the responsibility of kin and community in Gaelic society. People began preparing for their fate early on. 'It is a curious practice of newly married women to commence spinning and preparing linen for their shroud.'[85] It was expected that people would make direct contact with the corpse, which would literally bring one face-to-face with the reality of death.

> *Nuair a bhiodh iad ann an taigh-faire agus a bhiodh iad a' fàgail, chuireadh iad an làmh air làmh an neach a bha marbh 's a' chistidh, air neo air bathais an duine ... Agus 's e an t-adhbhar a bha aig feadhainn, an dòigh anns an robh iad a' creidsinn ann an leithid seo, gur h-e nan tachradh an tathasg aig an neach a bhiodh an sin a-rithist nach gabhadh tu eagal roimhe a dhèanadh deifir dhuit ...*[86]
>
> When they would be in the wake-house and about to leave, they would put their hand on the hand of the deceased in the coffin, or else on his forehead ... And people had as the explanation of why they

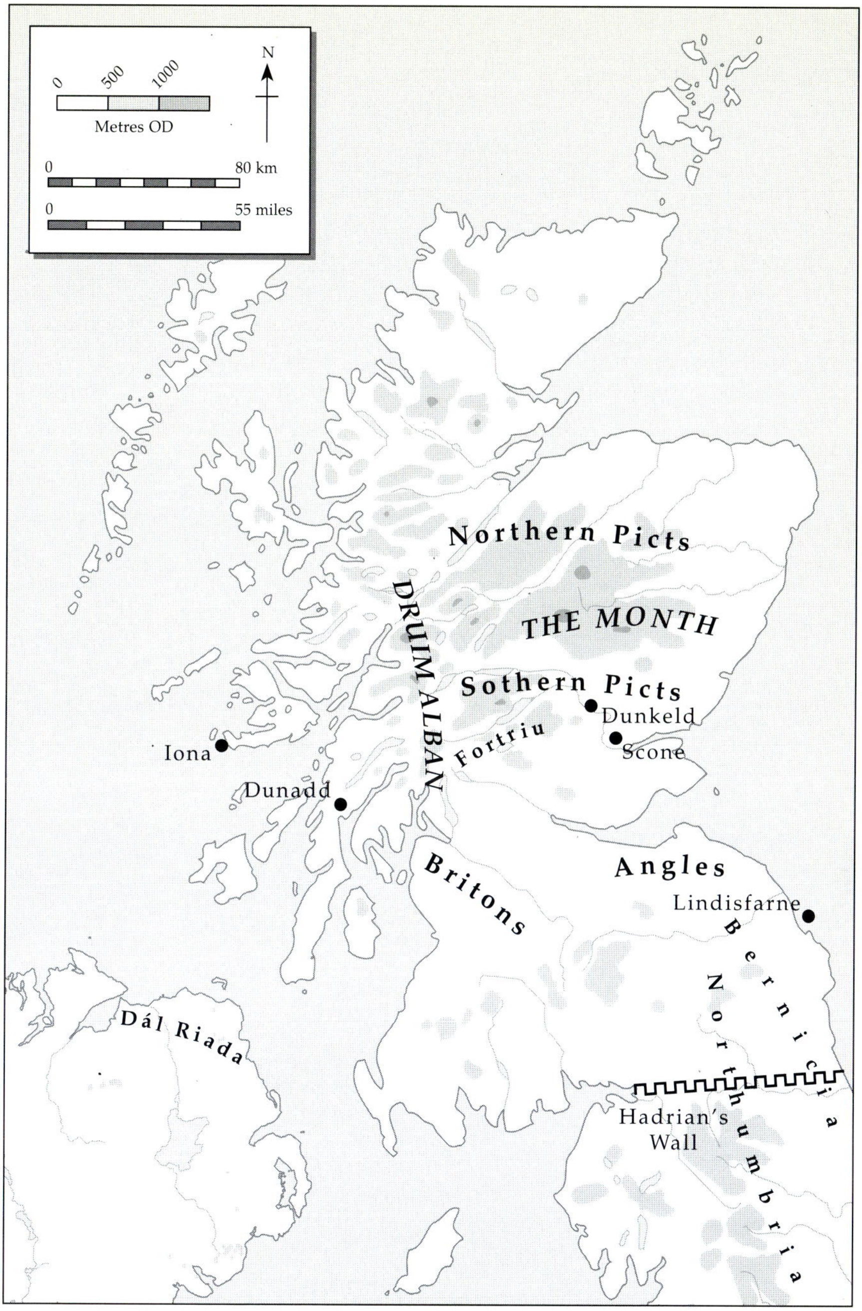

1 Early Medieval peoples.

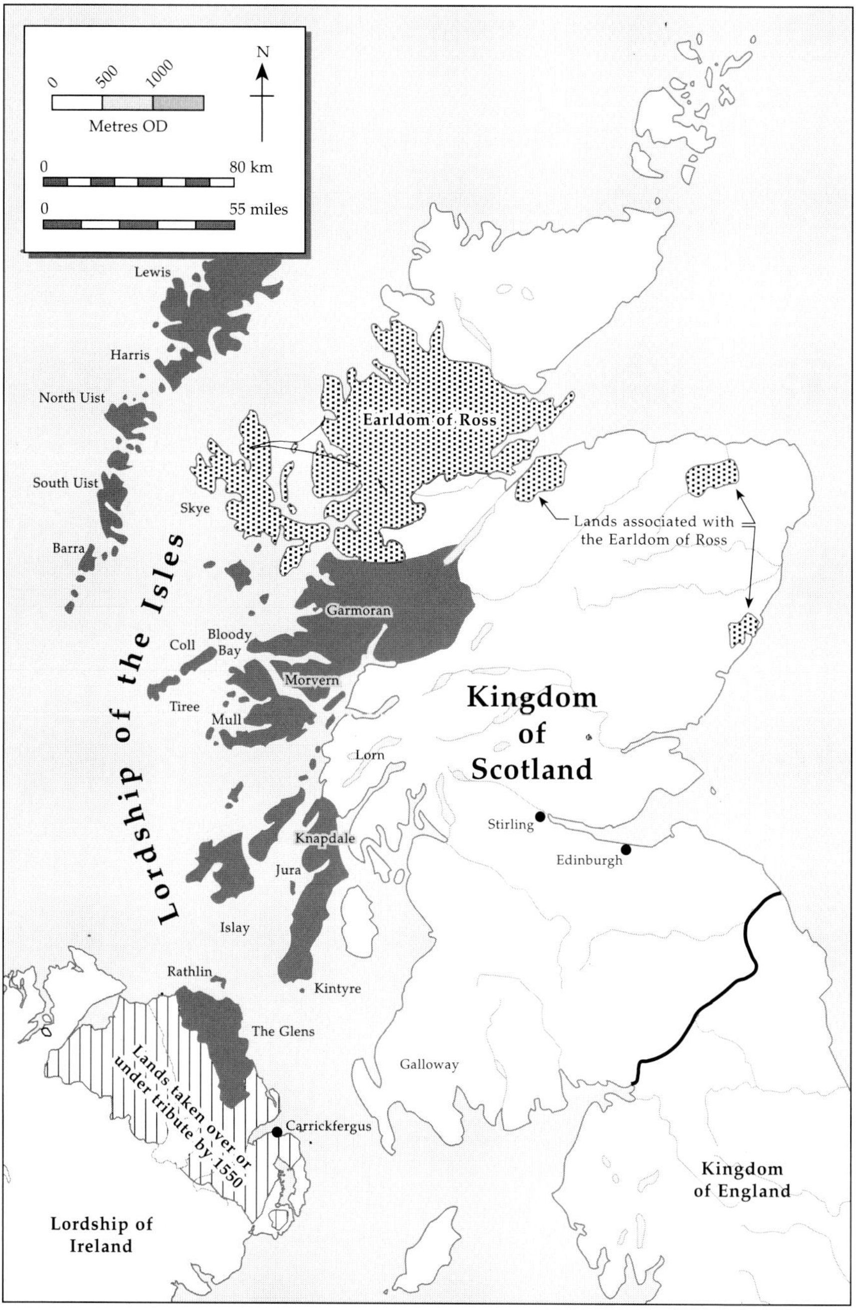

2 Lordship of the Isles.

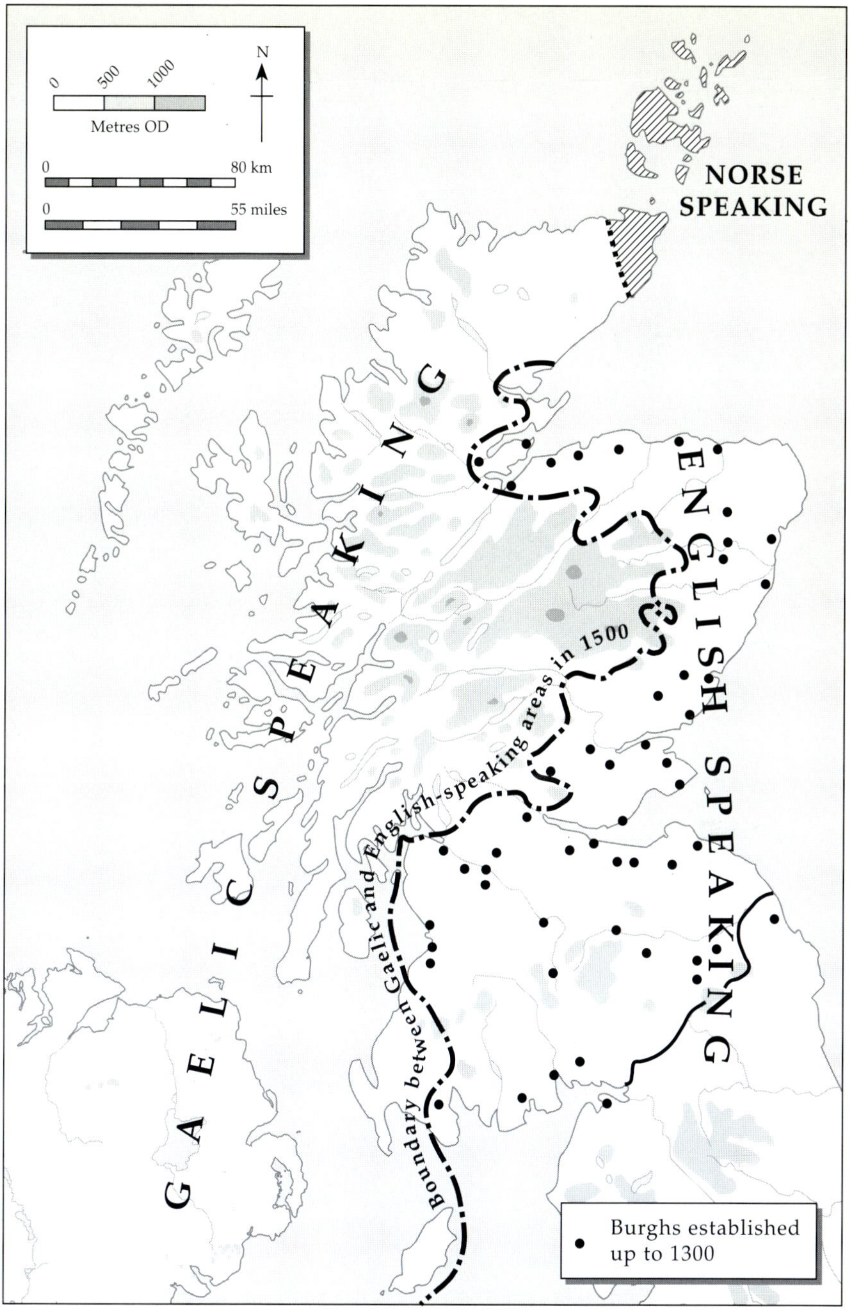

3 Language *c.*1500

4 Three Highland soldiers and a Highland woman in Inverness, from an early eighteenth-century drawing.

5 A thatched cottage in the isle of Islay, from a late eighteenth-century drawing. Note that the thatch is held down by rope.

6 The inside of a weaver's cottage in the isle of Islay, from a late eighteenth-century drawing.

7 Summer sheilings in the isle of Jura, from a late eighteenth-century drawing. Note that some of them are bee-hive shaped, and that a lattice of wood acts as a door.

8 Daily activities in the isle of Skye: two women work a quern, grinding corn, while a group of women sing a waulking song while they pound the tweed with their feet. Married women wear mutches, but the unmarried maidens have their heads bared. The shepherd, in Highland gear, gazes into the distance.

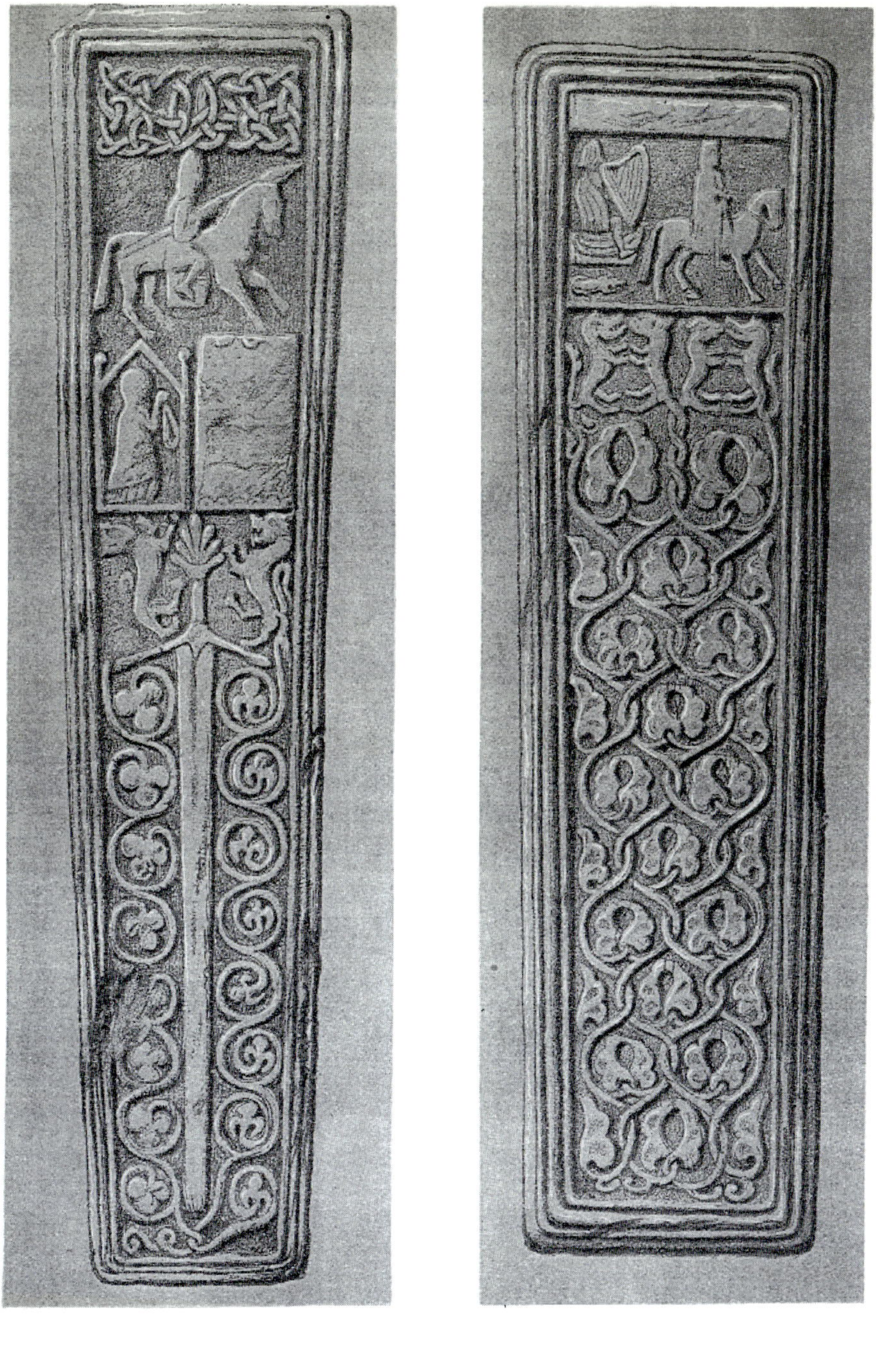

9 A late nineteenth-century drawing of two fourteenth- or fifteenth-century grave stones from the tombs of warriors in St Oran's churchyard, isle of Iona. Note how the cleric prays for the success of the warrior on the left, while the warrior on the right is set off to the sound of poetry and the *clàrsach*.

10 A late nineteenth-century drawing of a medieval grave-slab in Iona of an unidentified Gaelic warrior. (MacLean of Ross is only the title given by the artist.)

11 A late nineteenth-century drawing of a medieval grave-slab in Killean, Kintyre, of an unidentified Gaelic warrior. Note the depiction of the long-ship on his shield.

12 A drawing of the *Brecbennach* (often called the 'Monymusk Reliquary'), the portable shrine associated with St Columba, built about the year 700.

13 A drawing of the little religious house on *Innis Colum* (Englished as Inchcolm, 'St Columba's isle') in the Firth of Forth. It is built in the ancient manner, using only carefully placed stones.

14 A very fine brooch found in Hunterston, Ayrshire.

15 A mid-nineteenth century drawing of the isle of Iona.

> believed in doing this, that if the person's spirit should meet you again, you would not fear him in a way that would make any difficulty for you …

Wakes for the dead and burials were renowned for their excessive joviality before they were made more solemn by the new powers of the church in the eighteenth century. Food and drink was served to the men who had to carry the funeral bier over a potentially long distance to the graveyard. Keening women traditionally accompanied the death procession. Although they were replaced latterly by a bagpiper, the following indicates a transitional period between the two musical traditions:

> Burials are preceded by the large bag-pipe, playing some mournful dirge. They continue playing till they arrive at the place of interment, while the women sing the praises of the dead, clasping the coffins in their arms, and lie on the graves of their departed friends …
>
> On those occasions, there is great profusion of meat and drink brought to the place of interment, where the expenses generally bear a proportion to the rank and fortune of the person deceased, to prevent the imputation of meanness; and they seldom separate while the cask contains any spirits to wash down their sorrow: which seldom happens before their griefs are converted into squabbles, and broken heads, which some of them carry home as marks of remembrance for their lost friends.
>
> They seldom display much mirth at late wakes, as they do in many parts of Scotland; but sit down with great composure, and rehearse the good qualities of their departed friend or neighbour. Their grief soon subsides after they are buried; and many have speedily replaced a lost wife by some of their former acquaintance.[87]

There were too many joys, and tasks, in life to let death trouble one for too long. 'The ghost of a person who is grieved for too much by his nearest relative may return, for it is an act of insubordination against Providence to grieve too much for the dead.'[88] A person might be advised to bring his grief to a closure with the proverb, '*Is fhada tha bàs do sheanmhar 'nad chuimhne* (Your grandmother's death is long on your mind).'

Although life in traditional Gaelic society would not be appealing to most people raised in modernist societies, it was a fully functional organism that produced people with active minds and great vigor, as a quatrain from the Middle Ages asserts:

Is fearr sgíos cos bharr gnímh ghlain
Ná fos agus sgíos meanman;
mairidh sgíos meanman go bráth:
cha mhair sgíos cos acht aontráth.[89]

Tired feet after great achievement are better
Than inactivity and weariness of the spirit;
Weariness of the spirit lasts forever:
Feet are only tired for a space of time.

People expected life to be full of hardships and challenges, and were prepared to meet them. '*Chan eil air a' chruadal ach cruadhachadh ris* (The only remedy for hardship is to harden to it);[90] *Is beag a ghearaineas sinn, ge mòr a dh'fhuilingeas sinn* (Little do we complain, though we endure much).'

Life was not judged by the quantity of years that one might live, but by the achievement of honour and virtue. The belief that fame of song and story was far more lasting than life in the mortal world made Gaelic warriors fierce enemies.

> Yet they have great courage in fighting, and I have seen many of them suffer death with as constant resolution as ever Romans did … no men more desire [honour], affecting extremely to be celebrated by their Poets … and fearing more than death to have a rhyme made in their disgrace and infamy.[91]

Cyclic thinking

While our highly individuated modernist society only perceives human life as a linear process, a society aware of ancestry and in which all generations are in constant contact is more likely to perceive life as a constantly renewing cycle. While the notion of reciprocity has appeared several times already in relation to warfare, co-operation, and generosity, there are many clues that the cyclic metaphor informed many aspects of Gaelic life. 'The ancients believed that movement in nature was disposed toward the circular path … Not until the eighteenth century did the linear, directional concept of time become important.'[92]

The sun and stars of the heavens move in a cyclic motion and the celebration of the seasons follows a constantly renewing pattern. The performance of ritual is based on the idea of re-enacting the time-hallowed precedents of ancestors, transcending the bounds of time and invoking sacred time.[93]

In the traditional Gaelic naming scheme, the first son is named after his grandfather and the second after his father. The practice of 'recycling' these names is called in Gaelic *togail an ainm*.[94] This system reflects the idea of the survival of the dead in their descendants, but Gaelic poetry more explicitly elaborates this theme:

Cha do theast é uainn, ar linn:	It seems to me that he has not left us in Death:
Mairid a dheighmheic againn[95]	His excellent sons remain with us

Some of the euphemisms for death – *caochail* (to change), *siubhail* (to travel) – suggest that death is only a stage in a larger scheme of things, an idea, of course, entirely consistent with Christian theology. There are occasional glimpses, however, of cycles which are not so orthodox:

Chuir e toll ann am shlàinte	It has torn a hole in my health
Nach leighis plàsta no lighich	Which no poultice or doctor can heal
Gus an ginear mi 'm phàiste	Until I am born again as an infant
'S air cìoch mo mhàthar mi rithist.[96]	And suck at my mother's breast.

About the beliefs of his parishioners in the southern Gàidhealtachd of the late seventeenth century the Revd Robert Kirk wrote 'Tis ane of their Tenets, that nothing perisheth, but (as the Sun and Year) every Thing goes in a Circle, lesser or greater, and is renewed and refreshed in its Revolutions.'[97]

World turned upside down

King James VI made a concerted effort to break down the communal society of Gaeldom. The ideology of a cash economy can be seen in Statutes of Iona. The third and fourth of these provisions are aimed at eliminating the practice of *faoighe* (thigging) and hospitality. These banned the practice of giving free lodging and required everyone living in the Western Isles to either have a 'legitimate' trade or a source of income. This was, in large part, an attempt to oust the subsistence economy of the Gàidhealtachd – with its ethos of hospitality and reciprocity – and replace it with a cash economy generating income for the Crown.[98]

The second of the provisions sought to establish inns so that strangers travelling in the Highlands could buy lodging, and so that the Highlanders themselves would begin patronizing these new centres of public entertainment. It is important to realize that previous to this innovation, all grandiose entertainment was conducted by the chieftains in their halls, and neighbours had always been in the habit of giving each other food and provisions. In other words, the act of establishing inns is an attempt to break down the ethos of generosity and mutual reciprocity, and the unity of clan society under its hereditary leaders.[99]

There is evidence in Gaelic tradition that inns and taverns were viewed with suspicion and seen as outposts of external authority.[100] In any case, these franchises operated on money, which circumvents notions of honour, pride and familiarity in a small, kin-based society. 'The offer of money was often regarded in the Highlands as throwing suspicion on the motives and honesty of the person who offered it.'[101]

The new infrastructure of inns facilitated the cash economy. The Union of the Crowns of Scotland and England broke down trade barriers between the two nations, and the great demand in England for cattle suited the best export that the Gàidhealtachd could offer. The drovers – men who travelled with the droves of cattle – stayed in these inns on their journeys. Their externally-derived cash income instigated further change: instead of living according to sufficiency and paying a landlord in kind (provisions grown at home), land was to be treated as collateral on loan, to be paid with cash generated by exporting surplus products.[102]

In such an economy, the interests of the individual could come in conflict with those of his chieftain and clan, and the chieftain's power and wealth no longer relied solely upon his ability to summon fighting men. While the remoteness of Gaelic communities held no disadvantage in the traditional self-sufficient mode of living, it became a liability in a market economy.[103]

Gaels often looked warily upon towns. The following verse is attributed to John Morison, who flourished in the mid-seventeenth century, as his opinion of the people of the newly established burgh of Stornoway:

Cha tèid mis' a Steòrnabhagh,	I will not go to Stornoway
Chan eil mo chòmhnaidh ann	That is not where my home is:

Far am bheil na buirdeasaich
A chuir an cliù 'nam broinn;

Chan b' ionann mac an tuathanaich
Bho 'm faighinn faoighe shìl
Is bheirinn dha a-rithis e
Nuair bhiodh e air a dhìth.[104]

That is where the burgh-folk are
Who have put their fame into their bellies.

Not so the farmer's son
From whom I could thig seed
And I would give it back to him
When he was in need of it.

English officer Edmund Burt tells us in the 1720s that the government planned to create burghs in order to 'civilize' the Highlanders and entice them into the British cash economy:

> There was a civil Project on Foot, which was to build a Town after the English Manner, and procure for it all the Privileges and Immunities of a royal borough in Scotland. These Advantages, it was said, would invite Inhabitants to settle there, not only from the Lowlands, but even from England, and make it the principal Mart of the Highlands, by which Means the Natives would be drawn thither as to the Centre; and by accustoming themselves to Strangers, grow desirous of a more commodious Way of living than their own, and be enabled by Traffic to maintain it. And thus (it was said) they would be weaned from their barbarous Customs ...[105]

Another of the Statutes of Iona required that all men of substance send their sons to be educated in English in the Lowlands. This process not only changed the linguistic, religious, and cultural allegiance of many, but also gave them a newfound taste for luxury and the cash necessary to buy it. The effects are visible in Gaelic poetry within a generation of the enactment of these measures. As early as 1626, the poet Eóin Óg Ó Muirgheasáin said after the death of his patron, the MacLeod chieftain:

Ní fuighthear le féile nua
Éinfhear do chuirfeadh id chló;
Guais nách téid ó theasta tú
a clú feasta i méid is mó.[106]

It is impossible to find generosity
In anyone who could take your place;
There is a danger that, since you are dead,
The renown of your office will never be
increased.

By the middle of the seventeenth century chieftains were being routinely criticized by their poets for being away in the Lowlands or in London for long periods of time, and living beyond their means on clan expenses.

Gur fada leam an Sasann thu	I think you've been a long time in England,
'S a bhith 'gad chreach le spòrs.	Being ruined by gambling.
B' fhearr leam còt' is breacan ort	I would prefer you to wear a plaid and coat,
Na pasbhin 'chur air cleòc.[107]	Rather than in a cloak that fastens.

One of the most explicit statements of intent for replacing the Gaelic communal socio-economic system with an individualized, capitalist economy comes in a tract written immediately after Culloden. This tract describes Gaelic clan life as a form of servitude. Destroying this system, and assimilating the Highlanders into Anglo-British society, is claimed to bring them 'liberty' and 'happiness'. This is to be done by breaking up communal lands and the bonds of kinship.

> The Estates of the Rebel Chiefs are proposed to be vested in the Persons of their Tenants and Vassals. For, my Lord, their present strong Prejudices and Habits leading them to conceive the Interest of the Chief to be their own Interest, and these Prejudices being strengthen'd by family Affection and political Principles wrongly bias'd, a Gift made them of such a Quantity of Land as will raise them from their present State of Indigence to a State of comfortable Subsistance, and, in respect of their former, a State of Ease and Plenty, must, in the first place, not only immediately and feelingly convince them of a happy Change in their Circumstances, but present them with a new and very different Prospect of their own Interest. They must in this Case see, my Lord, and be persuaded, that their own true Interest is distinct and separated from the Interest of their Chiefs: For by experiencing the Happiness of their new Situation, the antient and strong Enchantment of implicit Submission and Family Attachment will at last dissolve; and, for the future, they will naturally desire, rather to live free, than return to Servitude; rather to promote and advance their own Interest, than that of their Chiefs.[108]

Another of the statements given in 1800 by the heir of the MacMhuirich dynasty of poets attests to the effect of the cash economy upon Gaelic society.

Ata daoine mearachd tha air bharail nach robh coibhneas no fialachd, deagh rùn no mòrdhalachd inntinn, fosgaireachd cridhe no carthannachd ann, an am na Fèinne, agus nach robh eòlas no cleachdadh aca air beusaibh matha air bith; ach gur h-ann bho chionn ghoirid thànaig na subhailcean-sa ann ar measg. 'Na aghaidh so, feudaidh sinn a dhèanamh soilleir gur h-ann a chaidh na subhailcean-sa a mhilleadh agus a chur air fògradh bhon a thòisich daoine ri gaol a ghabhail air airgead, air saoghaltachd, agus air fhiarachd thràilleil, a thug cealgaireachd ann ar measg. Ach roimhe sin bha daoine ag àrach duinealachd, bha iad blàth-chridheach cunbhalach agus seasmhach do an càirdean, 'nan sgiath agus 'nan dìon do an duine lag-chuiseach, ardaigneach ceannspreidheil agus cruadalach gus an naimhdean a smachdachadh.[109]

Those men are much mistaken who believe that neither kindness nor hospitality, disinterested magnanimity, generosity of heart, nor charity, existed in the age of the Fianna; that neither the knowledge nor practice of virtue existed in their times; but that these have lately been introduced into our country. In direct opposition to this, we can easily prove, that those virtues have been ruined, or driven into exile, since amongst us has come the love of money, worldliness, and slavish corruptions, which have introduced deceit and hypocrisy. Before this, people nurtured humanity; they were warm-hearted, determined, and unshakable in supporting their friends; were the shield and shelter of the feeble; high-spirited, headstrong and hardy in conquering their enemies.

The forced depopulation and impoverishment of the Highlands during the eighteenth and nineteenth centuries can be understood in much the same terms as modern Third World nations in which small-scale subsistence economies are suddenly replaced by dependent and volatile economies growing cash crops for export. Unmanageable population growth and economic crises almost invariably follow these rapid changes, and the bulk of the profits benefit a small number of local elite, who abandon their former comrades to poverty and impotence.

Even by the early twentieth century, when industry and commerce had been introduced to the Highlands, people were not only aware that such 'progress' had happened at the expense of native culture, but that the balance sheet could be read in a less than favourable light. While people may have felt that they were driven relentlessly forward by the grand project of Progress, they perceived that the lives of their predecessors were in many respects more satisfactory.

> I believe that taking simply happiness and contentment as the test, they were on the whole in a better condition formerly than they are now, notwithstanding the railways, libraries, and schools that abound in their midst. It will be said, of course, that we live in an age of progress, that it is our duty to press on, and endeavour to attain to a higher and a nobler life. Well, in this attempt, as carried on now, we may find more to eat and more to put on, and thus possibly improve the physical state, but what of the mental? … I do not mean, of course, that no progress or improvement has taken place in the general condition of the people in certain directions; but the genial, hospitable, guileless, lovable qualities, the Spartan simplicity that characterised their lives is not now what it was, and it seems to me that the tendency of the times is toward the obliteration of all these virtues.[110]

Another Gael in the early twentieth century looked back nostalgically upon the changes in the way of life of his native glen.

> It was a state of existence which, while partaking freely of very rough elements of civilization, yet had many redeeming features in its general economy. What though there was little circulation of money; there was none of the care and worry which the possession of it brings in its train, and there was, upon the whole, little real poverty and no starvation, while there was little 'wringing life out to keep life in'. What though the fashions were not studied; the people were well clothed, and in general there were good physiques. What though there was neither much style nor ceremony; these were not missed. There was, again, more time to enjoy existence … Excessive ambition is the minotaur of modern existence.[111]

CHAPTER 6

Nature and ecology

Culture and environment

There is a growing awareness about the failing health of the global environment. These problems become only more exacerbated as we continually push the limits of science and technology: the challenge is fundamentally a cultural one, not a technical one. Techno-consumer culture not only encourages us to have more profound and far-reaching effects on the environment than ever before, it makes it practically impossible to prosper without doing so.

The early modern 'cultural-evolution' myth characterized higher stages of civilization as having 'conquered' nature, while primitive societies were thought to live in wild nature, in a stage of savage primitivism. Since the age of the Romantic poets we have come to idealize and wax lyrical about nature and 'wilderness', but earlier generations saw such conditions as indications of an inferior race begging to be civilized, or dispossessed if it occupied desirable land.

The English officer Edmund Burt commented:

> So in the Highlands I have met with some Lairds, who surprised me with their good Sense and polite Behaviour, being so far removed from the more civilized Part of the World, and considering the Wildness of the Country, which one would think sufficient of itself to give a savage Turn to a Mind most humane.[1]

Likewise, immediately after Culloden a proposal for 'civilising that Barbarous People' saw the troublesome landscape as an obstacle to the taming of the people themselves, for 'the numbers of woods, mountains, and Secret Glens ... are also great allurements to incite that perverse Disposition that reigns amongst all Ranks of them, stimulated by the Rudeness of their Nature, unrestrained by Law or Religion.'[2]

René Descartes, arguably the father of scientific reason, laid the ideological foundations of modernist science and technology. His writings reflect anthropocentrism and the hubris of the early modernist mind which was already engaged in the conquest and exploitation of 'new worlds'.

> I perceived it to be possible to arrive at knowledge highly useful in life … to discover a practical [method] by means of which, knowing the force and action of fire, water, air, the stars, the heavens, and all the other bodies that surround us, as distinctly as we know the various crafts of our artisans, we might also apply them in the same way to all the uses to which they are adapted, and thus render ourselves the lords and possessors of nature.[3]

His ambition has been accepted and naturalized over centuries, although this imperial ideal is so fundamental to the modernist worldview that it is seldom acknowledged as the source of our ecological predicament. 'Man's dominion over nature was the self-consciously proclaimed ideal of early modern societies.'[4]

Land, it was rationalized in the early Imperial Age, was given by God to humankind for exploitation, and those peoples who did not maximize its fruits were unworthy of possessing it. The Gaels were among those inferior cultures which were supposed to be phased out for the greater good for humankind:

> The art of agriculture is no exception: in it, as in all the others, the accumulation of capital and the advance of knowledge and of skill dispense with half-employed and unproductive labour; … a population numerous, but accustomed to, and contented with, a low standard of living for themselves, and yielding no surplus for the support of others, gives place to a population smaller in amount, but enjoying a higher civilization, and contributing in a corresponding degree to the general progress of the world.[5]

Yet, the closer we come to extending our technology over the globe, the nearer we edge toward the extinction of life as we know it, choking the infinite diversity of organic nature which gave birth to humankind with the evolutionary dead-end of the machine.[6]

In discussing what it means to be 'indigenous' in non-modernist societies, John Mohawk notes that culture is adapted to reflect its environment.

> Traditional societies are socialized to existence in a specific place. That is to say, the most Traditional societies are indigenous in the sense that they believe they belong to the space they occupy ... Generation after generation expends energy thinking about what it means to be a people of a forest or desert, and that thinking process develops a conservatism about the ecology which is both healthy and, in the long term, necessary for survival ...[7]

Not only are the issues of biological diversity useful metaphors for issues of cultural diversity, but the two phenomena are inextricably linked in human history. 'Cultural diversity is as important as diversity in the natural world and, in fact, follows directly from it. Traditional cultures mirrored their particular environments, deriving their food, clothing, and shelter primarily from local resources.'[8]

Modernist society, on the other hand, attempts to move in the opposite direction, forcing diverse environments to fit into a single, homogenous mold. The modern home, with its artificial walls, floors, heating, and cooling, attempts to overcome the diversity of environments and climates. The modern consumer outlet provides a uniform supply of goods, clothing, and foods year-round. Modernist culture has a strong anti-indigenizing force wherever it is adopted, and people raised in this ethos do not have the same relationship to their environment as people in primal societies.

The naive view of primitive societies living in harmony with nature expects to see explicit expression of a love for nature and a desire for sustainability: people worshipping Mother Earth goddesses, rituals of nature cults, songs proclaiming the beauty of the wild, and so forth. The truth is more mundane, however. Those primal societies that did achieve an ecological balance – and there have been many failures – did so because of a simple approach to life, adapted to the local environment, that developed organically over many generations through continual observation of nature and social adjustments.

To look at the issue in reverse, we in techno-consumer society do not worship any God of Destruction, do not pray for ozone holes or oil spills, do not praise deforestation. In fact, 'green awareness' and sympathy for the environment, in broad terms, have never been greater. The fact is that while we speak of cherishing the environment, and advertisers make us feel good about buying eco-friendly products, we unconsciously continue to offer sacrifices to our cult of destruction on the altar of consumerism.

To perceive the relationship to environment in a primal society, then, we need to think about the values of that society and the way that it operates in its natural setting.

> In Native America, as no doubt in cultures the world over, there is no real will to conserve. Prayers are not offered for smaller harvests or fewer children. In fact, knowledge of all kinds is directed primarily toward human increase, not decrease. And yet, the element of reduction, like a tolling bell, makes itself heard through vast stretches of traditional lore.
>
> Stated in the broadest way possible, the pertinent themes ... seem bland enough. Young people growing up in traditional Native American society learn to think in terms of personality. They develop a sense of kinship. They come to recognize a need for restraint. They learn to accept death and they acquire techniques of renewal.[9]

Our culture, our very language, determines the way that we perceive the world and the conceptual categories we use in thinking about it.[10] The myths of modernism have confined our understanding of the universe to that of a machine, reduced to quantities and scientific laws, stripped of sacredness or inherent value. Let us consider the meanings of a few words in modern English to demonstrate the degree to which they reflect the values and mythology of modernist culture.

The word 'Improvement' has been used to describe the processes of humanizing the landscape: draining bogs and moorlands, micro-managing forests, introducing more efficient agricultural implements and techniques, and so on. What was 'improved' was the profit for humankind, not the well-being of the entire eco-system. While yields might have increased, and human-labour decreased, the result was only some multiple factor of previous 'primitive' conditions: limits still remain even after the ecological integrity is severely compromised.

We use the word 'development' in more recent times in a similar fashion. We speak of 'developing' a field or an industrial park, using a very different sense of the word than when we speak of 'child development'. When a child develops normally, there is a continual process of growth which allows him or her to become a happy and healthy adult. 'Develop' in modernist parlance, as pertaining to the environment, is little more than a euphemism for 'destroy and cover with concrete'.

Consider the associations and implications of other words, such as 'wilderness', 'progress', 'creation of wealth', 'innovation', 'civilized', 'rational', 'practical', 'useful', 'productive', and so on. Even the work of ecologists is constrained by the categories that we unconsciously inherit, for to think of the environmental crisis merely in terms of quantities of resources and their distribution is to be unable to transcend the mechanistic and reductionist view of the world which has created the problem itself.[11]

'Wilderness' can only be perceived when it stands in opposition to something else, namely landscape with visible human impact. It is no surprise that our modern sensibilities about nature are largely derived from the intellectual revolt against the Industrial Revolution during the Romantic Era. Thus, like the 'noble savages' themselves, the wild in nature was easily idealized only after it no longer posed any real threat to the established order. Non-industrialized societies seldom have a need to express their love of nature, for they live in what they expect to be the normal state of existence.

Land use

By the early modern period, Lowland culture and language had taken the better arable land, and the Gaels were left mostly with the higher ground, less productive for agriculture. Recent research suggests that the Highland economy was constantly shifting the ratio of land used for pastoralism and agriculture according to a number of factors such as demands for cash, population growth, and available labour.[12] An old proverb illustrates the importance of cattle in Highland life. '*Is fearr aon sine bà na bolla de'n mhin bhàin* (A single cow's teat is better than a bowl of meal).'[13]

Even so, crops of various sorts were grown and Highlanders found ways of creating a symbiosis between agriculture and pastoralism. After *Bealltainn* (May Day), the cattle were taken by the women and the children to the sheilings in the hills, away from the homesteads, so that the men could work on the houses and the farm-lands near the village. Shifting the cattle off the hills during the 'dark half' of the year allowed the flora to recover, and shifting them away from the home in the 'warm half' kept them out of the way of the work of cultivation.

People also kept a small number of goats and the old breed of Highland sheep – smaller and more delicate than the varieties which displaced the human population in the eighteenth and nineteenth centuries[14] – which needed to be watched to prevent their voracious appetites from doing too much damage.

> The cause of the flowers being so plentiful in the good old times was that neither my grandfather nor his forebears would ever hear of sheep coming near the place ... The stock consisted of sixty Highland milk cows and their sixty calves ... These were continually shifted from place to place, and this gave the plants and bulbs a chance of growing.[15]

The added nutrients of cattle manure enhanced the fertility of the soil. An old proverb says, '*Pàighidh am feamann am feurach* (The fertilizer will pay for the grazing)', meaning that the cost to the land for grazing the cattle will be paid back by the manure that they leave behind them. These areas would often be used for growing crops the next year.

> The thrifty owners of the cattle frequently went in the spring to the hills to make small rigs and furrows, and sow corn or barley in them where the cows had spent the night the previous year, as the soil would have been enriched with their droppings.[16]

Sheilings and cultivation were interwoven in the fabric of life and established the patterns of settlement and activity.

> The old humble sheiling existence was part of the agricultural system. It helped mightily to keep a large and hardy population, dependent on cultivation and grazing, spread out over the face of the country, people content with simple, natural life if they only had a bare sufficiency of absolutely necessary means of subsistence.[17]

One can see other practices in Highland life which demonstrate that Gaels were careful in their use of scant resources, and that they took advantage of the processes of use in recycling materials. The thatch of cottages, for example, made of bracken, rushes, or heather, absorbed the soot of the smoke during the year. When the thatch was taken off the houses in the summer, it was used as fertilizer on the fields.[18] In cold regions, cattle were kept in the same house as people (though in a separate compartment) during the winter, contributing to the warmth of the house and reducing fuel consumption.[19]

The agricultural and pastoral practices were not merely an economy which provided sustenance to them: it defined their seasonal calendar and customs, related to their values and worldview, suited their love of freedom and the outdoors, sustained their health, and nourished their sense of pride. The economic and social changes which were introduced later completely disrupted this pattern, forcing Gaels to abandon the sheilings and their very homesteads so that sheep, and later, deer-parks, could be put in their place. It is no wonder, then, that commentators could state 'The sheep reign deeply hurt the Highland people.'[20]

The improvers of the eighteenth century were appalled by the state of the Highlands, continually criticizing the ineffectual tools and techniques in use.[21] One example is the use of *feannagan*, rows of earth labouriously formed by digging parallel ditches, called 'lazy-beds' in English on the mistaken assumption that this was done because the Gaels were too lazy to plough the ground properly.[22]

The traditional Gaelic economy was geared toward maximizing the spread of the human community. Since goods were produced locally and consumed locally, the costs of production and location were not significant. As the new economic and agricultural regime took over, however, 'remoteness' became a handicap, costs had to be minimized, and profits maximized.[23]

One of the supporters of the old way of life was Duncan Campbell of Glenlyon who noted at the end of the nineteenth century:

> The ruined mills on many streams dumbly testify, and the records, in which rents in kind are enumerated, bear written evidence to the fact that under the old husbandry the scanty arable lands of the Highlands produced heavier crops than they produce at the present time. The old farmers had plenty of farm-yard manure, and, speaking in particular for my native district, the tenants used far back a good system of rotation … Farming implements were simple and rude compared to what they are now, most of them being at home, but in result cultivation was much better than it is now, and much more land was under crops.[24]

Likewise were the opinions of Osgood MacKenzie.

> I, who am more or less of a farmer myself, am prepared to prove that far more crop was raised out of the soil then than there is now. I remember having it constantly dinned into my ears when I was young

> that when the people were educated (and not till then) the land would be properly cultivated, and that then every croft would become perfect like a garden. But, alas! it has turned out the very contrary.[25]

Recent reassessments of Highland agriculture have vindicated these claims: 'Traditional Highland agriculture had achieved a relatively successful balance between the needs of the people and the availability of resources.'[26]

The outside perception of the Highlands is that of a barren and poor land, a land whose inhabitants were happy to flee to 'greener pastures'. This belief is, of course, a convenient rationale for those who would deny the injustices of the Clearances and prefer to believe that the 'improved condition' of the descendants of those exiles allows us to overlook this episode. Gaelic sources, however, show a deep sense of contentment and attachment to the Highlands. Edmund Burt recorded, for example, that 'the Natives of the Hills say they inhabit a Land of Milk and Honey'.[27]

The farmer was obliged to follow the established farming practices and attend to his land responsibly: '*Biadh a thoirt do'n fhearann mun tig an t-acras air; fois a thoirt da mun fàs e sgìth; a ghart-ghlanadh mum fàs e salach – comharran deagh thuathanaich* (To feed the land before it gets hungry; to give it rest before it gets tired; to clear it before it gets messy – the signs of a good farmer).' Assuming this was done, it was expected that people would be well fed.

Is cugallach an t-sealg	Hunting is precarious,
Is cearbadach an t-iasg;	Fishing is unreliable;
Cuir do mhuinghinn 's an talamh:	Put your trust in the land:
Cha d' fhàg e fear falamh riamh.[28]	It never left a man empty.

This is not to say that there were no bad years, blights, shortages, and famines from time to time. Non-industrialized societies have always been prone to such failures, and even industrialized society will soon exhaust the earth's limits. This is merely to state that people had faith in the bounty of the land and in the practices they inherited to yield the fruits of the soil to them. There is no evidence in Gaelic tradition that people lived in constant anxiety and discontent, eager to escape to some richer land, but rather felt that they inhabited a sacred and singular homeland.[29]

Nor should the preceding discussion be taken to suggest that the Highlands and Islands were in the same ecological state, after several thousand years of human habitation, as they were shortly after their emergence from the Ice Age. There are almost invariably heavy losses during the initial phase of human, or even animal, colonization as society learns to adjust to a new environment and finds ways of settling into sustainable modes of living.

Between human agriculture, grazing by animals, heavy winds, poor soil, the fragility of trees, and scorched-earth military campaigns, most of Scotland's forests were cleared by the early medieval period. On the other hand, there are wonderful landscapes in the Gàidhealtachd, such as the *machair* of the Western Isles, which exist because of human activity and around which have evolved a rich eco-system. People need to be observant of their eco-system and responsive to its needs, and cultures need to be assessed according to these criteria of sustainability over a long time-scale.

The cycle of the seasons

The Gaels celebrated the round of the year with seasonal festivals inherited from their pre-Christian past. The most important dates recognized were the 'Quarter Days', organized generally according to the solar year, but adjusted to the lunar calendar by holding celebrations on the new moon. The dark always preceded the light, and therefore the new day starts with dusk, just as the new year begins with the start of winter.

Because each of the Quarter Days marked the end of one season and the beginning of the next, they were held to be liminal periods during which the normal boundaries of space and time were less rigid, and more permeable, than at other times of the year. They were thus especially suited for healing rituals and the working of magic, but dangerous because the security of boundaries – between order and chaos, dead and living, past and future – was compromised and the community was vulnerable to the capricious forces that threatened the human order.[30]

The origins of the Quarter Days can be found particularly in the biological cycles of the domesticated animals of the Gaels and the climatic conditions common to northern lands.[31] The crops could only be planted and reaped when environmental conditions allowed, and the natural rhythms of animals had to be accommodated.

Samhainn, corresponding to modern Halloween, derives from a term meaning 'the end of the summer'. Life turned inwards: people and their livestock returned to permanent habitations, indoor work (such as making ropes and cloth) was the new focus, and the storytelling season began. Excess animals were slaughtered, taxes were rendered, and feasts were held. The young cattle were recognized as passing into the next stage of life: '*Oidhche Shamhna, theirear gamhna ris na laoigh.*'

Because cattle were in their peak health, having spent the warm months feeding on the mountain grasses, it was an ideal time for cattle raiding. This could be done in retaliation when a client refused to render his taxes, but even when done as an act of aggression, the cattle had to be strong enough to travel speedily along difficult terrain for long distances. A poem from the early eighteenth century refers to the theft of livestock during this season, which accords with the pranks, mischief, and chaos associated with this night:

An uair thig gealach bhuidh' na Samhna
'S thèid càch 'nan taighean-geamhraidh
Goididh mise 'ghobhar cheanndubh
Le cuid meann bho Eònachan Dubh.[32]

When the yellow Halloween moon comes
And everyone else is in their winter quarters
I will steal the black-headed goat,
Along with her kids, from Black Jonathon.

This part of the year was sometimes called 'a' *Mhìos Dhubh* (the Black Month)' and the darkest part of winter was called '*na Mìosan Marbha* (the Dead Months)'. This festival was strongly associated with the dead and the Otherworld, being a time when dead ancestors visited the living[33] and the Otherworld beings were moving to their winter quarters. Bonfires, called *samhnagan* in some places, were lit, people arrayed themselves in bizarre and grotesque costume, and played tricks on each other.

There were divination rituals held on this night to attempt to ascertain one's fortune during the coming year, death and marriage (for unmarried men and women) being the prominent themes. Apples and hazel nuts were especially associated with this night, as they were winter foodstuffs and were used in some of these rituals.[34] '*Is ann Oidhche Shamhna a chnagadh tu cnò* (Halloween night is when you would break a nut)'.

Some of the beliefs and rituals of the Celtic new year appear to have been transferred to the Gregorian New Year (31 December) during the process of Christianization. The community celebration of the turning of the Christian year, *Oidhche Challainn* (Kalend's Eve), resembles many from around the world meant to ward off evil and defend the neighbourhood from the forces of dearth. One description from the mid-nineteenth century also conveys the warmth and kindness reinforced by such celebration in the cold and dark season.

> A sheep or wether was skinned for the Kalends' feast in such a way as to leave the skin in the shape of a bag. A little piece of skin was left on the beast's chest, which was afterwards neatly removed, and called 'the Kalends' Strip'. This Kalends' Strip was then carried by the Kalends' Band: at a particular time of the night, every adult male would gather together and visit their friends' and neighbours' houses.
>
> The entire group had to go three times clockwise around each house, every man holding a staff in his hand, while repeating the following verse as he circled the house, and at the same time striking the walls with his staff:

Calluinn a' bhuilg bhuidhe bhoicinn	Kalends of the yellow buckskin bag
Buail an craicionn	Strike the hide
Air an tobhta.	Against the wall.
Cailleach 's a' chùil –	A hag in the corner –
Cailleach 's a' chill –	A hag in the churchyard –
Cailleach eile ceann an teine;	Another hag next to the fire;
Bior 'na dà shùil	A thorn in her two eyes
Bior 'na goile	A thorn in her throat
Èirich agus fosgail dhuinn!	Arise and open up to us!

> Each man then had to sing his verse before the door would be opened to him. This is an example of one of the verses.

Èirich thus', a bhean chòir
'S a bhean òg, a choisinn cliù:
Liobhair thus' a' Challuinn uait
Mar bu dual dhuit a thoirt dhuinn:
A' mhulchag air am bheil an aghaidh rèidh,
'S am fear nach do bheum sùil –
'S mur eil sin deas 'nad chòir
Fòghnaidh aran 's feòil dhuinn.

> Arise, o good wife,
> And you young wife who has earned celebrity;
> Offer up the Kalends goods
> As is your custom to give to us:
> The smooth-faced chunk of cheese,
> And the unspoiled supply of butter –
> If those are not in your command,
> Bread and meat will suffice for us.

> The door was then opened with great excitement and generosity; and then the Kalends' Strip was then brought forward and singed in the fire, and given to the eldest woman in the house. She put the half-burnt strip to her nose, and it was sent in a circuit around the people of the house.
>
> Then the festival-table was surrounded by the Kalends' Band; the table contained the best selection of food and drink, and there was conviviality, friendship, and enjoyment amongst all of those present.[35]

Other accounts describe the leader of the band donning an animal skin with the horns and hooves still attached, and making a terrible display to emphasize the threat of death and famine which he represents to the human community. Quite a number of *Duain Challainn* (Kalends' songs) survive, some of them simply wishing the household well and celebrating the revelries, others wishing the bad luck of the season to go to a rival township.[36]

Other rituals during this mid-point of the bleak and cold winter celebrate the expectation of renewal and new life. The last night of the year was called *Dàir na Coille* (the impregnation of the forest) in some areas from the belief that a wind from the west on this night would plant new life-forces into the trees and forests. This accords with the universal symbolism of the primeval forest and Tree of Life as the ultimate source of life. On New Year's morning, the head of a household brought a twig from a local fruit-bearing tree into the home, accompanying it with the saying '*Fàs is gnàths is toradh* (Growth, custom, and fertility).'[37]

Spring was ushered in by the celebration of *Latha Fèill Brìde* (St Brigit's Day). This festival marks the break of the reign of winter and the return of fertility. 'The ritual focus of the season was on motherhood, both human and animal'.[38] Feminine affairs were brought to the fore, and the renewed ability of animals to give milk was greatly anticipated. Care was taken that the lambs be born before the calves, for sheep could graze on the scant winter vegetation and thus provide milk to their young far better than the cattle could.[39]

St Brigit, a saint derived largely from a pre-Christian goddess, personifies many of the concerns of this festival. She was said to be the nursemaid of Christ and the protector of flocks and herds. One of the customs associated with this festival was the making of a figurine made of oats (or corn and hay), dressed with female apparel, which was laid by the door and kept lit all night with candles. The mistress of the house was to shout out the door '*A Bhrìd, a Bhrìd, thig a-steach is gabh do leabaidh* (O Brigit, o Brigit, come inside and take your bed)' when all was prepared, and they hoped to see the impression of St Brigit's staff there in the morning as an omen of a good crop for the year.[40]

Probably the most important celebration was that of *Bealltainn*, corresponding generally to May Day. While May Day rites and festivals are common in many nations, Gaelic customs particularly emphasize renewal, fire, the fortification of boundaries, and the return to outdoor life. *Bealltainn* marked the beginning of the bright half of the year, and is commonly called *Latha Buidhe Bealltainn* (the bright (or auspicious) May Day) in Gaelic.

Descriptions of the communal event of renewal and purification come down to us from the earliest records and continued in much the same form in places in the Highlands into the nineteenth century. All of the home-fires of the community were extinguished, a dangerous act which was not normally done. A specially selected group of men, usually some power of the sacred number three (nine, twenty-seven, or eighty-one men), expended their energy in producing the *teine-èiginn* (need-fire) which was used to kindle two bonfires. Embers were taken from this communal fire to re-light the hearth in each home.[41] The cattle, which had spent all of the winter indoors, were ritually cleansed by being driven between these fires.

A ceremony from this festival recorded in one part of the Highlands attempts to propitiate the predators that would normally feed on animals domesticated by humankind and removed from the natural food chain. According to the account, given only in English translation, herdsmen went out to the summer pastures and baked oatcakes. Bits of these were broken and tossed over their shoulders with the words, 'Here to thee, wolf, spare my sheep; there to thee, fox, spare my lambs; here to thee, eagle, spare my goats; there to thee, raven, spare my kids; here to thee, martin, spare my fowls; there to thee, harrier, spare my chickens.'[42]

Because *Bealltainn* marked another dangerous liminal time, there were a number of ceremonies which attempted to redefine and reassert boundaries. Households were guarded against damage by Otherworld beings who were roaming during this period by displaying branches of the sacred rowan tree. 'Branches of the mountain-ash [rowan], decorated with heath and flowers which had been carried thrice around the fires kindled at Beltane, were reared above their own dwellings, to remain until displaced by those of the succeeding season.'[43]

The choice of green verdure for the assertion of the forces of life which the human community needed symbolized the vital energies of the archetypal Tree of Life. 'The aim of the greenery was to fill and strengthen the house and farmyard and the householders with the new Spring strength, and to scare off everything evil and hostile to life and livelihood as well.'[44] A house's liminal spaces – neither indoors or outdoors, namely doorways and windows – were most vulnerable and most carefully guarded by these protective items.

The cattle would be taken as soon as *Bealltainn* (though in some places somewhat later) to graze on the high summer pastures and everyone rejoiced in the return to the outdoor life on the *àirigh* (sheiling). One of many songs describes the process of moving the cattle and equipment to the hills.

Fàgaidh sinn còmhnard-ghlinn le'r n-eallaichean,	We will leave the level glens with our burdens
Gu siubhal nam beann 's nan glac as aithne dhuinn	To travel the mountains and hollows we know so well,
Sòlas da-rìribh ceumadh bhealaichean	What great solace to travel the paths
'S ar sùil ri àirigh nam bò …	In anticipation of the cattle sheilings …
Bhith còmhnaidh feadh bheann bho àm na cuthaige,	To live amongst the mountains from the time of the cuckoo (May Day),
Gu toiseach a' gheamhraidh ùdlaidh dhubhailce	Up to the beginning of the dark and gloomy winter,
A' cuallach na sprèidh 's na glinn 's na mullaichean	Tending the herds in the glens and the summits
Chuir sunnd is càileachd 'nam pòr …[45]	Which put joy and vigor in their bodies …

The festival of *Lùnasdal* is in origin the celebration of the pan-Celtic god Lugh who appears in early Gaelic myth as a culture-hero, winning the science of agriculture for his people. The festival, held around the first of August, is a harvest festival of which only fragments remain. 'The pagan importance of *Lugnasad* was so pronounced that it was utterly transformed under Christian influence.'[46]

The main activity of this season was the weaning of lambs and the beginning of the mating season. Thus, while St Brigit's Day has a feminine focus, *Lùnasdal* has strongly masculine overtones. It was also a time when contracts for trial marriages were arranged.[47]

While there could be intense bursts of labour, people generally enjoyed a very leisurely pace of life, planning their schedule according to the rhythms of nature. The Gaelic word *aimsir* means 'weather, time, or season', reflecting the fact that the time of the year, the activities engaged in, and the climactic conditions were all inter-related.

Limits and constraints

While the only limits recognized by techno-consumer society are those of money, most non-industrialized societies are careful to observe taboos of usage, to constrain activity according to time-proved tradition, and to be content with what is sufficient. A culture which conceives of the universe as invested with personality and supernatural beings is able to impress these restrictions upon its members in a very persuasive manner.

> For all but the most dedicated, restraint for restraint's sake makes an easily broken rule. More effective than the bald injunction to save for tomorrow is the pressure exerted by inner forms of plants and animals and by other supernaturals, who demand a morality higher than greed and hold out the necessary threats to enforce it.[48]

The *machair* (sandy grasslands) of the Hebrides are a fragile, human-made ecosystem. A traditional allegory warned children of the delicate nature of that environment and of the price that they would pay for ruining it.

> The *teine-biorach* [will-o'-the-whisp] is a metamorphosis undergone by a girl from Benbecula who went to gather the roots of the 'rue' at night on the hillocks of the *machair*. There was a fine imposed upon all who did this, as the hillocks would soon crumble in consequence through sand-drift ...[49]

Even in agricultural areas, there is evidence of taboos prohibiting the rapid expansion of land under cultivation: 'Of old it was reckoned unlucky for a son to plough one foot more ground than his father.'[50] The Gaels did not farm more than was necessary and one description from Canada in the early nineteenth century suggests that at least some Highland immigrants continued in this manner:

> [They] make but indifferent farmers, accustomed to a hard and penurious mode of life, they are too easily satisfied with the bare existence that even indolence can procure in this country, and care little for raising themselves and their families to a state of comfort and abundance.[51]

The desire for a superfluous abundance of possessions is more characteristic of modernist society than primal society and there are many Gaelic proverbs which advise a person to be content with less, rather than more. '*Is fhearr an teine beag a gharas na an teine mòr a loisgeas* (The small fire that warms is better than the big fire than burns); *Tha gu leòr cho math ri cuirm* (Enough is as good as a feast); *Is math na dh'fhòghnas* (What is sufficient is good);[52] *Am fear as mò a gheibh, is e as mò a dh'iarras* (The man who gets the most wants the most);' and so on.

Such was the adoption of the virtues of frugality that the Gaels saw it as an ideal that typified them, and contrasted them to their enemies.

> By Accounts of the Plenty and Variety of Food at the Tables of the Luxurious in England, the People, who have not eaten with the English, conclude they are a likewise Devourers of great Quantities of Victuals at a Meal, and at other Times talk of little else besides Eating ... It is from this Notion of the People that my Countrymen [the English], not only here, but all over Scotland, are dignified with the title of *Poke Pudding*, which, according to the Sense of the Word among the Natives, signifies a Glutton.[53]

This contrast is also sometimes found in Gaelic poetry, such as in this depiction of 'big-bellied' Lowlanders.

Ní hionann an bhuidhen bholgmhor	Not alike are the big-bellied band
ar bhruach mberna	On brink of battle-gap
's na Gaoidhil ghasda Chlár Connla[54]	And the stalk-like Gaels of Connla's plain

The size of the human population itself also needed regulation. Warfare and disease incurred losses amongst the population, but there is also evidence that other measures were taken to limit population growth. As it was felt that individuals only function healthily when the integrity of the community itself is intact, most primal societies see little choice but to practice abortion and infanticide in order to stabilize their population. An eighteenth-century visitor to the Highlands reports that Lycopodium selago was taken by pregnant girls in order to induce abortion.[55] It is also possible that infanticide was practiced when necessary, for the motif appears in a number of Gaelic folk-tales.

Many parts of the landscape were inhabited by supernatural beings who required that humans respect their homes and, if they entered them at all, that they obey the regulations for use.

> There is a Valley between two Mountains on the East-side, called Glenslyte, which affords good Pasturage. The Natives who farm it, come thither with their Cattle in the Summer-time, and are possessed with a firm Belief that this Valley is haunted by Spirits, who by the Inhabitants are call'd the great Men; and that whatsoever Man or Woman enters the Valley, without making first an entire Resignation of themselves to the Conduct of the great Men, will infallibly grow mad.[56]

Not all supernatural beings were as beneficent or generous, however. There were two supernatural beings called Dàibhidh and Mòr that inhabited a hill in Glen Urquhart. They disapproved of the nearby villagers taking their cattle to summer pasture on their turf. After driving the cattle away a number of times, they became so incensed that Dàibhidh pulled up a large tree by the roots and chased off the men and beasts with the words:

Is leam-s' Doire-Dhamh is Doire-Dhàibhidh,
Is Boirisgidh bhuidh' nan alltan,
Is Ceann a' Chnoc mòr le fiodh is le fàsach:
A bhodachaibh dubh daithte, togaibh oirbh![57]

Doire-Dhamh and Doire-Dhàibhidh belong to me,
As well as bright Boirisgidh of the streams,
And great Ceann a' Chnoc with its woods and wilderness:
Go away, you black and singed wags!

The ecological consequence of such taboos and beliefs is that sanctuaries of unhumanized land, or at least lands with minimal human impact, can be maintained. Such spaces encourage bio-diversity, supply a refuge for wild animals and uncultivated plants, and provide an 'Other' with which to contrast the domesticated landscape. Such sanctuaries will be explored further in the next chapter.

There is also evidence of restraint in hunting practices. The most basic one was a recognition that hunting should be restricted to the bright months, between *Bealltainn* and *Samhainn*. The doe and hind were protected during snow fall, when they came to lower ground to feed, and custom sought to ensure that they were left alone to breed during the appropriate time of the year.[58] Just as important is that the hunter adopt the proper respect for life and not kill needlessly. 'My father never went out to kill a heavy bag. Such things were never boasted of in those times as now, when a man who shoots, say, one hundred brace in a day is looked up to as quite a hero.'[59]

An elaborate ceremony for the hunter in older times was recorded by Alexander Carmichael, explicitly naming what animals he was allowed to kill and which he should let go.

> A young man was consecrated before he went out to hunt. Oil was put on his head, a bow was placed in his hand, and he was required to stand with bare feet on the bare grassless ground. The dedication of the young hunter was akin to those of the *maor*, the judge, the chief, the king, on installation. Many conditions were imposed on the young man, which he was required to observe throughout life. He was not to take life wantonly. He was not to kill a bird sitting, nor a beast lying down, and he was not to kill the mother of a brood, nor the mother of a suckling. Nor was he to kill an unfledged bird, nor a suckling beast, unless it might be the young of a bird, or of a beast, of prey. It was at all times permissible and laudable to destroy certain clearly defined birds and beasts of prey and evil reptiles, with their young.

An tràth a dhùineas tu do shùil	The time you shall have closed your eyes
Cha lùb thu do ghlùin is cha ghluais	You shall not bend your knee or move
Cha leòn thu lach bhios air an t-snàmh	You shall not wound the duck that swims
Chaoidh cha chreach thu h-àlach uaip.	Never shall you bother her brood.

Eala bhàn a' ghlugaid bhinn	The white swan of the sweet gurgle
Odhra sgàireach nan ciabh donn	The speckled dun of the brown tuft
Cha ghearr thu it' as an druim	You will not cut a feather from their backs
Gu la bràth air bharr nan tonn ...	Till doom's day, on the crest of the wave ...
Chan ith thu farasg no blianach	You will not eat fallen fish or fallen flesh
No aon eun nach leag do làmh	Nor one bird that your own hand does not fell
Bi-sa taingeil leis an aon-fhear	Be thankful for the one
Ge do robh a naodh air snàmh.[60]	Even though nine may be swimming.

There is also evidence of a totemic system in which people inherited a special kinship to a particular type of animal for which they felt great empathy or else whose fate they were tied to. The best known example is that of the MacCodrums, who were said to be the descendants of a union between a seal-woman and a human man. There was a woman of the MacCodrums who, according to tradition, 'used to be seized with violent pains at the time of the annual seal hunt, out of sympathy, it was supposed, with her suffering relatives.'[61] Because of their kinship, no MacCodrum would ever kill a seal.

Another example comes from the now-depopulated island of Rum whose leaders appear to have had special affinity to the deer.

> The Mountains have some hundred of Deer grazing in them. The Natives gave me an account of a strange Observation, which they say proves fatal to the Posterity of Lachlin, a Cadet of Mack-Lean of Coll's Family; That if any of them shoot at a Deer on the Mountain Finchra, he dies suddenly, or contracts some violent Distemper, which soon puts a Period to his Life. They told me some Instances to this purpose: whatever may be in it, there is none of the Tribe above-nam'd will ever offer to shoot the Deer in that Mountain.[62]

Totemic restrictions appear in early Irish literature as aspects of the *geas*, special ritual prohibitions which are almost invariably broken by the hero and which bring about his ultimate downfall. These *gessi* were particularly 'attached to every member of the society interacting with the Otherworld',[63] those people who mediated between the human community and supernatural powers.

Such mythopoeic ways of understanding the cosmos, however, are broken down by the dynamics of a cash economy. 'The Indian's own religious values had been eroding from the day they began to hunt for foreign exchange instead of sustenance ... Do not sell that which I have placed on the earth for food.'[64] Nineteenth-century writers in the Highlands saw a similar exploitation of the landscape and its flora and fauna with the development of commercial fishing and hunting.

> And now, instead of those happy, exciting times, there are horrid bag nets all round the coast, which keep up a melancholy stream of fish, all going to London in exchange for horrid, filthy, useful lucre. My father, luckily for him, died ere the Gairloch salmon came to such degeneration.[65]

Humankind and nature

The development of modernist culture saw the gap between human civilization and the natural world widening into an unbridgeable chasm. In empowering the 'lords and possessors of nature', modernist thought has adopted the conceit that we are not an integral part of nature, but far above it, and that our own interests outweigh those of other forms of life.

> In early modern England the official concept of the animal was a negative one, helping to define, by contrast, what was supposedly distinctive and admirable about the human species. By embodying the antithesis of all that was valued and esteemed, the idea of the brute was as indispensable a prop to established human values as were the equally unrealistic notions held by contemporaries about witches or Papists.[66]

As people of modernist society – especially urbanites – became increasingly alienated from their animal relations, they depicted other peoples who lived in symbiosis, or at least close quarters, with animals as being animal-like in nature.

> By the sixteenth century it had become customary for the English to boast that they kept their domestic stock at a distance; they despised the Irish, the Welsh and the Scots because many of them ate and slept under the same roof as their cattle, 'very beastly and rudely in respect of civility', as a contemporary put it.[67]

Primal societies, however, believe that humankind is not the highest authority in the universe but shares the world with many forms of life with whom they have mutual interests and responsibilities, and a fundamental kinship.

That the Gaels took great delight in the natural world around them and were keenly aware of its many aspects is abundantly evident in the oral tradition. There is a huge number of proverbs dealing with weather lore which attest to close observation of the correlation of weather patterns and other natural phenomena, including the activities of animals. '*Tha an seillean fo dhìon: thig gailleann is sian* (The bee is sheltered: bad weather is coming); *Ge toil leam an ròn, cha toil leam naidheachd an ròin* (Although I like the seal, I don't like his tidings (since he comes ashore before storms))', and so on.

There are remarkable imitations of birds and animals in Gaelic verse which carefully duplicate their sounds and rhythms and their perceived characteristics. These were learned by generations of Gaels in order to allow them to identify the wildlife in their environment.[68]

Other traditional lore encapsulates the properties of herbs, especially for health and healing, such as, '*Lus Phàra liath, cuiridh e a' ghiamh as a' chnàmh* (Gray St Patrick's herb (grundsel) will take pain from the bone).' Martin Martin took particular pride in the traditional herbal lore of his Gaelic people, advising the scientists and physicians of the late-seventeenth century to investigate the traditional medicine of the Western Isles.

> The Inhabitants of these Islands do for the most part labour under the want of Knowledg of Letters, and other useful Arts and Sciences; notwithstanding which Defect, they seem to be better vers'd in the Book of Nature, than many that have greater Opportunities of Improvement. This will appear plain and evident to the judicious Reader, upon a View of the successful Practice of the Islanders in the Preservation of their Health, above what the Generality of Mankind enjoys; and this is perform'd merely by Temperance, and the prudent use of Simples ... A Man of Observation proves often a Physician to himself; for it was by this that our Ancestors preserv'd their Health till a good old Age, and that Mankind laid up that Stock of natural Knowledg, of which they are now possess'd.[69]

Rather than seeing themselves as existing outside of, or above, the world of plants and animals, primal people often sought to form bonds with these organisms in order to gain their characteristics or allegiance. Human individuals or kin-groups often bear animal-names, sometimes as an aspect of totemism, other times simply because of some perceived resemblance.

Many personal names in Gaelic derive from animal names: *Calum* (dove), *Rònan* (Little-seal), *Conan* (Little-hound), *Oisean* (Little-deer), and others. There are also traces of a custom of naming a child after animals. 'It is alleged (in Arran) to have been an ancient Highland custom, before surnames, to call a child by the name of the first thing which attracted the notice of the baptismal party on their way to church.'[70] This is very like the reading of omens according to what was encountered on the way to any significant enterprise, a practice common in Gaelic society until recent times.[71]

Some of the early tribal names in Scotland derive from animals and still continue in clan and territorial designations in present-day Gaelic. One of the peoples who dominated the far north were the Cat-people, and hence *Innse Cat* (Cat-isles) for Shetland, *Cataibh* for Caithness and part of Sutherland, and a whole host of Cat- place-names in the north. *Morair Chat* is still the title of the duke of Sutherland.[72] Another examples are the Orc (Whale- (or boar-) folk) for whom Orkney is named, and the horse-folk of Kintyre.

Other later clan names are also derived from animals: *Clann Chatain* (the cat-clan), *Mac Mhathain* (bear's son, 'Matheson'), *Mac Each[-thighe]arna* (the horse-lord's son, 'MacEachern') and a few others. There are many traditional animal nick-names for the communities of the Highlands, sometimes used as taunts or compliments, but often descriptive of some feature or habit of the people. '*Daimh mhòra Radharaidh, Buic Srath Ghairbh, Fithich dhubha Loch Carrann, Clamhanan Loch Bhraoin* (the big oxen of Raddery, the bucks of Strathgarve, the black ravens of Lochcarron, the kites of Lochbroom)'.[73]

Warriors often ornamented their weapons, shields, and armor with representations of fierce animals – especially boars, hounds, and eagles – and many such animals, possibly used as heraldic devices, can be seen on the elaborately carved Pictish stones. Warriors sometimes took animals names to themselves to dramatize their ferocity. The war-cry of the Camerons, '*A Chlann nan con, thigibh an seo is gheibh sibh feòil* (O clan of hounds, come here and you will have flesh)', is said to derive from a battle between the Camerons and the Robertsons.

Further suggestions of a previous totemic system in Gaelic society come from the evidence of dream-lore. Although the particular symbols may have differed from place to place, there are fragments of a system of interpretation of animals in dreams which is paralleled by other Gaelic lore and heraldry. A dream about a cat was taken as signifying a MacPherson or a Macintosh, both septs of the *Clann Chatain.*[74] A pig signified the Campbells, who have a boar in their crest and who according to later popular tradition were descended from Diarmad of the Fianna, who was killed by a boar.[75]

There are also examples of organisms with which the destiny of a family, dynasty or clan was twinned, so that the destruction of one heralded the extinction of the other. The tree is a particularly common marker of fate, and this may be a development of the ancient Celtic belief in the *bile* (sacred tree) as the *axis mundi* of the tribe.

> A well known prediction about the family was long current, to the effect that when the last son to succeed his father as hereditary smith should die, an old elm, whose mighty boughs overshadowed the smithy, would fall ... On the night that the old grandfather lay a-dying, a wild storm swept down the Glen. In the morning he was dead, and the elm lay prostrate before the smithy door.[76]

It has already been noted in Chapter Three that the organisms of the natural world had been divided into categories of noble and non-noble in traditional Gaelic cosmology, and that representatives of these categories could be used to convey praise or dispraise on account of these associations. This may be illustrated by contrasting two poems, the first an elegy for Alasdair MacDonald of Glengarry:

Chaill sinn darag làidir liathghlas
Bha cungbhail dìon air a chàirdibh;
Capall-coille bharr na giùthsaich,
Seabhag sùlghorm lùthmhor làidir ...

Bu tu am bradan anns an fhìor-uisg',
Fìreun as an eunlainn 's àirde;
Bu tu leomhann thar gach beathach,
Bu tu damh leathann na cràice ...

Bu tu 'n t-iubhar thar gach coillidh
Bu tu 'n darach daingean làidir
Bu tu 'n cuileann 's bu tu 'n draigheann
Bu tu 'n t-abhall molach blàthmhor

Cha robh do dhàimh ris a' chritheann
Na do dhligheadh ris an fheàrna;
Cha robh bheag annad de'n leamhan …

We have lost our mighty grey oak sapling
Who protected his kin;
The capercaillie of the pine-forest,
The vigorous, bright-eyed, mighty falcon …

You were the salmon of pure-water
An eagle from the highest aviary;
You were the lion who excels other creatures,
You were horned, broad-shouldered stag …

You were the yew above every forest
You were the mighty steadfast oak
You were the holly, you were the blackthorn
You were the rough-barked, blossoming apple tree
You had no relationship with the aspen
Or any alliance with the alder
There was none of the elm in you …

The second is a satire of Dr Samuel Johnson, written by one of many Gaels displeased with the comments he published after his trip to the Highlands. Derision is poured upon him by exploiting the ignoble associations of various animals and plants.

Gur tu an losgann sleamhainn tarr-bhuidh'
'S tu màigean tairgneach nan dìgean
Gur tu dearg-luachrach a' chàthair
Ri snàg 's ri màgaran millteach.
'S tu bratag sgreataidh an fhàsaich,
'S tu an t-seilcheag grannda bhog lìtheach …

A-measg nan iasg 's tu 'n dallag-mhùrlaig,
A' bhiast mhùgach sin mac-làmhaich,
'S tu 'n t-isean a meadhan na brèine
Am broc 's a shròn 'na chèir trì ràithean
A' mhial-chaorach dha'n ainm an t-sèalain …

Cha bu tu 'n draigheann na 'n cuileann
Na 'n t-iubhar fulannach làidir
Chan eil mìr annad de'n darach
No de sheileach dearg nam blàran
Tha 'chuid as motha dhìot de chrithinn
Ingnean sgithich is làmhan feàrna
Tha do cheann gu lèir de leamhan
Gu h-àraidh do theanga 's do chàirean ...[77]

You are the slimy, yellow-bellied frog
The horny toad of the ditches
You are the lizard of the bogs
Creeping and crawling in the grass.
You are the horrid caterpillar of the wild
You are the greasy, soft, ugly snail ...

In the fish-kingdom, you are the dog-fish,
That snuffling beast, the cat-fish,
You are the hatchling in the middle of stench
The badger whose nose is in his buttocks for three seasons
The sheep's parasite, the tick ...

You would not be the blackthorn or the holly
Or the strong, hardy yew
There isn't a trace of the oak in you
Or of the red willow of the fields
The greater part of you is made of aspen
Hawthorn talons and alder hands
Your entire head is made of elm
Especially your tongue and your gums ...

The assignment of ignoble status to particular species of the natural world does not necessarily mean that there was any attempt to extirpate them or squeeze them out of existence, however. The very existence of such a dichotomy is threatened unless both sides can be seen in opposition to each other.

Gaelic literature and oral tradition abound in symbolism and metaphor drawn from the natural world and reflect a profound sense of rootedness in the local environment. Poetry by the deer hunters of the old Gaelic world conveys a great deal of warmth and affection for the deer, and implies a bond of kinship between hunter and hunted. This can be seen, for example, in a remarkable piece of folk poetry attributed to *Domhnall mac Fhionnlaigh nan Dàn* from the sixteenth century, who asked to be buried in the skin of the last deer that he killed.[78] A short excerpt may convey the essence of the life of the hunter:

Nuair bhùireas damh Beinne Bige	When the stag of Beinn Bheag bellows
'S a bheucas damh Beinn na Craige	And the stag of Beinn na Craige roars
Freagraidh na daimh ud d'a chèile	Those stags will call to each other
'S thig fèidh a Coire na Snaige.	And deer will emerge from Coire na Snaige.
Bha mi on rugadh mi riamh	Ever since I was born I have always
An caidreabh fhiadh agus earb:	Been in the company of deer;
Chan fhaca mi dath air bian	The only skin colour that I have ever seen
Ach buidhe riabhach is dearg.	Is speckled yellow and red.
Cha do chuir mi dùil 's an iasgach,	I never had an interest in fishing,
Bhith 'ga iarraidh leis a' mhaghar;	To go seeking it with bait;
'S mòr gum b' annsa leam am fiadhach	I greatly prefer the deer-chase
Siubhal nan sliabh anns an fhoghar.	Travelling the moors in the autumn.
Is aoibhinn an obair an t-sealg	Blissful is the work of hunting
Aoibhinn a meanma is a beachd;	Blissful is its spirit and its meditation;
Gur binne a h-aighear 's a fonn	Sweeter the melody of it
Na long is i dol fo beairt.	Than equipping a ship.
Fad a bhithinn beò no maireann	For as long as I live,
Deò de'n anam ann mo chorp	As long as there is a spark of life in my body
Dh'fhanainn am fochair an fhèidh:	I will stay in the company of the deer:
Sin an sprèidh an robh mo thoirt.	That is the herd in which I put my esteem (rather than cattle).

Nature and traditional cosmology

Primal peoples see the universe not as a dead, mathematical model, but as a sentient entity, abounding with life which responds to the behaviour of its inhabitants. There is no distinction in Gaelic between 'natural' and 'supernatural': entities and forces whose existence is denied by scientific reason are held be to part of the natural order.[79]

There is in the Gaelic belief system the idea of an Otherworld which in some aspects mirrors our own world, and in other aspects is its complete antithesis. The Otherworld often intersects with our own, especially at liminal times and at sacred places. It is sometimes referred to as *an dà shaoghal* (The two worlds), a usage paralleled by a Gaelic term for Second Sight, *an dà shealladh* (The two sights).[80]

There are a number of accounts which testify to a belief in a sort of 'animism', that is, that everything has some sort of internal life-force, including what we would now consider 'dead matter'. The description of one of the last Gaels of Deeside, Walter 'Wattie Plants' Stewart, answers to this. 'He had no belief in physical laws. The whole phenomena of nature were the direct and immediate acts of spiritual beings. The government of the world was a disputed sway, and nature the battle-field between the two belligerent powers.'[81]

The writings of the Revd Robert Kirk of Aberfoyle in the seventeenth century also reflect a belief in animism. 'The Earth being full of Cavities and Cells, and there being no Place nor Creature but it supposed to have other Animals (greater or lesser) living in or upon it as Inhabitants; and no such thing as a pure Wilderness in the whole Universe.'

There are also examples of Nature attempting to maintain its integrity, despite the misbehaviour of humankind. The most common form of this belief is that holy wells move themselves if they are violated, and many examples from around the Gàidhealtachd have been noted.[82]

An example which I heard myself in Gaelic in Cape Breton will illustrate this. A man on whose land a well-known healing well was located decided to exploit this feature, a 'resource' which was, by tradition, to be freely shared by all. After he erected a fence around the well, intending to charge people for its waters, it dried up and reappeared some days later outside of the fence.

Some people interpreted a terrible flood in the year 1877 as vengeance against a rapacious landlord:

> The belief is common throughout the parish that the disaster is a judgment upon Captain Fraser's property. It is very remarkable, it is said, that all the destruction on Skye should be on his estate. What looks so singular is that two rivers should break through every barrier and aim at Captain Fraser's house. Again, it is strange that nearly all the dead

> buried in Uig in the last five hundred years should be brought up as it were against his house, as if the dead in their graves rose to perform the work of vengeance which the living had not the spirit to execute.[83]

Nature might simply withdraw her favours if not treated properly. This may be reflected in the proverb, common since the rent-racking of the modern economic regime and said of a number of places, '*Mur b'e eagal an dà mhàil, bheireadh Tiridhe an dà bharr* (If it wasn't for the fear of double-taxes, Tiree would yield double-harvest).' Perhaps more ordinary, but just as important in observation, is wisdom of the proverb '*Ma bheir thu an car a d' fhearann, bheir d' fhearann an car asad* (If you cheat your land, your land will cheat you).'[84]

Nature did, indeed, demand payment. People had to take care to offer a portion of the yields of their crops and beasts, sometimes literally the 'cream of the crop', back to the Otherworld forces. Payment was most commonly offered to the *sìthichean* (roughly corresponding to 'fairies' in English[85]).

> It used to be a common belief and saying in Islay that the top grain of corn on every stalk belonged to the Fairies, and this was confirmed by the fact that invariably at shearing time this grain was found to be wanting. The idea was that the Fairies had already taken it away as their own portion.[86]

Most areas had a stone upon which milk was offered to an Otherworld being, and the environs of these designated sites are said to have flourished all the more because of the practice.

> The allusion to paying 'the fairies their due on the fairy knowe' has reference to the custom, common enough on the western mainland and in some of the Hebrides some fifty years ago, and not altogether unknown perhaps at the present day, of each maiden's pouring from her *cuman-bleoghainn*, or milking pail, evening and morning, on the fairy knowe a little of the new-drawn milk from the cow, by way of propitiating the favour of the good people ... The consequence was that these fairy knolls were clothed with a richer and more beautiful verdure than any other spot, howe or knowe, in the country, and the lacteal riches imbibed by the soil through this custom is even now visible in the vivid emerald green of a shian or fairy knoll whenever it is pointed out to you.[87]

Retribution would be taken when the due was not paid. According to tradition, when Clan Ranald's new Protestant milkmaid began her service, she refused to recognize the 'popish' superstition of pouring milk libations on the stone. That same night the best cow in the fold was dead, and the cows gave blood, not milk, the next morning.[88]

The more sinister and devouring aspects of Nature are fully present in Gaelic tradition, especially in the form of the *cailleach* or *bodach* (female or male spectre) which inhabited many places in the landscape. Life is only possible because it feeds on other life, and thus Death is an ever-present condition of Life.

> In olden times almost every Highland hamlet had its hag, or *cailleach*. These extraordinary beings, whatever they were, according to common tradition, all frequented the wildest, weirdest, and most solitary parts of the districts where they were to be found, but yet very often such places as drovers, packmen, and travelers generally had from time to time to pass. An interesting feature of the belief in them was that while some of them were considered inimical, particularly to members of certain clans, others were looked upon as friendly.[89]

Rivers have a very long pedigree of reverence in Celtic tradition: 'That the continental Celts regarded rivers as divine appears from the names given them … [in Scotland] the feeling of divinity pervades and colours the whole system of our ancient stream nomenclature'.[90] The *cailleachs* and *bodachs* who personified such streams, however, were almost invariable baneful and required a certain number of human lives a year, as in the Lowland rhyme:

> Bloodthirsty Dee, each year needs three
> But Bonny Don, she needs but one.

The natural features of the landscape, being alive and commanding awe, could be engaged in poetic dialogue. While it sometimes is merely a poetic conceit requesting that some feature of the landscape, being an eyewitness to history, contribute its wisdom, at other times it appears to be a sincere form of address. At other times both sides of the dialogue merely echo human sentiment, though put in the 'mouth' of an animal, mountain, or other non-human entity.

A mid-eighteenth-century visitor to Ireland comments upon the composition of poetry to appease the capricious forces of a mountain, 'There is a custom among the country people, to enjoin every one that passes this mountain, to make some verses to its honour, otherwise, they affirm, that whoever attempts to pass it without versifying, must meet with misfortune.'[91]

One of a number of examples of poetic dialogue with nature from Scotland was composed by Domhnull 'Gobha' Siosal when he was leaving his homestead at the mountain called *a' Chìoch.* The poet takes advantage of the name of this mountain, for it means 'breast' on account of its shape.

Mi 'm shuidhe air a' Pholl-ruidhe	I sit here on Poll-ruidhe
'S m' inntinn trom fo bhonn bealaich …	And my thoughts are heavy at the foot of the path …
Chuir mo bhanaltrum cùl rium	My nurse-maid has turned her back on me
Chaill mi 'n cupan 'bha fallainn.	I have lost a wholesome drink.
Fhuair na Frisealaich còir ort	The Frasers have taken control of you
'S chaidh mis' 'fhogar le m' aindeoin.	And I have been forced out.
Ceithir bliadhna 's a fichead:	Twenty-four years:
Bha mi siud air do bhainne …	That is the time I fed on your milk …
'S tric a bha mi gu h-uallach	Many is the time I was playful
Air do ghualainnean geala …	On your fair shoulders …
'S fuar sèideadh do shròine	Cold are the blasts off your nose
Nuair a thòisicheas gaillionn.	When the storm begins.
(an sin fhreagair a' bheinn)	(Then the mountain replies)
De tha 'cur air mo phàiste	What is bothering my child
Rinn mi àrach gun ainnis? …	Who I raised without experiencing poverty? …

The image of the homeland as *muime* (nurse, foster-mother) is a common image in Gaelic nature poetry and reminds us of the mutual bonds and obligations formed in the course of fosterage in Gaelic society.

CHAPTER 7

Landscape and culture

Wilderness, civilization, and improvement

It seems strange to us, in an age when wildness and wilderness are praised and tourists go to places like the Scottish Highlands precisely to escape from 'civilization', to read the comments of visitors in earlier times. The English writer Daniel Defoe, sent as a spy into Scotland, wrote that the Highlands were 'a frightful country, full of hideous desert mountains, and unpassable except to the Highlanders who possess the precipices'.[1] Edmund Burt similarly wrote 'I verily believe there is not an Englishman, when he knew [the Highlands], but would think of a settlement there with more Horror than any Russian would do of banishment to Siberia.'[2]

It has been pointed out that the writing of Scottish rural history has been distorted by an Anglo-centric view. This was particularly established by the accounts of eighteenth-century English travellers which described the landscape as bleak and desolate, the agricultural methods primitive and inefficient, and the people lazy, ignorant, and stubbornly opposed to innovation.[3] This interpretation insinuates that the aberrant Scottish backwater only joined the ranks of civilization when it reformed itself according to English models of Improvement.

This view still pervades common attitudes about the Scottish landscape and land-use, which is not surprising given that standard Scottish school textbooks in the 1960s and 1970s began with statements claiming that pre-Union Scottish agriculture

> was backward in almost every respect ... Visitors from England, where agriculture was more highly developed than in any other country of Europe except the Netherlands, were much impressed by the backwardness of the farming and the poverty of the people.[4]

Neither the Gaels of Ireland or of Scotland developed cities, although monastic centres were a step in that direction. The Norse established what pre-Norman towns there were in Ireland along trade routes. The Gaels of Scotland never developed settlements corresponding to the burghs of the Lowlands.[5] The idea that the Gaels were culturally retarded and lacked the incentive to move out of the wilderness and into civilized cities appears as early as the twelfth century in the Anglo-Norman propaganda of Gerald of Wales.

> They live on beasts only, and live like beasts … While man usually progresses from the woods to the fields, and from the fields to settlements and communities of citizens, this people despises work on the land, has little use for the money-making of towns, contemns the rights and privileges of citizenship, and desires neither to abandon nor lose respect for, the life which it has been accustomed to lead in the woods and countryside.[6]

Such sentiments were expounded as a rationale for dispossessing the Gaels, such as in the 1610 tract by Sir John Davies.

> For if themselves were suffered to possess the whole country, as their septs have done for many hundreds of years past, they would never, to the end of the world, build houses, make townships or villages, or manure or improve the land as it ought to be; therefore it stands neither with Christian policy nor conscience to suffer so good and fruitful country to lie waste like a wilderness, when his Majesty may lawfully dispose it to such persons as will make a civil plantation thereupon.[7]

The 'wilderness' that European explorers imagined that they discovered when going to foreign lands was very seldom devoid of impact by humankind.

> The very word 'wilderness' in the sense of a natural landscape unaffected by human use has little meaning for most of aboriginal North America. To assert that Indians lived on pristine 'virgin land' not only ignores the human influences … but also 'naturalizes' Indians in a way that denies both their histories and their cultures.[8]

Likewise, to speak of the 'wilderness' of the Highlands is to neglect the ruins of Clearance villages, the crop furrows, sheilings, and signs of human settlement that permeate the landscape.

Although Gaelic culture has been separated from its Paleolithic origins for millennia, many of the general features of the Paleolithic worldview regarding Nature survived to a surprising degree.

Regarding the perception of Wilderness, Paleolithic Hunter-Foragers probably:

- believed that regardless of locale, Nature was their home.
- regarded Nature as intrinsically feminine.
- thought of Nature as alive.
- assumed that the entire environment of plants, animals, and landscape, was alive.
- inferred that divinity could be manifest in many forms and that metaphor and symbol was the means of divine access.
- believed that time was synchronous, folded into an eternal present.
- supposed that ritual was essential to maintaining the natural cycles of life and death.

Figure 7.1 (After Max Oelschlaeger 1991, p. 12)

There are two words one might use in Gaelic to express the concept of 'wilderness'. One is *dìthreabh* (that which is unplowed). The most common term is *fàsach* (that which is empty, i.e., of human habitation), semantically akin to 'desert' and 'desolation'. Gaelic cosmology contrasts the area of human activity – home and field – with the areas beyond normal human settlement, corresponding roughly to poles which Levi-Strauss referred to as 'the raw' and 'the cooked'.[9]

The differentiation between wilderness and community can also be examined from a social perspective. Culture is a means of imposing order and sense upon an otherwise chaotic and hostile universe. The order of the community is sustained not only by creating a physical layout on the landscape, but by enacting social regulations.

> The traditional community understood the world in terms of a distinction between itself and that which was outside ... A boundary by its nature orders, and order therefore became the defining criterion of the community ... Anything which upset the natural order of the community tended to be linked to the disorderly world outside.[10]

Unpredictable and potentially malevolent beings such as the *sìthichean* ('fairies') inhabited the wilderness and threatened to invade the community if the proper precautions were not taken. The violation of social and physical boundaries, either by disruptive internal forces or by intrusive external agents, could cause the disintegration of the norms of the community.

> I remember very vividly, when I was a little boy, seeing a wild hind grazing within the confines of the *baile* [homestead, or village]. Those who could read the signs realised that the natural order was being overturned and said: '*Se comhtharra cogaidh a tha seo* [this is an omen of war].' Not very long after that the Second World War began. That sighting, that metaphor of order invaded by the wild, helped those who witnessed it to arrange their experience.[11]

Behaviour could not be bound to the social norms of the community once one moved into the wilderness. The tales of the Fianna explored their lives as hunters and warriors in the wilderness, where they lived beyond the normal confines of the domestic community and could pose a threat to the order of the very society that they were meant to protect.[12]

The normal regulations of society were held in abeyance during death rituals. The keening woman in particular took on attributes which marked her as removed from the mundane order of society: she disheveled her hair, bore her breasts, drank the blood of the dead, and assumed the persona of one gone mad. This allowed her to stand outside the bounds of her community and to express her anger and pain without being confined by its codes of conduct.[13]

The ritual mourning of death is associated in Gaelic song with such common refrains as '*Dìreadh na beinne 's 'ga teàrnadh* (ascending and descending the mountain)'.[14] This reflects the journey of the dead beyond the bounds of community and the keening woman's transcendence of the boundaries of her society. 'In her self-presentation she acts out the disorder brought about by death, and her journey takes her not along roads but across country, through wild nature.'[15]

Town and country

Although a distinction was made between domesticated space and 'wild' space, houses were rather simple and transient affairs by modernist standards.

> The Gael has always been an outdoor man. 'Home' to him was the great outdoors, and his house was merely a convenient shelter from inclement weather. It was not an object of domestic luxury. Rather, it was a building erected to shut out the storm. In good weather it was normal to live out of doors ...[16]

There is no indication that the Gaels envied the Lowlanders in their cities. In fact, the Gaels took pride in their rural setting and disdained the mode of life of their neighbours. A common proverb in the Central Highlands was '*B' fhearr am meòg anns a' Ghàidhealtachd na am bainne blàth a bhiodh am Peairt* (Whey in the Highlands would be better than warm milk in the city of Perth).' Cathal Mac Mhuirich writes of the towns of their enemies as '*glórb-hailtibh Gall* (Noisy towns of non-Gaels)'.[17] The poet An Ciaran Mabach sang when in hospital in Edinburgh in the seventeenth century:

Ge socrach mo leaba	Although my bed is comfortable
B' annsa cadal air fraoch;	Sleep in the heather is better;
Ann an lagan beag uaigneach	In a remote little hollow
Is bad de'n luachar ri m' thaobh.	With my side against a tuft of rushes.

The praise of the superiority of the Highlands over the Lowland towns in later songs may be more proscriptive than descriptive. Many of the MacLeod chieftains that bardess Màiri nighean Alasdair Ruaidh praised in the late seventeenth and early eighteenth centuries were already becoming Anglicized and her poetry reminded them that they needed to stay loyal to their ancestral territory:

> *Cha b'e Machair nan Gall*
> *a chleachd thu, Fo d' bhonn*
> *Gionach no sannt Pàrlamaid.*
> *Bu roghainn dhut gleann, faghaid 'na deann*
> *Tadhal nam beann àrda dhut.*[18]

The Lowlands were not your haunt,
The greed and ambition of Parliament
Were not your habit,
You would prefer a glen, in pursuit of the hunt,
Frequenting the high mountains.

Many old songs extol life out on the sheilings and these usually are peppered with the names of places held dear to the poet:

Fhir a shiubhlas uam thar a' Bhealaich
Thoir uam soraidh gu Taobh Loch Eireachd
Gu Beinn Udlamain 's am bi 'n eilid
Gu Bràigh an Sgulain 's gu Loch an t-Searraich.

Là na h-Imrich nuair a dh'fhalbhainn
Rachainn timcheall air a' mheanbh-chrodh
Leiginn m' anail air a' Gharbh-Dhùn
'S air Lùb Bad Chearc gun caidlinn an-moch.

Nuair a thèid mi mach mu'n chabhsair
Leam chan èibhneas ceòl nan àrd-chlag:
An crodh a' geumnaich mach mu'n àiridh
'S a' ghrian a' tearnadh fo sgèith Beinn Eallar.[19]

O man who travels away from me over the Pass
Take my greeting to Loch Errocht
To Beinn Udlamain where the deer hinds are
To Bràigh an Sgulain and to Loch an t-Searraich.

When I would set off on the day of departure
I would go around the calves
I would take my rest at Garbh-Dhùn
And I would sleep late at Lùb Bad Chearc.

When I set out around the city streets
The music of the bells is no joy to me:
(I prefer) the lowing of the cattle on the sheiling
As the sun sets over Ben Alder.

The Gaels seem to have taken their exclusion from the gentler agricultural lands as a badge of identity and pride. One poet exclaimed: '*Cha dùth do Ghall àrd bheann a dhìreadh* (Lowlanders are not inherently disposed to climbing high mountains).'[20] The intrusion of Lowland life into the Highlands and Gaelic society is a subject of songs in the eighteenth and nineteenth centuries. When the York Company culled timber from the forests of Glenmore, the natives were provoked to sabotage their operations and to comment in verse:

Siud an gleannan rìoghail fallainn	Yonder is the wholesome royal glen
Ann am fanadh làn daimh	In which full-grown stags would linger
Mo mhollachd do'n phannail	My curses on the company
A chuir thairis a bharrachd.	Who took away its foliage.
'N àite an crònain anns an doire	Instead of deer crooning the thicket
Gu faramach mar b' àbhaist	Noisily, as they used to do,
'S e 's beus dhuinn nis anns gach badan	What is usual now in every grove
Slachdarnais Ghallda.[21]	Is the clamorous noise of foreigners.

The forest was an archetypal wilderness, an intermediary zone between the human world and the Otherworld. It was the refuge of wild animals and brigands (called in Gaelic *ceatharnaich-choille* (forest-warriors)) and the backdrop of Otherworld encounters. An outlaw from ordinary society was said to be *fo choill* (under forest).

Despite these darker associations, one of the most common metaphors for human individuals and society, as part of a very complex system of symbolism and kennings, is the forest. Shakespeare's image of the moving wood of Birnam is taken from this Celtic stock-image. It is found, for example, in this praise of the men of Braemar and of their chieftain, who, as their leader and protector, is depicted as the over-arching shelter of the forest.

Chan eil am Màr o cheann gu ceann deth
Ceann-fine idir ach Mac Fhionnlaigh
'S e fèin, no chlann aig, riamh cha d' ionnsaich
Cùl a thionndadh 'n còmhraig.

E mar chraoibh mhullaich dhuillich bhlàthail
Dh'fhàs gu h-ùrar dosrach làidir

Dh'fhàs gu geugach meurach cràchdach
Cha b' ann an gàradh Lònaig.

Dh'fhàs e 'n lios nan craobhan rìomhach
Mar dharaig àrd nan gallan dìreach
'S tha chlann mar choill' gun mheang gun chrìonaich
Nach lùb le siantaibh Lònaig.[22]

The only chieftain in Braemar, from one end
To the other, is MacKinlay,
And neither himself or his descendents ever
Learned to turn their backs to battle.

He is like the leafy, flowering, top-most tree
Which has grown strong, fresh, full of boughs,
Full of branches, limbs, and sprouts –
He is not to be found in Lonak's garden walls.

He has grown in the orchard of regal trees
Like a tall, straight oak sapling
And his descendents are like a flawless forest,
No rotten wood among them,
They will not bend in the bad weather from Lonak.

The forest represented the familiar 'eco-system' of kith and kin in this rhetorical system and the forlorn poet could bemoan his condition using these images:

'S mi craobh choimheach na coire
A bha roimhe seo 'n coille
'S cha bu doimheamh an doire as 'n do bhuaineadh[23]

I am the misplaced tree of the corry
Who was previously in the forest
And the grove from which it was taken was not troubled

Such conventions remind us to be careful about interpreting all Gaelic nature poetry, especially that containing tree metaphor, literally, for different layers of meaning and symbolism may be present. The celebrated poem written by the Tiree bard who found himself exiled in the forests of Canada needs to be analyzed in this light to appreciate its implications fully:

Gum bheil mi 'am ònrachd 's a' choille ghruamaich
Mo smuaintean luaineach, cha tog mi fonn:
Fhuair mi an t-àit' seo an aghaidh nàduir
Gun thrèig gach tàlant a bha 'nam cheann

I am here all alone in the gloomy forest
My thoughts are restless, I cannot be merry:
I am in this place unnaturally,
Every talent that was in my head has failed me

Marriage to territory

The ancient Celtic ceremony of the marriage of the chieftain to his territory has already been mentioned several times. That cults of the territorial goddesses were carried into Scotland from Ireland is demonstrated by the existence of Irish goddess names in Scotland: *Banba* (in names such as 'Banff') and *Ealg* (in the name 'Elgin').[24] Little survives to show that the Gaelic nation-state of Scotland developed a national goddess myth comparable to that of Ireland, however, and this may be due to socio-political discontinuities, as well as to Scotland not being a self-contained geographical entity.

There is evidence, however, that the smaller Gaelic subkingdoms had local tutelary goddesses to whom the local rulers were ritually married. The earl of the Lennox is celebrated by Muireadhach Albanach Ó Dálaigh as being a suitable mate for Leven, the goddess for whom the river, loch, and territory were named. When Eoin Mac Suibhne sails into his ancestral territory, the streams bid him welcome and the branches of the trees bow down to him.[25]

Particularly pertinent, however, is the lore surrounding localized Otherworld beings such as the *gruagach* and the *caoineachag*. These may be, at least in part, derivatives of tutelary land goddesses.

Many of the offerings of milk mentioned in the last chapter were given onto a stone dedicated to the local *gruagach*. 'There is hardly a district in the Highlands which does not possess a *leac gruagaich* … whereupon the milk libation was poured.'[26] While the *gruagach* is often credited with watching after the cattle herd from which the libations come, they also appeared to be specifically attached to 'families of name and note'.[27]

> The small island of Inch, near Easdale, is inhabited by a [*gruagach*], which has followed the MacDougalls of Ardincaple for ages, and takes a great interest in them. He takes care of their cattle in that island night and day, unless the dairymaid, when there in summer with the milk-cattle, neglects to leave warm milk for him at night in a knocking-stone in the cave, where she and the herd live during their stay in the island. Should this perquisite be for a night forgot, they will be sure in the morning to find one of the cattle fallen over the rocks with which the place abounds.[28]

The *caoineachag* (weeper), whose close relation is the *bean-nighe* (washer-woman), was a spectre who foretold death seldom seen but frequently heard keening before a death. She shares a common descent with the Irish banshee, who has been shown to derive from the territorial goddess who laments the death of her spouse, the king/chieftain, and by extension, all of those native Gaels who live on her 'body'.[29] Before the night of the Massacre of Glencoe, the local *caoineachag* caused a number of people to flee because of the warning in her song:

Tha caoineachag bheag a' bhròin	The little sorrowful weeper
A' dòrtadh deòir a sùla,	With her eyes full of shedding tears,
A' gul 's a' caoidh cor Chlann Domhnuill	Crying and lamenting the fate of Clan Donald:
Fàth mo leòin! nach d' èist' an cumha.[30]	Pity that the keen was not heard.

The Stewarts of Kincardine were said to have a being called the *Làimh-dhearg* (Red-hand) attached to them. In one anecdote this being took away the knives of the young heir when he went hunting and reprimanded him for killing too many of the deer of the spectre's haunts.[31]

The bond formed between territory and clan was particularly focused around the graveyards of ancestors.

> Particular clans had certain hills to which the spirit of their departed friends had a peculiar attachment. *Tom Mòr* was that appropriated to the house of Gavra, a branch of Clan Pherson; and *Orc*, another hill, was regarded by the house of Crubin, of the same clan, as their place of meeting in a future state, and their summits were supernaturally illuminated when any member of the families died.[32]

Courts of law, seasonal rituals, inaugurations, and festivities were regular causes for a clan to gather at some site of significance in their territory. Place-names significant either in clan history, or as gathering sites, feature in many of the slogans used by clans to call men to war.

The beings which inhabited places could sometimes be hostile, however, especially to particular kin-groups. The sea was personified as a woman. If a man drowned and his body was not found, the sea was said to want to keep him as her lover. The being which inhabited a wild area in the hills of Glenmoriston was called *Cailleach a' Chràich*, and she was particularly malicious to MacMillans and MacDonalds.[33] A poem describing the death of men in the snows of the forests of Gaick personifies the area as a hostile and wanton woman:

Gàdhaig dhubh nam feadan fiar
Nach robh ach 'na strìopach riamh –
'Na bana-bhuidsich a' toirt 's a lìon
Gach fear leis 'm bu mhiannach laighe leatha.[34]

Dark Gaick of the crooked, whistling glens
Who was never anything but a harlot,
A witch who would take into her net
Every man who would want to lie with her.

Clan names sometimes appear in territorial names, just as many chieftains had territorial sobriquets. *Dùthaich Mhic Aoidh* (MacKay Country) is the Gaelic nick-name for the area in the north of Sutherland once dominated by the MacKays. Strath in the Isle of Skye is called *Srath Mhic Fhionghuin* (Strath of MacKinnon) to differentiate it from all of the other 'strath's in Scotland.

The Gaelic word *dùthchas* does not correspond to any one word in English, but ties together a sense of inheritance and territory. One's *dùthchas* is one's set of hereditary qualities, one's culture, and one's homeland. The adjective *dùthchasach* describes that which is indigenous, native, and inherited, and the same word can refer to a native of some particular place. This demonstrates that place is integrated into a sense of identity and ancestry in Gaelic tradition.

It is also significant that in Gaelic tradition people belong to places, rather than places belonging to people. *Buinidh mi do* ... means 'I belong to ...', a phrase describing one's place of birth, commonly used in Lallans speech in the same sense.

Although most professional Gaelic poetry celebrated people, and most especially the leaders of Gaelic society, the praise of people is almost invariably accompanied by the praise of their homeland. It is also true that the praise of place hardly ever neglects to praise those living on it. A poet would only bother composing a satire about a place to insult those who belonged to the area. In the Gaelic worldview, people and place are inextricably linked.

A poem in praise of Kintyre from the eighteenth century provides a suitable example, for it begins by praising the land and ends by praising its people:

Soraidh soir uam gu Cinn-tìre
Le caoine dìsle agus fàilte
Gun àrd no ìosal a dhearmad
Eadar an Tairbeart is Abhart.

Banaltra Galldachd is Gàidhealtachd
Ge do thrèig i nis a h-àbhaist
Bha drùdhadh gach tìr d'a h-ionnsaigh,
Is cha dùraig aon neach a fàgail …

Is e a glòir 's a sgèimh thar gach aoinni,
A h-uaisle flathail rìoghail stàtail:
'S an cùirtibh maiseach meadhrach mùirneach
Bha an sinnseara cliùiteach 'gan àiteach.

Clann Domhnaill na fèile is an t-suaircis
'Gam buaine ceannas nan Innse:
Is cian bunadh na treibhe as uaisle
'S an tìr mhaisich bhuadhaich rìoghail.[35]

Send a greeting east from me to Kintyre
With sincerity and a welcome
Without neglecting places high or low
Between Tarbert and Dunaverty.

The nurse-maid of Gael and non-Gael,
Although she no longer follows custom
That once drew all lands toward her,
No one would wish to leave her.

Her crowning glory above all
Is her royal, stately nobility:
In merry, delightful, resplendent courts
Did renowned ancestors inhabit her.

Clan Donald of generosity and civility
Who long held sway over the islands:
The origin of that noblest kindred is ancient
In that lovely, royal, propitious land.

The sacred in the landscape

It is a universal idea that at the centre of each territory is some sacred focal point, an *axis mundi*, connecting the mortal world with the higher and lower powers.[36] The feature most often associated with this centre point in Gaelic tradition is the sacred tree and it is no coincidence that a *bile* (sacred tree) was associated with inauguration sites and early Christian dedications.

Several poets claim Scotland as a whole for the Clan Donald because they were said to control 'a house and a half of Scotland', a formula common in Gaelic lore.[37] What is significant, however, is the site of this house.

Sliochd nan Collaidhean garga	The offspring of the fierce Collas
Le'n do chuireadh Cath Ghairbheach	Who gave battle at Harlaw
'S Domhnall Ballach nan Garbh-chreach	It is Donald Ballach of the war-raids
Rinn Taigh nan Teud aig leth Alba 'na chrìch[38]	Who made Taigh nan Teud, the centre-point of Scotland, a boundary

This location, *Taigh nan Teud*, is traditionally the centre of Scotland and a claim to the centre symbolizes a claim to the whole territory.[39] *Taigh nan Teud* is close to the yew tree of Fortingall, the oldest living tree in Europe and undoubtedly a venerated site in ancient times. The place-name Duneaves (*Taigh-neimhidh* in local vernacular Gaelic) in this parish contains a word derived from ancient Celtic term *nemeton*,[40] designating a sacred place which commonly included trees or groves.

Many other *bile* and *nemeton* sites exist in Scotland, particularly in conjunction with seats of power, holy wells, graveyards, and sites associated with the early saints. In early Irish tradition, a *bile* was said to be an enormous tree, big enough to shelter the entire tribe and stretching high into heaven, and similar descriptions appear in the lore of some trees in Scottish tradition.

The *bile* is one of the most high status kennings of praise for a social leader. The use of this term implies a parallelism between the territorial function of the sacred tree and the social function of the social leader: the king or chieftain is the pre-eminent member of the tribe who shelters his people and connects them with the Otherworld powers. The seventeenth-century lord of Applecross is described with these images:

A' chraobh thu b' àirde anns a' choille	You were the highest tree in the forest
Thar gach preas bha thu soilleir	You were visible above every thicket
A' cumail dìon air an doire	Keeping the grove protected
Le d' sgèimh ghuirm fo bhlàth dhuilleag[41]	With your verdant beauty of blooming foliage

There were a number of trees or groves in Scotland, often located near other holy sites, which no Gael would consider tampering with. 'There is a small coppice near to the well, and there is none of the Natives venture to cut the least branch of it, for fear of some signal judgment to follow upon it.'[42]

The holy well was another common feature in the landscape. Such wells were resorted to for healing and were visited by pilgrims on the Quarter Days, which were believed to be the times when the water was most efficacious. A few of these wells are still visited and are typically marked by shreds of cloth left tied on nearby trees and shrubs.

There was once a practice of setting aside a designated portion of land, a portion which was dedicated to the Otherworld powers in thanksgiving. The names of this plot in Lowland tradition, such as the 'Guid Man's Field' and 'Cloutie's Croft', contain nicknames for the devil and demonstrate that this practice was perceived as being pagan.

> It was the custom throughout Scotland to leave a portion of land untilled, which was called, 'the good man's croft,' or 'the old man's fold,' a practice which the Elders of the Kirk in 1594, exerted their utmost influence to abolish, without effect.[43]

This practice is not well recognized in the Highlands because Gaelic culture in the agriculturally viable parts of the Highlands was quicker in disappearing than in other areas. It is evident, however, that it was practiced in Gaelic-speaking areas in the eighteenth and nineteenth centuries such as Highland Aberdeenshire.

> In a good many parts of the country there were pieces of land left uncultivated, though there was no natural obstacle to their being so ... In Congarff there were two such spots. They had a rampart of stones round them to prevent any man or beast from going over them. They had also to be some distance from water ... They were sprinkled yearly with milk on the first of April (O. S.). This oblation was to keep the evil one out of 'the hoose, the milk-hoose, the byre an' the barn'. If the guideman [farmer] crossed the forbidden ground, he lost the best tooth in his head ...[44]

When the layers of structure and symbolism which encrust the complex of ideas surrounding the *sìthichean* and Otherworld in Gaelic tradition are examined, it becomes clear that this is not a static belief system but a dynamic one. While there are undoubted continuities from the pre-Christian period to recent times, there have also been many times when new ideas have created new patterns and old beliefs have been forgotten, re-analyzed, and amalgamated with others.

It appears that the *sìthichean* were originally the pre-Christian Gods of the Gaels, for early sources tell us as much, and folk custom and belief into the twentieth century confirm their divine origins.[45] According to legend, the *sìthichean* live in a parallel world primarily accessible from round hillocks (plural *sìtheinean*) and mountains prominent throughout the Scottish landscape.

One of the most significant of these is *Sìth Chailleann* (Englished as 'Schiehallion'), a mountain revered by the ancient Caledonians. *Sìtheinean* are, however, omnipresent in the landscape and have such an arresting power upon the Scottish imagination as to enter Lowland lore largely unchanged from their Celtic origins. The people in the Lowlands of Perthshire and Angus, for example, believed that fairies lived in the Sidlaw hills (a place-name containing the Gaelic element *sìdh*) and were careful to protect their wives and children from fairy-abduction.[46]

While the *sìthichean* are not merely the dead, there are many points of contact between dead ancestors and the *sìthichean*.[47] Graveyards were often fairy haunts[48] and Robert Kirk goes so far as to equate the sites of *sìthichean* and the dead:

> There be many Places called Fairie-hills, which the Mountain People think impious and dangerous to peel or dis-cover, by taking Earth or Wood from them; superstitiously believing the Souls of their

> Predecessors to dwell there. And for that End (some say) a Mote or Mount was dedicate beside every Church-yard, to receive their Souls till their Adjacent Bodies arise, and so become as a Fairy-hill …

It is significant that burial mounds and ancient tumuli are notable features of many sacred tribal sites such as seats of power and clan gathering places. 'Graveyards are themselves focal points in the landscape and function as inverse omphali, sacred places which link this world to the one above and below.'[49] The festival of St Michael in South Uist was held around the burial ground in the middle of the island.[50] The gathering-place of the Stratherrick Frasers was *Tom na h-Iùbhraich*, a site containing a sacred yew tree and ancient burial ground. The clan met there for pronouncements of law and horse races, and a number of traditions of the *sìthichean* were attached to the place. Baron courts were held at *Tom nan Aingeil* ('Fire (or Angel) Hillock') in Killin, Perthshire, a site associated with the *sìthichean.*[51]

There is sometimes an overlap between the fairy-knoll and the good man's croft.

> In Kinchraige there was a knoll with a sandy slope and large old fir trees growing toward the summit which was always held sacred to supernatural influences. It was observed that anyone who ploughed on this mound was certain to die afterwards. When a farmer's cattle were dwindling away and dying a mystic fire was raised here and the cattle driven through the fire … the knoll itself [was called] the *dùn.* Once a large tree disappeared from the *dùn,* and was supposed to have been spirited away by the fairies to a neighbouring hillock or fairy mound. From the inhabitants of the hillock a local violinist named MacKillop professed to derive some of his best tunes.[52]

Other sites were conferred special status because of their association with magical creatures. The divine cow-goddess has a number of manifestations in Gaelic lore and one of these is the *Glas Ghaibhneann,* the cow of the smith Goibhniu who brought her inexhaustible milk-supply to those in need. This cow has literally left her mark all over the Highlands and Islands, and a poetic litany of place-names lists her favourite pastures in Skye:

Gleann Dail an Diùranais,
Gleann Uig an Tròntarnais

Gleann sgiamhach Sgàladail
Gleann àlainn Ròmasdail
Glacagan Beinn Tianabhaig
Is Slaopan mèadhaineach nan Torr.[53]

A white cow-goddess appears in a number of other guises in Gaelic lore, including as the goddess *Boand* for whom the river Boyne in Ireland was named.[54] This name is probably the root of the name of the river Boyne in northern Scotland.[55] According to clan legend, a white cow led the founder of the Macintyres to where he should settle his family.

A character called the *Cailleach Bheur* appears in many Gaelic folk-tales and she may be an amalgam of a number of different early Earth Goddess figures and archaic beliefs. As to her age, she used to say, '*Nuair a bha 'mhuir 'na coille 's 'na crìonaich/ Bha mise 'n sin 'am nìonaig òig* (When the ocean was a forest of shrivelled trees/ I was then a young maiden)'.[56] She was said to regain her youth every hundred years in the waters of Loch Bà until a dog pre-empted her bath, breaking the conditions of the magical ritual and bringing an end to her life.[57]

The *Cailleach Bheur* was so enormous that the waters of the Sound of Mull only came up to her knees.[58] There are a number of landscape features associated with her, some of which she was said to have created, such as the ruins of her abode in Tiree and the marks of her ploughing on *Sìth Chailleann.*[59]

The Gaelic landscape was full of sites and features which were deemed to be sacred, physically connecting people with their ancestors and with the mysterious forces of the universe. It contained places which were the focuses of reverence and reserved for divine purposes. It may be initially surprising that a number of these sites, holy since pre-Christian times and associated with pagan legend, were used as gathering places for Presbyterian Communions.[60] Such continuities, however, can be found in unexpected places and remind us that so many of the discontinuities in Gaelic society are very recent.

Place-names and place-lore

The Scottish landscape is notable for its extremely high density of place-names: every discernible feature – stones, clumps of trees, hollows, pools, streams, and so on – had a distinctive name to identify it. There are a number of practical reasons why this was so. People needed to be able to pinpoint any location in the landscape with great preciseness, particularly because they owned livestock which could be shifted over a wide range of territory.

Another significant characteristic of Gaelic place-names is the perceived correspondence between human body parts and landscape features. The word for practically every human feature could be used to describe a natural feature: *ceann* (head, end), *aodann* (face, surface), *gualann* (shoulder, mountain ridge), *bràigh* (upper chest, uplands), *cìoch* (breast, pointed hills), *druim* (back, mountain ridge), *tòn* (buttocks, eminence), *bod* (penis, stone pillar), *fèith* (vein, bog-channel), and so on. This practice makes the landscape understandable in human terms and reinforces the sense of the landscape as a living entity. A stanza from a variation of *Òran na Comhachaig* makes this analogy:

Loch mo chridhe sin, Loch Trèig	Loch Trèig, my beloved loch,
Loch mu'm faighear fèidh is earb	The loch around which deer are found,
'G am bheil an slios farsuing rèidh	Which has the long, smooth side
Mar gum biodh an taobh aig mnaoi.[61]	Just like the side of a woman.

The act of naming, for many cultures, is a cosmogenic act: naming is culturally tantamount to creation, explaining, and making manifest, the essence of that place. A landscape which has been endowed with names is a landscape which has been culturally domesticated and made intelligible. A tale explaining the origin of a place-name often relates to the formation of the place or some culturally significant event which happened there.[62]

These cosmogenic acts of naming are highly prominent in early Irish literature and also appear in Scottish Gaelic lore. One variant of a widely distributed folk-tale explains that Loch Ness was formed when the waters of a well overwhelmed a woman who went to it for water. When she saw that the flood had filled the glen, she said, '*Tha loch a-nis ann*', a pun meaning both 'There is now a loch' and 'Loch Ness is there.'[63]

Gaelic literature and tradition displays a preoccupation with place-names and the lore of places. The professional Gaelic literati created a learned genre devoted to it called *Dinnshenchas*. Place-lore pervades vernacular Scottish Gaelic tradition as well. Much local poetry is peppered with litanies of place-names. 'It is probable that mostly all the names connected with every countryside in the Highlands have been fashioned into rhyme.'[64] Such poetry rejoices in familiar places, demarcates clan territory, recalls history, and delights in the sound of names.

B' fhada thathaich mi na glinn	I visited for a long time those glens
Eadar Spé agus Pataig;	Between the Spey and Pattack;
Cha robh creag, no craobh, no linn	There wasn't a rock, tree, or pool
Feadh nan crìoch sin nach b' aithn' dhomh.[65]	Throughout that territory I didn't know.

Such place-lore functions as tribal myth, proving the veracity of legend by fixing it in the landscape and demonstrating the inter-relation of people and place by co-relating their histories. 'The landscape and the place-lore which was its reflex in tribal myth and history functioned together as an effective mnemonic index of a large part of native tradition.'[66] George Brown, one of the last Gaelic tradition-bearers of Deeside, was typical of those generations which inherited this store of local knowledge.

> His fund of this kind of lore seemed inexhaustible. There was not within the district the ruins or site of an old church or chapel regarding which he had not gleaned some legend. The names of hills, glades, glens, corries, streams, and even pools and rapids in the river, had each its legend which accounted for its origin or related some circumstance connected with it.[67]

The landscape was teeming with the memories and tales of ancestral deeds and the names of previous inhabitants, and people took pride in understanding their environment in terms of this place-lore. It is little wonder, then, that this place-lore is a reflection of the sense of place and identity.

> A man who loves his own hearthstone, and all it stands for, always carries into every conflict a principle of more sacred steadfastness than the homeless, nameless, characterless and hopeless outcast who has no anchorage for his soul ... When I was young we learned at our fireside the native names of our towns, rivers, clan and family names – our genealogy, the story of our people and the ideals which ought to be ours ...[68]

A number of anecdotes relate how local place-name rhymes were used to assert a person's belonging to a particular place or to boast of their knowledge of its environs. In a tale set in the remote past, a woman was kidnapped by pirate raiders and taken to their country as a servant. When one of her sons who does not recognize her comes into the home in which she is working and is about to be murdered, she warns him to leave. She proves that they are related and that he can trust her by means of a quatrain of place-name rhymes from their homeland:

Cille Mo Ruibhe fo sgèith a' chuain
Camus Fhionnairidh fhuar nam beann
Robasdan a' choirce ghlais
'S ann leam a b' ait a bhith ann.[69]

Cille Mo Ruibhe under the ocean's wing
Chilly Camus Fhionnairidh of the mountains
Robasdan of the green oats
How I would love to be there.

That people took the history in names seriously is attested by the fact that place-names containing references to the Fianna were cited as proof positive for their existence during the Ossianic controversy. '*Ata ainm nan ceudan àiteachan anns a' Ghàidhealtachd anns an robh iad 'nan còmhnuidh agus a' tathaich* (There are hundreds of place-names in the Highlands where they (the Fianna) lived and visited).'[70]

Place names and place-lore are vital resources in the articulation of Gaelic cultural experience and in the sense of nationhood:

> Partly through genealogy, partly through lists of allies and through place-names there is generated in this poetic tradition a complex sense of territory, not just the territory to which the poet belongs but also a sense of a more extended territory which is at the least potentially friendly ...
>
> The poetic 'map' which the bards draw with place-names is comparable with the 'map' of political unity. The native Gael who is instructed in this poetry carries in his imagination not so much a landscape, not a sense of geography alone but a formal order of experience in which all these are merged. What is to a stranger an expanse of empty countryside – magnificent or drab according to prevailing notions – to the native sensibility can be a dynamic, perhaps even heroic territory, peopled with figures from history and legend.

... The rhetorical systems which contain these elements, interlocking and lighting up, as it were, in their entirety no matter where we make contact, could not fail to keep alive the unity of the Gaelic nation.[71]

In an excerpt of a poem by William Ross, the poet beseeches the mountain Blàbhainn to tell him of the deeds of his ancestors, who belonged to this territory, although he himself was born elsewhere. The mountain, in turn, as the witness to his people and their history, tells of their relations:

O 's ionmhuinn leam na chì mi thall!	O wonderful is what I see over yonder!
Rìbhinn nam beann nach fann gruaim	Queen of mountains, of stern aspect,
'S dh'aithnichinn fèin do thulach àrd	I would certainly recognize your high peak
Ge cian a thàrladh mi uat.	Even if I travelled far from you.
O! Bhlàbhainn àrsaidh, 's fàiltich' frìth	O ancient Blàbhainn, of welcoming forest,
Bhiodh mo shinnsear-s' annt a' sealg;	My ancestors would hunt in you;
Freagair dhomh le comas diamhair	Answer me privately,
O nach robh mi riamh 'gad fhalbh.	Since I have never traversed you.
'S labhair an tuairsgeul o shean	Tell me the story from olden times
Le bhith toirt fainear gach àm	By paying constant attention
O na lathaichean a chuaidh	To days past,
Dh'ionnsaigh an tràth thruaigh so th' ann ...	Up to the wretched times of the present ...
Ach chualas fathann grathuinn uam	But I heard something in the distance
Tabhann duanaig le guth fann –	Offering a verse with a weak voice:
'Bu truagh leam do ghlaodh bhith teirbeirt	'Sad to me that your call is dispersed
Mar chaora thearbaidh air chall.	Like a lost lamb separated from the others.
'B' eòl domh d' aitim 's b' ait am beus	'I knew your people, great their quality,
Bhith siubhal slèibhe gun sgìos;	Travelling moorland tirelessly;
Ach rè seal bha mise 'g iondrainn	But for a while now I have been missing
Torghain do bhuidhne 'nam fhrìth' ...'	The din of your people in my deer-forest ...'

William Ross is not merely making a poetic conceit: he is seeking to acquaint himself with the story of his people by learning the places and names which are an inseparable part of their history. It may be significant that many of those interested in Gaelic in recent times are hill-walkers and explorers who have become aware of the densely named landscape. The meaning and memories of these places are dumb and empty without Gaelic to explain them.

It is commonly said that the place-names of the western seaboard and the Hebrides are mostly Norse. While many of the larger features accessible from the ocean were named by the Norse during the era of their dominance, the vast majority of place-names identify small features and have been coined by Gaelic speakers in the post-Norse period. Even a cursory glance at a detailed map of the areas of strongest Norse influence, such as the coast of Lewis, shows that the majority of place-names are Gaelic and semantically meaningful to Gaelic speakers.

Sense of place

Among the other inventions of the British Imperial Age was the idea of the 'wandering Celt', a figure driven constantly around the globe just as restlessly as his supposed Aryan ancestors.[72] This is little more than a rationalization for the relentless harassment of Irish, Scots, and Welsh out of their homelands and into the distant colonies. Evidence for such an archetype is almost impossible to find in Gaelic sources, for attachment to home and sorrow for exile are the primary themes of this era.

A version of the popular tale of Deirdre written in a Scottish manuscript relates Naoise's joy upon returning to Ireland. ' "Better than everything is one's own native land," said Fergus, "for the greatest prosperity does not bring joy unless one sees his native land." "That is true," said Naoise.'[73]

People's beliefs and predilections are seldom expressed until they are challenged. The Clearances denied the Gaels the right to their homeland for the first time. It is no wonder that exile is the prominent theme of nineteenth century, and although it is sometimes full of feeble sentimentality and maudlin nostalgia, there can be little question that the trauma expressed is sincere.

Mun tàinig Diùc ann, no aon de shinnsir,
No Deòrsa rìoghail a rìoghachd Hanòbhair
Bha 'n t-eilean ìosal, bu lìonmhor àirigh
Aig clann nan Gàidheal 'na àite còmhnaidh.

Gach eilean ìosal, no beanntan àrda,
'S gach gleann bha 'g àrach nan Gàidheal còire:
Tha mòran fàs dhiubh, gun duin' ach cìobair
O Mhaol Chinn-tìre gu Taigh Iain Ghròta ...[74]

Before the Duke, or any of his ancestors, came
Or King George from the kingdom of Hanover
The low-lying island, full of sheilings,
Belonged to the Gaels as their habitation.

All of the low-lying islands, and high mountains,
And all of the glens which nourished the goodly Gael:
Many of them are empty, except for a shepherd,
From the Mull of Kintyre to John O Groat's ...

Attachment to homeland was particularly expressed in the desire to be buried amongst one's ancestors.

> Of all people Highlanders think most of the reverence due to their dead, and of the privilege of being under the shadow of the old place of worship while living, and when dead of being buried in ancestral graves. In their minds old churches and churchyards seem to unite the living with the dead of many generations.[75]

The London government, aware of the Gaelic attachment to place and code of honour, made banishment to the colonies one of the penalties of breaking the 1746 Act of Proscription. The oath stated

> I ... do swear, and as I shall answer to God at the great day of judgment, I have not, nor shall I have in my possession any gun, sword, pistol, or arm whatever, and never use tartan, plaid, or any part of the Highland garb; and if I do so, may I be cursed in my undertaking, family, and property, may I be killed in battle as a coward, and lie without Christian battle in a strange land, far from the graves of my forefathers and my kindred; may all this come across me if I break my oath.

The laments for sailors dwell morbidly on the condition of the body, torn by the sea without proper interment. The elegies for Gaels who died away from home display anxiety about the place of their burial.

Och is mis' th' air mo sgaradh	Och, how I am grieved
Nach tug iad thu thairis	That they did not take you across
Dhol air tìr air an Ealaidh	To land in Ealaidh
Dhol fo dhìon anns a' charraig	To go safely into the headland
Ann an reilig nam manach	In the holy burial ground
Mar ri d' athair is do sheanair,	Along with your father and grandfather
Is ioma treun laoch a bharrachd	And many brave warriors besides,
Far am faodamaid teannadh mu d' chàrnan.[76]	Where we would be able to gather around your cairn.

There are also numerous anecdotes about the lengths to which people went in order to return to their homeland so that they could die there and be buried among their ancestors. A woman of ninety-one years of age came from Strathbraan (in the Highlands) to visit her daughter living in Perth (in the adjacent Lowlands). Although she was healthy when she arrived, she came down suddenly with a fever.

> One evening a considerable quantity of snow had fallen, and she expressed a great anxiety, particularly when told that a heavier fall was expected. Next morning her bed was found empty, and no trace of her could be discovered, till the second day, when she sent word that she had slipt out of the house at midnight, set off on foot through the snow, and never stopped home till she reached home, a distance of twenty miles. When questioned some time afterwards why she went away so abruptly, she answered, 'If my sickness had increased, and if I had died, they could not have sent my remains home through the deep snows ... God forbid that my bones should lie at such a distance from home, and be buried among *Goill na Machair* [the Lowlanders].'[77]

Such beliefs testify to a strong attachment to place and the marked uniqueness of places. Although many emigrants rejoiced in their freedom from tyranny during the Clearances, many others chose to stay and to raise their voices in protest against the injustices which inflicted them and their country. A common sentiment is that the wheel of fortune will eventually turn in favour for the Gaels, and that they will have a chance once again to repopulate their homeland. A Strathglass poet expressed this using the ubiquitous tree imagery:

Tha mi an dòchas gun tionndaidh a' chùis mar as còir
Gun tig iad a dh'ionnsaigh an dùthchais bho thòs;
Na fiùranan àlainn chaidh àrach ann òg
Gun cluinneam sibh 'thàmh ann an àros nam bò.

Ged a thuit a' chraobh-mhullaich 's ged a fhrois i gu barr
Thig planndais a stoca an toiseach a' bhlàiths;
Ma gheibh iad mo dhùrachd mar a dhùrachdainn daibh
Bidh iad shuas an Cnoc Fhionn 's e bhur dùthchas an t-àit' ...

Cha b'i 'mhachair bu taitneach le na Glaisich dhol ann
Nuair a thigeadh an samhradh, ach bràighe nan gleann
Bhiodh aran, ìm, agus càise, 'gan àrach gun taing
Crodh-laoigh air an àirigh, bliochd is dàire anns an àm.[78]

I hope that the matter will be resolved so that justice prevails
That they will return to their original *dùthchas*;
Those handsome saplings who were raised there,
May I hear them inhabiting the grand-hall of the cattle.

Although the top-most tree has fallen, and it has been stripped completely
New growth from its stock will come with new warmth;
If they are granted all that I would hope for them
They will be up on Cnoc Fhionn, as that is their *dùthchas* ...

It is not to the Lowlands that the Strathglass folk would wish to go
When the summer comes, but into the hills
They would live on bread, butter, and cheese
Calves would be in the sheilings, dairy and calving all in good time.

Observant Gaels realized that the Highlands and Islands were being increasingly subject to policies unconcerned about, and even hostile to, Gaelic sensibilities and that such policies would in the long run assimilate both people and place.

> We need, to-day, to see to it that our land is not made a playground for strangers without thought of our history or our personality – or that our people are not to be compelled to become lookers-on at a

> picnic, gathering up what trippers leave behind them ... Kinlochleven and Inverlochy, springing up around the Aluminum and Electric Power industries, and the National Afforestation Schemes, bring all kinds of alien influences among our people, with forms of thought and speech and outlook entirely at variance of our own, and these must be watched and guided lest them become denationalizing centres.[79]

The world is increasingly characterized by *anomie*, a sense of alienation, rootlessness, and placelessness as people are moved around the globe like uniform machine parts according to the needs of 'economies' and their homelands are transformed into shopping malls, freeways, business parks, and suburbs. Gertrude Stein is reputed to have said of the American city of Oakland: 'When you get there, there is no there, there.'[80]

Our attitude to nature and its subservient relationship to the whims of human desire is institutionalized in our commodification of land and exploitation of resources. Professing 'respect for the Earth' while we allow such material processes to continue is hypocritical and we surely cannot allow this alienation to continue forever. Environment is fundamental to human existence and territory is fundamental to cultural development and identity. 'We cannot separate our place on earth from our lives on the earth, nor from our vision nor our meaning as a people.'[81]

The Gaelic poet Iain Crichton Smith comments about the anomie of modern society:

> The urban world in which so many inhabit is not in itself an attractive one, and it is quite possible that the contradictions in society itself are so deep that it may not be able to supply its own people with the necessities of life. Nor will anyone be satisfied with the impression of sordidness that he gets from traveling through British cities, the breakdown of transport, the graffiti which shows the aggression of the 'homeless,' the language of hatred, ferocious and misspelt, the feeling that one has of an urban world breaking down: the rushing from late trains to vandalised telephones, as if this was a land where people no longer feel at home.[82]

The current phase of techno-consumer culture threatens to cover the globe with a computerized control system, yet the very success of this enterprise will inevitably undermine its foundation, and that of life upon the earth.[83] Wilderness, and wildness, are necessary complements to human civilization and were conditions necessary for the evolution of humankind.[84]

Although we may assume to have conquered Nature and to have evolved beyond it, our connection to it has proven crucial in our continuing struggle to understand ourselves and our future. Henry David Thoreau's statement that 'In wildness is the preservation of the world' is not an irrational attempt to escape from reality but a profound insight into the human condition.[85]

The *sìthichean* are associated in Gaelic tradition with the wilderness and the area beyond human cultivation, and the Otherworld often appears as a metaphor for the Unconscious and the human creative faculty.[86] It is therefore interesting to note how native Gaelic associations of the wilderness – physical and metaphysical – correspond to more recent ideas of wilderness as the source of life and imagination in human ecology. Carl Jung wrote, 'Deep inside us is a wilderness. We call it the unconscious because we can't control it fully so we can't will to create what we want from it. The collective unconscious is a great wild region where we can get in touch with the sources of life.'[87]

The belief of most portable, multinational religions is that this world is a place of suffering and misery and that we are waiting to be taken to some heavenly paradise. This is not too different from the techno-utopian belief that our savior, science, will grant us a better life on some other planet or in a virtual reality. This is quite different from the views of most primal peoples, affectionately attached to their motherland and rooted to their locale by myth and ancestral spirits.

CHAPTER 8

Language

Language is a highly complex phenomenon which can be analyzed from a number of different vantage points: as an historical artefact, it can reveal cultural events and interactions with other linguistic groups; as a cultural artefact, it reflects the worldview, values, and belief system of its speakers; as an auditory phenomenon, it is intimately related to music, song, and magic; as a creative medium for communication, it is the material from which story, poetry, and all sorts of narrative genres are built; and so on.

Our first language is often called our 'Mother Tongue', recalling our childhood and our sense of security within our family and community. The most personal and immediate impact of language extinction is the dissolution of those ties and a feeling of loss as a fundamental aspect of our own personal and cultural identity disappears.

When people, or cultures, lose their language, communication does not cease altogether: rather, they are pulled into another ethno-linguistic matrix. The transition from one cultural milieu to another is usually accompanied by all sorts of tension and mixed feelings: shame, achievement, disorientation, stress, guilt, and isolation. Such signs are visible in the Gaelic record accompanying the long conflict with the English-speaking world.

Historical developments

The study of the development of Gaelic has until recently been dominated by a view predisposed to treat the Munster Irish dialect – being closest to the high-register, literary form of Classical Gaelic – as 'standard', and other dialects as derivatives of this idealized form. Old Irish has commonly been considered to be a uniform language free of dialectical variants, and the period of Common Gaelic between Ireland and Scotland was imagined to unite the speech of the countries into the thirteenth century.[1]

Recent research is challenging such orthodoxies and demonstrating that divisions between Eastern and Western forms of Gaelic can be seen as early as the Old Irish period. Scottish Gaelic also shows marked affinities with Brittonic languages, in opposition to Western Gaelic features, but whether this is due to a Brittonic 'substratum' (that is, Pictish and Cumbric speakers whose original language influenced the way they learnt and spoke Gaelic) or to mutual interaction and development is not yet clear.

Although speakers may be biased toward their own dialects, Scottish Gaelic is surprisingly uniform, especially in contrast with the divisions between the dialects of Irish. John Francis Campbell, the nineteenth-century pioneer of folklore, said of his travels in Scotland:

> Speaking from my own experience, I can converse freely in Lorne Gaelic with Scotch Highlanders in every district of Scotland, and with natives of Rathlin … but though there are such shades of difference, a Highlander used to hear[ing] languages variously spoken should have no difficulty in understanding any dialect of Gaelic spoken in Scotland, and most of the Irish dialects.[2]

Any language is enriched when a large body of people use it, and the greater the range of domains which they are engaged in, and the greater level of registers which they employ, the more the language will be extended, developed, and diversified.

Some of the most learned people of Europe in the Middle Ages were Gaelic speakers. The Latin learning of Christendom found an early home among the Gaels, no doubt in part because they already had well-developed native institutions of learning. Classical learning was soon translated into vernacular Gaelic and instigated an era of intense intellectual activity.

A seventh-century scholar composed a grammar for Gaelic and a ninth-century scholar compiled an etymological dictionary, the first for any vernacular European language. For at least a century in the early Middle Ages, Gaeldom's Latin learning surpassed anything to be found in England, Italy, or France, and pupils came in flocks to imbibe it, learning Gaelic to do so.[3] We can be in no doubt, then, that Gaelic had developed a sophisticated vocabulary to deal with literature, linguistics, law, and other domains.

These fields continued to be developed and practiced throughout the Middle Ages. Gaelic is one of only four languages – besides Arabic, Greek, and Latin – in which the learned medical tracts of medieval Europe were written.[4] When the Protestant religion sought to promote itself in the Gàidhealtachd, the language of choice was this high-register Classical Gaelic. Gaelic vocabulary dealing with theological matters has continued to be highly developed and expressive.

It is important to emphasize that Gaelic was not a rudimentary language, spoken only by peasants and appropriate only for poetry and rural activities, but a sophisticated tongue with many registers, used for many intellectual and practical applications. If Gaelic seems impoverished and ineffectual in the modern age, it is only because the natural life-course of the language has been severely disrupted, suffering attack, neglect, a loss of speakers, and their domains of activity.

The invention of the science of historical linguistics in the seventeenth and eighteenth centuries was particularly concerned with the origins of languages and cultures. 'Primitive' people and their languages were considered to be closer to the source of things – which in the Biblically-oriented world-view meant the Ark and the Tower of Babel – and such 'primitive' languages were assumed to be closely related to one another.

While Gaelic antiquities, such as language, were worthy of recording and scrutinizing for their scientific value, they were not encouraged as living entities. Chapter Two has already discussed the provision in the Statutes of Iona which required all men of wealth to send their heirs to school in the Lowlands where they would be taught English, and the following legislation in 1616 which sought to replace Gaelic – identified as a primary cause of the barbarity of the Highlanders – with English. The establishment of the Society in Scotland for the Propagating Christian Knowledge in 1709 marks a renewed effort to systematically extinguish Gaelic.

The teaching of English was made a noble cause in the 'Progress' of the Highlands, which was assumed to bring with it civilization and easy union with the English. Daniel Defoe, in his reports from the Highlands to the English government, claimed that 'there is reason to apprehend that in a few Years, Ignorance, Popery and the Irish language will be utterly extirpated; and in their stead, Virtue, Loyalty, and Industry, will take place.'[5]

Little wonder, then, with such institutionalized attacks on Gaelic language and culture, that the men of the Gaelic learned order should try to formulate a response. The Welsh scholar Edward Lhuyd compiled the first comparative study of Celtic languages and a volume of his research, *Archaeologia Britannica*, was published in 1707, demonstrating the antiquity of the Celtic languages and the affinities between them. The preface to this volume contained a number of poems by people involved in his project, including three by Scottish Gaels who demonstrate a good mastery of the professional Gaelic poetic tradition. One of them, the minister of Kildalton in Islay, said of Lhuyd:

Do duisgeadh riot as an úaigh
An chanamhuin chruaidh do bhí faoi smál
Teanga bhí cían faoi gheasaibh ...

You have stirred from the grave
The hardy language that has been repressed,
The tongue that has long been held down ...

Another minister composed a more ambitious poem, stressing the antiquity of Gaelic in human history, summarizing the national origin legend, and lamenting the fall of the language from its once exalted position in Scottish society:

B'i bh' oide-múinte luchd gach dúthcha 's teangth'
Chuir Gaill is Dúbhghaill chuice an t-iúl 's a nclann.
Nois dh'fholbh si úainn gu tur, mo núar 's mo chreach,
'S tearc luchd a gaoil, b' e sud an saogh'l fa seach.
Thuit i 'san túr mar-aon le h-úghdraibh féin
'S na Flaith' mbudh dúth i, ghabh d'a cumhdach spéis.
Reic iad 'san chúirt i air caint úir ó n-dé
'S do thréig le táir, budh nár leo ngcán'mhain féin.
Air sár O Liath biodh ádh is cuimhne 's buaidh
Do rinn gu h-úr a dúsgadh as a h-uaimh.

She [Gaelic] was the educator of every country and tongue
Lowlanders and other foreigners once entrusted their children and future to it.
Now she has been lost to us completely, o my shame and my loss,
Few are those who love her, what a change has come upon the world!
She has fallen from the [Kingly] Tower, along with her authors
And the Princes for whom she should be a Mother Tongue, who used to love her,
In their courts they have sold her for a newly arrived language,

> Scornfully abandoned, they are ashamed of their own language.
> May goodly Lhuyd enjoy success, renown, and prosperity
> As he has newly awoken her from the grave.

To claim at the beginning of the eighteenth century that Gaelic was nearly dead is poetic hyperbole, but it is surely significant that the Gaelic intelligentsia realized the fall in status of Gaelic in the cultural life of the nation, and perceived that it was persecuted and threatened.

The most important intellectual figure to champion the Gaelic cause in the eighteenth century was Alasdair mac Mhaighstir Alasdair, a well-educated minister's son who was a central figure in the Jacobite Rising of 1745. He published a book of Gaelic poetry in 1751, hoping to raise the prestige of Gaelic and to entreat the people of the Lowlands to join with the Highlanders on new cultural enterprises. Although his thinking reflects the ideology of cultural evolution dominant in his time, the scope and ambition of his vision is remarkable, as is evidenced in his introduction to Gaelic poetry.

> Nor need it surprise any one, that this genius should be found among a people so remote from the commerce of nations famous for arts and sciences, and now relegated to an obscure, neglected corner, who considers, that the Celtic nation, of which they are a small, but precious remain, once diffused itself over a great part of the globe. From its bosom have issued the conquerors of Rome, the planters of Gaul, Britain, Ireland …
>
> It would be agreeable, to trace the progress of their genius as far as it is now possible to discover it, through all of its modifications and changes …
>
> An agreeable inquiry, surely! and one would not think displeasing, even to the inhabitants of the lowlands of Scotland, who have always shared with them the honour of every gallant action, and are now first invited to a participation of their reputation for arts …

One of the songs in this 'seditious' book, which is reported to have been burnt at the Mercat Cross in Edinburgh, is a eulogy to the Gaelic language. Although the poet indulged in some boastful exaggeration, he also drew on earlier poems and traditions about the language and was sincerely attempting to bolster self-esteem by recalling its glories in Scotland's past:

Mhair i fòs	Still she survives,
'S cha tèid a glòir air chall	And her sound will not be extinguished
Dh'aindeoin gò	Despite the guile
Is mì-rùn mhòir nan Gall.	And the ill will of the non-Gaels.
'S i labhair Alba	She was the speech of Scotland,
'S Galla-bhodaiche fèin	And even the Lowland rabble,
Ar flaith, ar prionnsaidh'	Our nobles, our princes,
'S ar diùcanna gun èis.	And our dukes, impeccably.
An taigh-comhairl' an Rìgh,	In the counsel chamber of the King
Nuair shuidheadh air binn a' chùirt	When the court sat for session
'S i 'Ghàidhlig lìomhtha	It was refined Gaelic
Dh'fhuasgladh snaoim gach cùis.	That resolved every issue.
'S i labhair Calum	It was the speech of famous
Allail a' chinn mhòir	King Malcolm Canmore,
Gach mith is maith	Every commoner and nobleman
Bha 'n Alba, beag is mòr.	Who was in Scotland, great or small.

The antipathy toward all things Gaelic was particularly accentuated by the association between Jacobitism and the Highlands and observers consistently commented on the oppression of the language. One Gaelic scholar wrote in 1778:

> But when I look back into the former times of the Gael, whose history a native might be supposed more immediately fond of, finding it so much involved in obscurity, or suppressed and obliterated by the policy of a neighbouring monarch, I could sit down and weep over its fall, execrating the policy of usurping invaders, ever destructive to letters, humanity, and its rights.[6]

It is not surprising in this post-Culloden era of cultural invasion that we see native Highlanders turning against the language of their ancestors and toward the language of prestige, English. All of the institutions in the Highlands – churches, schools, industry – reinforced the belief that Gaelic was primitive and useless, and that English was the language of Progress and success. The Revd Thomas Munro wrote of the people of Kiltearn in 1845:

> English being the language universally spoken by the higher classes, the mass of the people attach a notion of superior refinement to the possession of it, which makes them strain every nerve to acquire it; and it is no uncommon thing for those who have lived for a short time in the south to affect, on their return, a total forgetfulness of the language which they had so long been in the habit of using.[7]

With native Gaelic institutions swept away, and no base from which to create a counter-attack, the sense of inferiority inevitably grew with the ever-tightening grip of the English-speaking world.

> The language and lore of the Highlands being treated with despite has tended to crush their self-respect, and to repress that self-reliance without which no people can advance. When a man was convinced that his language was a barbarism, his lore as filthy rags, and that the only good thing about him – his land – was, because of his general worthlessness, to go to a man of another race and another tongue, what remained … that he should fight for?[8]

This shift in attitude did not change suddenly, or at the same rate, or time, in every locale. An anti-Gaelic journalist of the mid-nineteenth century noted, 'There is little doubt that they will stick bitterly to their Gaelic, as they do to other barbarous things.'[9]

A genre of song was created in response to the attacks on the Gaelic language. Poets in the eighteenth and nineteenth century wrote songs in praise of Gaelic, a subject which would not have occurred to earlier generations. Canadian Gaels who went away for a space of time to the English-speaking world for work and pretended to have 'lost their Gaelic' upon return. Poets ridiculed such pretensions and the functions of such songs must have included keeping the moral high ground for the Gaels and warning potential emigrants against such impious behaviour.

Saoilidh mi gur amadanachd	I think that it is foolish
Do neach a bhith cho stàrnail	For anyone to be so conceited as to
Ged bhiodh e 's na Staitean bliadhn'	Be away in the States for only a year
Gun dìochuimhnich e a' Ghàidhlig.	And to presume to have forgotten Gaelic.
Tha mòran ann ar dùthaich –	There are many in our land –

Tha mi 'n dùil gum bheil e nàir' dhaibh –	I think it is to their disgrace –
Gun Bheurla aca chuireadh a-mach an cù	Who don't have enough English to put out the dog
'S cha chan iad aon ghuth Ghàidhlig.[10]	But refuse to speak in Gaelic.

Language extinction can be likened to murder, if an invading society goes so far as to actually eradicate the population or physically replace the social mechanisms for language transmission. This scenario, however, seldom accurately describes language shift. Language extinction has also been likened to 'suicide', as though a language, on account of its own inadequacies, voluntarily decides to terminate its existence. This second scenario oversimplifies the social and cultural associations of language in the context of cultural invasion, and blames the victim for its failure to overcome the invader.

Under the English-only policies established by the United States government in the late nineteenth century in the schools managed by the Bureau of Indian Affairs, pupils were punished and humiliated for speaking their native languages. In the short term, however, this policy had little success, as many Native American communities were far from Anglo-civilization and had little incentive to assimilate. In the longer term, however, it did instill low-self esteem and discouraged resistance against the erosion of native language and culture. In the case of Navajo, for example, the language declined not during the reign of antagonistic education policies, but later when it was confronted with the expansion of Anglo-America.[11]

There is no doubt that children were beaten in school for speaking Gaelic. While this is often pointed to as the reason that Gaelic declined, it is not sufficient to explain changing linguistic allegiances, as persecution just as often cultivates rebellion. Rather, we should see memories of beatings in school as a symbol articulating the sense of oppression and injustice of alien institutions.

Extinction happens when people choose to stop speaking a language and not to teach it to their children. What we must question are the conditions under which such 'decisions' are made, the cultural forces which act on people's lives and form their opinions, and the consequences they face if choosing allegiance to their mother tongue. The twentieth century's greatest scholar of language shift, Joshua Fishman, notes that dislocation – physical, demographic, social, and cultural – typically presages language loss.[12] Language loss, then, is part of a severe catastrophe in the fabric of society.

In the case of Gaelic, cultural invasion and conquest were long established processes that infiltrated society from the top down and were built into nearly every aspect of Highland life. An allegiance to Gaelic has long meant marginalization, prejudice, and stigma, not due to any characteristics of the language itself, but because the dominant cultural forces in Britain have been Anglo-centric and anti-Gaelic.

Some of the responses to the Education Act of 1872 have already been noted, but efforts against the damage done by this legislation continue to the present. One response to the anti-Gaelic prejudice in schools exemplifies the difficulties of struggling with a culturally-invaded mind:

> Men who have drunk so deeply of the imperial springs of English diplomacy that not only can they witness the terrible plight of their own people with sublime equanimity, but they can, with equally supreme indifference, survey disruptive international forces that rock the whole world …
>
> The Gaels have no reason to be happy with such a gospel, although they have listened to it for a long time. And what applies to the Gaels here applies equally to the rest of the people of Scotland. The welfare of one is bound up with the welfare of all …
>
> This insidious virus has permeated our being and has given us an inferiority complex with regard to ourselves and our language, and a false standard of values with regard to everything. And when those to whom we should look for leadership, distinguished men, presumably wise and learned, reveal such distorted views and disseminate such deplorable doctrines, what can we expect from the common herd but confusion of ideas, despair, and inertness?[13]

It is not the languages of societies which are powerful, wealthy, healthy, and self-confident which die, but rather the languages of the dispossessed, the oppressed, the poor, and the dispirited. Thus, language recovery and maintenance are not merely linguistic exercises, but issues of social justice, particularly high priorities for societies recovering from cultural invasion. Reclaiming one's language is part of reclaiming one's self-worth and the redress of past injuries.[14]

Language and culture

While the term *Gàidhealtachd* is thought of in recent times as referring to the geographical Highlands of Scotland, it originally referred to a cultural space, that is, Gaelic-speakers and the places occupied by them, which extended into the geographical Lowlands in some places into the nineteenth century. Similarly, *Galldachd* referred to the Lallans-speaking people and the space they occupied. Only in recent times has the equation of Highlands and Gaelic-speakers, and Lowlands and Lallans-speakers, become fixed in both Gaelic and English tradition. Before this time, the term *Garbh-chrìochan* (Rough-country) was typically used to describe the geographical Highlands, and a' *Mhachair (Ghallda)* (the (foreign) grassy plain) to describe the geographical Lowlands.[15]

The Gàidhealtachd was determined by linguistic and cultural criteria. Gaelic speakers witnessing the extinction of the language on the mainland have made statements such as '*Chan eil an seo ach Galldachd an-diugh* (This place is un-Gaelic now)' to describe the cultural result of language extinction.[16] The poet Domhnull 'Gobha' Siosal pleaded that Strathglass be left as a Gaelic area and not be assimilated into English-speaking society:

Seall gur Gàidhealtachd Glais:	Observe that Strathglass is a Gaelic place:
Na dèan Galld' i le lagh[17]	Do not force it into being un-Gaelic

Into the twentieth century, Gaels spoke of the Gàidhealtachd as extending '*bho h-Irt gu Peairt* (from St Kilda to Perth)' and Gaelic-speaking communities survived in many places throughout this region. Some individuals lived long enough to be recorded by workers of the Gaelic Linguistic Survey, which operated from the 1950s to the 1980s, in peripheral regions such as Loch Lomond-side and Aberdeenshire.

The songs of the Clearances recognize the cultural assimilation that so often accompanies language shift and deplore the transformation of exiles.

Tha sliochd nan suinn a dh'àiticheadh
Na glinn ud a chaidh fhàsachadh
An diugh mar Ghoill gun Ghàidhlig ac'
Air sràidibh bhailtean móra ...

Nam biodh gach frìth air àiteachadh
Le fir tha srì ri bàtaichean

Bhiodh suaimhneas feadh na Gàidhealtachd
'S bhiodh fuaim na Gàidhlig beò innt'.[18]

The warrior race who used to dwell
In those glens which were emptied
Have lost their Gaelic and became foreign
On the streets of big cities ...

If each deer-forest were inhabited
By men who dealt with the boats
There would be tranquility throughout the Gàidhealtachd
And the sound of Gaelic would live there.

As the great 'container of culture', language reflects and propagates the world-view of the culture which uses it: 'language plays a central role in all knowledge and thought, indeed, in culture and therefore life'.[19] A number of examples of words have been discussed, such as *nàire*, *dùthchas*, and *Gàidhealtachd*, which illustrate a Gaelic perspective on the world and social relations which do not have any single equivalent in English (although they can be explained in English). Likewise, our examination of the usages of English words such as 'development' and 'improvement' revealed that they reflect modernist ideology.

The very attack on Gaelic was based on the premise that English would bring in its wake civility and Progress, whereas Gaelic

> maintains and fosters those ancient habits and modes of thinking, which repel what the people cannot be taught to consider improvements ... Opinions are formed in it, and consecrated by it; it constitutes, not only the vehicle of ideas, but almost the ideas themselves; and it will be in vain to attempt to change the current of thought and action in the Highlands, while the language is allowed to remain.[20]

Words are not discrete units as much as bundles of associations. Each language reflects the associations and conceptual categories of the culture which speaks it. As one example, Gaelic divides the colour spectrum up differently than the colour system in English, so that one colour word in Gaelic may correspond to two or more colour words in English, and vice-versa. No direct translation exists in traditional usages. Beyond this, colours can be used to describe qualities: *buidhe* (similar to 'yellow-white') can also be used to mean 'lucky' or 'grateful'; *bàn* (similar to 'white') can also be used to mean 'empty', and can imply holiness; and so on.

Language is the ideological glue that holds the matrix of culture together. When this glue is dissolved by some agent, and the fabric of society is unwound and absorbed by a new ethno-linguistic glue, the matrix takes on some new and different shape.

To use another metaphor, language is the map which makes the cultural landscape visible. When one does not have access to language, landmarks and culturally specific orientation are no longer discernible or navigable. While it may be possible to translate from one ethno-linguistic system to another, the integrated worldview and panorama is not directly accessible except through the original medium.

It would be unusual for a man who knows no French to claim to be a Frenchman or a woman who knows no English to claim to be an Englishwoman. Well into the twentieth century, the term 'Highlander' was understood to be not just someone who originated in the geographical Highlands, but someone who was a Gaelic speaker.

> What constitutes a Highlander? … I say those who are born in the Highlands and speak the language of the Highlanders are genuine Highlanders, and none others. To test this position, I venture to assert that the present Lochiel, by descent and birth the chief of a Highland clan, is not a Highlander; he is simply an English gentleman. He can enter into all the ideas, thoughts, tastes and emotions of Englishmen; but he is entirely cut off from any such intimate relationship with Highlanders so long as he is unacquainted with the language in which their thoughts are conveyed. I do not say this by way of blame to Lochiel, it is perhaps more his misfortune than his fault; indeed I believe he sees it as a misfortune to him, and has the manliness to acknowledge it.[21]

Such perceptions about the way in which language defines identity are not new in the Highlands, as the report of Edmund Burt in the first quarter of the eighteenth century about the town of Inverness shows: 'It is not only the Head borough or County-Town of the Shire of Inverness, which is of large Extent, but generally esteemed to be the Capital of the Highlands; but the Natives do not call themselves Highlanders, not so much on Account of their low [geographical] Situation, as because they speak English.'[22]

The sense of place discussed in Chapter Seven depends to a great degree upon understanding the language in which the place names were coined. A poet, probably in response to the Education Act of 1872, warned of the possibility of a day when people would not be able to pronounce or even understand the names of things and places around them. His warning is worth giving in some length:

Ochan nan och! an caochladh truagh
'S a' Ghàidhealtachd thig 's gach taobh mun cuairt
Ma thèid a cànain chaoin 'na suain
Le cion an t-sluaigh a labhras i!

Luchd-àiteachaidh nan gleann 's nan stùc,
Thaobh ainm gach nì is àite 's an dùthaich
An teangaidh Ghalld' chan urrainn lùb
Bidh iad gun tùr, gun aithne orr'!

Gach creag is sliabh, gach stùc is càrn
Gach lag is cnoc, is slios, is learg
Gach glaic is tulaich, eas, is allt:
Bidh iad gu dall is aineolach! . . .

Chan aithne 'chainnt, 's cha tuig a fuaim
Bho nì no àit' a tha mu'n cuairt,
Oir reic am parantan, mo thruaigh!
Iad uil' le'n uaill 's le'n amaideachd.

Rinn tràillean dhiubh do'n t-Sas'nach mhòr
'S an toirt fo chìs do chainnt a bheòil;
A' Ghàidhealtachd 'chur fo chleòc –
Nach cian an ceò a chaidleas oirr'! . . .

Beinn Cruachan fhèin as guirme snuadh,
Bidh 'cridh' fo chràdh ri tuireadh truagh
A chionn 's nach cluinn i chaoidh gu buan
Ach goileam cruaidh nan Sasannach.

Beinn Ghlòdh nan eag – cha bheag an t-ioghn'
A cridh' bhith goirt 's fo sprochd a' caoin'

'S nach cluinn i 'chànain mhilis chaoin
Bh' aig luchd a gaoil, na h-Athallaich.

'S Beinn Labhr', bidh i 'na lasair dheirg –
Ri luchd an fhoghluim bidh i 'm feirg,
A chionn 's gun mheall an sluagh le'n ceilg
'Gan cur an geimhlean Sasannach.

Gach creag is stac, gach sgorr is stùc,
Togaidh am fonn le co-sheirm ciùil
Gu tiamhaidh trom le mulad is tùrs
Chionn cainnt na dùthch' nach maireann i:

M'an tachair siud, a luchd mo spèis,
Grad èiribh suas ri guaillibh 'chèil'
A' boideachadh gu daingeann treun
Nach strìochd, nach gèill, 's nach tachair e.

Nach ceadaich sibh gum bi 'nur dùthaich
A' chànain ghaoil 'ga chur air chùl
Le tràillean leibideach gun fhiù
D'an ainm 's d'an cliù bhith fasanta.[23]

Ochan nan och! What terrible change could
Come into the Gàidhealtachd from all sides
If its gentle language is put to sleep
Because of the lack of people who speak it!

O inhabitants of the glens and peaks,
The Lowland tongue can't get around the
names for things and places in our country:
They won't understand or recognize them!

Every craig and moor, every peak and cairn,
Every hollow and hill, side, and slope
Every defile and knoll, waterfall and stream:
They will be blind and ignorant! …

They won't recognize the language, or understand the sound
Of the things and places around them,

Since their parents sold it all – woe is me! –
In their pride and foolishness.

They were made slaves to the great Englishman,
and yoked to his speech;
The Gàidhealtachd put under a veil –
Long does the mist rest over it! …

Even Ben Cruachan of greenest hue
Has a broken heart and grieves mournfully
Since it will never again hear anything
But the harsh chatter of English.

Jagged Ben-y-Gloe, little wonder her heart
Is sore and she keens sadly
Since she cannot hear the sweet, gentle
Language of her beloved Atholl-folk.

And Ben Lawers will be incensed –
She will be angry at the educational board
Since they deceived people treacherously
Putting them into English chains.

Every craig, precipice, peak, and cliff,
They will raise a wailing, sad chorus
in their sorrow
Because the tongue of the homeland perished:

Before any of that happens, o beloved people,
Rise up in support of each other,
Giving solemn and steadfast vows,
That you will never submit, and that it will not happen.

Never allow your country
To turn its back on its language
Because of worthless, dirty slaves
Who have the repute of wanting to be trendy.

Gaelic poets have always had a substantial role in maintaining and innovating the language, pushing its ability to express new ideas to the limit, keeping the vocabulary rich and flexible, and providing a rich store of literary allusions and precedents to draw from.

> Had it not been for the bards of the past centuries, we wouldn't have the Gaelic we have today … and when you have an interest in those kind of men, you like to understand what they've been singing or talking about. I think the bards keep the language going, and the day they go, goes our language, goes our heritage, goes our identity.[24]

It is little wonder that a great deal of the knowledge and literature of the Highlanders has gone to the grave with the language. About the Gaelic traditions of Deeside, it was commented:

> It is not difficult to assign a sufficient reason for the loss of this lore. A change of manners, of taste, or of occupation among a people does much to obliterate the recollection of a literature, born and bred in a state of society that has passed away and lost its interest. But more effectual than any or all of these is a change of language.[25]

Once the most vibrant and traditional of Gaelic communities in exile, the cultural integrity and vitality of Cape Breton was sustained by the strength of Gaelic itself:

> The degree to which the people have remained truly Highland may be measured by their retention of the Gaelic language. Only by retaining their language can the people preserve their oral traditions and their music; when they lose the language they lose with it much that marks them off from other people settled in the New World.[26]

It was similarly noted about the last Gaelic tradition-bearers in Newfoundland:

> The real identity was in the fabric of the people themselves: their language, their lore, their lifestyle, all woven into the very essence of their individuality. Most important of all to Allan's generation was the mother tongue. They realized only too well that the Gaelic language had been the vehicle for carrying their Scottish traditions from one generation to the next. With its rapid decline, the traditions it upheld would be forced to follow.[27]

For all this, however, it must be realized that while language provides the map to the cultural landscape, it is possible for the process of external acculturation to affect a culture so much as to make its landscape resemble that of another more dominant one. This cultural convergence is mirrored by linguistic convergence, so that the two languages become ciphers for the same ideas.

The process of linguistic and cultural convergence can currently be seen to be taking place in the Gaelic world, for example, in colour terminology. Rather than referring to different ranges of the colour spectrum, Gaelic colours are taking on the shades of similar English words, so that the two languages are becoming interchangeable ciphers for the same colour values.[28]

Prepositions are the most idiomatic elements in language, and the idiosyncrasies of each preposition must be learned in a new language. The preposition 'for' in English can correspond to the prepositions *air*, *air son*, *do*, *rè*, and a host of others in traditional Gaelic usage, depending on the particular meaning. At the present, however, it appears that many Gaelic speakers are settling into a one-to-one correspondence between most English and Gaelic prepositions, which would mark a dramatic break from the historical usages in the language.

While all languages are bound to change, they usually change at such a subtle rate that it is hardly noticeable during a single lifetime. It is clear that Gaelic is being rapidly influenced and changed by contact with the English language in every aspect, to the extent that the oldest and youngest speakers have a difficult time communicating with each other. This cannot be seen as a process of 'natural' internal innovation.

One of the reasons to maintain the language is to be able to access the immense wealth of wonderful literature and tradition which represent generations of accumulated wisdom and experience. Yet, the increasing gap in language may prevent transmission and comprehension of this material, which is not only emblematic of Gaelic identity, but implicitly expresses a Gaelic-specific worldview. From a cultural perspective, the consequence of this process is troubling.

It is disappointing to see that, at least thus far, there is little consciousness in the Gaelic community about these issues, and hardly any forum for discussing language planning and the results of linguistic divergence and convergence.

Music and language

One of the special features of Gaelic is its time-significant vowel system. Vowels can either be short or long in the amount of time that they are held,[29] and these lengths are semantically significant: the only different between *bàta* (boat) and *bata* (stick) is that the former has an initial 'a'-sound which is held longer than the latter.

This vowel system, along with the obligatory initial-syllable stress, forces speech utterances to conform to a particular rhythmic pattern. This contributes to Gaelic's characteristic cadences and speech rhythms.

Contrary to popular belief, music is not a 'universal language', but rather a culturally-specific construct which can vary widely in form, content, style, and purpose in different societies.[30] We must not blindly accept the aesthetics of Western art music, the dominant musical tradition in Europe for several centuries, if we are to understand the music of other cultures.

The biases inherited from Western art music include the assumption that music must be aesthetically pleasing, that it is simply a form of art, that it is meant to be performed by professionals and enjoyed by an audience, and that it can, and should, be recorded and learned via a written notation. Gaelic musical tradition follows the conventions of most others in the world in that music is seen as a functional part of ordinary life: all members of the community actively participate in it, learning and transmitting it orally.

The voice is the oldest and most basic musical instrument, and when researching the music of a nation, one should begin by examining the native song tradition. Heroic poetry can be found in societies around the world, and such poetry nearly always conforms to similar characteristics.

> Heroic poetry seems always to be chanted, usually to some simple stringed instrument ... This is quite a different art from the melodies which accompany lyric poetry, give pleasure for their own sake, and are as likely to obscure as to illustrate the words. Heroic poetry puts the words first and subordinates the music to them. What it uses is really no more than recitative. To use a regular tune like that of a song would have made the task of heroic poets much more difficult and have interfered with the clear presentation of the tales which they have to tell.[31]

This accords very well with what we know of the syllabic metres of the *filidh* and the survivals of Ossianic poetry in Scottish Gaelic. Donald Campbell, in his 1862 *Treatise on the Language, Poetry and Music of the Highland Clans* tells us, 'The airs of the historical poems were, properly speaking, not melodies, but a musical and pleasing style of reciting poetry.'[32]

It has already been mentioned that the Gaelic terminology for singing a song is the same as that for reciting poetry. 'The broad general principle is that the rhythm in which a song is sung is determined by the rhythm in which it would be spoken.'[33]

This reflects the fact that Gaelic songs are not merely pretty objects of art but specific thoughts which the singer is meant to communicate clearly to the audience. In his introduction to the *Killin Collection*, editor Charles Stewart notes, 'The words occupy the first place, the music only the second ... The words and music implicitly follow the idiosyncrasies of the language.'

Like many other cultures, although the music was subservient to the words, the tune was perceived as indivisible from the words which were married to it. The terms *luinneag*, *fonn*, and *sèis(t)* refer both to chorus vocables and the tune, as 'the separate concepts of words and music of a song did not exist.'[34]

Gaelic songs usually exist in variants, reflecting regional differences and personal styles. The fact that songs can be found in different forms does not mean, however, that Gaelic tradition accepts any change as equally valid: 'in each society limits are placed on musical creativity'.[35] Gaelic music has its own musical aesthetics which determine what 'dialectical' differences fall within its standards, and which go beyond them:

> The fact that an air could assume so many forms does not mean that it could assume any form. Some things were possible within the tradition: other things were not ... All we are entitled to ask is whether a version of a song is consistent with the tradition, and then to ask how good it is, judging by the musical standard of what is best in the tradition.[36]

While the vocables – sounds which are meaningless semantically – which can be found in Gaelic song, especially in the work song tradition, may not carry any semantic weight, they are nonetheless not random or insignificant. 'Gaelic singers feel a close association between the vocable refrain and the melody of the song – as if the vocables had a definite mnemonic function as far as the music is concerned.'[37]

The general principle is that vowel length is significant, with the same values as in Gaelic words, and that vowel position corresponds to pitch, the lower notes being articulated further back in the mouth. The pitch order (high to low) is i, e, a, o, u. This corresponds very closely to *canntaireachd*, the traditional oral mnemonic used to transmit and teach bagpipe tunes, a system which was far better suited to this purpose than 'standard' written musical notation, as nineteenth century collectors discovered.[38]

The pervasiveness of Gaelic song has already been noted. From the time their mother sang them to sleep with lullabies people were surrounded by the constant strain of song. As the Gaelic language itself is the foundation of the style of Gaelic song, so did language and song produce the idiom of Highland instrumental music. That is to say, the style of Highland instrumental music is based on the song tradition, for, as can be found in all folk cultures, instrumentalists were in the habit of playing tunes that they and their audience were already familiar with as songs.

This is particularly evident in the fact that the bagpiper took the place of singers when occasion called for it, and he must have taken the appropriate repertoire of songs into his collection of tunes. Parties of reapers are sometimes described as working to the sound of the pipes,[39] and there is no reason to doubt that he would have played the tunes of their reaping songs. When the practice of keening was effectively banned, the bagpiper led the procession and often seems to have adapted the music of the keening songs.

The *port-a-beul* (mouth-music) song tradition in particular was used for encoding tunes and learning them and many of the words to these tunes played on the fiddle and bagpipe have been preserved. The traditional Gaelic style did not vary whether one was singing, or playing fiddle or pipes.[40] Charles Stewart in his introduction to the *Killin Collection* describes the utility of this repertoire of song to instrumentalists: 'Every old reel and strathspey, being originally a *port-a-beul*, has its own words. Now, if you wish to play with genuine taste, keep singing the words in your mind when you are playing the tune.'

If there is any doubt that the Gaelic language formed the basis of the idiom of Highland instrumental music, one need only consider the stringent rules which govern Gaelic speech rhythms, and ask what the odds are that reel and strathspey tunes could accidentally correspond exactly to these speech characteristics. Indeed, one of the most unique characteristics of Scottish music, the 'Scotch snap', is paralleled in Gaelic speech and is most likely to have derived from Gaelic song.

The reliance of instrumentalists upon the Gaelic words as the source of their music has its corollary in the belief that instruments could be made to speak

Gaelic words. Given that the length and pitch of notes could represent particular vowels, and that other cultures with similar speech characteristics have developed talking musical instruments, this is within the bounds of possibility.[41]

> Of old the Highlanders believed that their pipers could actually communicate all requisite tidings by making the instrument almost speak the same as if by words. There are several traditions of parties having been rescued from danger and death by the distant warning notes of the *pìob mhòr*. In this there is nothing incredible to any who know the surprising execution with which pipers of skill can handle their chanters.[42]

One of the highest compliments paid to a fiddler referred to his ability to make the fiddle communicate as effectively as a Gaelic singer: 'I never heard any one who could make the fiddle speak Gaelic so beautifully!'[43]

With this close correlation between language and musical idiom, it is no surprise that fiddlers in Cape Breton, who preserved a particularly conservative Gaelic musical idiom and learned fiddle tunes via the Gaelic song tradition, recognize a change in style in the young generation of non-Gaelic speaking fiddlers. Without the anchor which the language and the song tradition provide, new generations are most likely to be drawn into the mainstream of English-language style fiddlers.[44]

Music is thus another example of the many aspects of Gaelic culture which are reliant upon language.

Bu mhòr am beud gum bàsaicheadh	It would be a great tragedy if this
A' chànain as fheàrr buaidh;	language of great worth should die;
'S i as treis' thoirt greis air àbhachd	It is most effective in a bout of wit
'S a h-uil' àit 'n tèid a luaidh;	wherever it is spoken;
'S i 's fheàrr gu adhbhar-gàire	It is the best for raising a laugh
'S as binne bhlàithe fuaim	It has the most melodious and warm sound
'S i ceòl nam pìob 's nan clàrsach	It is the music of the pipe and the harps
Luchd-dàn' is dhèanamh dhuan.[45]	Of the poets and the song makers.

Words, names, and magic

Humankind has been uttering magic spells for as long as we have been able to speak. Indeed, there is every reason to think that the practice of magic played no small part in the development of language and human civilization. 'The right use of words created for the first time a new world seemingly under human control: any departure from meaningful order, any confusion of tongues, was fatal to this magic.'[46]

As in many societies, people's daily tasks, and especially new, long, or difficult enterprises, were initiated by a blessing in traditional Gaelic society. 'They set about few actions all the year without some Charm or superstitious Rite interwoven.'[47] 'There were ceremonies and blessings for all the more important duties engaged in.'[48]

Those who defended Gaelic culture against charges of primitivism and superstition pointed out that Christian prayer works on much the same principle. 'Those that defend the Lawfulness of Charms call them a continued Miracle, which by Heaven's compassion to men's infirmities convey virtue.'[49]

> I think the ordinary mind may find it difficult to see wherein lies the difference between the simple-minded peasant who, with implicit faith in its efficacy, mutters a prayer with the view of stopping the toothache or curing a colic, and the modern ecclesiastic who, by a prayer, hopes to stamp out the influenza.[50]

The knowledge of names in primal societies is a form of power, for 'All things and beings are properly named'.[51] A name reveals the nature of something and can allow a person access to it and an understanding of it. The primal philosopher probed into the mysteries of the universe, at least in part, by dissecting and theorizing about names and words.

Early Gaelic literature shows a preoccupation with names and the origins of words. While these ancient attempts at etymology may not find the approval of modern historical linguists, they reflect a mytho-poeic approach to of the nature of names and the universe.[52]

Names could be invoked in order to assume the qualities and powers of the things they referred to. 'It was customary also with ancient practiced Magicians ... to change the names of ordinary things with those of Creatures that had some like operation to that which they designed to bestow.'[53]

Gaelic folklore warns that that names should not be revealed lest they give someone power over that thing or person. A child's name was not uttered until he or she was baptized, for it might be heard by malicious beings who would gain power over them by use of that name. Similarly, 'In the night time they will not call upon children by their name, least the Devil get power over them.'[54] A dog was thought to be a useful ally when confronted by a ghost, unless one mentioned the dog's name and allowed the ghost to thus control it.[55]

There are many variants around the Highlands of a folk-tale in which a man's magical enemy disables his weapons one by one after he mentions their names. It is only when he disguises the name of his dagger, which his opponent does not recognize, that he is able to use it to effect.

The universal idea of the 'Noa term' – a name used in order to avoid calling something or someone by their true name – is very common in Gaelic tradition and there may be a number of motivations for avoiding using true names.

The common word for deer is Gaelic is now *fiadh* (wild-thing), but this seems to be a Noa term in origin, perhaps used to avoid drawing the deer's attention. Respect was shown for the *sìthichean* by referring to them as 'the good people', although in reality they could be very malicious.[56] Smallpox, which took many lives until the nineteenth century, was portrayed as a comely maiden and referred to in Gaelic as *am Bòidheach* (the beautiful one),[57] perhaps as a way of avoiding her wrath. The Gaelic word for fire, *teine*, was avoided by many when referring to indoor flames, and instead the term *aingeal* was used. One person said that 'He felt if he should say *teine* that fire would be apt to come and put the place on fire.'[58]

We have already seen that from ancient Gaelic times kings and poets were expected to maintain truth and that breaching the bounds of truth brought about dire consequences. These ideas continued to resonate in Gaelic oral tradition until very recently.

A folk-tale recorded in the latter half of the nineteenth century describes how the judgment seat kicked, and the king's neck was twisted, when he pronounced false judgments. The identity of the rightful king, who was then but a mere shepherd, was revealed by his ability to utter truths and correct the king's mispronouncements.[59]

CHAPTER 9

Belief, tradition, and science

Highlanders have long been stereotyped as ignorant and superstitious, clinging on to rituals and beliefs abandoned long ago by more advanced civilizations. The undoubted cultural conservatism of Gaeldom made it the subject of inquiry by folklorists from the inception of the study of folklore in the nineteenth century, but we ought to question the negative implications of words like 'myth' and 'taboo' in the light of modern scholarship. Despite the dismissive attitude of Modernism to these social regulators, there is no doubt that they were key in the history of culture and the human intellect:

> In short, the whole sphere of early man's existence which the modern scientific mind, in its consciousness of intellectual superiority, rejects, was the original source of man's self-transformation from an animal into a human person. Ritual, dance, totem, taboo, religion, magic – these provided the groundwork for man's later higher development.[1]

By examining the content, context, and application of such cultural features, we can learn a great deal about the values and belief systems of the cultures that have created and transmitted them.

Custom, ritual, and belief in society

Customs and rituals are mechanisms which perpetuate a culture's order and organization and secure its value and belief system. Although the rituals of Gaelic society reflect aspects of its cosmological framework, we could also examine them in the organization and operation of society itself. One description of the celebration of *Bealltainn* reveals an important social detail of the ceremony:

> It was then the custom for each family in the district to receive a brand from the sacred fire to kindle the domestic hearth. But those who were in arrears of rent, had failed to pay their just debts, had been guilty of theft or meanness, or were known to have committed certain offenses against good morals were deprived of the privilege ...[2]

The eighteenth-century antiquarian John Ramsay of Ochtertyre offers the following rationale for this exclusion: 'If any of them had been guilty of murder, adultery, theft, or other atrocious crime, it was imagined either that the fire would not kindle, or that it would be devoid of its usual virtue.' Whether this explanation was a traditional explanation or Ramsay's own inference, the social function of such ritual was to renew the bonds of the community and to enforce the boundary between those inside it and those outside of it.

A similar anecdote in a semi-fictional account of *Oidhche Challainn* (New Year's Eve) as celebrated in a remote Highland glen recalls that two men were excluded from the festivities because of some crime committed. Their ostracism from the ritual made their sentence known to all in the community, and they appear to have left the area altogether after this event.[3]

The values of a culture may also be defended by the threat of supernatural retribution, so that 'superstition' is used as a higher law in ensuring the maintenance of social norms. Certain aspects of social life were under the guardianship of supernatural beings, such as the *Glaistig*:

> The *Glaistig* was also offended at littleness and meanness of mind ... Those who looked down on fools and people of weak intellect, or ill-treated them, she paid off by putting dust or soot in their meat. Akin to this was her punishment of neglect in servants.[4]

Even well-established standards of conduct were policed by supernatural agents:

> To tell a lie about anything meant practically to hand it over to the fairies. Should a needy person apply for charity in the shape of meal or milk, and the possessor deny the possession of such, the party would afterward find that the meal or milk had mysteriously disappeared.[5]

Anthropologists observe that the more dangerous or unpredictable activities of primal societies are those most likely to be accompanied by magic. These ritual activities and arcane forms of knowledge are meant to inform people of potential dangers, to help them avert disaster, and to ensure success. While practical knowledge, basic skills, and simple technology allowed mastery over some endeavours, one had to resort to the powers of magic to overcome more formidable hazards.

A good example of this is in Gaelic society is the reading of the *còmhdhail* (encounter). If a man was on his way to go sailing, or to war, and he encountered a person or animal, he might abandon the entire enterprise if the entity encountered was read as a bad omen. 'Much of the success in any work or enterprise is believed to depend on the [*còmhdhalaiche*], or first person or creature that presents itself.'[6] A common Gaelic imprecation was '*droch còmhdhail ort!* (may you have an evil omen-encounter)'.

Warfare was accompanied by rites and objects of magic. Soldiers, even to the First World War, were believed to be protected from injury by the *seun*, a magical spell of protection. Clans often possessed a *clach bhuadhach* (magic, or victory, stone) which they carried into war to help them secure victory,[7] and it might be noted that Robert the Bruce carried the *Brecbennach*, St Columba's reliquary, to Bannockburn for the same purpose. In traditional tales, warriors on their way to battle are often given advice – things to do, or places to avoid – by women who have magical foreknowledge.

Seafaring was another such dangerous activity and it is the context in Gaelic society which seems the most concerned with using Noa terms. Martin Martin provides a long list of customs and Noa terms observed by men while they were at sea, such as calling the island of Eigg only by the pseudonym *Eilean nam Ban Mòra* (the Island of the Great Women).[8] A number of charms and Christian blessings for ships departing for sea have been composed in Gaelic, one of them published in the 1567 Gaelic adaptation of the Book of Common Order.

Prophecy, divination, and second-sight are common phenomena in primal societies and help to reinforce the notion of a well-ordered universe knowable by people with the proper skills or talents. *An Dà Shealladh* (literally 'the two sights', but 'the Second Sight' in English) was considered a curse and not a blessing which could come unasked for, but people sought knowledge about future events or distant objects via a number of techniques.

There were a great number of portents concerning death and any number of signs observed in the recent past might be recalled later when a member of a community died. Other omens were less grim. When the hero makes his dramatic appearance in folktales, he is often told, 'It was foretold that you would come.' A seventeenth-century account states that signs foretelling the arrival of travellers were commonplace.

> Upon my landing (says he) the Natives receiv'd me very affectionately, and address'd me with their usual Salutation to a Stranger: 'God save you, Pilgrim, you are heartily welcome here; for we have had repeated Apparitions of your Person among us (after the manner of the Second Sight) and we heartily congratulate your arrival …'[9]

A description of 'prophecy' in Hopi culture is relevant to understanding its role in Gaelic society. 'Prophecy is not prediction, even though it purports to be so … It is a way of articulating and defining contemporary events within the context and language of "tradition".'[10] In Gaelic society 'a seer's vision or precognition did not imply that the event was predestined and absolutely bound to happen. In fact it was the seer's duty to warn of the approaching danger.'[11] Tradition was thus used creatively as a resource to inform society of events that could potentially occur so that people could act on, or against, them.[12] The authority of tradition was itself legitimized by such endeavours.

The fact that divination is less proactive than in earlier times seems to reflect the loss of self-determination:

> The individuals concerned [previously] had some freedom to take evasive action. But it is not so now, in the minds of those who believe in such matters … Fate is now fixed. Is this a reflection of Gaelic historical experience, which is so much an experience of ethnocide?[13]

The performance of songs and tales had important social and psychological functions. Storytelling is a ritual activity in most societies, and the choice of tale might depend on the occasion: on the eve before battle, stories of victorious warriors might be told; at a wedding, stories of elopement and romance might be told; and so on.[14] Song, dance, and other activities would accompany such stories. At a psychological level, these many forms of narrative can provide catharsis, light relief, guidance, affirmation, and subjects for introspection.

Although there are no longer any *cèilidh* houses at which to conduct research of this sort directly, the evidence suggests that such contexts had an important role in the socialization of members of the community. It was at such events that people related the narratives, in song or story, that expressed their united sense of identity and confirmed their worth within their community. Moreover, the genres of tradition propagated the worldview and value-system of Gaelic culture.

> Folktales contain an important didactic component, being closely allied with social strategies and life plans for those living within a given society. Looking at the deep structure of stories, researchers have found that they not only embody fundamental paradigms of the culture but often express the 'primitive' societies' concepts of universal truths which have served as guides, conscious and otherwise, to reciters and listeners throughout their lifetimes.[15]

These storytelling activities appear to contribute to the health of Navajo society both in their content and form:

> It seems to me arguable that the 'pretty languages' (by which my informant's daughter simply meant the especially beautiful words) of the Coyote stories may have a direct therapeutic relationship to the more all-embracing Navajo concept of well-being. Thus, the narrator of a Coyote tale, using beautiful language to express ideas conducive to a beautiful life (from a Navajo point of view), actually engages in that sense of well-being and applies it to his listeners as the story is performed.[16]

It is not too much to suggest that this was also the case in Gaelic society. When one examines the high-register language used by traditional storytellers and the delight in word-play to be found in their tales – alliteration, rhyme, runs, proverbs, archaistic phrases, and other devices – it is not hard to see that they are drawing upon the high-art of the Gaelic intelligentsia and ennobling their audience by their participation in what they knew was an elite art form.

Belief systems and peace of mind

Primal societies regulate their activities according to the rhythms of nature rather than the artificial regularity of the clock and calendar, giving themselves plenty of time for non-labour oriented activity. So long as they observe the proper rituals and tasks, there is no reason to feel any stress about the future but rather a sense of contentment and security. Likewise, for the Gaels:

> Charting and celebrating the recurrence of the seasons and their long-term constancy must have offered a kind of existential security for early peoples in the face of the terrible uncertainties of harvests, health and human nature. This order in nature was not something for which humans had to assume responsibility and so, unlike the Christian concern with personal damnation and salvation, it was not a cause of anxiety. There was a solid otherness to natural seasonal rhythms which must have imparted a feeling that social life had grown organically out of its framework …[17]

Although the modernist conception of the universe as a machine has enabled large corporate bodies to gain greater control over the material world, there are many ways in which individuals now exercise less control over their lives than in primal societies. We are no longer in direct control of our means of production, but are held hostage by some enormous, abstract entity called 'the economy' which reigns over most of the aspects of our lives. Our lives are now troubled with a stress unknown in primal societies.

The concept of personal free-will and self-determination is also a significant departure, for the attendant institutions of Modernism allow, in theory, greater control over one's environment and life than in primal societies. As we perceive ourselves to be individuals, empowered to achieve anything we desire, our personal responsibility for success and failure is much greater than in societies in which a person's role and expectations are largely governed by ancestry and by fate. Our life's journey is thus less certain and more vulnerable to failure and disappointment.

One of the many functions of the rich and complex layers of tradition which have evolved around the *sìthichean* (Otherworld beings) concerns human defects. It was believed that children could be stolen by the *sìthichean* and replaced by a baby who was sickly, ill-behaved, misshapen, or deformed in some way. Thus children who were in some way 'abnormal' were explained as having been changelings, and it was believed that being kind to the changeling would cause the real child, being nursed in the Otherworld, to receive similarly kind treatment.[18]

While such beliefs may seem irrational and self-deceptive to modernists, they contain both explanative power and psychological significance. In the present day, parents of physically or mentally handicapped children can be burdened by a deep sense of guilt for a child's state. By explaining such abnormalities as the consequences of actions outside human control, the weight of shame or guilt can be minimized.

It is a shock to those who know a person to see him or her transformed into a stranger due to mental illness or dysfunction. The abduction of a person by the *sìthichean* who is replaced by a physically identical 'dummy' seems a suitable way to describe a person who is now 'away with the fairies' mentally.[19] Preternatural abilities and mental aberrations, and terrible disasters, were explained in Gaelic tradition as bestowed by these Otherworld beings.

Human beings have a wonderful capacity for being able to hold mutually conflicting beliefs with equal conviction. Although the *sìthichean* have been partially rationalized within Christian cosmology by explaining them as the angels that fell with Lucifer when he rebelled,[20] many other aspects of these two belief systems cannot be reconciled easily with each other on the same terms and were believed independently of one another.

When an Irish clergyman was asked what his congregation really believed, he had three different answers: that they believed in the teachings of the Church and in divine reward and punishment after death; that when a human being dies, he dies as an animal dies, and that is that; that the dead remained in the churchyard malevolently watching the living.[21] Examples from Scottish tradition can be found for all three of these beliefs, and we shouldn't be surprised if a single individual expressed belief in all three of these at different times in different contexts.[22]

The anxiety in most primal societies that a person be properly buried, often involving a complex and costly ritual, is explained as important because it prevents the vindictive return of his ghost. At least from a psychological standpoint, such strong emphasis on burial rituals ensures that the living will come to terms with the reality of death and to complete the process of mourning.

Modernism describes the world in terms of atomic elements obeying universal scientific laws. This conceptualization does not necessarily enable people to deal with the challenges of their daily lives any more effectively than in primal societies which viewed the world as acted upon by beings and forces, explicable in terms of symbol and metaphor. A person who can only imagine the brain as a network of biological wiring, for example, is much less empowered to stop his nightmares and manipulate his dreams than a person who conceives of dreams in symbolic terms.

Thomas Hobbes dismissed life in primal societies as 'nasty, brutish, and short', and many modernists accordingly interpret non-industrial societies in these terms: all superstition is 'ignorance' and slavish adherence to irrationality, while science and progress liberate humankind from the shackles of unthinking tradition. While the more privileged in modernist society have been materially rewarded, progress has come with great spiritual and emotional deficits. It should be questioned whether the quantitative directives of modernist life and the endless cycle of overwork and passive consumerism are any more meaningful than the life-styles of primal societies in which members have direct control over the means of production and are in close communion with each other and their environment.

In primal thought, an individual is not merely an entity that lives, briefly, in a fixed space and time. Through ritual, story, and song, they can transcend the ordinary limits of time and be connected to ancestors and to descendants, to those who had come before and those still yet to come. They have a unique and vital role to play in family and community, sharing their joys and sorrows. They love their homeland and are nurtured by it. Because of the perceptions of the continuities of life, and an acceptance of its inevitabilities, they do not fear death with the same paralyzing anxiety as people in modernist society do.

To label this belief system as 'superstition', or even 'paganism', is to underestimate its grounding in the universal human experience, for nearly all cultures and religions, including many forms of Christianity, have reflexes of these fundamental Truths. Humankind seems to have an innate need for a connection with the sacred, for each society attempts to fulfill this need by re-imagining the divine according to its own aesthetics. Not only does this impulse seem to be deeply rooted in the psyche, the relationship between humankind and the environment is better served when a sense of the sacred is cultivated and humans do not presume themselves to be 'the measure of all things'.

'Folk' science and native epistemology

Some of the aspects of so-called 'superstition' demonstrate the same powers of observation and causal reasoning as can be found in modern science. The modernist typically underestimates the magnitude of the achievements of early humankind and the amount to which we still depend on the discoveries, inventions, and attainments of the Stone Age.

> Those who are still contemptuous of the errors of pre-scientific lore overlook the large accretions of positive knowledge that justified it; and this knowledge was often more important than the physical tools employed. Long before Bronze Age technics had fully utilized the earlier improvements in horticulture and agriculture, archaic man had done the preliminary work of exploration so well that except for a few plants like the cultivated strawberry and the boysenberry, all our present domestic plants and animals are Neolithic end-products ...[23]

The massive amount of information regarding the natural world in Gaelic tradition attests to many generations of observation, experimentation, and reasoning. Lore was continually practiced, refined, and passed on to succeeding generations, and should not be undervalued. Martin Martin gives us a few remarks about the manner of proto-scientific inquiry in the Gaelic world:

> Many of the Natives, upon occasion of sickness, are disposed to try Experiments, in which they succeed so well, that I could not hear of the least Inconvenience attending their Practice ... [One native herbalist] pretends to judg of the various qualities of Plants, and Roots, by their different Tastes; he has likewise a nice Observation of the Colours of their Flowers, from which he learns their astringent and loosening qualities; he extracts the Juices of Plants and Roots, after a Chymical way, peculiar to himself, and with little or no charge.[24]

He lists a number of traditional remedies and medical techniques of the islanders,[25] and clearly believed that their many observations about natural phenomena would impress his audience. Such experimentation was done in many aspects of life, as in this survey of the best source of fertilizer:

> There is a curious custom in Bernera ... They take the [sea]ware home and spread it on a little bit of ground, marking the place where it has been spread. This is a kind of test, and should that bit of ground yield a good crop that season, it is taken as a good augury for the season following, and when the time comes round for manuring the land they go to that part of the shore for their seaweed from which they had previously taken the test sample.[26]

Since pre-Christian times the Gaels have read omens from the flight of birds, *a' leughadh nan eun*, and to recent times birds have heralded significant events, especially changes in the weather. Although many different signs could be read to provide different sorts of information about the weather, birds were believed to be particularly good indicators. Given the climate-specific migrations of birds, such traditional lore is at least in part the result of sound patterns of reasoning.

All ancient people observed that the moon influenced the tides, and many peoples generalized the moon's influence over all liquids in living creatures. As early as the Greek philosopher Pliny there are recommendations that plants should be planted and harvested at particular phases of the moon. The most detailed account in a Gaelic context is by Gerald of Wales, who, although he was an Anglo-Norman, elaborates on these beliefs in his book on Ireland in a way which is compatible with the surviving Gaelic folklore.

> Indeed, Phoebe is to such an extent a source and influence on all liquids, that according to her waxing and waning she directs and controls not only the waves of the sea, but also the bone-marrow and brains in all living things as well as the sap of trees and plants. When she is deprived of her full light you will notice that all things lose their fullness.[27]

As discussed in Chapter Six, the belief in dangerous beings inhabiting the wilderness encouraged the maintenance of regions with minimal human impact. Another of the functions of such lore was to keep children and adults from wandering into unsafe territory. Such cautionary tales must have kept many people from crossing such regions unprepared and during dangerous conditions.

This is not to claim that all aspects of the Gaelic belief system correspond to modern scientific knowledge. What must be acknowledged is that traditional Gaelic ontology – the explanation of the ultimate nature of the world – is not inherently any less sophisticated or valid than that of modernist science. They operate in different value systems, and are geared toward different modes of production: Gaelic ontology is tied to a small-scale, kin-based, subsistence economy, while modernist science is part of the matrix of the large-scale exploitation of resources as practiced by specialized fields of knowledge.

The absence of a recognizable technical vocabulary does not necessarily imply that people in primal societies did not recognize, discuss, or manipulate complex concepts. Common sense alone dictates that intellectual giants the likes of Einstein or Da Vinci appear in every era of all human societies, but that the field of their endeavours is largely directed by the cultural foci of the societies they belong to.

We are only just beginning to realize that the native intellectual traditions of primal societies can be highly expressive and sophisticated, without requiring the technical jargon characteristic of modernist science. The absence of the terminology of modern psychology, for example, did not prevent Gaels from discussing the pathologies and dysfunctions of the mind – rather, a rhetorical system based on the metaphors of the Otherworld was used as a medium of discourse. It also appears that this same rhetorical system was used for expressing ideas regarding the unconscious and the creative faculty.[28]

Underneath the simple, tangible images and 'clichés' that typify the panegyric code runs a deep and quiet stream which has fed and shaped the Gaelic worldview and provided a framework for discussing the intellectual subjects relevant to Gaelic society. Although it is easy to recognize the use of kenning and metaphor in Gaelic literature to refer to concrete people and things, we need to be sensitive to the deeper layers of meaning and rhetorical systems which co-exist in this rich milieu.

The conventions of the panegyric code are not merely sycophantic flattery or idle poetic musings: they encapsulate the principles of Gaelic socio-political institutions using native concepts in which metaphor, physical reality, and cosmological ideal are interwoven and articulated using parallel language. This mythopoeic understanding of the cosmos allows all topics of discourse to be discussed using the same language, rather than creating terminology which artificially segregates human civilization and knowledge from the rest of nature.

An advocate of native Hawaiian epistemology urges that we 'validate other ways of knowing that are more empowering, more meaningful, more fun, and more rigorous in the kinds of ways that engender community, extend culture, and strengthen commitment to the things and ways of value.'[29]

Resistance against false 'progress'

It is often difficult for people in modernist societies to understand why their technology causes terrible disruptions in less 'developed' countries and why these countries may even resist such innovations. What may not be obvious to the modernist, who sees invention and innovation as worthy goals in themselves, is that technology is not free of the values of the society that produced it. 'Along with the thing comes the idea, and the idea is often culture-specific. Without the idea, without the worldview it represents, the object is often of little value or use.'[30]

Despite the fact that many human functions in industrialized society have been replaced by 'labour-saving' machinery and people have been effectively barred from leading productive lives, we continue to produce machines which are even more 'efficient'. Few other cultures have desired to create machinery when a surplus of human labour was available, and an anecdote from Gaeldom illustrates the same point:

> One of these was a young man of a very ingenious turn of mind. He spent years inventing a machine that would work on a principle somewhat like that of the powerloom which afterwards came ... he gave a demonstration to his neighbours and asked their opinion about the machine. One of them replied: 'Yes, you have invented a wonderful machine. It will make weaving easy. It will save a great deal of labour. But, believe me, in the days to come your name will be execrated for taking away the means of livelihood of so many poor people.' Next day, it is said, the young man smashed to pieces the invention ...[31]

There was also a long-standing resistance against the introduction of the spinning wheel in Gaeldom, apparently on account of pride of workmanship with the traditional methods:

> I myself knew of an old lady, not many years deceased, who would suffer no such complicated machines to enter her house; but kept eight good old women in her house, spinning on as many orthodox distaffs, to the last; and gave for a reason, what I believe is true, that the yarn, though more abundant, was never equally strong or even, when produced from a wheel, as that spun in the primitive mode.
>
> With this intrepid opposer of innovation died the good old faith in distaffs: but the smaller spinning-wheel, adapted to flax, had many enemies to encounter before it got a footing in the Highlands; which it never obtained till the country was disarmed [that is, 1746]; and the good women used to speak most pathetically of the '46, as the sad era which introduced little wheels and red soldiers into the country.[32]

When new foods are forced upon a population, it is often due to some change in economic circumstances. There was a rapid change of means of production in the mid-eighteenth century as the areas once used for sheilings were taken over by the new estate owners, Gaels were forced into marginal land and had to grow alien and unpalatable crops for their sustenance. The introduction of kail, traditionally associated by Gaels with their Lowland enemies, was an unwelcome one.

> I know that all country people, whose minds are not enlarged by proper education, are great enemies to all innovations, which they think will ruin them. This I am well assured, was the case with regard to Kail or cabbages, which was introduced into the Highlands not above 100 years ago. When the Heretors, who had seen the advantages of Kail in England and Holland, proposed to their tenants to plant them in their yards, they first resisted, and when the Heretors planted them, they pull'd 'em out by the roots, till the Heretors at last compell'd 'em by fines in their Baron Courts to allow them to grow, and now they could not live without them.[33]

The introduction of the potato by estate managers in the eighteenth century met with the same opposition, for eating tubers growing under the soil was perceived by Gaels as being beneath their dignity.[34] South Uist is said to be the first place in the Scottish Gàidhealtachd where potatoes were grown, having been discovered by the chieftain of Clan Ranald while visiting his kinsman in Antrim. Although he insisted that his dependents plant the potato crop, 'Only after being imprisoned did they consent to do so, and when the crop was raised they deposited it at the chief's gate, saying that though he could make them plant the strange roots he could not make them eat them.'[35]

Before long, however, the population had little choice but to accept this convenient nutritional resource. Over-reliance on this single crop – a condition contrary to previous ages of Gaelic society – was to prove disastrous for the natives of both Ireland and Scotland in the mid-nineteenth century, however, as the potato blight destroyed this temporary, artificial buttress.

The culture which imports technology from a more powerful, dominant culture typically finds itself becoming dependent upon it and placed in a subservient position. 'Technological borrowings are not often accomplished without a heavy price being exacted from the stability of the recipients' culture.'[36] This imbalance makes the borrower feel vulnerable and can provoke a sense of resentment. When the London government sent its military to build roads in the Highlands, in order to better police the area after the failed Jacobite Rising of 1715, not everyone was enthusiastic about the plans of improvement:

> The Objections made to these new Roads and Bridges by some in the several Degrees of Condition among the Highlanders, are in Part as follows: viz. –
>
> I. Those Chiefs and other Gentlemen complain, that thereby on easy Passage is opened into their Country for Strangers, who, in Time, by their Suggestions of Liberty, will destroy or weaken that Attachment of their Vassals which it is so necessary for them to support and preserve.
>
> That their Fastnesses being laid open, they are deprived of that Security from Invasion which they formerly enjoyed.
>
> That the Bridges, in particular, will render the ordinary People effeminate, and less fit to pass the Waters in other Places where there are none …
>
> II. The middling Order say the Roads are to them an Inconvenience, instead of being useful, as they have turned them out of old Ways …

That the roads did in fact produce these effects is confirmed by comments from the nineteenth century:

> The people, on the other hand, not only complained that they brought in strangers, but that they broke up their old customs. They said that the rough, stony ways were not suited to their unshod horses, and that they preferred the grass and the heather. It is curious to find objections of the same sort rife in Asia Minor in the present day.[37]

It has been further noted that the building of railroads in the late nineteenth century had the same effect of allowing dominant Anglo-centric culture fast and easy access to the Gàidhealtachd and that socio-linguistic decline followed swiftly thereafter. Electronic media such as television and radio are high-tech parallels to these older roadways. Although minority cultures may respond by attempting to develop equivalent mass-media programs of their own, they are inevitably upstaged by the greater prestige and resources of dominant cultures.

From early times, Scottish writers have commented upon the ruggedness of the Highlanders. A mid-sixteenth-century account by the bishop of the Isles is typical of these observations:

> They have all, not only the greatest contempt for pillows, or blankets, but, in general, an affection of uncultivated roughness and hardiness, so that when choice, or necessity induces them to travel in other countries, they throw aside the pillows, and blankets of their hosts, and wrapping themselves round with their own plaids, thus go to sleep, afraid lest these barbarian luxuries, as they term them, should contaminate their native simple hardiness.[38]

King James V wrote similarly of them at about the same time:

> The people are tenacious of old customs, traditional manners and rites: they cannot tolerate the introduction of anything which menaces ancestral practice, and if any man ... fails in a manner of accepted custom, they consider it an imperfection or it fills them with aversion and contempt.[39]

It would be going too far to suggest, however, that Gaelic society never actually changed. Rather, when it was self-reliant, it was able to adopt those elements which were consistent with its own sensibilities and to adapt them according to its own cultural norms. The examples cited above demonstrate that it was not merely a matter of 'ignorance' that the 'benefits' of English life did not easily penetrate Highland life: people consciously chose to reject those elements which they felt were not compatible with the Gaelic cultural matrix.

The makeup of the oral tradition gives us similar testimony. While the song genre commonly referred to as the 'international (or Child) ballad' was sweeping the rest of Europe in the Middle Ages, Gaeldom only saw fit to allow a handful of these items into its repertoire. This is no doubt because the Gaelic oral tradition was already well developed, and there was no new niche which the international ballad could fill.

The seventeenth century, on the other hand, saw the introduction of the fiddle into the Gàidhealtachd. It is during this same period that social-dancing and step-dancing were also introduced. It is significant, however, that these music and dance traditions took on the distinctive Gaelic idiom and were re-fashioned according to internal aesthetics.

Protestant progress and cultural attack

Protestantism was introduced into Scotland during a time when England was emerging as a major commercial and imperial force, and when ambitious Lowland Scots were eager to unite in a pan-British political entity in order to capitalize on this new power. The Scottish commissioners who attempted to arrange the marriage between Queen Elizabeth of England and earl of Arran James Hamilton justified it on the grounds that Britain 'is a comon countrey to us both, one that speaketh your owne language, one of the same religion.'[40]

The Protestant Reformation in Scotland was a catalyst in transforming Scotland's cultures, languages, and religions according to Anglo-centric principles. Assimilating Scotland into England, it was believed by some, would allow the two former enemies to form a union destined to become the new world empire and to bring a new order of civilization to the world. The ideology of progress, civility, civilization, industry, and improvement were thus united with the mission of the Reformation and the conversion to the English language, while Gaelic and Catholicism were equated with rebellion against authority, barbarity, ignorance, laziness, and heathendom.

The agenda initially behind the schools of the Society in Scotland for the Propagating Christian Knowledge (SSPCK), established by Royal Charter in Edinburgh for educating the Gaels, is neatly expressed in the Memorial to the Court of Police in 1716: 'Nothing can be more effectuall for reducing these countries [the Highlands and Islands] to order and making them usefull to the Commonwealth than teaching them their duty to God, their King and Countrey, and rooting out their Irish language.'[41] While the SSPCK was later forced to change its educational policies to a more Gaelic-friendly stance, the general attitude of improvement according to the norms of the English-speaking world remained.

The kirk records and regulations all around Scotland attest to the attempts to stamp out conduct considered immoral, customs considered 'popish' or 'pagan', and reverence paid to local sites holy since pre-Christian times. While the conversion to Christianity a millennium earlier had been able to incorporate much of the pre-existing notion of the sacred into a Christian ethos, the new religious order would not tolerate any deviance from the new austere orthodoxy.

Many of the ancient customs associated with ancient Celtic holidays were once practiced all around Scotland, but various institutions attempted to banish 'immoral', 'uncivil', or 'heathenish' practices. Various measures were passed by burgh councils and kirk sessions outlawing dancing, guising, and dramas at Yule-time,[42] and *Samhainn* customs such as bonfires, dancing, and nut divination.[43]

Local customs showing veneration to holy sites were also targeted. The church prohibited the decoration of holy wells in 1649,[44] and the practice of the 'Goodman's croft' was so tenacious that the church made an appeal to the Scottish Parliament to enact a law against it:

> Anent the horrible superstition used in Garioch and divers parts of the country in not labouring a parcel of ground dedicated to the devil under the name of the Goodman's croft: the Kirk for remedy thereof has found meet that a request be made to the Parliament that an act may proceed from the Estates, ordaining all persons, possessors of the said lands, to cause labour the same betwixt and a certain day appointed thereto: otherwise in case of disobedience, the said land to fall into the king's hand to be disposed to such persons, as please his majesty, who will labour the same.[45]

The Parliament does not seem to have granted the church its wish, and the practice only came to an end at the beginning of the nineteenth century because economic pressures caused a reallocation of lands. The kirk session records of the seventeenth century are replete with charges against individuals who maintained these ancient local dedications.[46]

It should not be surprising that Gaelic charms were also attacked by the church. A note in the kirk session records of Kenmore in 1700 is typical of attitudes towards traditional rituals and cures: 'It was enacted this day that because the Session was troubled with people suggested to use enchantments, any who were found to use any charms should be reported guilty of witchcraft.'[47]

It may be more surprising that Protestantism, being vehemently anti-Catholic and inclined toward scientific rationality, was disdainful of many forms of traditional knowledge such as herbal lore. Such knowledge often incorporated saints' names and traditions, or even those of earlier, pre-Christian figures. St John's wort is called *lus Chaluim Chille* (Columba's plant); meadow-sweet is called *crios Chù Chulainn* (Cù Chulainn's belt); and so on. While the attack on traditional lore in England happened well before similar events in Highland Scotland, the processes show much similarity:

> Vehement Protestants, deeply sensitive to any apparent survivals of popery or paganism, were, like some of their medieval predecessors, strongly hostile to the notion that vegetation might have any protective power and were unsympathetic to the symbolic use of plants ... This Protestant attack on older ways of looking at the natural world was now strongly reinforced by the writings of scientists.[48]

The retarding effects of Catholicism upon the Highlands were imagined to be naturalized into the landscape itself:

> For the Balefull influence of the Popish religion, wherever it is generally professed in the Highlands, is visible, even in the face of the Country. There, not only the morals and manners of the People, but the very Soil, is more rude and uncultivated.[49]

The Gaels were by custom used to following their leaders in all customs and values, and so long as these leaders were loyal to Gaelic values the fabric of society continued to be resilient and flexible. The assimilation of Gaelic chiefs into Anglo-British society, and the role of Protestantism in this process, introduced a new and sometimes irreconcilable strain into the life of many clans. The strong-arm tactics of some chiefs in forcibly converting their followers tarnished Protestantism in some regions.

> The Inhabitants of Rum adhered strictly to the Popish Religion, till about the beginning of this Century, when in one Day, they were all converted from Popery, and in a single manner. Maclean of Coll, their chieftain, being himself a Protestant, insisted that they should renounce the Roman Catholick Religion. He came to the Island with a Protestant Minister, and ordered all the People to appear at a certain Place, on Sunday, at publick Worship. They came to the Place, but refused to go into the House, where the Protestant Service was to be administred. The Chieftain reasoned with them, but they became more refractory. At last, he seized the most resolute Man among them, and having drubbed him heartily with his Cane, drove him into the House. Upon this, they all followed, without any further Opposition, and so the Reformation in this Island was accomplished. From that Day, they have ever since continued Staunch Protestants and there are but two Women among them at present of the Popish Persuation.

> Their neighbours, however, in the Popish Islands of Egg and Canna, still continue to call the Protestantism of Rum by the name of [*Creideamh a' chall bhuidhe*, 'religion of the yellow stick'][50]

The Established Church rapidly moved into the power vacuum of the post-Culloden Highlands and the role of leadership was taken up by ministers drawn from the native learned classes. Not all such men were hostile to secular culture in all of its forms, and indeed they often undertook important rescue work such as collecting and editing poetry that would have otherwise been left neglected. By injecting the learned tradition into religious contexts, they enriched and extended the registers and domains of the Gaelic language. Unfortunately, however, they tended to internalize the subordinate status of Gaeldom projected by the outside world and to make reformation their duty. A sermon to the SSPCK in 1750 describes the Highlands as a 'missionary field' needing civilizing:

> Here society still appears in a rude and imperfect form. Strangers to industry, averse from labour, inured to rapine, the fierce inhabitants scorned all the arts of peace, and stood ready for every bold and desperate action. Attached to their own customs, from ignorance and habit, they have hitherto continued a separate people, and though the religion established among them be the same which we enjoy, its progress hath been imperfect, and the fixed pastors were never able to surmount the disadvantages of their situation or the obstinacy of their people.[51]

SSPCK supporters claimed in the later eighteenth century that the civilizing mission of the schools was succeeding:

> The establishment of charity-schools hath wrought a happy change in many places: ignorance hath been in a great measure dispelled; the English language hath made considerable progress; the arts of civilization have been in some degree introduced; and thousands have been educated in the principles of loyalty and the Protestant religion.[52]

While the era of the Moderate ministers lasted, and before social disruptions rent the fabric of Gaelic life too deeply, secular culture still continued with much of the vitality that it had in earlier times. By the end of the eighteenth century, however, the Puritan model of the 'inner community' which turned its back on the vanity of the world fueled the impulses of the Evangelical movement[53] and produced ministers notorious for their condemnation of secular culture, folklore, and popular amusements.

> These pious men set their faces harshly against the traditional practices that they condemned absolutely and upon which they fixed the mark of sin. They were men sincere in their moral conduct, hard, unbending in their opinions and zealous for belief. With them came many changes to the people's lifestyle ...[54]

While even these men show many of the characteristics and skills of traditional Gaelic heroes – prophecy, poetic flyting, and so on – religious poetry and songs from this era display an inferiority-complex and a desire for the superior civilization of the English-speaking world. The Revd James MacGregor wrote of the process of 'educating' the Gaels:

Bha na Gàidheil ro aineolach dall,	The Gaels were totally blind and ignorant,
Bha ionnsachadh gann 'nam measg;	Little learning did they have;
Bha 'n eòlas cho tana 's cho mall ...	Their knowledge was shallow, and slow ...
'Nis togaidh na Gàidheil an ceann,	Now the Gaels will raise their heads,
'S cha bhi iad am fang nas mò	And they will no longer be in a rut,
Bidh ac' àrd-fhoghlum nan Gall	They will have the great learning of the
Is tuigse neo-mall 'na chòir ...	Non-Gaels and swift knowledge along with it ...

The early nineteenth-century poetry of Pàdraig Grannd, a Baptist minister from Strathspey, contains harsher words against Gaelic secular culture and is worth quoting from in some length:

> *'S an t-seann seanchas, bha Gàidheil ainmeil*
> *A-measg dhaoine, b'ainmig an leithid ann,*
> *Le gaisg' is cruadal, is creach air uairibh,*
> *Is bha am fuil cho uaibhreach a' toirt buaidh dhaibh ann,*
> *Gun tuigse, gun chiall ac', mu thimcheall siorraidheachd ...*
>
> *B'e ar cleachd o'r n-òige bhith aotrom gòrach*
> *Gun neach a' seòladh dhuinn slighe nas fearr;*

Bhitheadh tional mòr anns na taighean-òsda dhinn
Bhitheadh seinn air òrain, bhitheadh spòrsa is gàire …
Le cainnt ro dhìomhan mu thimcheall Fianntaibh …

Bhitheadh eagal mòr orra roimh na bòcain
Is iad a' faicinn mòran diubh nach bitheadh ann;
Bhitheadh gisriag is orthaichean is seachnadh chòmhlaichean
Is mòran seòlaidhean ann 'nan ceann;
Bhitheadh aca Sìtheachan anns gach sìthean
A bheireadh sìos leò mnathan is clann;
Is bhitheadh iad cuid a' bruadair 's an sluagh 'ga mhìneach –
Is gun ghuth air Bìobull bhith idir ann.

Nach truagh ri innseadh gum biodh na mìltean
De anamain prìseal cho anabarra dall
Is gun tèid iad dìreach an aghaidh na fìrinn
Is nach creid iad nì dheth a bhith gu an call;
Sibhse a tha cuir Bhìobull is luchd teagaisg fìrinneach
Dh'ionnsaigh Innseanach fada thall:
Nach cuir sibh pairt dhiubh 's gach eilean Gàidhealach
Oir is truagh bu bhràth dhuinn ma bhitheas sinn mall …

In olden lore, the Gaels were famous
Amongst people, there were not many like them,
With great feats and hardiness, and an occasional foray,
Their vainglorious blood brought them victory,
But they lacked sense and understanding of the eternal …

It was our habit since youth to be light-hearted and foolish,
Lacking anyone to show us a better way;
We would gather together in the hostelries
And there would be the singing of songs, having fun and laughter …
With vain and idle talk about the Fianna …

They would fear ghosts greatly
And they saw many of them which did not exist;
There would be superstitions, and charms, and the avoiding of omen-encounters,

And they had many such practices;
They believed that fairies dwelt in every fairy-hillock,
Who would take women and children down with them;
And some would have dreams which others would interpret –
And there was not a single mention of the Bible.

Terrible to say, but there were thousands
Of precious souls which were exceeding blind
And they were in direct opposition to the truth
And they did not believe that any of it was to their loss;
O all of you who are sending Bibles and honest missionaries
To the Indians so far away:
Will you not send some of them into all of the Gaelic islands,
For the judgment against us will be harsh if we react slowly …

Hector Urquhurt, one of the collectors of traditional tales for the pioneer folklorist John Francis Campbell, said of the *cèilidh* house in his youth, 'The minister came to the village in 1830, and the schoolmaster soon followed, who put a stop in our village to such gatherings.'[55] Campbell advised another of his collectors in 1859, 'Do not trouble yourself to go to ministers and school-masters except for information as to the people. The educated generally know nothing of the amusements of the people.'[56]

This 'educational' process also had the result of stigmatizing Gaelic as the backward language of peasants and rebels. When inspecting SSPCK schools in 1825, it was observed that 'There seems to be in the minds of the people … a very general prejudice against using the Gaelic as a school language.'[57]

Rather than simply weaving the rites, customs, and tenets of religion into the natural fabric of life, Protestantism intellectualized religion in a way never before experienced in Gaelic society. It became a cause of controversy and a bone of contention, even more so because of the conflicting interests of the different strands of Highland society in the post-Culloden phase. In his original 1830 text, James Logan remarks that religious strife was an injurious innovation in Highland life:

> It has been remarked that the Highlanders seldom or ever meddle with religion, and the late General Stewart has some very sensible remarks on their tolerant spirit, mixed, however, with regret that sectaries should have been able to infuse among them a spirit of cavilling and

> dispute on religious topics. He deplores that, instead of the contented, plain, Christian-like satisfaction formerly to be found among them, they occupy themselves too frequently in 'disputes of interminable length'. The example of the chief was formerly almost sufficient authority for the religion which the clan professed.[58]

In the 1876 edition of his work, however, the editor notes sadly that religion had tightened its grip even further on the Highland mind and become a cause of debate and dissension. 'Within recent years this evil has largely increased, and one is sorry to be obliged to confess that in many parts of the Highlands fanaticism and religious rancour and bitterness have taken the place of that love and "good will toward men" which are the characteristics of genuine Christianity.'

Even if we accept the premises of Modernism and decide that the transformation of Highland society according to modernist principles was necessary, it is clear that this process was executed in such a way as to violate Gaelic cultural norms and to demean many of the positive and self-affirming aspects of Highland life. It also attacked the mythopoeic worldview of Gaelic cosmology and the reverence due to the sacred embodied in the local and familiar landscape. Frances Tolmie had relevant insight into the origins and the demise of the so-called 'fairy-faith'.

> The fairy-lore originated in a cultured class in very ancient times. The peasants inherited it; they did not invent it. With the loss of Gaelic in our times came the loss of folk-ideals. The classical and English influences combined had a killing effect; so that the instinctive religious feeling which used to be among our people when they kept alive the fairy-traditions is dead. We have intellectually-constructed creeds and doctrines which take its place.[59]

In order to bring the Highlanders to accept the remodeling of their society according to the values and structures of the English-speaking world, it was necessary to convince them of the inherent superiority of the civilization of their former enemies. Gaels converted to this new ideological orientation could be employed to effect the same change upon other peoples in the colonies of the Empire.

Many of those in the various branches of the Presbyterian church have defended it as the only institution which supported Gaelic and have claimed that Gaelic may not have survived at all if it were not for the aid of the church. While there may be an element of truth in such statements, we would be better off asking where Gaelic would be now had there been the full array of secular institutions which keep any typical society healthy. When many Gaelic communities retreated into the shelter of the church, the blessings were mixed, and the cultural reforms implemented by clergy were not balanced by native secular institutions.

It should be noted, however, that there is nothing inherent in Protestantism or Calvinism themselves which caused the gloom, despair, and fatalism which is so marked in the Highlands, and in Scotland as a whole. Rather, we need to examine the cultural and political circumstances in which these religious institutions operated, and the attitudes formed due to these circumstances.

A similar cultural decline happened in rural Ireland following the Great Famine of the 1840s. Catholic priests assumed positions of moral authority in the social collapse, some of them declaring the catastrophe to be a judgment against the sinners of their parishes and leading zealous campaigns to rid their communities of musicians, whom the priests believed incited the population to acts of immorality. The crusades of such priests, the shift of language from Irish to English, and the effects of rapid Modernization caused a huge part of the repertoire of the Irish musical tradition to be lost.[60] In cultural terms, the Famine 'effected a distinct psychological change in the Irish character.'[61]

At the same time that secular society was experiencing this dislocation, Ireland's state institutions were internalizing Anglo-Protestant norms:

> The Irish Catholicism which developed in the nineteenth and twentieth centuries was puritanical since its clergy was drawn from a middle class which consciously modeled itself on the Protestant elite with its strong Victorian values. Hence, much of the popular religion as practised by Catholics was felt to be a source of shame and scandal to them in the eyes of their Protestant neighbors.[62]

The Presbyterian Gaelic communities of Cape Breton, in the eastern Maritimes of Canada, provide us with a contrast. At the same time that many communities back in Scotland were discouraged from indulging in worldly pleasures, the vibrant musical traditions of Presbyterian Cape Breton, which sided with the Free Church in the Disruption of 1843, suffered no noticeable deterioration because of religious influence.[63]

To paint a more complete picture of Highland life, it must also be realized that a number of communities, both in the Highlands and Islands, have remained Catholic to the present day. Although some of these, such as South Uist, have been great preserves of tradition, none of them have been able to isolate themselves from the wider assaults on Gaelic society.

The greatest Gaelic poet of the twentieth century, Somhairle MacGilleain, was at pains to emphasize that Calvinism did not mute all oral tradition in his family, and that he was 'very sceptical of the Scottish writers who seemed to attribute most of Scotland's ills to Calvinism'.[64] He also reminds us that the greatest Gaelic poet of the nineteenth century, Màiri Mhòr nan Òran, from Presbyterian Skye, displays a zest for life, a hearty optimism, a critical mind about religion, and an appeal for action in her poetry.[65] Her rootedness in this world, for all of its goods and evils, is confirmed in such passages as:

Ach bhon is luibh an dìomhanas	But since worldly vanity is a plant
A riaraicheas an fheòil	Which satisfies the flesh
Tha i leantainn rium cho daingeann	It clings to me as solidly
'S tha am barr-iall ris a' bhròig.	As the shoe-lace to the shoe.

The New Age movement has kindled interest in alternative spiritualities among a large segment of society, and 'Celtic spirituality' appears to be enjoying a wide popularity in these circles. Many of those involved want to 'reclaim' the pre-Christian beliefs of their ancestors, which they believe they have some right to on account of their 'race'. It is inevitable that religious systems should reflect the societies which create and use them, and it is not surprising that the reconstituted spirituality typically offered by most New Age evangelicals differs in style, substance, and context from its traditional antecedents.

New Age spirituality tends to reflect the individualist orientation of modernist society. Books and courses focus on personal development and spiritual self-realization: 'Awaken the Goddess in you', 'Listening to your inner Shaman', or 'Tao and Business Success'. Ritual, celebration, and spirituality, like all practices, revolve around the family and community in traditional Gaelic society and focusing on the individual, and removing him from his larger social context, would be thought to be unhealthy and unsound apart from exceptional circumstances.

Although Celtic literature has been misrepresented as being inherently mystic and ethereal, it is always concrete, detailed, personal, and specific. In short, spirituality is never divorced from other aspects of life, and one cannot hope to understand Gaelic spirituality without putting it in its larger cultural and linguistic context.

CHAPTER 9

Past and future prospects

Gaeldom in health

No healthy society silently succumbs to pressure from external forces, nor does it entirely reject all external stimuli. Rather, a fully functional and self-confident society assesses ideas from outside sources according to its own internal value and belief systems, adapts those ideas which are perceived to be beneficial to it, and rejects those which disturb or conflict with its own norms and aesthetics.

For as long as Gaelic society was able to control its own destiny, it was able to both maintain a strong sense of continuity with its past and to adapt those ideas from the outside world which were perceived as being beneficial to it. Not only could ideas be accommodated, but many would-be invaders – Vikings, Anglo-Normans, and Lowlanders – were assimilated into Gaelic society.

Syncretism is manifest in our earliest written evidence in Gaelic, for the very existence of writing was inspired by contact with the Roman world. The first script created by Gaels, however, *ogam*, is not a direct borrowing from Latin but rather a unique writing system particularly suited for inscriptions on stone and wood.

Although Gaelic scholarly tradition was greatly influenced by contact with the Classical Mediterranean tradition carried as part of the cultural baggage of Christianity, this contact had the effect of augmenting, rather than eclipsing or displacing, most aspects of native Gaelic tradition. The various early linguistic projects of the Gaelic scholars of the early Christian era were meant to raise the status of Irish to that of Latin,[1] a feat that should not be underestimated. Once this syncretism was under way, Gaelic was used as the medium of composition and learning for scholarly pursuits.

Ethnocentrism is a universal phenomenon. 'The illusion of superiority and centrality is probably necessary to the sustenance of culture. When rude encounters with reality shatter that illusion the culture itself is liable to decline.'[2] Like other peoples, Gaelic myth gave the Gaelic realms a uniquely exalted place in the world and made the Gaels the descendants of gods and divine heroes.

Once the Gaelic world made contact with the civilization and literature of Christendom, the heir of the Roman Empire, the early Gaelic scholars found imaginative ways of harmonizing this new learning with their own native traditions without doing their inherited worldview irreparable harm or disrespect. They rewrote their own mythic history so that it could fit into the framework of Christian cosmology and the annals chronicling the important events of the Mediterranean world.[3]

This mythopoeic exercise reached its creative apogee in the eleventh century *Lebor Gabála Érenn* (Book of the Takings of Ireland) which gives an account of the waves of settlers coming into Ireland. With Gaeldom's stress on ancestry and the belief of ennoblement by blood, it is little wonder that most of the important peoples and events of Christian and Classical literature were incorporated in one way or another into this narrative: Noah's grandson Japhet is made the progenitor of the first wave of settlers to come into Ireland; the daughter of Pharaoh of Egypt is made the ancestress of the Gaels themselves, coming through the Mediterranean and conquering Scythia and Spain on their way; and so on.

The Gaelic language was claimed to have been fashioned from the best features of the seventy-two languages of the world at the time of the Tower of Babel by Gaedel Glas, a linguist of great ability for whom the Gaels were named. This is reminiscent of the belief common into recent times that Gaelic was spoken in the Garden of Eden.

The tales of the Ulster Cycle were made to synchronize with the time of Christ, and although druids and other pagan characters figure in these tales, they clearly find ways to make themselves friendly to the principles of Christianity, and even to presage its introduction into Ireland. Some of these figures were worked into vernacular versions of Biblical lore. St Brigit, for example, was made into the *muime* (foster-mother) of Christ.

It is with this framework of syncretism, asserting the prestige of the native while incorporating it into an externally-derived schema, that we can understand the vitality and survival of otherwise 'pagan' Gaelic gods and heroes. Although the Gaels have considered themselves to be Christians since the early Middle Ages they were able to retain many of the pre-Christian elements of their culture and assert them as models of excellence and standards of virtue. This is not evidence that they were still pagan, but rather an indication of their pride in their culture and their ability to absorb many of the elements of Christian ideology into their own cosmology without completely altering its essence.

In the folktales of the Fianna common throughout the Scottish Gàidhealtachd, this band of select warriors was said to have defended Scotland and Ireland from all invaders and threats to peace. Tales tell of hostile foreign armies, some of them fantastic (such as the Cat-head people) and others corresponding to real peoples, such as the Vikings (from folk-memories of real conflicts), Greeks (who would have been familiar from tales from the Classical world), and Turks (entering tradition as enemies of Christendom during the Crusades). That all of these invaders are defeated by Gaelic forces is surely an indication of the self-confidence of Gaeldom.

All cultures have some source of prestige which asserts its own sense of self-esteem and sophistication. This is often some form of art expressed in a high register, supported by the efforts of the elite and most expressly addressed to them. Such art generally serves to ennoble all of society and to act as an articulation of cultural identity.

It was the nobility themselves, and the effusions of the Gaelic intelligentsia that they supported, which provided the source of prestige which ennobled Gaelic society as a whole. As long as Gaelic society was functioning healthily, such high-register art originating in the nobility as clan sagas, Ossianic ballads, and eulogies to chieftains were treasured artefacts amongst all members of the clan.

The pedigrees of the nobility were common knowledge to all and blood ties to them were particularly esteemed. Kinship bound society together, maintained the bonds of affection between ranks, and gave pride to the humblest follower. Thus it is that to the nineteenth century, the lowest Gael is described as feeling as dignified and headstrong as any of his superiors:

> However tame and simple a Highlander may seem to be in dealing with the gentry, yet when harshly treated, or deprived of what he thinks his due, his mutinying is the more formidable that there is a method and temper in it, which is not easily diverted and keeps steady to its point.[4]

Although there were more tangible local and familial loyalties, there can be no doubt that a pan-Gaelic identity and consciousness did exist. A nation does not become conscious of its own identity until it encounters another one different to it and the markers of identity in Gaelic oral narrative increase in occurrence as the conflict with the English-speaking world gathers pace. Many of these expressions of identity have already been discussed, but it is worth reiterating that, like other societies, the emphasis in most texts is on language, clothing, food, and manners.

The Gaels spoke 'melodious, eloquent' Gaelic, dressed in the tartan plaid (and trews), ate (moderate amounts of) venison and dairy products, drank red wine, were fierce as warriors, were gentle, generous, and honourable as allies, and lived a life of freedom in the countryside. Their enemies spoke 'harsh' English,[5] dressed in dark, dour cloaks and hats, ate (excessive amounts of) cabbage and uncouth foods, drank whiskey, were effeminate, clumsy and unskilled at war (relying upon unsportsman-like technology), were greedy and morally suspect, and lived in dense, noisy, and unclean towns. This is a simplified stereotype collated from many widely scattered fragments, yet one which is consistent in Gaelic tradition.[6]

Cultural invasion and decline

The Gaelic identity of Scotland as a whole had suffered deterioration since the Anglo-Norman takeover of the national court in the twelfth century, but outside of royal spheres of authority, and particularly in the uplands and western seaboard of Scotland, a Gaelic kingdom in miniature survived and often thrived.

The seventeenth century marks a turning point in Gaelic history for English-speaking society was finally able to muster forces – both military and ideological – which launched a cultural invasion into the heart of Gaelic culture. The assimilation of clan elite into English-speaking society marked the decline of their allegiance to Gaelic cultural norms and of their patronage of the arts which lent prestige to Gaelic society and articulated its identity and concerns.

This process was did not happen everywhere to the same degree at the same time. Still, this assimilation tore at the fibre of Gaelic society and split its consciousness between a Gaelic past and an Anglo-centric vision of Progress. It was noted of one Gael that 'The changes in the country in his time had been so great, that he used to say "he had lived in two worlds".'[7] Success in the new regime meant assimilating to English norms, and scorning Gaelic culture.

> In the course of twenty-five years after the Rebellion [1746] a number of noblemen and gentlemen, whose estates lay in the Highlands, had died, and were succeeded by young men of very different manners and sentiments. Some of these had been educated in England and the low country, where they had formed new friendships and connections. They had been accustomed from their infancy to hear their country vilified and ridiculed by all about them. No wonder, then, that they should return prepossessed against it – a species of prejudice of all others the most unfortunate to a man's self and his dependents. To the persons and pretensions of their tenants, as well as to their language and customs, they were in a great measure strangers. Instead of treating such of them as were supposed to be of the same lineage with themselves in the manner their fathers used to do, they affected to estimate them by their dress and economies ...[8]

Gaels had come to expect cultural attack from the English-speaking world,

> But to see chieftains, or such as affected the manners of chieftains, repay their attachment with coldness and contempt, filled the middling and lower classes of people with grief and indignation. From being an affectionate cheerful people, a great proportion of them became sullen, suspicious, and restless.[9]

Gaelic society thus deprived of its native aristocracy and prestige culture had less of a stable anchor to steady it once economic hardships increased and social problems escalated.

> The tacksmen and subtenants, formerly, or nearly, on an equal footing, were wont to plead their cause, on equal terms, before a common chief. At present they are obliged to be much more submissive to their tacksmen than ever they were, in former times, to their lairds or lords. Formerly, they were a free, animated, and bold people, commanding respect from their undaunted courage, and repelling injuries from whatever quarter they came, both by words and actions. But, now they must approach even the tacksmen with cringing humility, heartless, and discouraged, with tattered rags, hungry bellies, and downcast looks ... Formerly, a Highlander would have drawn his dirk against even a laird, if he had subjected him to the indignity of a

> blow: at present, any tyrannical tacksman, in absence of the laird or lord, whose presence alone can enforce good order and justice, may strike a *scallag*, and even a subtenant, with perfect impunity. What degree of spirit and virtue is to be expected from a people so humbled, so enslaved?[10]

The assimilation of the native intelligentsia into the ranks of the Presbyterian ministry expedited the 'improvement' of Gaeldom along Anglo-centric lines and hindered the possibility of a critique of Anglo-British Imperialism from an alternative point of view.

It is a psychological and sociological truism that people who are self-confident are more apt to take risks while those in crisis tend to cling to the safety of conservatism and avoid decisions with uncertain outcomes. Once they have accepted the position of inferiority assigned to them, those most harassed and restrained by external forces are those also most likely to exercise what little self-control left to them in ways which are self-denying and self-destructive.

The Ghost Dance and Peyote Cult of Native America of the late nineteenth century could be read as cultural parallels to the failed Highland Jacobite cause and the subsequent austere severity of Highland religion. The Ghost Dance was practiced by many tribes who hoped that it would invoke the Great Spirit to regain the country for the natives and to make the White Man, and his civilization, disappear. When this cult showed itself to be ineffectual, or when it was forcibly terminated by state authorities, the Peyote Cult offered itself as an alternative, but rather than inspiring action, it encouraged passive resignation and surrender to the new order. Likewise, it was noted that many communities of the Gàidhealtachd lost their sense of involvement in the physical (and political) world in exchange for a belief in a personal spiritual struggle:

> Some characteristics of the Free Church services may be noted ... There is an air of settled gloom on the faces of many of the people – intensified on the Sabbath day. It seems to partake of a religious character. The ministers, catechists, and elders nearly all oppose dancing and every kind of music. Surely they are short-sighted! A sort of fatalism is the most apparent result of the religion of the natives of Gairloch. It has a depressing effect when illness comes.[11]

The Anglo-British Empire was bolstered by a racial ideology that the Teutonic-Gothic peoples of England and the Scottish Lowlands were destined for global greatness.[12] Once Gaeldom no longer posed a threat to the Anglo-Saxon order, it was pilfered for elements to add local colour to the Empire and accentuate its ability to absorb diverse ethnicities. It could also be argued that the appropriation of select elements of Gaelic culture was a means of assuaging the guilt of those who witnessed, participated in, and benefited from the cultural genocide of the Highlands.

From the eighteenth century to the twentieth century, institutions have been established which act as patrons for particular Gaelic-derived arts: piping, singing, Scottish Country Dancing, Highland Dancing, and so on. These institutions, however, have isolated particular elements from their larger cultural and linguistic contexts. Being removed from the other genres with which they are inter-related, and which give them meaning and balance, has made them vulnerable to distortions and non-Gaelic aesthetics. Even more problematic, however, is the fact that these institutions have been created with the express purpose of 'improving peasant arts' to resemble whatever ideas and trends were fashionable at the time so that Gaelic culture could appear more 'refined' to dominant, urban, Anglo-British culture. 'We need only look at the previous century to see that Gaeldom has been vulnerable to varieties of runaway cultural engineering which have deeply affected its concept of itself.'[13]

An Comunn Gàidhealach (the Highland Society) was established in 1891 with the express aim of encouraging the Gaelic language and tradition. It has been the patron of an annual competition called the *Mòd*, modeled on the Welsh *Eisteddfod*. While ACG has made some important contributions to the promotion of Gaelic, particularly in its early years when it produced Gaelic textbooks edited by William J. Watson, a number of factors have prevented it from being the radical and independent institution it would have needed to be to lead cultural change.

The 'improver' mentality of the *Mòd* is exemplified in its long-standing emphasis on a late-nineteenth-century stage style of singing which was previously unknown to Gaelic tradition and which has entirely displaced local styles where they were not strong enough to resist the mission of improvement. The danger of such 'innovation' is that now, more than a century later, the *Mòd* style sounds out of date and unfashionable, while the traditional Gaelic style still sounds timeless and unique.

The old clan chiefs were the patrons of colleges which developed a native tradition of bagpipe music, but such centres suffered the same fate as the bardic schools. Contrary to popular belief, the bagpipes have suffered not from any act prohibiting their use after Culloden – no such act ever existed – but from the lack of native institutions. The British military became the principal patron of bagpiping and competitions in the Lowlands and at Highland Games were the new means of achieving prestige in the piping world. As these contexts were far removed from the Gaelic world, they enabled the introduction of ideas and styles once foreign to Gaelic music. Improvers made bagpiping a 'literate art' (in contrast to previous oral and aural styles of teaching), regularized tunes according to written notation and Western art music ideas of musicality (leveling out the Gaelic idiom), and changed the tempo.[14]

The Scottish Country Dance Society was formed in 1923 with the intention of 'improving' and standardizing Scottish social dancing so that people could have a single corpus of dances no matter where they were. Teachers, armed with books of dance positions (influenced by ballet aesthetics) and formations, could then 'correct' undisciplined village dancers and iron out local variations that existed all across Scotland.[15] Highland dancing was created from the Gaelic folk dance repertoire but formalized with the conventions of ballet, and required athletic rigor to be performed at competitions. Both of these 'improvements' have changed the nature and style of folk dance and usurped control from the communities which created them in their many diverse variations.

Any traditional *cèilidh* features spontaneous music, dancing, song, poetry, folk-tale, and so on. The timing and style of dancing was a natural regulator for the style of musical accompaniment, be that *puirt-a-beul* (mouth music) or bagpiping. The repertoire of song would have fed into the stream of tunes played by instrumentalists. Stories provide not only the backdrop to many songs, but also employ the same linguistic and literary skills and conventions which underpin oral tradition as a whole. 'Taken all together symbolic systems constitute an essential source for the visions contained within the cultures.'[16] In other words, for traditional Gaelic culture to retain its integrity, all of these expressions must be seen as inter-related aspects of the same culture and need to be nurtured and experienced together, rather than taken under the aegis of separate institutions. Those institutions which do not even recognize the Gaelic language as an essential skill for participating in the culture need to be seriously questioned.

When a person uses some marker of identity so that it is distorted out of proportion, taken out of context, or misrepresented entirely, he is engaging in an act of *cultural exaggeration.* This is particularly liable to happen to minority cultures which do not control the relevant political and cultural institutions, and thus have no way of asserting their own identity and history. Images of them are likely to be created and manipulated by the dominant culture for its own purposes, usually to create a rationale for its own superiority and to project an anti-image of itself upon subordinate ethnicities.

Some Native Americans attempting to make money from tourism wear feathered head-gear and buckskin costume regardless of how accurately it represents their own tribal tradition simply because this Hollywood image is what tourists expect an Indian to look like. The term *tartanism* is a shorthand for Scottish cultural exaggeration which attempts to provide a veneer of ethnicity by ornamenting an object or activity in tartan, or in other such stereotypical markers of identity.

Tartan was perceived in the eighteenth century by Gaels as an authentic cultural marker, and it is the case that kilts, Highland dress, and tartan have been re-embraced in Scotland as national symbols of identity. Be that as it may, tartanism is most pronounced in those attempting to captivate a non-native audience, or in those with very little real connection to the culture. Those who actually participate in Gaelic culture have no need for cultural exaggeration, as has been noted amongst communities in Nova Scotia: 'Tartanism seems to play an important role in Nova Scotia not among Gaelic speakers but among those English monoglots with Highland ancestry. For them, the trappings of tartanism enable them to feel that they have not been cut off from their heritage.'[17]

It is ironic that Scotland contributed so much to the ideology of nationalism in Europe, yet was unable to benefit from this movement as other nations did in the eighteenth, nineteenth, and twentieth centuries. James MacPherson's reinterpretation of Gaelic Ossianic material for an English-speaking audience was the harbinger of the Romantic movement and an early expression of the noble savage. This rhetoric of ethnicity, misguided as it often was, provided the impetus for the science of folklore and the intellectual framework for political nationalism.[18] The literary battleground created by MacPherson's Ossian was the backdrop for an argument about the nature of Scotland itself:

> The furious Ossianic controversy was not, in fact, purely literary. How could it be when so many of Macpherson's assailants, then and now, were so obviously ignorant of the Gaelic literary tradition? No, in the

> Ossianic controversy the real argument was about Scottish national identity. The anti-Ossianists, like Pinkerton, sought to obliterate Scotland's Celtic past and to prove that from the beginning the Scottish nation was of Germanic, and therefore Lowland, origin.[19]

The Celtic element of the Scottish nation had been too disadvantaged in the eighteenth and nineteenth centuries to provide an ethnic myth around which people could rally and find pride. While self-confident Teutonism, whose 'truth' was confirmed by the success of the Anglo-British Empire, had a compelling magnetic pull for Lowlanders, tartanism, 'rather than laying the foundations for a Gaelic-inspired Scottish romantic nationalism, it emasculated Scottish nationalist urges through cultural sublimation.'[20]

Whatever else might be said about nationalism, it was (and remains) an inevitable consequence of the process of modernization.[21] By providing a secure sense of ethnic identity, it allows a society to assimilate external ideas and innovations without feeling that its own culture is endangered. This enhanced the ability of nations in the nineteenth and twentieth centuries to adopt aspects of modernism. Gaeldom was never allowed such an opportunity, and modernization in Scotland as a whole was undertaken in the faith that Anglicization and progress were synonymous.

As unfortunate as these events might be, the most tragic consequence of cultural invasion has been the internalization of the anti-Gaelic prejudice of the English speaking world. The belief that Gaeldom represents a failed civilization, and that English civilization holds the key to all progress, was an ideology implicit in the strategies of the London government, the Presbyterian church, and the educational system since the seventeenth century. The acceptance of this myth has prevented Scotland from understanding its past properly and imagining a new future.

The prevalence of this inferiority complex plagues Scotland as a whole, and until the assumptions that underlie this fallacy are seriously undermined, cultural revitalization will be held up by doubt, apathy, and self-loathing.

> The regressive response empirically exhibits itself in increasing incidents of such things as alcoholism, extreme passivity and indolence, the development of highly ambivalent dependency relationships, intragroup violence, disregard of kinship and sexual mores, irresponsibility in public officials, states of depression and self-reproach, and probably

a variety of psychosomatic and neurotic disorders. Some of these regressive action systems become, in effect, new cultural patterns.[22]

Development and recovery

Cultural revitalization has been the response of many societies which have suffered social disruption, geographical dislocation, linguistic decline, economic deprivation, and psychological damage since the Age of Empires: 'A revitalization movement is defined as a deliberate, organized, conscious effort by members of a society to construct a more satisfying culture.'[23] Revitalization movements have taken different forms according to differing circumstances, some of them focusing on religious identities, others on linguistic revival, and, in cases where nations have emerged from crumbling Empires, as nationalist aspirations.

It is not hard to see that the present plight of Gaeldom is not too different from scores of other disempowered and dispossessed minorities around the world. Only those who have a strong determination to survive, and can harness that aspiration to good effect, will be able to weather the winds of change. Those who lack self-esteem or vision will be sure to disappear in the rapids of modernism.

To the present, French- and Mi'kmaq-speaking communities have found ways to strengthen their communities in Nova Scotia, while the once-vibrant Gaelic community has all but disappeared. While many minority communities in the European Union have been able to exploit new opportunities and create educational, political, and economic institutions which benefit them, Scottish Gaelic communities are still in unmitigated decline.

Petty parochial prejudices will have to be set aside in order to think critically about what will provide the maximum benefit for Gaelic language and culture as a whole, rather than letting allegiance to a single dialect, community, religion, or kin-group blind the decision-making process. The ranks of a new intelligentsia who not only speak Gaelic but are also sensitive to the sensibilities of tradition and culture and who have the technical skills to lead cultural revitalization are still to be filled properly. The siege mentality which rejects persons from the outside, regardless of their sincerity and capabilities, in preference to those with Gaelic but inadequate skills, will also be detrimental to revitalization.

The potential for cultural revitalization exists only because of the tireless efforts and persistent dedication of a small number of activists. The lack of political power in the Gàidhealtachd over many generations has cultivated apathy and a lack of involvement in decision making, and new more pro-active behavior must be learnt in order for these communities to re-empower themselves. Although government agencies have begun to give Gaelic more support, this will make little real impact unless demand emanates from, and development is under the direction of, local communities themselves.

It remains to be seen whether these efforts will be successful and enable Gaeldom to survive as anything like a recognizable community through the twenty-first century. So many of the necessary prerequisites seem to be missing, most especially a critical mass of people with the imagination to see beyond the deprivation of the recent past into the richness of cultural resources available in Gaeldom and who have the social and political will to realize those potentials.

It is always easier to be a victim than to move past the stage of victimization, for a victim can relegate his personal responsibility to events that occurred in the past and are beyond his control. To move beyond victimization means to take charge of the present and to accept responsibility for success and failure. Cultural revitalization has only happened when societies have decided to take their fate into their own hands and Gaeldom has yet to take such measures.

The myth of economic determinism has too large an influence in perceptions about Highland life and history and too many people still associate Gaelic with poverty. Many Gaels themselves are too preoccupied with the material reference points that defined the living space of Highland life in the recent past – crofts, thatched houses, peat fires, etc – to see the value and belief systems, language and oral tradition, that were the real lifeblood Gaelic identity. These can be transferred to new living spaces with a different material culture.

As many Gaels self-consciously jettison the reminders of poverty from their lives in a headlong rush toward modernism and material wealth, there is a serious danger of violating the integrity of Gaeldom's cultural matrix. The desire for external validation – the need to prove that Gaeldom is 'normal' according to the dominant standards of the English-speaking world – is frequently evident and reveals a fear of disapproval from the outside world and a lack of faith in the internal world of Gaeldom.

When explaining the rationale of Gaelic-language television, a native Gaelic-speaking producer at the BBC said, 'We've tried to make Gaelic sexy, to show people who don't speak the language that we are as normal, as

Nineties, as anyone else.'[24] Why would anyone who was confident about their culture be preoccupied with convincing others that it was not abnormal or behind the times?

This quest for external validation causes many aspects of Gaelic tradition to be neglected in preference for translating what is essentially the culture of the English-speaking world into Gaelic. By adopting external norms and ideas, and by assuming that they hold the key to all Progress, Gaelic will lose its own cultural matrix. Gaelic and English could become slightly differing ciphers for the same set of ideas and aesthetics.

A great deal of the energy currently in the Gaelic movement is directed towards education, which is in principle a necessary and worthy activity. The lack of funding available to Gaelic education, and the requirement that children in Gaelic schools come out with the same 'facts' as children in English-medium schools, means that educational materials are essentially the same for both sets of children. This in turn inhibits the ability of Gaelic-medium schools to exploit knowledge and experience specific to Gaelic culture.

We still wait for the day when oral tradition will be harnessed to give children a Gaelic view of the world and express knowledge with Gaelic-specific concepts and genres. Why not draw upon traditional Gaelic rhymes, riddles, and folktales to teach them about animals, plants, and nature, rather than simply translate English-language textbooks? Why not teach them songs about historical events in order to give them the first-hand perceptions of those involved, rather than simply reading over history lessons? Using traditional materials with natural Gaelic idioms would also prevent against the cultural and linguistic drift so pronounced amongst young people at the moment.

Music is usually pointed out as a signal indication of the existence, even success, of the Gaelic 'renaissance', yet most of what is happening indicates external acculturation and *cultural asset stripping*, rather than internal innovation and rejuvenation. In accordance with the concept of being a 'celebrity', musicians are praised for individual achievement and innovation, rather than acclaimed for their mastery of traditional idioms, their respect for the tradition from which they inherit their repertoire, and their role in the community. Reflecting modernist notions of progress, importance is placed on 'absorbing influences', 'pushing back boundaries', and 'doing newer and bigger things'.

When aiming for a wide consumer market unacquainted with the nuances of Gaelic language and culture, the information content and other traditional aesthetic considerations are de-emphasized in order to 'bring the product to the widest possible market'. In other words, the process of cultural asset stripping appropriates only those elements that can be readily assimilated into mainstream Western art music and consumed by a mass market. We should question whether it really does a service to Gaelic culture to transform its resources according to foreign aesthetics and expectations, and what opportunity costs this entails.

Albums of 'Celtic music' – a marketing term with little real meaning – often cater to the 'Celtic twilight' notion of Gaels as semi-pagans singing haunting, mystical songs. One can hear laments sung as though they were fairy songs, battle songs sung as though they were somber meditations, dance songs totally altered in timing and execution. In short, many musicians have appropriated items from the Gaelic music tradition and refashioned them into exotic commodities according to their own agendas, rather than honouring their content, style, and idiom.

It has already been shown that the Gaelic musical tradition has had periods of change, and new ideas and instruments have been incorporated into it over the centuries. There are important differences, however, in the techno-consumer age regarding these processes of change. In previous eras, change was in the control of the Gaelic community itself, which was able to decide which innovations were within its own accepted aesthetic parameters. A global market, however, now takes the focus of control outside of the Gaelic community and consumer demand dictates how Gaelic music is performed and presented.

The Gaelic music 'revival' has done very little to benefit to cultural revitalization. Musicians playing Gaelic music seldom contribute to the financial needs of their ailing ancestral communities and usually live in the English-speaking world where the music business is based when they are not on tour. The existence of individuals who are musical virtuosos does not indicate that a culture's music is healthy, for folk tradition is based on the active participation of communities and on inter-generational transmission. Little of this is yet operative in the Gaelic world, especially where language is concerned.

Many of the important issues regarding development boil down to a basic question: Is Gaelic culture merely a deviant, subordinate, peasant subculture which needs to be improved and developed according to the norms and aesthetics of the English-speaking world? Or is Gaelic culture an entity unto itself, with its own independent aesthetics and cultural logic, to be judged according to its own standards, valid in its own right, free to develop according to its own needs and resources?

The answer should be the same as comparing Tibetan culture with Chinese, Estonian culture with Russian, Icelandic culture with Danish, or Sami culture with Scandinavian: 'diversity is desirable in cultures as well as in biology, and what is good for North America, Japan, or England is not necessarily good for Gaels'.[25]

It is unwise for Gaelic to follow too closely to the trends and culture of the English-speaking world. Adopting the fashions of the English-speaking world will reinforce its position as a second-class poor-relation chasing after a goal moving too rapidly for it to ever capture. Gaelic 'pop' music made in the 1970s, which at the time was an attempt to 'modernize' Gaelic music, sounds like a derivative of to 1970s English music. Traditional Gaelic styles do not go out of fashion, but hold their own on their own ground.

There are those who dismiss the agenda of cultural revitalization with the same statement made to reject the aspirations of environmentalists: 'You cannot go back'. The problem with such a retort is that it buys into the idea of linear cultural evolution, that all societies move in a single direction called 'progress' and that any desire to re-activate portions of the cultural matrix abandoned in the relentless march of progress is regressive.[26] Yet, it should be clear that the ultimate consequences of the current path that techno-consumerism is forging leads to a corporate mono-culture which is ecologically suicidal and morally bankrupt.

We rather need to remember that each society has its own underlying cultural matrix which directs its many activities and forms its value and belief system. Acknowledging that culture is a complex and dynamic tapestry gives us the freedom to reintegrate archaic threads which can alter the texture of the tapestry in advantageous ways.

History did not stop with the sons of Malcolm, with Culloden, with the Clearances, or with the 1872 Education Act. It is an ongoing process with which we should be actively engaged. Just as the decline of Gaelic was not an inevitable or natural event, but rather the result of antagonist policies and actions, neither should we accept that nothing can be done to change the status of Gaelic in the future. Rather, we should look at what our goals for the future look like, and decide how to create policies and conditions which enable that future to come about.

Many Native Americans can be heard to say, 'It is an exciting time to be alive.' It is not merely that many First Nations have started the long road to recovery as they revitalize their native languages and cultures. They also realize that the once smug assumptions of modernism, which fueled the ideology of their repressors, are no longer tenable. The Baconian experiment has rendered humankind the lord and possessor of nature and we are masters of everything but ourselves. Science and technology have unleashed forces of ecological destruction, cultural oppression, spiritual impoverishment, suffering, and poverty at a scale never before known. The more that the modernist world descends into its self-created social, spiritual, and ecological dilemmas, the more interest people have in the principles of primal cultures.

Scotland has similar reasons for optimism. Involvement in the European Union is a reminder that a diversity of nations and cultures, some of them very small in comparison with Scotland, co-exist as peers in the same broad political framework. Indeed, the growing voice of ethnic minorities within the United Kingdom itself has helped to challenge the Anglo-centric hegemony. A greater awareness of the social, ecological, psychological, and spiritual virtues of Gaelic culture could make it the basis of a vibrant and sustainable post-modernist culture.

Confronting the processes of the cultural invasion of Gaeldom could help to heal the divisions which have torn Scotland's psyche and conspired to keep it powerless. It could renew the vigour of Scottish culture from within and reinforce the sense of place and identity which has only recently been disrupted from its ancient roots. It could change Scotland from being a mediocre periphery of the Anglo-American world to being at the centre of a Gaelic/Scottish world. All of this together could help give Scotland the self-confidence necessary to seize control of its own future and reclaim its status as a proud European nation among peers.

The rehabilitation of Gaelic language and culture will require a careful process of planning and implementation by many people with a broad range of skills. Only then can the prophecies of the return of the Gaels to their rightful place in the Scottish nation be fulfilled and Gaelic once again return from exile on the margins to the fore in the Scottish cultural matrix.

Notes

Most proverbs which are not referenced can be found in the various editions of NGP.

INTRODUCTION

1 Robert Dodgshon 1998, pp. 3, 32, 102, 107, 242.
2 Richard Kearney 1985, pp. 10-12.
3 Eric Cheyfitz 1991, p. xiv.

CHAPTER 1
THINKING ABOUT CULTURE

1 Ernest Gellner 1991, p. 207.
2 Séan de Fréine 1978, p. 35.
3 Ernest Gellner 1991, p. 11.
4 Ruth Megaw and Vincent Megaw 1999, p. 53.
5 Paul Ricoeur, in Richard Kearney 1985, p. 260.
6 Jaan Puhvel 1987, p. 1.
7 Max Oelschlaeger 1991, pp. 9-10.
8 Jaan Puhvel 1987, p. 2.
9 Richard Kearney 1985, p. 32.
10 Max Oelschlaeger 1991, pp. 68-9 and the rest of Chapter Three; Lewis Mumford 1970, Chapters Three and Four, p. 199.
11 Max Oelschlaeger 1991, p. 202.
12 Séan de Fréine 1978, pp. 34-5; Paul Ricoeur in Richard Kearney 1978, pp. 261-2.
13 Lewis Mumford 1966, p. 96.
14 Lewis Mumford 1970, pp. 172-5, 197-209.
15 David Dickson 1974, pp. 9-11, 43, Chapter 7; Morris Berman 1990, *passim.*
16 Ronald Wright 1992, p. 207.
17 David Dickson 1974, p. 66. See also Barre Toelken 1979, pp. 251-5.
18 David Dickson 1974, p. 67.
19 Lewis Mumford 1966, p. 131.
20 John Shaw 1993, pp. 1, 10.
21 Armin Geertz 1994, p. 5.
22 Theodore Allen 1994, pp. 7-8, 22-3, 27-8, 69.
23 Ronald Wright 1992, p. 281.
24 Ibid., p. 124.
25 Ibid., p. 24.
26 Ibid., pp. 212-21.
27 Lewis Mumford 1970, p. 197. See also pp. 198-202, 206-7; 1966, pp. 4-5, 23; Charles Withers 1988, pp. 62-3.
28 David Dickson 1974, pp. 44; 53.
29 Max Oelschlager 1991, pp. 6-7.
30 Theodore Allen 1994, p. 31.
31 Arthur Williamson 1982, *passim*; Nicholas Canny 1973, pp. 588-9.
32 Nicholas Canny 1973, p. 581.
33 Ibid., p. 588.
34 Eric Cheyfitz 1991, p. xiv.
35 Quoted in Charles Withers 1988, pp. 110-11.
36 From the 'Inquiry into the Distress in the Highlands and Islands', *The Scotsman*, 30 January 1847.
37 Colin Kidd 1993, p. 279.
38 Lewis Mumford 1970, p. 208.
39 Max Oelschlaeger 1991, p. 65.
40 Lewis Mumford 1966, p. 57.
41 Helena Norberg-Hodge 1991, p. 149.
42 Paulo Freire 1996, p. 134.
43 Craig Beveridge and Ronald Turnbull 1989, p. 5.
44 Fritz Fanon 1967, p. 169.
45 Quoted in Theodore Allen 1994, p. 29.
46 Ibid., pp. 33-4.
47 Ronald Wright 1992, p. 7.
48 *The Scotsman*, 26 September, 1997.
49 Myles Dillon and Nora Chadwick 1967, p. 17. See D. Ellis Evans 1997, *passim*, for a more recent defense of this.

50 *Agricola* §11.
51 John MacInnes 1978, p. 456.
52 See Alan Bruford 1985.
53 Myles Dillon and Nora Chadwick 1967, p. 15.
54 John Koch 1991, p. 18.
55 Myles Dillon and Nora Chadwick 1967, p. 16.
56 John Waddell 1991, p. 7.
57 William J. Watson 1926, p. 6.
58 John Koch 1991, p. 21.
59 Ibid., p. 22.
60 Myles Dillon and Nora Chadwick 1967, pp. 108-9.
61 See Alfred Smyth 1984, Chapter Two.
62 Proinsias Mac Cana 1985, p. 73.
63 Ibid., p. 64.
64 Ruth and Vincent Megaw 1999, p. 33.
65 Máire Mac Neill 1962, p. 356.
66 Margaret Bennett 1992, pp. xvii-xviii.
67 Michael Lynch 1992, p. xvii.
68 I.F. Grant 1961, p. 279.
69 John MacInnes 1992a, p. 121.
70 J.G. Campbell 1900, p. ix.
71 I.F. Grant 1961, pp. 279-80.
72 John MacInnes 1989b, p. 379.
73 William J. Watson 1926, p. 198.
74 Hamish Henderson 1989, p. 265.
75 Thomas Charles Edwards 1995, pp. 723, 733.
76 John MacInnes 1989a, p. 92.
77 John Koch 1991, p. 22.
78 John MacInnes 1989a, p. 93.
79 Charles Withers 1988, p. 66.
80 Fergus Kelly 1988, p. 113.
81 Proinsias Mac Cana 1985, p. 65.
82 John MacInnes 1981, pp. 152-3.
83 John MacInnes 1989a, pp. 98-9.

CHAPTER 2
A GAELIC HISTORY OF SCOTLAND

1 B.A. Crone 1993, p. 251.
2 Anna Ritchie 1995, p. 22.
3 Graham and Anna Ritchie 1991, pp. 101-5.
4 Alfred Smyth 1984, pp. 53-5; Michael Lynch 1992, p. 5.
5 Anna Ritchie 1995, p. 21.
6 John Waddell 1991, *passim.*
7 Alfred Smyth 1984, p. 43.
8 W.F.H. Nicolaisen 1996, pp. 4-5; Michael Lynch 1992, p. 7.
9 Alfred Smyth 1984, p. 48.
10 W.F.H. Nicolaisen 1976, p. 173.
11 Alfred Smyth 1984, pp. 47-8; Katherine Forsyth 1997, p. 23; W.F.H. Nicolaisen 1976, Chapters 8 and 9.
12 W.F.H. Nicolaisen 1996, pp. 15-19.
13 Alfred Smyth 1984, pp. 49-51.
14 Ibid., p. 49.
15 Alex Woolf 1998, passim. For comments about the political motivations of assuming a non-Celtic identity for the Picts, see William Fergusson 1998, Chapter Twelve.
16 Michael Lynch 1992, p. 8; Alfred Smyth 1984, pp. 43-4.
17 William J. Watson 1926, pp. 391-95.
18 Michael Lynch 1992, pp. 17-19.
19 Alfred Smyth 1984, pp. 79-80
20 Ibid., pp. 25-6.
21 R.B. Warner 1995, *passim.*
22 Thomas Charles-Edwards 1995, p. 710.
23 Kenneth Jackson 1972, p. 50.
24 William J. Watson 1926, pp. 390, 459-60.
25 Ibid., p. 436.
26 W.F.H. Nicolaisen 1996, pp. 6-10.
27 Michael Lynch 1992, p. 32; John Bannerman 1989, pp. 126-32.
28 Michael Lynch 1992, p. 36.
29 John Bannerman 1989, p. 127.
30 Michael Lynch 1992, p. 35; see also Alfred Smyth 1984, pp. 134-5.
31 Alfred P. Smyth 1984, pp. 14, 40; Michael Lynch 1992, pp. 8-11.
32 J.E. Caerwyn Williams and Patrick Ford 1992, p. 67.
33 John Lorne Campbell 1945, p. 12.
34 Michael Lynch 1992, p. 17; Alfred P. Smyth 1984, pp. 68-71.
35 Alfred Smyth 1984, pp. 177-9; Michael Lynch 1992, pp. 22-3.
36 Alfred Smyth 1984, pp. 176-82.
37 Ibid., pp. 187-9.
38 Benjamin Hudson 1996, p. 200.
39 Davit Broun 1997, p. 9.
40 Michael Lynch 1992, p. 44; Alfred Smyth 1984, pp. 231-3.
41 Alfred Smyth 1984, p. 157.
42 W.F.H. Nicolaisen 1976, p. 133; John Bannerman 1988, p. 2.
43 G.W.S. Barrow 1981b, p. 14.

44 Michael Lynch 1992, p. 53.
45 G.W.S. Barrow 1981b, p. 43.
46 Ibid., p. 29.
47 Michael Lynch 1992, p. 79. See also Michael Lynch 1992, p. 82; G.W.S. Barrow 1981b, pp. 70, 76.
48 See, for example, John Bannerman 1989, pp. 148-9; G.W.S. Barrow 1981b, p. 107.
49 Michael Lynch 1992, pp. 82-3.
50 Ibid., p. 63.
51 G.W.S. Barrow 1981b, pp. 51-2.
52 John Bannerman 1993, p. 23.
53 G.W.S. Barrow 1989, p. 70.
54 Alexander Allerdyce 1888, p. 388.
55 G.W.S. Barrow 1989, passim; Michael Lynch 1992, p. 68.
56 John MacInnes 1992a, p. 106; John Bannerman 1989, *passim.*
57 Michael Lynch 1992, pp. 118-19; John Bannerman 1993, p. 38.
58 Michael Lynch 1992, pp. 96, 125.
59 Archibald Constable 1892, p. 38.
60 John Bannerman 1977, p. 216.
61 Ibid., pp. 213-5; John MacInnes 1981, p. 147.
62 Jean Munro 1981, p. 126.
63 John MacInnes 1981, p. 148.
64 G.W.S. Barrow 1989, pp. 67-8.
65 Michael Lynch 1992, pp. 68-9.
66 Charles Withers 1984, p. 23.
67 George Buchanan, pp. 103-4.
68 W.D.G. Sellar 1989, *passim.*
69 John MacInnes 1992a, p. 102; 1989a, pp. 92-3.
70 Michael Lynch 1992, p. 68.
71 Archibald Constable 1892, p. 50.
72 Michael Lynch 1992, p. 168; David Sellar 1981, pp. 108-9.
73 Arthur Williamson 1996, pp. 46-54; Dòmhnall Uilleam Stiùbhart 1996, p. 205.
74 Arthur Williamson 1996, pp. 62-6.
75 Terence McCaughey 1989, pp. 173-4.
76 Michael Lynch 1992, pp. 189, 196-7.
77 Arthur Williamson 1982, pp. 34-43.
78 Terence McCaughey 1989, p. 177; Victor Durkacz 1983, pp. 1-5; John L. Campbell 1945, pp. 40-1.
79 Terence McCaughey 1989, pp. 178-9.
80 Arthur Williamson 1982, pp. 44-5.
81 Robert Dodgshon 1998, Chapter Five.
82 Charles W.J. Withers 1988, pp. 88-90; Allan Macinnes 1993, pp. 35, 43.
83 Jane Dawson 1987, pp. 113-17; Allan Macinnes 1993, pp. 35-7.
84 Allan Macinnes 1993, p. 35.
85 Charles Withers 1988, pp. 112-14; Allan Macinnes 1993, pp. 38-41; John L. Campbell 1945, pp. 44-5; 1994, Chapter Six; Dòmhnall Uilleam Stiùbhart 1996, p. 56.
86 John MacInnes 1992a, p. 107.
87 Charles Withers 1988, p. 113.
88 Dòmhnall Uilleam Stiùbhart 1996, pp. 118-19, 196; Allan Macinnes 1993, pp. 40, 45-6.
89 Allan Macinnes 1993, pp. 41-3, 46, 49; 1996, pp. 46-7.
90 Allan Macinnes 1996, Chapter Four.
91 John L. Campbell 1945, pp. 45-6.
92 Michael Lynch 1992, p. 304.
93 Jane Dawson 1994, p. 247.
94 Michael Lynch 1992, p. 304; Dòmhnall Uilleam Stiùbhart 1996, p. 84; John L. Campbell 1945, p. 43.
95 John L. Campbell 1945, pp. 46- 9; Charles Withers 1988, pp. 120-2.
96 John L. Campbell 1945, pp. 50-1.
97 *OIL*, p. 228.
98 Michael Lynch 1992, p. 327.
99 *BSC*, p. 18.
100 Michael Lynch 1992, pp. 328-34.
101 William Gillies 1988b, pp. 54-61.
102 John Simpson 1988, p. 10; Donald Fraser 1988, pp. 40-1.
103 Revd G.V.R. Grant 1988, p. 30; Donald Fraser 1988, p. 43; Allan Macinnes 1996, p. 179.
104 John Simpson 1988, pp. 11-12.
105 John MacInnes 1981, pp. 152-6; 1989a, p. 98; William Gillies 1988b, pp. 56-7; *HSFF*, p. 4.
106 *HSFF*, p. 118.
107 For example, *HSFF*, 214, 240-2, 252, etc.
108 For example, John Dewar 1964, p. 82; John Grant Michie 1908, p. 55; Marianne McLean 1991, p. 20; Allan Macinnes 1996, pp. 212-13.
109 Margaret MacKay 1980, p. 6.
110 *Old Statistical Account for Scotland* (1791-9), Kirkmichael Parish, Banffshire.

111 William Gillies 1988b, p. 67.
112 Henry Mackenzie 1805, pp. 50. See also John MacInnes 1989a, p. 99. For a poem written a hundred years earlier with the same import, see *EB*, p. 100.
113 Alexander Allardyce 1888, p. 396.
114 Duncan Campbell 1910, pp. 119-20.
115 Anne Grant 1811, p. 126.
116 Duncan Campbell 1910, pp. 53, 91; John MacInnes 1982, p. 239; 1989b, p. 383.
117 John MacInnes 1982, pp. 233-4; 1989b, pp. 385-7; 1992a, pp. 117-18; John Gibson 1998, pp. 138-9, 171-3.
118 John MacInnes 1989b, pp. 386-7; Donald Meek 1996, pp. 19-20.
119 Alexander Campbell 1804, p. 208.
120 Liz Curtis 1984, p. 65.
121 Derick Thomson 1994, pp. 44-7.
122 Donald Meek 1995, pp. 34-8.
123 Charles Fraser-Mackintosh 1877, p. 418.
124 *BG*, p. xxiii.
125 Colin Kidd 1995, p. 46.
126 Julian D'Arcy 1996, pp. 37, 39.
127 Michael Lynch 1992, p. 112.
128 Colin Kidd 1995, p. 66.
129 Somhairle MacGill-eain 1985, p. 19.
130 Donald Meek 1996, p. 34.
131 Terence McCaughey 1989, p. 198.
132 John MacInnes 1982, p. 239; 1989b, p. 388; Terence McCaughey 1989, pp. 194-5, 203.
133 Victor Durkacz 1983, pp. 159-64.
134 John L. Campbell 1945, p. 62.
135 'An Deis Odhar' by Murchadh MacPhàrlain.
136 George Foster 1973, pp. 56-7.
137 Charles Withers 1988, pp. 59-61; Dòmhnall Uilleam Stiùbhart 1996, p. 57.

CHAPTER 3
GAELIC ORAL TRADITION

1 John MacInnes 1981, p. 142.
2 The following is largely based on Morton Bloomfield and Charles Dunn 1989, Chapters One, Two and Three.
3 Ibid., p. 8.
4 Ibid., p. 9.
5 Fergus Kelly 1976.
6 Morton Bloomfield and Charles Dunn 1989, pp. 30-1; Myles Dillon and Nora Chadwick 1967, pp. 126-7.
7 Morton Bloomfield and Charles Dunn 1989, pp. 6, 7.
8 Gearóid Mac Niocaill 1972, pp. 43-4.
9 Morton Bloomfield and Charles Dunn 1989, p. 7.
10 See ibid., Chapter Three, for a discussion of these.
11 William Gillies 1988a, p. 246.
12 Ibid.
13 Ibid., pp. 247, 250; J.E. Caerwyn Williams and Patrick Ford 1992, p. 164.
14 William Gillies 1988a, p. 247; J.E. Caerwyn Williams and Patrick Ford 1992, p. 160.
15 J.E. Caerwyn Williams and Patrick Ford 1992, pp. 161-2.
16 Ibid., pp. 162-3; William Gillies 1988a, pp. 250-1.
17 IBP, p. 8.
18 Only some subset of these may be valid for any particular dialect, however. See John Shaw 1992-3, p. 40.
19 William Gillies 1988a, p. 248; J.E. Caerwyn Williams and Patrick Ford 1992, p. 155; John MacInnes 1968, *passim*; John MacInnes 1986, p. 95.
20 *GC*, pp. 92-4.
21 Proinsias Mac Cana 1978, p. 462; Joan Radner 1990, p. 177.
22 Iain MacAonghuis 1986, *passim.*
23 Archibald Brown 1908, p. 118.
24 William Gillies 1988a, p. 245.
25 Kenneth Jackson 1957, p. 128.
26 Benjamin Hudson 1996, §152.
27 John Bannerman 1989, *passim.*
28 Derick Thomson 1977; Ronald Black 1977, p. 343; Wilson McLeod, personal communication.
29 Katherine Simms 1990, p. 617.
30 Martin Martin 1716, p. 104.
31 Ronald Black 1973, *passim.*
32 William Gillies 1988a, pp. 253-4; Proinsias Mac Cana 1979, pp. 448, 478.
33 William Gillies 1988a, p. 257; Proinsias Mac Cana 1979, p. 458.
34 *BA*, lines 1859-62.
35 William Gillies 1988a, pp. 245, 247, 253, 254; John MacInnes 1981, pp. 437-8, 449;

Proinsias MacCana 1985, p. 69; John L. Campbell 1994, p. 49.
36 John MacInnes 1968, pp. 33-7.
37 Ibid., p. 33.
38 John MacInnes 1978, p. 495.
39 The term 'Gaelic panegyric code' was coined by Dr John MacInnes and is systematically explored by him in John MacInnes 1978. For the uniformity of verse style, see John MacInnes 1981, p. 157.
40 Although the line of transmission from court to commoner was not always direct. See John MacInnes 1968, p. 32.
41 Quoted in John MacInnes 1981, p. 145.
42 James Logan 1876, p. 315.
43 Donald MacAulay 1976, p. 46; see also Breandan Ó Madagáin 1985, pp. 175-6; Thomas A. McKean 1997, Chapter Five; Barre Toelken 1979, p. 193.
44 Allan MacDougall 1829, p. 185.
45 *Highlander*, 2 June, 1877.
46 Donald Meek 1995, p. 25.
47 Breandán Ó Madagáin 1985, pp. 215, 131.
48 John MacInnes 1968, p. 40; Breandán Ó Madagáin 1985, pp. 182-4.
49 Breandán Ó Madagáin 1985, pp. 177-8.
50 Breandán Ó Madagáin 1993, *passim.*
51 William Gillies 1988a, p. 255; Thomas A. McKean 1997, p. 131; John MacInnes 1966, pp. 60-1.
52 John MacInnes 1978, pp. 447-8.
53 Ibid., pp. 448-52.
54 William J. Watson 1914-19, p. 219.
55 *BA*, poem 15.
56 *Celtic Magazine* 7 (1881), pp. 50-1.
57 Martin MacGregor 1998, *passim.*
58 George Henderson 1898, p. 87.
59 Herbert Campbell 1926, p. 217.
60 William Gillies 1977, *passim.*
61 Alexander Allardyce 1888, p. 411.
62 Frances Tolmie 1911, p. 235.
63 John MacInnes 1968, p. 37; *EB*, pp. 279-80.
64 William Shaw 1778, pp. 123-4.
65 See for example *MC*, pp. xi, 33; Frances Tolmie 1911, p. 236.
66 *NGP*, p. 134.
67 John MacInnes 1969, *passim.*
68 James Logan 1876, p. 309.
69 Revd W. Forsyth 1900, p. 277.
70 William Mackenzie 1892, p. 99.
71 *Tocher* 38, p. 8.
72 John Francis Cambell 1860/1994, vol. 1, p. 5.
73 James Logan 1876, pp. 237-8.
74 See also Breandán Ó Madagáin 1985, p. 189; Alexander MacDonald 1914, p. 252.
75 John Dewar 1964, p. 259.
76 William Gillies 1987, p. 63.
77 James Logan 1876, p. 221.
78 Thomas A. McKean 1997, pp. 142-5.
79 Ibid., p. 145.
80 John F. Campbell 1860/1994, p. 34; see also John Shaw 1987, p. xxxvii.
81 John Shaw 1987, p. xxii. See also John Shaw 1993, pp. 6-7.
82 Alexander Allardyce 1888, pp. 408-9.
83 Duncan Campbell 1910, p. 120.
84 John Shaw 1993, p. 5.
85 From 'The Moving Picture' by Angus Peter Campbell in *As an Fhearann: from the land*, 1986; see also John Shaw 1993, pp. 2-3.
86 John Lorne Campbell 1990, p. 20.
87 *An Teachdaire Gàidhealach* 1836, pp. 228-9.

CHAPTER 4
THE ORGANIZATION OF SOCIETY

1 Charles Withers 1988, p. 62.
2 Arthur Williamson 1996, pp. 65-6.
3 From page 14 of *A Second Letter to a Noble Lord containing a plan for effectually uniting and sincerely attaching the Highlanders to the British Constitution*, published anonymously in 1748.
4 T.C. Smout 1969, p. 47. See also Allan Macinnes 1996, p. 6; Roger Dodgshon 1998, pp. 10, 13.
5 Nerys Patterson 1994, Chapter Two; John Bannerman 1977, p. 209.
6 John Mohawk 1990, p. 94. See also Nerys Patterson 1994, p. 29.
7 R.W. Munro 1981, pp. 122-3.
8 Edmund Burt 1754, vol. 2, pp. 105-6.
9 Derick Thomson 1994, p. 44.
10 John Bannerman 1988, p. 5.

11 Osgood MacKenzie 1921, p. 59.
12 Anne Grant 1811, p. 47.
13 John Bannerman 1977, p. 224.
14 Calum MacPhàrlain 1908, p. 56.
15 John MacInnes 1981, pp. 144-5; Dauvit Broun 1997, pp. 6-7.
16 Edmund Burt 1754, vol. 2, p. 86.
17 N.B. Aitchison 1994, p. 63.
18 Proinsias MacCana 1979, p. 456.
19 *HSFF*, p. 5.
20 Written by James Dalrymple in 1681, quoted in William Fergusson 1998, p. 153.
21 Edmund Burt 1754, vol. 1, p. 106.
22 Michael Lynch 1992, p. 85; W.D.H. Sellar 1989, pp. 13-14; Rosemary Ommer 1986, p. 128; John Bannerman 1998, p. 86.
23 Donncha Ó Corráin 1972, p. 39.
24 John L. Campbell 1975, p. 57.
25 John Bannerman 1977, pp. 221, 225-6.
26 Anne Grant 1811, p. 256.
27 Ibid., p. 206.
28 Ibid., pp. 306, 302. See also Robert Dodgshon 1998, p. 45.
29 Quoted in William Fergusson 1998, p. 66.
30 Walter MacFarlane 1900, Genealogical Collections I, pp. 182-3. See also R.W. Munro 1981, pp. 119-22.
31 Katherine Simms 1990, p. 609.
32 Martin Martin 1716, pp. 101-2.
33 Ibid., pp. 209-210.
34 Rosemary Ommer 1986, p. 125.
35 I.F. Grant 1961, pp. 31, 57; Robert Dodgshon 1998, pp. 95, 97.
36 John L. Campbell 1975, p. 45.
37 Colm Ó Baoill 1994, lines 544-9. Further discussion and examples in *West Highland Free Press*, 21 June 1996.
38 Martin Martin 1716, p. 97.
39 R.W. Munro 1981, p. 119.
40 Martin Martin 1716, p. 108.
41 J.R.N. Macphail 1914, p. 45.
42 Martin Martin 1716, pp. 103-4.
43 Allan Macinnes 1996, p. 57; Robert Dodgshon 1998, p. 89.
44 John MacInnes 1991, p. 383; 1981, p. 157.
45 Nerys Patterson 1994, pp. 11-12; R.W. Munro 1981, p. 121; I.F. Grant 1961, pp. 11-12.
46 William J. Watson 1916, p. 133.
47 Æneas J.G. MacKay 1892, pp. 45-6.
48 Quoted in I.F. Grant 1961, p. 27.
49 Iain Crichton Smith 1986, p. 44.
50 John Michie 1908, p. 316.
51 W.D.H. Sellar 1985, p. 12.
52 Myles Dillon and Nora Chadwick 1967, p. 133.
53 Alexander MacDonald 1925, p. 281.
54 Revd John Lane Buchanan 1793, p. 114.
55 Alexander MacDonald 1925, p. 288.
56 Herbert Campbell 1926, p. 200.
57 R.W. Munro 1981, p. 126; Allan Macinnes 1996, pp. 11-12, 51; Robert Dodgshon 1998, pp. 11, 34, 35.
58 R.W. Munro 1981, pp. 126-7.
59 Allan Macinnes 1996, p. 10; Robert Dodgshon 1998, pp. 34, 40.
60 J.F. Campbell 1861/1994, vol. 2, p. 374, 'The Story of Conall Gulban'.
61 Martin Martin 1716, p. 109.
62 Donald Meek 1978, no. 642.
63 BA, p. 273.
64 See 'The Quern Dust Calendar', *West Highland Free Press*, 4 December 1998 for some discussion.
65 John Lorne Campbell 1975, p. 76.
66 Duncan Campbell 1910, p. 65.
67 Alexander MacDonald 1925, pp. 298-9; *BA*, p. 274.
68 Dòmhnall Uilleam Stiùbhart 1999, forthcoming.
69 Anne Grant 1811, p. 50.
70 Richard Jenkins 1990, p. 305.
71 See Lisa Bitel 1996, Chapter Seven, for echoes of this in Early Irish literature.
72 Nerys Patterson 1994, pp. 310-1; Dòmhnall Uilleam Stiùbhart 1999, forthcoming. An anecdote illustrating the separate maintenance of this wealth can be seen in John Dewar 1964, p. 101.
73 Dòmhnall Uilleam Stiùbhart 1999, forthcoming.
74 Mary Mackellar 1888, p. 146.
75 Angus Matheson 1952, p. 374.
76 Nerys Patternson 1994, pp. 211, 288, 311-15.
77 Somhairle MacGill-eain 1985, p. 125.
78 Angus Matheson 1952, p. 360.
79 John Dewar 1964, pp. 235-6.

80 Colm Ó Baoill 1997, lines 945-6.
81 Also called *mnathan-tuiridh*.
82 *CG* 5, p. 344.
83 Angela Bourke 1993, *passim*.
84 Alan Bruford 1996, p. 63; Angela Bourke 1993, p. 161.
85 Discussed and quoted in John MacInnes 1968, pp. 37-8.
86 J.C. Watson 1937-8, pp. 50-1.
87 Domhnall Uilleam Stiùbhart 1999, forthcoming; Angus Matheson 1964-6, pp. 7-10.
88 Thomas Owen Clancy 1996, p. 55.
89 John MacInnes 1966, pp. 63-4; Nerys Patterson 1994, p. 306.
90 John MacInnes 1978, p. 482.
91 Dòmhnall Uilleam Stiùbhart 1999, forthcoming.
92 John Dewar 1964, p. 167.
93 Dòmhnall Uilleam Stiubhart 1999, forthcoming.
94 Ibid.
95 Ibid.
96 Ibid.
97 Quoted in Liam Breatnach 1996, p. 113. For some discussion of these principles in early Gaelic society, see Nerys Patterson 1994, Chapter Four.
98 Revd John Lane Buchanan 1793, pp. 48-9.
99 Rosemary Ommer 1986, p. 126.
100 Colmán Etchington 1996, p. 131.
101 W.J. Watson 1927-8, stanzas 4-5.
102 Allan Macinnes 1996, p. 18.
103 David Stewart 1885, pp. 41-3.
104 Edmund Burt 1754, vol. 2, p. 177.
105 R.W. Munro 1981, p. 124.
106 Lewis Mumford 1964, p. 359.
107 Anne Grant 1811, p. 51.
108 Robert Dodgshon 1998, pp. 42, 48-50, has a slightly different interpretation.
109 R.W. Munro 1981, pp. 122-3.
110 I.F. Grant 1961, pp. 177, 198, 257.
111 Roland Smith 1929, p. 122.
112 George Foster 1973, pp. 60-1; Robert Dodgshon 1998, pp. 27, 36, 107.
113 Allan Macinnes 1996, pp. 71, 142; Robert Dodgshon 1998, p. 113.
114 Iain Crichton Smith 1986, pp. 49, 43.

CHAPTER 5
THE OPERATION OF SOCIETY

1 Proinsias Mac Cana 1985, pp. 64-6, 76.
2 John MacInnes 1989a, p. 95.
3 John MacInnes 1991, p. 382. See also John MacInnes 1989a, pp. 94-6; Alan Macinnes 1993, p. 39.
4 Allan Macinnes 1996, pp. 65-6.
5 John MacInnes 1989a, pp. 94-6 for several more examples.
6 Paruig Turner 1813, p. 220.
7 John MacInnes 1991, p. 389.
8 George Buchanan, p. 161.
9 Alexander Allardyce 1888, p. 408.
10 *Celtic Magazine* 1, p. 485.
11 Martin Martin 1716, pp. 101-2.
12 *BA*, lines 909-10.
13 *BG*, lines 5188-91.
14 W.J. Watson 1914-9, p. 221.
15 George Henderson 1898, p. 283.
16 Michael Lynch 1992, pp. 42, 53; W.D.H. Sellar 1989, passim; John Bannerman 1998, p. 113.
17 Hugh MacDonald, quoted in W.D.H. Sellar 1989, pp. 3-4.
18 J. Carmichael Watson 1940, §21-2.
19 Donald Meek 1978, no. 488.
20 Alexander Allardyce 1888, p. 419.
21 I.F. Grant 1961, pp. 100-5.
22 Ibid., p. 44.
23 N.B. Aitchison 1994, p. 69.
24 W.D.H. Sellar 1989, p. 16.
25 John Bannerman 1974, p. 155.
26 I.F. Grant 1961, pp. 87, 216; Allan Macinnes 1996, p. 20; Robert Dodgshon 1998, p. 66.
27 G.W.S. Barrow 1989, p. 74.
28 W.F. Skene 1890, p. 432. About *coinnmed* and *cuid-oidhche* see John Bannerman 1988, p. 9.
29 W.D.H. Sellar 1989, p. 17.
30 W.J. Watson 1927-8, §6.
31 Donald Meek 1995, poem 24, lines 21-4.
32 Alexander MacDonald 1925, p. 298.
33 T.M. Charles-Edwards 1978, p. 136.
34 James Logan 1876, pp. 46-7.
35 G.W.S. Barrow 1989, p. 75; W.D.H. Sellar 1989, p. 16.
36 James Logan 1876, pp. 142-3.

37 Nerys Patterson 1994, pp. 126-7.
38 Alexander Allardyce 1888, p. 394.
39 Revd Duncan Campbell 1978, no. 30.
40 T.M. Charles-Edwards 1978, pp. 123-4, 130.
41 This is mentioned in Heptads 12, 13, and 14 of the *Senchas Màr.* Thanks to Dr Liam Breathnach for these references.
42 Morton Bloomfield and Charles Dunn 1989, pp. 6-8.
43 *GC*, p. 174.
44 NLS MS. 72.1.39, f. 29.r, kindly provided to me by Wilson McLeod.
45 *OIL*, lines 1701-6.
46 For example, in *OIL* lines 735-8, and line 2852.
47 Traditional text of *Mo Rùn Geal Òg.*
48 Anne Grant 1811, p. 118.
49 I.F. Grant 1981, p. 72; Alexander Nicolson 1994, p. 17.
50 Colm Ó Baoill 1997, lines 223-30.
51 Donald Campbell 1978, no. 365.
52 Revd John Lane Buchanan 1793, pp. 100-1.
53 Colm Ó Baoill 1997, lines 810-11.
54 William MacGillivray 1996, pp. 24, 44-5.
55 James Logan 1876, pp. 368-70.
56 Duncan Campbell 1910, p. 99.
57 Margaret Bennett 1992, pp. 91-3.
58 Revd John Lane Buchanan 1793, pp. 109, 111.
59 Nerys Patterson 1994, pp. 288-9.
60 Donald Meek 1978, no. 639.
61 Revd John G. Campbell 1895, p. 135. This closely parallels the dialogue between Deirdre and Naoise.
62 Traditional text of *Mo Rùn Geal Òg.*
63 Alwyn Rees and Brinley Rees 1961, pp. 93-4.
64 Margaret Bennett 1992, pp. 6-30.
65 Ibid., pp. 38-9.
66 Ibid., pp. 7-8, 28; Alexander Allardyce 1888, p. 423.
67 Charles Fergusson 1878, p. 133; John Ramsay 1888, p. 423.
68 Mary Mackellar 1888, p. 152.
69 Joseph Nagy 1987, pp. 161-2.
70 Ibid., p. 163. See also Kim McCone 1995, passim.
71 *BA*, lines 313-6.
72 Joseph Nagy 1987, pp. 171-2.
73 Nerys Patterson 1994, pp. 124-5.
74 Ibid., pp. 294-304.
75 James Logan 1876, p. 373. An example is given in Alexander MacDonald 1914, p. 22.
76 Proinsias Mac Cana 1980, pp. 74-5; Lisa Bitel 1996, pp. 51-6.
77 K.C. Craig 1944, p. 49.
78 Alexander Allardyce 1888, p. 420.
79 Margaret Bennett 1992, pp. 98-103.
80 William G. Stewart 1851, p. 192.
81 Archibald Brown 1908, p. 182.
82 At least two examples survive: Alexander Nicolson 1994, p. 217, and *CG* 2, p. 214.
83 Alexander MacDonald 1914, p. 148.
84 Alexander Cameron 1894, p. 477.
85 James Logan 1876, p. 375.
86 John Shaw 1987, p. 420.
87 Revd John Buchanan 1793, pp. 169-70.
88 Alexander MacBain 1888, p. 240.
89 *BA*, poem 37.
90 Donald Meek 1978, no. 297.
91 Graham Kew 1998, p. 102, from an early seventeeth-century manuscript describing Ireland. I have modernized the spelling.
92 Yi-Fu Tuan 1974, p. 148.
93 Alwyn Rees and Brinley Rees 1961, pp. 105-6.
94 George Henderson 1911, p. 19.
95 *BA*, lines 1943-4.
96 Donald MacPherson 1868, p. 4.
97 His treatise, which has been edited several times, is called *The Secret Commonwealth of Elves, Fauns, and Fairies.*
98 Raghnall Mac 'ille Dhuibh, *West Highland Free Press*, 4 December 1998; Allan Macinnes 1993, p. 40; John L. Campbell 1994, Chapter Six. This measure was also aimed at the many Scottish Gaelic mercenaries who travelled and fought widely in Scotland and Ireland.
99 Ibid.
100 Raghnall Mac 'ille Dhuibh, *West Highland Free Press*, 22 November 1998.
101 Alexander Stewart 1928, p. 66.
102 Rosemary Ommer 1986, p. 129; Allan Macinnes 1996, pp. 71, 142; Robert Dodgshon 1998, p. 113.

103 Robert Dodgshon 1998, pp. 12. 107, 111.
104 *CD*, p. 212.
105 Edmund Burt 1754, vol. 2, pp. 335-6.
106 John MacDonald 1955-8, §17.
107 *OIL*, lines 1566-9. For other examples, see lines 1135, 1511, 1514, 1879, 1901, and 1909.
108 *A Second Letter to a Noble Lord* ..., 1748, pp. 22-3.
109 First given in Henry MacKenzie 1805 and reprinted in W.J. Watson 1929, p. 135.
110 *Celtic Review* 1, pp. 379-80.
111 Alexander MacDonald 1914, pp. 8-9.

CHAPTER 6
NATURE AND ECOLOGY

1 Edmund Burt 1754, vol. 2, pp. 268-9.
2 Quoted in Charles Withers 1988, p. 64.
3 Quoted and discussed in Lewis Mumford 1964, pp. 77-9. See also Max Oelschlager 1991, pp. 86-7.
4 Keith Thomas 1983, p. 29. See also Lewis Mumford 1964, pp. 172-3.
5 Quoted in Iain Fraser Grigor 1979, p. 13.
6 See discussions in Lewis Mumford 1966, pp. 36-7; Max Oelschlager 1991, Chapter Ten.
7 John Mohawk 1990, p. 94.
8 Helena Norberg-Hodge 1991, pp. 182-3.
9 John Bierhorst 1994, p. 10.
10 Yi-Fu Tuan 1974, Chapters 6 and 7; Max Oelschlaeger 1991, pp. 325, 350.
11 Max Oelschlager 1991, pp. 318, 339.
12 Robert Dodgshon 1998, Chapters 6 to 9.
13 Mary Mackellar 1888, p. 149.
14 I.F. Grant 1961, pp. 78-81.
15 Osgood MacKenzie 1921, p. 27.
16 Mary Mackellar 1888, p. 141.
17 Duncan Campbell 1910, p. 262.
18 I.F. Grant 1961, p. 160; Osgood MacKenzie 1921, p. 79; Alan Macinnes 1996, p. 18.
19 Robert Dodgshon 1998, p. 209.
20 Duncan Campbell 1910, p. 618.
21 Robert Dodgshon 1998, p. 213.
22 I.F. Grant 1961, p. 94.
23 Robert Dodgshon 1998, pp. 12, 107, 111, 235-6.
24 Duncan Campbell 1910, pp. 52-3.
25 Osgood MacKenzie 1921, p. 155.
26 Marianne McLean 1991, pp. 18-19.
27 Edmund Burt 1754, vol 2, p. 264.
28 Donald Meek 1978, no. 565. See also no. 150.
29 Max Oelschlaeger 1991, pp. 14-7.
30 Alwyn Rees and Brinley Rees 1961, pp. 89-94.
31 Nerys Patternson 1994, pp. 120-1.
32 William Matheson 1965, p. 167.
33 Dáithí Ó hÓgáin 1991, p. 403; *Scottish Studies* 9, p. 205.
34 Ronald Black 1996, p. 50; *EB*, pp. 174-5; W.G. Stewart 1851, p. 163.
35 *An Gàidheal* 2 (1873), p. 135.
36 'The Quern Dust Calendar', *West Highland Free Press*, 21 January 1994.
37 Donald Meek 1978, no. 462.
38 Nerys Patterson 1994, p. 129.
39 Ibid., pp. 130-1.
40 Martin Martin 1716, p. 119; Alexander Allardyce 1888, p. 447.
41 A strikingly similar ritual was performed in a number of Native American cultures, with the explicit symbolism of renewing life. See John Bierhorst 1994, p. 269.
42 Thomas Pennant 1772. We might read this in terms of the symbolism of asserting boundaries between 'wild' and 'humanized' food.
43 John Dalyell 1834, p. 9.
44 Patricia Lysaght 1993, p. 41.
45 Lachlann MacKinnon (no date), p. 25.
46 Nerys Patterson 1994, p. 141.
47 Ibid., pp. 143-5.
48 John Bierhorst 1994, p. 123.
49 John L. Campbell 1958, p. 240.
50 Revd W. Forsyth 1900, p. 161.
51 Charles Dunn 1968, p. 109.
52 *RC* 2, p. 499.
53 Edmund Burt 1754, vol. 1, pp. 118-9.
54 William J. Watson 1927-8, §13.
55 *West Highland Free Press*, 31 July 1998, p. 17.
56 Martin Martin 1716, p. 85.
57 William MacKay 1914, pp. 425-6.
58 Nerys Patterson 1994, pp. 123-4.
59 Osgood MacKenzie 1921, p. 142.

60 *CG* 1, pp. 310-13.
61 George Henderson 1910, p. 262.
62 Martin Martin 1716, p. 273.
63 Tom Sjöblom 1994, p. 164.
64 Ronald Wright 1992, p. 233. See also Barre Toelken 1979, p. 254.
65 Osgood MacKenzie 1921, p. 94.
66 Keith Thomas 1983, p. 40.
67 Ibid., p. 94.
68 A selection of bird imitations can be heard on track 25 of *Celtic Mouth Music*, ISBN 1-55961-341-6.
69 Martin Martin 1716, pp. x-xii.
70 W. Mackenzie 1914, p. 116. The same practice is mentioned in John Dewar 1964, p. 58.
71 This was referred to as *còmhdhail*, but is also similar to the reading of the *frìth*. A similar naming custom is mentioned in John G. Campbell 1895, p. 29.
72 William J. Watson 1926, pp. 29-30.
73 Ibid., p. 29.
74 John MacInnes 1981, p. 143.
75 Ibid., p. 160. See also George Henderson 1911, pp. 109-30.
76 K.W. Grant 1925, p. 48.
77 Raonuill Macdomhnuill 1776, p. 320.
78 George Henderson 1911, p. 54.
79 John MacInnes 1992b, p. 1; Max Oelschlaeger 1991, p. 16.
80 John MacInnes 1989c, pp. 12, 18-20. Some examples of *an dà shaoghal* can be found in K.C. Craig 1944, p. 37; 'Òran mu'n Èideadh Ghàidhealach' by John MacCodrum; W.M. MacKenzie 1914, p. 262.
81 John Grant Michie 1908, p. 172.
82 A selection of these are in Joseph Macpherson 1929, p. 55.
83 Originally printed in the newspaper *The Highlander*, but quoted in Francis Thompson 1984, p. 9.
84 Donald Meek 1978, no. 693.
85 The Gaelic fairy is very unlike the fairy as depicted in modern English lore, however: he or she looks very much like a human, and does not have wings or other such features.
86 M. MacLeod Banks 1937, p. 93.
87 Revd Alexander Stewart 1883, pp. 21-2.
88 George Henderson 1911, p. 254. Variants can be found in *CG* 5, p. 387; W.Y. Evans-Wentz 1966, pp. 92, 95.
89 Alexander MacDonald 1914, p. 228.
90 William J. Watson 1926, pp. 426-7.
91 Written by Charles Smith in 1756, quoted in Máire Mac Neill 1962, p. 137. The poem given in *CG* 5, p. 386, and the tradition attached to it, appears to be a Scottish example of this practice.

CHAPTER 7
LANDSCAPE AND CULTURE

1 Quoted in Charles Dunn 1968, pp. 8-9.
2 Edmund Burt 1754, vol. 2, p. 340.
3 Craig Beveridge and Ronald Turnbull 1989, Chapter Three; Robert Dodgshon 1998, p. 213.
4 From the *History of Scotland for Schools* by I.M.M. MacPhail, quoted in ibid., p. 42.
5 I.F. Grant 1961, p. 242.
6 John O'Meara 1982, pp. 101-2.
7 From *The Plantation of Ulster* (1610), quoted in Patrick Sheeran 1984, p. 195.
8 Richard White and William Cronon, quoted in John Bierhorst 1994, p. 141.
9 John MacInnes 1992b, pp. 17-18; Barbara Rieti 1991, p. 3; Max Oelschlaeger 1991, p. 28. For the same opposition in Native American thought, see John Bierhorst 1994, p. 141.
10 Diarmuid Ó Giolláin 1991, pp. 200-1.
11 John MacInnes 1992b, p. 19.
12 Joseph Nagy 1987, *passim*.
13 Angela Bourke 1993, *passim*.
14 John MacInnes 1983, p. 9.
15 Angela Bourke 1993, p. 165.
16 Francis Thompson 1984, p. 49.
17 Ronald Black 1973, §17. A similar image occurs in *BG*, line 6810 ('*Òran na Comhachaig*').
18 William Matheson 1965, p. 165.
19 Thomas Sinton 1906, pp. 11-12.
20 Paruig Turner 1813, p. 111.
21 Revd W. Forsyth 1900, pp. 188-9.
22 Revd Charles Robertson 1926, p. 8.
23 *EB*, lines 879-81.

24 William J. Watson 1926, pp. 226-32.
25 Thomas Owen Clancy 1998, pp. 258, 304.
26 *CG* 2, p. 306.
27 Alexander MacBain 1888, p. 13.
28 John F. Campbell 1860/1994, vol. 1, p. 61.
29 Dáithí Ó hÓgáin 1991, p. 45.
30 *CG* 2, p. 245.
31 Revd W. Forsyth 1900, pp. 52-3.
32 James Logan 1876, p. 354.
33 Alexander MacDonald 1914, p. 229.
34 Ibid., p. 204. Also given in Thomas Sinton 1906, p. 286.
35 *BG*, lines 4912-19, 4988-95.
36 Alwyn Rees and Brinley Rees 1961, pp. 148, 159-60; John MacInnes 1978, p. 458; Yi-Fu Tuan 1974, p. 19.
37 Several examples are given in W.J. Watson 1927-8, p. 77.
38 Quoted in Alexander MacDonald 1914, p. 2.
39 John MacInnes 1981, p. 154.
40 William J. Watson 1926, pp. 247-8.
41 *GC*, p. 176.
42 Martin Martin 1716, p. 141.
43 James Logan 1876, p. 93.
44 M. MacLeod Banks 1939, pp. 196-7, about sites in Congarff, Aberdeenshire, with Gaelic names: *Dail nan Damh* (Delnadamph, 'Stag-haugh') and *Torr na Càise* (Tornahaish, 'Cheese-hillock'). Recorded about 1915 from someone who heard it from a man of eighty-three years of age who died in 1894.
45 Heinrich Wagner 1981, *passim*; John Koch 1991, *passim.*
46 Margaret Bennett 1992, p. 11.
47 John MacInnes 1992b, pp. 5, 7; 1989c, p. 10.
48 See, for example, W. M. Mackenzie 1914, p. 271.
49 Patrick Sheeran 1984, p. 203. See also Alwyn Rees and Brinley Rees 1961, p. 166.
50 *CG* 1, p. 207.
51 Revd William Gillies 1938, p. 260.
52 *The People's Journal*, 14 August 1886.
53 John MacInnes 1985, pp. 18-19.
54 Proinsias Mac Cana 1988, p. 335.
55 William J. Watson 1926, pp. 230, 469.
56 John Mac Cormick 1923, p. 69.
57 Ibid., p. 65.
58 Ibid., p. 67.
59 K.W. Grant 1925, pp. 7-8.
60 John MacInnes 1982, pp. 240-1.
61 Thanks to Pat Menzies for this material.
62 Proinsias Mac Cana 1988, p. 321.
63 See for example John F. Campbell 1860/1994, tale 34.
64 Thomas Sinton 1906, p. 2.
65 Ibid., p. 7.
66 Proinsias Mac Cana 1988, p. 333.
67 John Michie 1908, p. 150.
68 Lauchlan MacLean Watt 1937, p. 43.
69 From the private collection of Colonel Lachie Robertson of Elgol. This quotation and a variant of the anecdote appear in Donald Meek 1978.
70 William J. Watson 1929, p. 135.
71 John MacInnes 1981, p. 158.
72 Seán de Fréine 1978, pp. 17-18.
73 From the Glenmasan MS., printed in *Celtic Review* 1, p. 109.
74 Donald Meek 1995, poem 35, §5, 6.
75 Duncan Campbell 1910, p. 170.
76 *BG*, lines 3746-3753.
77 *Celtic Magazine* 10, p. 392.
78 Ibid., p. 346.
79 Revd Lauchlan MacLean Watt 1937, p. 38.
80 Quoted in Patrick Sheeran 1984, p. 206.
81 Ronald Wright 1992, p. 312.
82 Iain Crichton Smith 1986, pp. 42-3.
83 Max Oelschlaeger 1991, pp. 8, 327, 348.
84 Ibid., p. 8-9; Lewis Mumford 1966, pp. 35-7.
85 Max Oelschlaeger 1991, Chapter Five; Paul Shepard 1992, pp. 72-4.
86 John MacInnes 1992b, pp. 9-10, 18.
87 Quoted and discussed in Dolores LaChapelle 1992, p. 233.

CHAPTER 8
LANGUAGE

1 Derick Thomson 1994, p. 90.
2 John F. Campbell 1860/1994, vol. 1, p. 84.

3 J.E. Caerwyn Williams and Patrick Ford 1992, pp. 67, 88, 91.
4 John Bannerman 1998, p. 97.
5 Quoted in Charles Withers 1988, p. 110.
6 William Shaw 1778, p. xi.
7 Given in the entry in the Statistical Account for Scotland for that parish.
8 Quoted in Charles Withers 1988, p. 333.
9 'Notes of a Winter Tour in the Western Isles', written by the editor of the *Fifeshire Journal*, 11 February 1847.
10 Charles Dunn 1953, p. 133.
11 James Crawford 1994.
12 Joshua Fishman 1991, pp. 55-67.
13 *An Gàidheal* 1938, p. 116.
14 James Crawford 1994.
15 Wilson McLeod, forthcoming.
16 John MacInnes 1989a, p. 90.
17 Colin Chisholm 1883, p. 223.
18 'Fògradh ar Gàidheil', by Murchadh Mac a' Ghobhainn.
19 Max Oelschlager 1990, p. 325. See also Lewis Mumford 1966, p. 87; Barre Toelken 1979, pp. 225-7, 234, 277.
20 Written by J. MacCulloch 1824, quoted in Charles Withers 1988, p. 334.
21 *Highlander* 18 December 1875.
22 Edmund Burt 1754, vol. 1, p. 35.
23 Composed by Gilleasbuig Mac Iain, printed in *An Gàidheal* 3 (1874), pp. 143-4.
24 Calum MacNeacail (no date), p. 15.
25 John Michie 1908, p. 113.
26 Charles Dunn 1968, p. 138.
27 Margaret Bennett 1989, p. 192.
28 Sharon MacDonald 1997, pp. 249-51.
29 There are also epenthetic vowels (also called 'helping' or 'svarabhakti' vowels) which are introduced between some combinations of adjacent consonants, but which are always short and unstressed.
30 Bruno Nettl 1983, p. 36.
31 Maurice Bowra 1966, pp. 38-9.
32 p. 154. See also Breandán Ó Madagáin 1985, pp. 178-84.
33 William Matheson 1955, p. 78. Exceptions are discussed on p. 79.
34 John MacInnes 1966, p. 52.
35 Bruno Nettl 1983, p. 41.
36 William Matheson 1955, p. 76.
37 John MacInnes 1966, p. 47.
38 John Shaw 1992-3, p. 49.
39 I.F. Grant 1961, p. 107.
40 John Gibson 1998, pp. 4, 87, 144.
41 John Shaw 1992-3, pp. 49-50.
42 Revd Alexander MacGregor 1852, p. 2.
43 *An Gàidheal* 3 (1874), p. 228.
44 John Shaw 1992-3, pp. 42-4.
45 *ODB*, lines 3988-95.
46 Lewis Mumford 1966, pp. 87-8.
47 Stewart Sanderson 1976, p. 113.
48 William MacKenzie 1892, p. 177. See also Mary Mackellar 1888, p. 142; Breandán Ó Madagáin 1985, p. 167.
49 Stewart Sanderson 1976, p. 105.
50 William MacKenzie 1892, p. 100.
51 Morton Bloomfield and Charles Dunn 1989, p. 9.
52 Proinsias Mac Cana 1988, pp. 335-7; Tom Sjöblom 1994, p. 161.
53 Stewart Sanderson 1976, p. 107.
54 John L. Campbell 1975, p. 75.
55 John Shaw 1987, p. 424.
56 Diarmuid Ó Giolláin 1991, p. 201.
57 Anne Grant 1811, p. 169.
58 John L. Campbell 1958, p. 22.
59 John F. Campbell 1860/1994, tale 35 'Conall'.

CHAPTER 9

BELIEF, TRADITION, AND SCIENCE

1 Lewis Mumford 1966, p. 71.
2 James MacDonald 1893, p. 273.
3 'Litir o Fhionnladh Pìobaire', in *Fear Tathaich nam Beann* 1848, re-edited in *Caraid nan Gàidheal*, p. 394.
4 John G. Campbell 1900, p. 161.
5 Alexander MacDonald 1914, p. 226.
6 Alexander Allardyce 1888, p. 457.
7 Called a *leug* by John Ramsay in ibid., pp. 452-3 (though misspelled as *leugh* in the publication).
8 A list of marine Noa terms also appears in John G. Campbell 1900, p. 239.
9 Martin Martin 1716, pp. 19-20.
10 Armin Geertz 1994, pp. 6, 7.
11 John MacInnes 1992b, p. 17.

12 John MacInnes 1989c, pp. 12-13.
13 John MacInnes 1992b, p. 17.
14 Alwyn Rees and Brinley Rees 1961, pp. 14-20, 210-12.
15 John Shaw 1993, p. 9.
16 Barre Toelken 1979, p. 187.
17 Nerys Patterson 1994, p. 147.
18 Barbara Rieti 1991, pp. 41-6; John G. Campbell 1900, p. 39.
19 Barbara Rieti 1991, p. 44.
20 John MacInnes 1982, p. 228.
21 Ibid., p. 229.
22 See Armin Geertz 1994, pp. 318-19, for a discussion of how a worldview can contain multiple and inconsistent belief systems.
23 Lewis Mumford 1966, p. 135.
24 Martin Martin 1716, p. 197.
25 For example, pp. 175-90.
26 From the Robert MacLagan MSS of the late nineteenth century, quoted in M. MacLeod Banks 1939, p. 13.
27 § 36.
28 John MacInnes 1992b, pp. 8-10.
29 Manu Aluli Meyer 1998, p. 40.
30 Barre Toelken 1979, p. 255. See also George Foster 1973, pp. 5, 92, 111.
31 Alexander Stewart 1921, p. 173.
32 Anne Grant 1811, pp. 124-5.
33 Revd W. Forsyth 1900, p. 160, from a letter written in 1764.
34 See, for example, I. F. Grant 1961, p. 56.
35 William Matheson 1938, pp. 205-6.
36 Barre Toelken 1979, p. 251.
37 Revd W. Forsyth 1900, p. 160.
38 R.W. Munro 1961, p. 43.
39 Quoted in John Bannerman 1977, p. 239.
40 Arthur Williamson 1982, p. 41.
41 Quoted in Charles Withers 1988, p. 122.
42 M. MacLeod Banks 1941, pp.195, 202, 232, 238-242.
43 M. MacLeod Banks 1941, pp. 173-4.
44 M. MacLeod Banks 1941, p. 41.
45 Quoted in Joseph MacPherson 1929, p. 135.
46 Ibid., pp. 136-8.
47 Revd William Gillies 1938, p. 307.
48 Keith Thomas 1983, p. 78. See also p. 84.
49 Margaret MacKay 1980, p. 4.
50 Ibid., p. 197.
51 Revd W. Forsyth 1900, p. 92.
52 Quoted in Charles Withers 1988, p. 136.
53 Donald Meek 1998, p. 6.
54 Quoted in John Gibson 1998, p. 173.
55 John F. Campbell 1860/1992 vol. 1, p. 6.
56 Quoted in John Gibson 1998, p. 141.
57 Quoted in Charles Withers 1988, p. 136.
58 James Logan 1876, p. 367.
59 W.Y. Evans-Wentz 1966, p. 99.
60 Gearóid Ó hAllmhuráin 1999, pp. 40-4.
61 Ibid., p. 43.
62 Diarmuid Ó Giolláin 1991, p. 206.
63 John Gibson 1998, pp. 200-1.
64 Somhairle MacGill-eain 1985, p. 10.
65 Ibid., pp. 70-4.

CHAPTER 10
PAST AND FUTURE PROSPECTS

1 Thomas Charles-Edwards 1995, p. 722.
2 Yi-Fu Tuan 1974, p. 31.
3 J.E. Caerwyn Williams and Patrick Ford 1992, pp. 90-5.
4 Alexander Allardyce 1888, p. 536.
5 It is worth noting that the common term for English, *Beurla*, is in origin *beul-ràdh* (mouth-talk), implying 'foreign babble'. Lallans, the English of the Scottish Lowlands, is called a' *Bheurla Ghallda.*
6 Most of these features are listed in John MacInnes 1989a, *passim.*
7 Revd W. Forsyth 1900, p. 251.
8 Alexander Allardyce 1888, p. 508.
9 Ibid., p. 510.
10 Revd John Lane Buchanan 1793, pp. 49-51. See also Duncan Campbell 1910, p. 643.
11 John Dixon 1886, p. 121.
12 Colin Kidd 1995, *passim.*
13 John Shaw 1993, p. 10.
14 The whole process of the 'Improvement' and de-racination of Gaelic bagpiping is detailed in John Gibson 1998.
15 See 'Stepdancing: Why we must learn from past mistakes', Margaret Bennett, in *West Highland Free Press*, 14 October 1994.
16 John Shaw 1993, p. 8.

17 Jonathan Dembling 1997, p. 38.
18 Colin Kidd 1995, pp. 45-6.
19 William Fergusson 1998, pp. 311-12.
20 Colin Kidd 1995, p. 47.
21 George Foster 1973, pp. 64, 66, 73.
22 Anthony Wallace 1956, p. 265.
23 Ibid., p. 264.
24 *New Woman* September 1991 (Special supplement: *New Woman Scotland*), p. 6. Thanks to Dr Michael Kennedy for this reference.
25 John Shaw 1993, p. 8.
26 Paul Shepard 1992, pp. 78-80.

Abbreviations

BA	William J. Watson, 1937, *Bàrdachd Albannach O Leabhar Deadhan Lios-Mòir*, Edinburgh: Scottish Gaelic Texts Society.
BG	William J. Watson, 1959 (revised edition) *Bàrdachd Ghàidhlig*, An Comann Gàidhealach.
BSC	Colm Ó Baoill, 1972, *Bàrdachd Shìlis na Ceapaich*, Edinburgh: Scottish Gaelic Texts Society.
CD	William Matheson, 1970, *An Clàrsair Dall*, Edinburgh: Scottish Gaelic Texts Society.
CG	Alexander Carmichael, 1900-1971, *Carmina Gadelica*, 6 vols, Edinburgh.
EB	Colm Ó Baoill, 1979, *Eachann Bacach agus bàird eile de Chloinn Ghill-eathain*, Edinburgh: Scottish Gaelic Texts Society.
GC	Colm Ó Baoill and Meg Bateman, 1994, *Gàir nan Clàrsach*, Edinburgh: Birlinn Ltd.
HSFF	John L. Campbell, 1984, *Highland Songs of the Forty-Five*, Edinburgh: The Scottish Gaelic Texts Society.
IBP	Osborn Bergin, 1970, *Irish Bardic Poetry*, Dublin Institute for Advanced Studies.
MC	Revd A. MacDonald and Revd A. MacDonald, 1911, *The MacDonald Collection of Gaelic Poetry*, Inverness: The Northern Counties Publishing Company.
OIL	Annie M. MacKenzie, 1964, *Òrain Iain Luim*, Edinburgh: Scottish Academic Press.
NGP	Alexander Nicolson, 1881, *A Collection of Gaelic Proverbs and Familiar Phrases.*
RC	Alexander Cameron, *Reliquiæ Celticæ*, vol. 1, 1892; vol. 2, 1894; Inverness: Northern Counties Publishing Company
SGS	*Scottish Gaelic Studies.*
SHR	*Scottish Historical Review.*
TGSI	*Transactions of the Gaelic Society of Inverness.*
ZCP	*Zeitschrift für Celtische Philogie.*

Bibliography

Adam, Frank, and Sir Thomas Innes, 1970 (8th edition), *The Clans, Septs & Regiments of the Scottish Highlands*, Stirling: Johnston and Bacon.

Aitchison, Norman B., 1994, 'Kingship, Society, and Sacrality: Rank, Power, and Ideology in Early Medieval Ireland', *Traditio* 49, pp. 45-75.

Allen, Theodore, 1994, *The Invention of the White* Race, London and New York: Verso.

Allardyce, Alexander, 1888 (ed.), *Scotland and Scotsmen in the Eighteenth Century*, vol. 2, Edinburgh and London: W. Blackwood and Sons.

Almqvist, Bo, Séamas Ó Catháin and Pádraig Ó Héalaí, 1987 (ed.) *The Heroic Process*, Dún Laoghaire: Glendale Press.

Anderson, Marjorie O., 1980, *Kings and Kingship in Early Scotland*, Edinburgh: Scottish Academic Press.

Banks, M. MacLeod, 1937, *British Calendar Customs: Scotland, vol I*, London: Folk-Lore Society.

—, 1939, *British Calendar Customs: Scotland, vol II*, London: Folk-Lore Society.

—, 1941, *British Calendar Customs: Scotland, vol III*, London: Folk-Lore Society.

Bannerman, John, 1974, *Studies in the History of Dalriada*, Edinburgh: Scottish Academic Press.

—, 1977, 'The Lordship of the Isles', in (ed.) J. Brown, *Scottish Society in the Fifteenth Century*, London, pp. 209-240.

—, 1988, 'The Scots Language and the Kin-based Society', in *Gaelic and Scots In Harmony* (ed.) Derick Thomson, University of Glasgow, pp. 1-19.

—, 1989, 'The King's Poet and the Inauguration of Alexander III', *SHR* 68, pp. 120-49.

—, 1993, 'MacDuff of Fife', in *Medieval Scotland* (ed.) Alexander Grant and Keith Stringer, Edinburgh University Press, pp. 20-38.

—, 1996, 'The Residence of the King's Poet', *SGS* 17, pp. 24-35.

—, 1998, *The Beatons*, Edinburgh: John Donald.

Barrow, G.W.S., 1981a, 'The Sources for the History of the Highlands in the Middle Ages', in Loraine MacLean 1981, pp. 11-22.

—, 1981b, *Kingship and Unity*, Edinburgh University Press.

—, 1984, *Robert Bruce and the Scottish Identity*, Edinburgh: Saltire Society.

—, 1989, 'The lost Gàidhealtachd of medieval Scotland', in William Gillies 1989, pp. 67-88.

Bennett, Margaret, 1989, *The Last Stronghold*, Edinburgh: Canongate Publishing Ltd.

—, 1992, *Scottish Customs From the Cradle to the Grave*, Edinburgh: Polygon.
Berman, Morris, 1990, 'The Cybernetic Dream of the 21st Century', in John Clark 1990, pp. 12-32.
Beveridge, Craig and Ronald Turnbull, 1989, *The Eclipse of Scottish Culture*, Edinburgh: Polygon.
Bierhorst, John, 1994, *The Way of the Earth*, New York: William Morrow and Company.
Bitel, Lisa, 1996, *Land of Women: Tales of Sex and Gender in Early Ireland*, Ithaca: Cornell University Press.
Black, Ronald, 1973, 'A Manuscript of Cathal Mac Muireadhaigh', *Celtica* 10, pp. 193-209.
—, 1977, 'The Genius of Cathal MacMhuirich', *TGSI* 50, pp. 327-65.
—, 1996, 'James Macintyre's Calendar', *SGS* 17, pp. 327-65.
Bloomfield, Morton and Charles Dunn, 1989, *The Role of the Poet in Early Societies*, Cambridge: D.S. Brewer.
Bourke, Angela, 1993, 'More in Anger than in Sorrow: Irish Women's Lament Poetry', in *Feminist Messages: Coding in Woman's Folk Culture* (ed.) Joan Radner, Urbana: University of Illinois Press, pp. 160-82.
Bowra, Maurice, 1964, *Heroic Poetry*, London.
Breatnach, Liam, 1996, 'Law', in Kim MacCone and Katherine Simms, pp. 107-22.
Bromwich, Rachel, 1991, *Trioedd Ynys Prydein*, University of Wales Press.
Broun, Dauvit, 1997, 'The Birth of Scottish History', *SHR* 76, pp. 4-22.
Brown, Archibald, 1908, *The History of Cowal*, Greenock: Telegraph Printing Works.
Bruford, Alan, 1985, 'Colour Epithets for Gaelic Chiefs', in *Shadow: The Newsletter of the Traditional Cosmology Society* vol. 2 no. 1, 14-23.
—, 1996, 'Workers, Weepers and Witches: the status of the female singer in Gaelic society', *SGS* 17, pp. 61-70.
Buchanan, George, 1827, *The History of Scotland*, Glasgow: Blackie, Fullarton & Co.
Buchanan, Revd John Lane, 1793, *Travels in the Western Hebrides From 1782-1790*.
Burt, Edmund, 1754, *Burt's Letters from the North of Scotland* (two volumes).
Byrne, Francis John, 1973, *Irish Kings and High Kings*, New York: St Martin's Press.
Campbell, Alexander, 1804, *The Grampians Desolate*.
Campbell, Alexander, 1926, 'The Manuscript History of Craignish' (ed.) Herbert Campbell, in *Miscellany of the Scottish History Society*.
Campbell, Duncan, 1910, *Reminiscences and Reflections of an Octogenarian Highlander*, Inverness: Northern Counties Publishing Company.
Campbell, John Francis, 1860, *Popular Tales of the West Highlands* (new edition) Edinburgh: Birlinn, 1994.
Campbell, John Gregorson, 1891, *Waifs and Strays of Celtic Tradition IV: The Fians*, London: Alfred Nutt.
—, 1895, *Waifs and Strays of Celtic Tradition V: Clan Traditions and Popular Tales*, London: Alfred Nutt.
—, 1900, *Superstitions of the Highlands and Islands*, Glasgow: James MacLehose and Sons.

—, 1902, *Witchcraft & Second Sight in the Highlands and Islands of Scotland*, Glasgow: James MacLehose and Sons.

Campbell, John Lorne, 1945, *Gaelic in Scottish Education and Life*, Edinburgh: Saltire Society.

—, 1958, *Gaelic Words and Expressions from South Uist and Eriskay*, Dublin Institute for Advanced Studies.

—, 1975, *A Collection of Highland Rites and Customes*, London: Folklore Society.

—, 1990, *Songs Remembered in Exile*, Aberdeen University Press.

—, 1994 (3rd edition) *Canna: The Story of a Hebridean Island*, Edinburgh: Canongate Press.

Canny, Nicholas P., 1973, 'The Ideology of English Colonization: From Ireland to America', *William and Mary Quarterly* 30, pp. 575-98.

Charles-Edwards, Thomas M., 1978, 'Honour and Status in Some Irish and Welsh Prose Tales', *Ériu* 29, pp. 123-41.

—, 1995, 'Language and Society amongst the Insular Celts AD 400-1000', in Miranda Green 1995, 703-36.

Cheyfitz, Eric, 1991, *The Poetics of Imperialism*, Oxford University Press.

Chisholm, Colin, 1883, 'Òrain agus Sgeulachdan Shrath-Ghlais', *TGSI* 10, 220-39.

Clancy, Thomas Owen, 1996, 'Women Poets in Early Medieval Ireland', in *The Frailty of Her Sex? Irishwomen in their European Context* (ed.) Katherine Simms and Christine Meek, Dublin: Four Courts Press.

—, 1998 (ed.), *The Triumph Tree*, Edinburgh: Canongate.

Clark, John, 1990 (ed.), *Renewing the Earth: The Promise of Social Ecology*, London: Green Print.

Collins, Kevin, 1990, *The Cultural Conquest of Ireland*, Dublin: Mercier Press.

Constable, Archibald, 1892 (ed.), *John Major's History of Greater Britain (1521)*, Edinburgh: Scottish History Society.

Craig, K.C., 1944, *Sgeulachdan Dhunnchaidh*, Glasgow: Alasdair Matheson & Co.

Crawford, James, 1994, 'Endangered Native American Languages: What Is To Be Done, and Why?', www.ncbe.gwu.edu/miscpubs/crawford.

Crone, B.A., 1993, 'Crannogs and Chronologies', *Proceedings of the Society of the Antiquities of Scotland* 123, pp. 245-54.

Curtis, Liz, 1984, *Nothing but the same old story: The Roots of Anti-Irish Racism*, London: Information on Ireland.

D'Arcy, Julian, 1996, *Scottish Skalds and Sagamen*, East Linton: Tuckwell Press.

Dalyell, John, 1834, *The Darker Superstitions of Scotland*, Edinburgh: Waugh and Innes.

Dawson, Jane, 1987, 'Two Kingdoms or Three? Ireland in Anglo-Scottish Relations in the Middle of the Sixteenth Century', in *Scotland and England 1286-1815* (ed.) Roger A. Mason, Edinburgh: John Donald, pp. 113-38.

—, 1994, 'Calvinism and the Gàidhealtachd in Scotland', in *Calvinism in Europe 1540-1620* (ed.) Andrew Pettegree, Alastair Duke and Gillian Lewis, Cambridge University Press, pp. 231-53.

de Fréine, Seán, 1978, *The Great Silence* (2nd edition), Dublin: Mercier Press.

Dembling, Jonathan, 1997, *Joe Jimmy Alec Visits the Mod and Escapes Unscathed: The Nova Scotia Gaelic Revivals* (unpublished Masters Thesis at Saint Mary's University).

Dewar, John, 1964, *The Dewar Manuscripts* vol. 1 (ed.) Revd John MacKechnie, William MacLellan: Glasgow.

Dick, Cairistiona agus Iain Bannerman, 1987, *Dal Riata*, Glaschu: Gairm.

Dickson, David, 1974, *Alternative Technology*, Glasgow: William Collins Sons & Co. Ltd.

Dillon, Myles and Nora Chadwick, 1967, *The Celtic Realms*, London: Weidenfeld and Nicolson Ltd.

Dodgshon, Robert, 1998, *From Chiefs to Landlords*, Edinburgh University Press.

Dorian, Nancy, 1981, *Language Death: The Life Cycle of a Scottish Gaelic Dialect*, Philadelphia: University of Pennsylvania Press.

Dunbar, James Telford, 1962, *History of Highland Dress*, Edinburgh: Oliver & Boyd.

Dunn, Charles, 1968, *Highland Settler* (reprint) 1991, Breton Books.

Durkacz, Victor Edward, 1983, *The Decline of the Celtic Languages*, Edinburgh: John Donald.

Dwelly, Edward 1911, *The Illustrated Gaelic-English Dictionary*, Gairm: Glasgow 1977.

Eliade, Mircea, 1958, *Patterns in Comparative Religion*, London: Sheed and Ward.

Etchington, Colmán, 1996, 'Early Medieval Irish History', in Kim MacCone and Katherine Simms, pp. 123-54.

Evans, D. Ellis, 1997, 'Celticity, Celtic Awareness and Celtic Studies', *ZCP* 49-50, pp. 1-27.

Evans-Wentz, W.Y., 1966, *The Fairy-Faith in Celtic Countries* (reprint) University Books.

Fanon, Fritz, 1967, *The Wretched of the Earth*, Penguin Books.

Fergusson, William, 1998, *The Identity of the Scottish Nation*, Edinburgh University Press.

Fishman, Joshua, 1991, *Reversing Language Shift*, Clevedon, England: Multilingual Matters.

Forsyth, Katherine, 1997, *Language in Pictland*, Utrecht: de Keltische Draak.

Forsyth, Revd W., 1900, *In The Shadow of Cairngorm*, Inverness: Northern Counties Publishing Company Ltd.

Foster, George, 1973 (2nd edition), *Traditional Societies and Technological Change*, New York: Harper & Row.

Fraser, Donald, 1988, 'Some Highland Causes of the '45', in Lesley Scott-Moncrieff, pp. 35-52.

Fraser-Mackintosh, Charles, 1877, 'The Depopulation of Aberarder in Badenoch', *Celtic Magazine* 2, pp. 418-25.

Freire, Paulo, 1996 (new edition), *Pedagogy of the Oppressed*, London: Penguin Books.

Geertz, Armin, 1994, *The Invention of Prophecy: Continuity and Meaning in Hopi Indian Religion*, University of California Press.

Gellner, Ernest, 1991, *Plough, Sword and Book*, London: Paladin.

Gibson, John G., 1998, *Traditional Gaelic Bagpiping*, Edinburgh: NMS Publishing.

Gillies, Rev. William, 1938, *In Famed Breadalbane* (reprint) 1980, Strathtay: Clunie Press.
Gillies, William, 1987, 'Heroes and Ancestors', in Bo Almqvist, et. al., pp. 57-74.
—, 1988a, 'Gaelic: The Classical Tradition', in *History of Scottish Literature* vol. 1 (ed.) R.D.S. Jack, Aberdeen University Press, 245-61.
—, 1988b, 'The Prince and the Gaels', in Lesley Scott-Moncrieff, pp. 53-72.
—, 1989 (ed.), *Gaelic and Scotland/ Alba agus a' Ghàidhlig*, Edinburgh University Press.
—, 1991, 'Gaelic Songs of the 'Forty-Five', *Scottish Studies* 30, pp. 19-58.
Grant, Alexander and Keith Stringer, 1993, *Medieval Scotland*, Edinburgh University Press.
Grant, Anne, 1806, *Letters from the Mountains.*
—, 1811, *Essays on the Superstitions of the Highlanders of Scotland.*
Grant, Revd G.V.R., 1988, 'The '45: A Disastrous Mistake', in Lesley Scott-Moncrieff, pp. 23-34.
Grant, I.F., 1961, *Highland Folk Ways*, London: Routledge & Kegan Paul.
—, 1981 (2nd edition) The MacLeods, Edinburgh: Spurbooks.
Grant, K.W., 1925, *Myth, Tradition and Story from Western Argyll*, Oban Times Press.
Green, Miranda, 1995 (ed.), *The Celtic World*, London and New York: Routledge.
Grigor, Iain Fraser, 1979, *Mightier than a Lord*, Stornoway: Acair Ltd.
Henderson, George, 1898, *Leabhar nan Gleann*, Edinburgh: Norman MacLeod.
—, 1910, *The Norse Influence on Celtic Scotland*, Glasgow: J. Maclehose.
—, 1911, *Survival in Belief among the Celts*, Glasgow: J. Maclehose.
Henderson, Hamish, 1989, 'The Ballad and Popular Tradition to 1660', in *History of Scottish Literature* vol. 1 (ed.) R.D.S. Jack, Abderdeen University Press, pp. 263-83.
Hubert, Jane, 1994, 'Sacred beliefs and beliefs of sacredness', in *Sacred Sites, Sacred Places* (ed.) David Carmichael, Jane Hubert and Brian Reeves, London and New York: Routledge, pp. 9-19.
Hudson, Benjamin, 1996, *The Prophecy of Berchán*, Westport, Connecticut: Greenwood Press.
Jackson, Kenneth, 1957, 'The Duan Albanach', *SHR* 36, pp. 125-37.
—, 1972, *The Gaelic Notes in the Book of Deer*, Cambridge University Press.
Jenkins, Richard, 1991, 'Witches and Fairies: Supernatural Aggression and Deviance Among the Irish Peasantry', in Peter Narváez, pp. 302-35.
Johnson, Samuel and James Boswell, 1996, *Journey to the Hebrides* (ed.) Ian McGowan, Edinburgh: Canongate Classics.
Kearney, Richard, 1985 (ed.), *The Irish Mind*, Wolfhound Press.
Kelly, Fergus, 1988, *A Guide to Early Irish Law*, Dublin Institute for Advanced Studies.
Kew, Graham, 1998, 'The Irish Sections of Fynes Moryson's Unpublished Itinerary', *Analecta Hibernica* 37, pp. 3-137.
Kidd, Colin, 1993, *Subverting Scotland's Past*, Cambridge University Press.
—, 1995, 'Teutonist Ethnology and Scottish Nationalist Inhibition, 1780-1880', *SHR* 74, pp. 45-68.

Kirk, James, 1998 (ed.), *The Church in the Highlands*, Edinburgh: Scottish Church History Society.

Koch, John T., 1991, 'Ériu, Alba and Letha: When was a language ancestral to Gaelic first spoken in Ireland?', *Emania* 9, pp. 17-27.

LaChapelle, Dolores, 1992, 'Not Laws of Nature but Li (Pattern) of Nature', in Max Oelschlaeger, pp. 220-44.

Logan, James, 1876 (2nd edition), *The Scottish Gael, or Celtic Manners as Preserved among the Highlanders.*

Lynch, Michael, 1992, *Scotland: A New History*, London: Pimlico.

Lysaght, Patricia, 1993, 'Bealtaine: Irish Maytime Customs and the Reaffirmation of Boundaries', in *Boundaries & Thresholds* (ed.) Hilda Ellis Davidson, Woodchester, England: Thimble Press, pp. 28-43.

MacAulay, Donald, 1976 (ed.) *Nua-Bhàrdachd Ghàidhlig*, Edinburgh: Canongate.

MacBain, Alexander, 1888, 'Highland Superstition', *TGSI* 14, pp. 232-72.

McCaughey, Terence P., 1989, 'Protestantism and Scottish Highland Culture', in *An Introduction to Celtic Christianity* (ed.) James Mackey, Edinburgh: T&T Clark, pp. 172-205.

MacCana, Proinsias, 1978, 'Regnum and Sacerdotium: Notes on Irish Tradition', *Proceedings of the British Academy* 65, pp. 443-75.

—, 1980, *The Learned Tales of Medieval Ireland*, Dublin Institute for Advanced Studies.

—, 1985, 'Early Irish Ideology and the Concept of Unity', in Richard Kearney, pp. 56-78.

—, 1988, 'Placenames and Mythology in Irish Tradition: Places, Pilgrimages and Things', in *Proceedings of the First North American Congress of Celtic Studies* (ed.) Gordon MacLennan, University of Ottawa, pp. 319-41.

McCone, Kim, 1995, 'Cúlra Ind-Europach na Féinne', in *An Fhiannaíocht: Léachtaí Cholm Cille* 25 (ed.) Pádraig Ó Fiannachta, Maigh Nuad: An Sagart, pp. 7-29.

McCone, Kim, and Katharine Simms, 1996 (ed.), *Progress in Medieval Irish Studies*, Maynooth: Dept of Old Irish.

Mac Cormick, John, 1923, *The Island of Mull*, Glasgow: Alex MacLaren & Sons.

McCrone, David, 1992, *Understanding Scotland: The Sociology of a Stateless Nation*, London: Routledge.

Macdomhnuill, Raonuill, 1776, *Comh-chruinneachaidh Órannaigh Gàidhealach [the Eigg Collection]*, Duneidiunn.

MacDonald, Alexander, 1914, *Story and Song from Loch Ness-side*, Inverness: The Northern Counties Publishing Company.

MacDonald, James, 1893, 'Stray Customs and Legends', *TGSI* 19, pp. 272-86.

MacDonald, Sharon, 1997, *Reimagining Culture: Histories, Identities and the Gaelic Renaissance*, Oxford: Berg.

MacDougall, Allan, 1829, *Òrain, Marbhrannan, agus duanagan Gàidhealach*, Inverness.

MacDougall, Revd James, and Revd George Calder, 1910, *Folk Tales and Fairy Lore*, Edinburgh: John Grant.

MacGill-eain, Somhairle, 1985 (ed.), William Gillies, *Ris a' Bhruthaich*, Stornoway: Acair Ltd.

MacGregor, Revd Alexander, 1852, *The Lays and Laments of the Gael*, Edinburgh.

MacGregor, Martin, 1998, 'Church and culture in the late medieval Highlands', in James Kirk, pp. 1-36.

MacInnes, Allan I., 1993, 'Crown, Clans and Fine: The "Civilizing" of Scottish Gaeldom, 1587-1638', *Northern Scotland* 13, pp. 31-56.

—, 1996, *Clanship, Commerce and the House of Stuart, 1603-1778*, East Linton: Tuckwell Press.

MacInnes, John, 1966, 'The Choral Tradition in Scottish Gaelic Songs', *TGSI* 46, 44-65.

—, 1968, 'The Oral Tradition in Scottish Gaelic Poetry', *Scottish Studies* 12, pp. 29-44.

—, 1976, 'The Gaelic Literary Tradition', in *Scottish Literature in the Secondary School*, Edinburgh.

—, 1978, 'The Panegyric Code in Gaelic Poetry and its Historical Background', *TGSI* 50, pp. 435-98.

—, 1981, 'Gaelic Poetry and Historical Tradition', in Loraine MacLean, pp. 142-63.

—, 1982, 'Religion in Gaelic Society', *TGSI* 52, pp. 222- 42.

—, 1983, 'Sùil air Bardachd na Gàidhlig', in *For a Celtic Future* (ed.) Cathal Ó Luain, Dublin: The Celtic League, pp. 4-24.

—, 1985, 'Gleanings from Raasay Tradition', *TGSI* 56, pp. 1-20.

—, 1989a, 'The Gaelic Perceptions of the Lowlands', in William Gillies, pp. 89-100.

—, 1989b, 'Gaelic Poetry in the Nineteenth Century', in *The History of Scottish Literature* vol. 3 (ed.) Douglas Gifford, Aberdeen University Press, pp. 377-95.

—, 1989c, 'The Seer in Gaelic Tradition', in *The Seer in Celtic and Other Traditions* (ed.) Hilda E. Davidson, Edinburgh: John Donald, pp. 10-24.

—, 1991, 'Clan Sagas and Historical Legends', *TGSI* 58, pp. 377-94.

—, 1992a, 'The Scottish Gaelic Language', in *The Celtic Connection* (ed.) Glanville Price, Gerrards Cross, pp. 101-30.

—, 1992b, 'Looking at Legends of the Supernatural', *TGSI* 59, pp. 1-20.

McKay, Margaret M., 1980 (ed.), *The Rev. Dr John Walker's Report on the Hebrides*, Edinburgh: John Donald.

McKean, Thomas A., 1997, *Hebridean Song-Maker*, Edinburgh: Polygon

Mackellar, Mary, 1888, 'The Sheiling: Its Traditions and Songs', *TGSI* 14, pp. 135-53.

Mackenzie, Henry, 1805, *Report of the Committee of the Highland Society of Scotland appointed to enquire into the nature and authenticity of the Poems of Ossian*, Edinburgh.

MacKenzie, Osgood, 1921, *A Hundred Years in the Highlands* (new edition) 1949, London: Butler & Tanner Ltd.

Mackenzie, W.M., 1914, *The Book of Arran* vol. 2, Glasgow: Hugh Hopkins.

Mackenzie, William, 1892, 'Gaelic Incantations, Charms, and Blessings of the Hebrides', *TGSI* 28, pp. 97-182.

MacKinnon, Lachlan (no date), *Cascheum nam Bàrd* 3, Inverness: Highland Printers.

MacLean, Loraine, 1981 (ed.), *The Middle Ages in the Highlands*, Inverness Field Club.

McLean, Marianne, 1991, *The People of Glengarry*, Toronto: McGill-Queen's University Press.

MacLennan, Gordan, 1988 (ed.), *Proceedings of the First North American Congress of Celtic Studies*, Ottawa.

Mac Mathúna, Liam, 1997, 'The Christianization of the Early Irish Cosmos?: *muir mas, nem nglas, talam cé*', *ZCP* 49/50, pp. 532-47.

MacNeacail, Calum (no date), 'Calum Ruadh: Bard of Skye', *Scottish Tradition* 7, School of Scottish Studies of Edinburgh University.

Mac Neill, Máire, 1962, *The Festival of Lughnasa*, Oxford University Press.

Mac Niocaill, Gearóid, 1972, *Ireland Before the Vikings*, Dublin: Gill and MacMillan.

MacPhàrlain, Calum, 1908, *Binneas nam Bard*, Stirling.

Macpherson, Donald, 1868, *An Duanaire*, Edinburgh.

MacPherson, Joseph, 1929, *Primitive Beliefs in the Northeast of Scotland*, London.

Mallory, J.P., 1989, *In Search of the Indo-Europeans*, London: Thames and Hudson.

Martin, Martin, 1716 (2nd edition), A *Description of the Western Isles of Scotland*.

Matheson, Angus, 1952, 'Gleanings from the Dornie Manuscripts', *TGSI* 41, pp. 310-81.

Matheson, William, 1938, *The Songs of John MacCodrum*, Edinburgh: Scottish Gaelic Texts Society.

—, 1955, 'Some Early Collectors of Gaelic Folk-song', *The Proceedings of the Scottish Anthropological and Folklore Society* vol. 5, no. 2, pp. 67-82.

—, 1965, 'Further Gleanings from the Dornie Manuscripts', *TGSI* 45, pp. 148-95.

Meek, Donald, 1978 (ed.), *The Campbell Collection of Gaelic Proverbs and Proverbial Sayings*, Gaelic Society of Inverness.

—, 1995, *Tuatha is Tighearna/ Tenants and Landlords*, Edinburgh: Scottish Gaelic Texts Society.

—, 1996, *The Scottish Highlands: The Churches and Gaelic Culture*, Geneva: WCC Publications.

—, 1998, 'God and Gaelic: Reflections on Religious Faith, Language, and Culture', paper presented at *Aithne nan Gàidheal*, Belfast.

Megaw, Ruth and Vincent Megaw, 1999, 'Celtic Connections Past and Present: Celtic Ethnicity Ancient and Modern', in *Celtic Connections* (ed.) Ronald Black, William Gillies, Roibeard Ó Maolalaigh, East Linton: Tuckwell Press, pp. 19-81.

Meyer, Manu Aluli, 1998, 'Native Hawaiian Epistemology: Exploring Hawaiian Views of Knowledge', *Cultural Survival Quarterly* Spring 1998, pp. 38-40.

Michie, John Grant, 1908 (2nd edition), *Deeside Tales*, Aberdeen: D. Wyllie & Son.

Mohawk, John, 1990, 'Distinguished Traditions', in John Clark, pp. 91-6.

Mumford, Lewis, 1966, *The Myth of the Machine: Technics and Human Development*, New York: Harcourt Brace Jovanovich, Inc.

—, 1970, *The Myth of the Machine: The Pentagon of Power*, New York: Harcourt Brace Jovanovich, Inc.

Munro, Jean, 1981, 'The Lordship of the Isles', in Loraine MacLean, pp. 23-37.

Munro, R.W., 1961, *Munro's Western Isles of Scotland (1549)*, Edinburgh: Oliver and Boyd.

—, 1981, 'The Clan System – Fact or Fiction', in Loraine MacLean, pp. 117-29.

Nagy, Joseph, 1987, 'Fenian Heroes and their Rites of Passage', in Bo Alqvist, et al., pp. 161-82.

Narváez, Peter, 1991 (ed.), *The Good People*, Lexington: University Press of Kentucky.

Nettl, Bruno, 1983, *The Study of Ethnomusicology*, Urbana: University of Illinois Press.

Nic-a-Phearsoin, Màiri, 1891, *Dàin agus Òrain Ghàidhlig*, Inverness: A. agus U. MacCoinnich.

Nicolaisean, W.F.H., 1976, *Scottish Place-Names*, London: Batsford.

—, 1996, *The Picts and their Place-names*, Rosemarkie: Groam House Museum.

Nicolson, Alexander, 1994 (2nd edition), *History of Skye*, Portree: MacLean Press.

Norberg-Hodge, Helena, 1991, *Ancient Futures: Learning from Ladakh*, London: Rider.

Ó Baoill, Colm, 1994, *Iain Dubh*, Aberdeen: An Clò Gàidhealach.

—, 1997, *Duanaire Colach*, Aberdeen: An Clò Gàidhealach.

Oelschlager, Max, 1991, *The Idea of Wilderness*, New Haven and London: Yale University Press.

—, 1992 (ed.), *The Wilderness Condition*, San Francisco: Sierra Club Books.

Ó Giolláin, Diarmuid, 1991, 'The Fairy Belief and Official Religion in Ireland', in Peter Narváez, pp. 199-214.

Ó hAllmhuráin, Gearóid, 1999, 'Amhrán an Ghorta: The Great Famine and Irish Traditional Music', *New Hibernia Review / Iris Éireannach Nua* 3 :1 (Spring/Earrach 1999), pp. 19-44.

Ó hÓgáin, Dáithí, 1991, *Myth, Legend & Romance: An Encyclopedia of the Irish Folk Tradition*, London: BCA.

Ó Madagáin, Breandán, 1985, 'Functions of Irish Song in the Nineteenth Century', *Bealoideas* 53, pp. 130-216.

—, 1993, 'Song for Emotional Release in the Gaelic Tradition', in *Irish Musical Studies* 2 (ed.) Gerard Gillen and Harry White, Blackrock: Irish Academic Press, pp. 254-75.

O' Meara, John J., 1982 (ed.), *The History and Topography of Ireland (by Gerald of Wales)*, New York: Penguin Books.

Patterson, Nerys Thomas, 1994, *Cattle Lords & Clansmen*, Notre Dame: University of Notre Dame Press.

—, 1995-6, 'The English Just Are', *Planet: The Welsh Internationalist* 114, pp. 72-7.

Puhvel, Jaan, 1987, *Comparative Mythology*, Baltimore and London: John Hopkins University Press.

Radner, Joan, 1990, '"Men Will Die": Poets, Harpers, and Women in Early Irish Literature', in *Celtic Language, Celtic Culture* (ed.) A.T.E. Matonis and Daniel Melia, Van Nuys: Ford & Bailie, pp. 172-86.

Rees, Alwyn and Brinley Rees, 1961, *Celtic Heritage*, New York: Thames and Hudson.

Rieti, Barbara, 1991, *Strange Terrain*, Memorial University of Newfoundland.

Ritchie, Anna, 1995, 'The Archaelogical Evidence for Daily Life', in *A Pictish Panorama* (ed.) Eric Nicoll, Balgavies, Angus: Pinkfoot Press.

Ritchie, Graham and Anna, 1991, *Scotland: Archaeology and Early History*, Edinburgh University Press.

Robertson, Revd Charles, 1926, 'Gaelic Poems Collected in Braemar', *TGSI* 33, pp. 2-43.

Sanderson, Stewart, 1976 (ed.), *The Secret Commonwealth & A Short Treatise of Charms and Spells*, Ipswich: Folklore Society.

Schneider, Marius, 1957, 'Primitive Music', *New Oxford History of Music* vol. 1.

Scott-Moncrieff, Lesley, 1988 (ed.), *The '45: To gather an image whole*, Edinburgh: Mercat Press.
Sellar, David, 1981, 'Highland Family Origins – Pedigree Making and Pedigree Faking', in Loraine MacLean, pp. 103-16.
Sellar, W.D.H., 1989, 'Celtic Law and Scots Law: Survival and Integration', *Scottish Studies* 29, pp. 1-27.
Shaw, John, 1987 (ed.), *Sgeul gu Latha/Tales Until Dawn*, Kingston and Montreal: McGill-Queen's University Press.
—, 1993, 'Gaelic Cultural Maintenance: The Contibution of Ethnography', unpublished paper presented at Fasgnag II, Sabhal Mór Ostaig, Isle of Skye, Scotland.
—, 1992-3, 'Language, Music and Local Aesthetics, Views from Gaeldom and Beyond', *Scottish Language* 11/12, pp. 37-61.
Shaw, William, 1778, *An Analysis of the Gaelic Language* (reprint) 1972, Menston, England: Scolar Press.
Sheeran, Patrick, 1984, 'Genius Fabulae: The Irish Sense of Place', *Irish University Review* 18, pp. 191-206.
Shepard, Paul, 1992, 'A Post-Historic Primitivism', in Max Oelschlaeger, pp. 40-89.
Simms, Katherine, 1990, 'Images of Warfare in Bardic Poetry', *Celtica* 21, pp. 608-19.
Simpson, John, 1988, 'The Causes of the '45', in Lesley Scott-Moncrieff, pp. 1-13.
Sinton, Thomas, 1906, *The Poetry of Badenoch*, Inverness: Northern Counties Publishing Company.
—, 1910, *By Loch and River*, Inverness: Northern Counties Publishing Company.
Sjöblom, Tom, 1994, 'On The Threshold: The Sacredness of Borders in Early Irish Literature', in *Ulidia* (ed.) J.P. Mallory and Gerard Stuckman, Belfast, pp. 159-64.
Skene, W.F., 1860, *Celtic Scotland* vol. 3 (2nd edition) 1890, Edinburgh: David Douglas.
Smith, Iain Crichton, 1986, *Towards the Human*, Loanhead: Macdonald Publishers.
Smith, Phillip, 1994, 'On the Fringe and in the Middle: The MacDonalds of Antrim and the Isles 1266-1586', *History Ireland* Spring 1994, pp. 15-20.
Smith, Roland, 1929, 'A Prophecy Ascribed to Cendfaelad', *Revue Celtique* 46, pp. 120-5.
Smout, T.C., 1969, *History of the Scottish People*, London.
Smyth, Alfred P., 1984, *Warlords and Holy Men: Scotland AD 80-1000*, Edinburgh University Press.
Stewart, Revd Alexander, 1883, *Nether Lochaber*, Edinburgh: William Paterson.
Stewart, Alexander, 1928, *A Highland Parish*, Glasgow: Alex MacLaren & Sons.
Stewart, David, 1885 (new edition), *Sketches of the Characters, Institutions and Customs of the Highlanders*, Edinburgh.
Stewart, William G., 1851 (2nd edition), *The Popular Superstitions and Festive Amusements of the Highlanders of Scotland*, Edinburgh: Oliver and Boyd.
Stiùbhart, Dòmhnall Uilleam, 1996, '*An Gàidheal, A' Ghàidhlig agus A' Ghàidhealtachd Anns an t-Seachdamh Linn Deug*' (unpublished Ph.D. thesis) Edinburgh University.
—, 1999 (forthcoming), 'Women in the early modern western Gàidhealtachd', in *Women in Scotland 1100-1750* (ed.) Maureen Meikle, et al., East Linton: Tuckwell Press.

Thomas, Keith, 1983, *Man and the Natural World*, Oxford University Press.
Thompson, Francis, 1984, *Crofting Years*, Edinburgh: Luath Press.
Thomson, Derick, 1977, 'Three Seventeeth Century Bardic Poets: Niall Mór, Cathal and Niall MacMhuirich', in *Bards and Makars* (ed.) Adam J. Aitken, Mathew P. McDiarmid and Derick Thomson, University of Glasgow Press, pp. 221-46.
—, 1992, *The MacDiarmid MS Anthology*, Edinburgh: Scottish Gaelic Texts Society.
—, 1994 (ed.), *The Companion to Gaelic Scotland* (2nd edition) Glasgow: Gairm.
Toelken, Barre, 1979, *The Dynamics of Folklore*, Boston: Houghton Mufflin.
Tolmie, Frances, 1911, *One Hundred and Five Songs of Occupation from the Western Isles of Scotland* (reprint) Llanerch Publishers, 1997.
Tuan, Yi-Fu, 1974, *Topophilia*, New York: Columbia University Press.
Turner, Paruig, 1813, *Comhchruinneacha de Dh'Orain taghta Ghaidhealach*, Duneidionn.
Waddell, John, 1991, 'The Question of the Celticization of Ireland', *Emania* 9, pp. 5-16.
Wagner, Heinrich, 1981, 'Origins of Pagan Irish Religion', *ZCP* 38, pp. 1-28.
Wallace, Anthony, 1956, 'Revitalization Movements', *American Anthropologist* 58, pp. 264-81.
Warner, R.B., 1995, 'Tuathal Techtmar: A Myth or Ancient Literary Evidence for a Roman Invasion?', *Emania* 13, pp. 23-32.
Watson, James C., 1937-8, 'Carmina Gadelica', *Yorkshire Celtic Studies* 1.
—, 1940, 'Cathal Mac Muireadhaigh Cecinit', in *Féil-Sgríbhinn Eóin Mhic Néill* (ed.) an t-Athair Eóin ua Riain, Ath Chliatha, pp. 167-79.
Watson, William J., 1914-9, 'Classical Gaelic Poetry of Panegyric in Scotland', reprinted and supplemented from *TGSI* 29, pp. 194-235.
—, 1916-17, 'Marbhnadh Donnchaidh Duibh', *An Deo-Gréine* 12, pp. 132-4.
—, 1926, *The History of the Celtic Placenames of Scotland* (reprint) Edinburgh: Birlinn, 1993.
—, 1927-8, 'Unpublished Poetry – III', *SGS* 2, pp. 75-91.
—, 1929, *Rosg Gàidhlig*, An Comunn Gàidhealach.
Watt, Revd Lauchlan MacLean, 1937, 'Celtic Glimpses', *TGSI* 38, pp. 10-45.
Williams, J.E. Caerwyn and Patrick K. Ford, 1992, *The Irish Literary Tradition*, Cardiff: University of Wales Press.
Williamson, Arthur, 1982, 'Scotland, Antichrist and the Invention of Great Britain', in *New Perspectives on the Politics and Culture of Early Modern Scotland* (ed.) John Dwyer, Roger A. Mason and Alexander Murdoch, Edinburgh: John Donald, pp. 34-58.
—, 1996, 'Scots, Indians and Empire: The Scottish Politics of Civilization 1519-1609', *Past & Present* 150, pp. 46-83.
Withers, Charles W.J., 1984, *Gaelic in Scotland 1698-1981*, Edinburgh: John Donald.
—, 1988, *Gaelic Scotland: The Transformation of a Culture Region*, London and New York: Routledge.
Woolf, Alex, 1998, 'Pictish matriliny reconsidered', *Innes Review* 49.2, pp. 147-67.
Wright, Ronald, 1992, *Stolen Continents: The Indian Story*, Random House: London.

Index